SIXTEENTH-CENTURY READERS, FIFTEENTH-CENTURY BOOKS

This innovative study investigates the reception of medieval manuscripts over a long century, 1470–1585, spanning the reigns of Edward IV to Elizabeth I. Members of the Tudor gentry family who owned these manuscripts had properties in Willesden and professional affiliations in London. These men marked the leaves of their books with signs of use, allowing their engagement with the texts contained there to be reconstructed. Through detailed research Margaret Connolly reveals the various uses of these old books: as a repository for family records; as a place to preserve other texts of a favourite or important nature; as a source of practical information for the household; and as a professional manual for the practising lawyer. Investigation of these family-owned books reveals an unexpectedly strong interest in works of the past and the continuing intellectual and domestic importance of medieval manuscripts in an age of print.

Margaret Connolly is Senior Lecturer in Medieval Studies at the University of St Andrews. Her previous publications include *Insular Books: Vernacular Manuscript Miscellanies in Late Medieval Britain* (2015), edited with Raluca Radulescu; *The Index of Middle English Prose, Handlist XIX: Manuscripts in the University Library, Cambridge* (2009); *Design and Distribution of Late Medieval Manuscripts in England* (2008), edited with Linne Mooney; and *John Shirley: Book Production and the Noble Household* (1998).

Cambridge Studies in Palaeography and Codicology

FOUNDING EDITORS
Albinia de la Mare
Rosamond McKitterick *Newnham College, University of Cambridge*

GENERAL EDITORS
David Ganz
Teresa Webber *Trinity College, University of Cambridge*

This series has been established to further the study of manuscripts from the Middle Ages to the Renaissance. It includes books devoted to particular types of manuscripts, their production and circulation, to individual codices of outstanding importance, and to regions, periods, and scripts of especial interest to scholars. The series will be of interest not only to scholars and students of medieval literature and history, but also to theologians, art historians, and others working with manuscript sources.

OTHER TITLES IN THE SERIES

William Noel *The Harley Psalter*

Charles F. Briggs *Giles of Rome's De regimine principum: Reading and Writing Politics at Court and University, c.1275–c.1525*

Leslie Brubaker *Vision and Meaning in Ninth-Century Byzantium: Image as Exegesis in the Homilies of Gregory of Nazianzus*

Francis Newton *The Scriptorium and Library at Monte Cassino, 1058–1105*

Lisa Fagin Davis *The Gottschalk Antiphonary: Music and Liturgy in Twelfth-Century Lambach*

Albert Derolez *The Palaeography of Gothic Manuscript Books: From the Twelfth to the Early Sixteenth Century*

Alison I. Beach *Women as Scribes: Book Production and Monastic Reform in Twelfth-Century Bavaria*

Yitzhak Hen and Rob Meens, editors *The Bobbio Missal: Liturgy and Religious Culture in Merovingian Gaul*

Marica Tacconi *Cathedral and Civic Ritual in Late Medieval and Renaissance Florence: The Service Books of Santa Maria del Fiore*

Anna A. Grotans *Reading in Medieval St Gall*

Alexandra Gillespie and Daniel Wakelin, editors *The Production of Books in England 1350–1500*

Susan Rankin *Writing Sounds in Carolingian Europe*

SIXTEENTH-CENTURY READERS, FIFTEENTH-CENTURY BOOKS

Continuities of Reading in the English Reformation

MARGARET CONNOLLY

CAMBRIDGE
UNIVERSITY PRESS

CAMBRIDGE
UNIVERSITY PRESS

University Printing House, Cambridge CB2 8BS, United Kingdom

One Liberty Plaza, 20th Floor, New York, NY 10006, USA

477 Williamstown Road, Port Melbourne, VIC 3207, Australia

314-321, 3rd Floor, Plot 3, Splendor Forum, Jasola District Centre, New Delhi - 110025, India

103 Penang Road, #05-06/07, Visioncrest Commercial, Singapore 238467

Cambridge University Press is part of the University of Cambridge.

It furthers the University's mission by disseminating knowledge in the pursuit of education, learning and research at the highest international levels of excellence.

www.cambridge.org
Information on this title: www.cambridge.org/9781108445528
DOI: 10.1017/9781108652421

© Margaret Connolly 2019

This publication is in copyright. Subject to statutory exception and to the provisions of relevant collective licensing agreements, no reproduction of any part may take place without the written permission of Cambridge University Press.

First published 2019
First paperback edition 2022

A catalogue record for this publication is available from the British Library

Library of Congress Cataloging in Publication data
NAMES: Connolly, Margaret, 1965– author.
TITLE: Sixteenth-century readers, fifteenth-century books : continuities of reading in the English reformation / Margaret Connolly, University of St Andrews, Scotland.
DESCRIPTION: Cambridge, UK ; New York, NY : Cambridge University Press, 2018. | Series: Cambridge Studies in Palaeography and Codicology | Includes bibliographical references and indexes.
IDENTIFIERS: LCCN 2018025222 | ISBN 9781108426770
SUBJECTS: LCSH: Books and reading – England – History – 16th century. | Manuscripts, Medieval – England. | Roberts, Thomas, 1470–1542 – Books and reading. | Roberts, Edmund, 1520–1585 – Books and reading. | Gentry – Books and reading – England – History – 16th century. | Roberts, Thomas, 1470–1542 – Library – Marginal notes. | Roberts, Edmund, 1520-1585 – Library – Marginal notes. | BISAC: LANGUAGE ARTS & DISCIPLINES / Publishing.
CLASSIFICATION: LCC Z1003.5.G7 C66 2018 | DDC 028.90942/09031–dc23
LC record available at https://lccn.loc.gov/2018025222

ISBN 978-1-108-42677-0 Hardback
ISBN 978-1-108-44552-8 Paperback

Cambridge University Press has no responsibility for the persistence or accuracy of URLs for external or third-party internet websites referred to in this publication, and does not guarantee that any content on such websites is, or will remain, accurate or appropriate.

In memory of my parents
   Marian McCabe Connolly (1929–2018)
   Thomas Connolly (1923–96)

Contents

List of Illustrations	*page* viii
Acknowledgements	xi
List of Abbreviations	xiii
Note on Transcription Policy	xv
Introduction	1
1 Family Matters: The Roberts Family of Willesden	18
2 Private Faces in Public Places	48
3 Devotional Reading in the Reigns of Henry VII and Henry VIII	77
4 Out of the Cloister, Out of the Family	129
5 Books and Their Uses	165
6 Devotional Reading in the Reigns of Mary Tudor and Elizabeth I	200
Conclusion: Newly Reformed Readers?	231
Postscript: After the Family: The Manuscripts' Later Histories	245
Appendices	253
i *Timeline of Key Events during the Lifetimes of Thomas and Edmund Roberts*	253
ii *Summary List of Contents of the Manuscripts Owned by the Roberts Family*	254
iii *Manuscripts and Printed Books of Uncertain Association*	257
iv *Other Families Named Roberts*	259
Bibliography	268
Index of Manuscripts and Early Printed Books	295
General Index	298

Illustrations

Maps
1 Map of Willesden and Neasden. — *page* 19
2 Map of the parish of St Clement Danes, London. — 49

Tables
1 Family tree: Suggested patrilineage of Thomas Roberts of Willesden. — 28
2 Family tree: The wives and children of Thomas Roberts. — 30
3 Family tree: The children and grandchildren of Edmund Roberts. — 36
4 Family tree: The children and grandchildren of Dorothy Roberts and Alan Horde. — 54

Figures
1 Oxford, Bodleian Library, MS Rawlinson C. 299, f. 1^r. Note of Battle of Barnet and Thomas Roberts's birth. Reproduced by permission of the Bodleian Libraries, the University of Oxford. — 25
2 Tomb brass of Edmund Roberts in St Mary's Willesden; rubbing, from London, British Library, MS Additional 32490, CC. 31. Reproduced by permission. © The British Library Board. — 39
3 London, British Library, MS Harley 1859, f. 218^v. Memorandum of Thomas Roberts's admission to the Inner Temple; copy of the indulgence naming Ralph and Johanna Roberts. Reproduced by permission. © The British Library Board. — 50
4 London, British Library, MS Harley 1859, f. *1^v. Inscription by Edmund Roberts; copy of sergeant's oath in the hand of Thomas Roberts. Reproduced by permission. © The British Library Board. — 52
5 TNA, E 210/10147. Indenture written by the hand of Thomas Roberts. Reproduced by permission of the National Archives. — 53
6 London, British Library, MS Harley 2322, f. 4^r. Roberts ownership inscription at top right corner. Reproduced by permission. © The British Library Board. — 81

List of Illustrations

7 London, British Library, MS Harley 2322, f. 61ᵛ. Thomas Roberts's annotations in the text of the Ten Commandments (part of the *Pore Caitif*). Reproduced by permission. © The British Library Board. — 89

8 London, British Library, MS Harley 2322, f. 25ᵛ. Thomas Roberts's Latin annotations in the text of the Creed (part of the *Pore Caitif*). Reproduced by permission. © The British Library Board. — 91

9 Cambridge, MA, Harvard University, Houghton Library, MS Richardson 22, f. 69ʳ. Erased English rubric to Latin prayer. — 109

10 Cambridge, MA, Harvard University, Houghton Library, MS Richardson 22, f. 89ᵛ. End of Long Charter of Christ and start of final text, showing change of scribal hands. — 126

11 Manchester, John Rylands Library, MS English 98, f. 48ʳ. Nicholas Love, *Mirror of the Blessed Life of Jesus Christ*; marginal marks in the section that discusses the Pater Noster. Copyright of The University of Manchester, reproduced with permission. — 136

12 Manchester, John Rylands Library, MS English 98, f. 137ᵛ. Birth records of Thomas Roberts's children, and note of his death. Copyright of The University of Manchester, reproduced with permission. — 144

13 Tomb brass of Dorothy Horde in St Mary's, Ewell; rubbing, from London, British Library, MS Additional 32490, LL 13. Reproduced by permission. © The British Library Board. — 155

14 Oxford, Bodleian Library, MS Rawlinson C. 894, f. vᵛ. Birth records of the children of Edmund Roberts. Reproduced by permission of the Bodleian Libraries, the University of Oxford. — 173

15 Oxford, Bodleian Library, MS Rawlinson C. 299, f. 3ᵛ. Medical recipes added by Thomas Roberts. Reproduced by permission of the Bodleian Libraries, the University of Oxford. — 182

16 Cambridge University Library, MS Ii.6.7, f. 4ʳ. Book of Hours: July section from the calendar with added obits. Reproduced by kind permission of the Syndics of Cambridge University Library. — 192

17 Cambridge University Library, MS Ii.6.2, f. 68ᵛ. Ownership inscriptions added by Thomas and Edmund Roberts. Reproduced by kind permission of the Syndics of Cambridge University Library. — 198

List of Illustrations

18 Cambridge University Library, MS Ii.6.2, f. 109^r. Inscriptions by Thomas, Edmund, and Francis Roberts. Reproduced by kind permission of the Syndics of Cambridge University Library.   218

19 Oxford, Bodleian Library, MS Rawlinson C. 894, f. 34^r. Annotations and underlining by Edmund Roberts in 'A Tretyse of Gostly Batayle'. Reproduced by permission of the Bodleian Libraries, the University of Oxford.   226

Acknowledgements

This book grew out of an encounter with two books of ours, CUL Ii.6.2 and Ii.6.7, as I was surveying manuscripts at Cambridge University Library for the Index of Middle English Prose. I wrote an article about these family books, but in the process I began to uncover far more information than could be accommodated in a short essay; I thus embarked on a fascinating journey to unravel the biographical and professional stories of these sixteenth-century readers and the codicological complexities of their eight fifteenth-century manuscripts. For allowing me to consult and quote from materials in their care, and for extending many courtesies to me as a reader, I would like to thank the staff at Cambridge University Library, the British Library, the Bodleian Library, the John Rylands Library, The National Archives, London Metropolitan Archives, the library of Westminster Abbey, and the library of Trinity College Dublin. For permission to reproduce images from medieval manuscripts in their care I am grateful to the British Library, the Bodleian Library, Cambridge University Library, the John Rylands Library, University of Manchester, The National Archives, and the Houghton Library, University of Harvard. For preparing the family trees I thank Leo Mewse of the University of St Andrews Print and Design Unit. For the award of a grant which has fully covered the costs of the illustrations to this volume, I would like to thank the trustees of the Marc Fitch Fund. For other financial assistance which has facilitated research trips I am grateful to acknowledge the support of the Wellcome Trust (Medical Humanities Grant No. 104798/Z/14/Z); the Society for the Study of Medieval Languages and Literatures; the British Academy (Neil Ker Memorial Fund); the Bibliographical Society, for the award of the Pantzer scholarship in 2015; and Trinity College Dublin, for the award of a Long Room fellowship in 2016.

Some of the material in Chapter 6 first appeared in preliminary form in 'Sixteenth-Century Readers Reading Fifteenth-Century Religious Books', *Middle English Religious Writing in Practice*, edited by Nicole R. Rice (Brepols, 2013); a fuller account of the medical manuscript described here in

Acknowledgements

Chapter 5 may be found in 'Evidence for the Continued Use of Medieval Medical Prescriptions in the Sixteenth Century', *Medical History* 60 (2016). Over the last eight years I have spoken to various audiences about this material, and have benefitted from their responses: my thanks to all who have listened to me on this topic at various conference meetings of the Early Book Society; in lectures at University College Dublin and Trinity College Dublin, at the University of Lausanne, and at The National Archives; and also at the University of St Andrews at seminars of the Medieval and Renaissance Research Group and the Centre for Medieval and Early Modern Law and Literature. Students on my early modern palaeography courses at St Andrews, and my colleague Rachel Hart, Keeper of Manuscripts and Muniments, have helped to save me from some errors in deciphering sixteenth-century script. The perceptive suggestions made by the two readers for the Press (one of whom, Michael Johnson, subsequently identified himself to me) have sharpened the focus of the final typescript. I am also grateful to the series editors, Tessa Webber and David Ganz, and to Linda Bree, for their support of this project, as also to Emily Hockley and Tim Mason for guiding it through to publication. A. I. Doyle shared his notes with me about manuscripts connected with the Roberts family, and remained interested in the slow progress of this book; he died whilst it was in its very final stages but I am glad to have the opportunity to record his contribution here. For academic help of various kinds in relation to this book I am indebted above all to Julia Boffey; I would also like to thank Lorna Hutson, Julian Luxford, and Kate Rudy. For help with specific points I thank Virginia Bainbridge, Robert Crawford, Marlene Hennessy, E. A. Jones, Holly James-Maddocks, Veronica O'Mara, Niamh Pattwell, Nicole Rice, Tess Tavormina, John Thompson, and Daniel Wakelin. For help of a different, but equally important kind, I thank my friends in the Ceres Book Group, and my family: Michael, Robert, and Isabelle. My mother heard much about this book and died whilst it was in production. I dedicate it to her memory, and to the memory of my father.

Abbreviations

BL	London, British Library
BodL	Oxford, Bodleian Library
BRUC	*A Biographical Register of the University of Cambridge to AD 1500*, ed. by A. B. Emden (Cambridge: Cambridge University Press, 1963)
BRUO	*A Biographical Register of the University of Oxford to AD 1500*, ed. by A. B. Emden, 3 vols. (Oxford: Clarendon, 1958)
CBMLC	Corpus of British Medieval Library Catalogues
CAR	*Calendar of Assize Records, Surrey Indictments Eliz I*, ed. by J. S. Cockburn (London: HMSO, 1980)
CCR	*Calendar of the Close Rolls*
CFR	*Calendar of the Fine Rolls*
CIPM	*Calendar of Inquisitions Post Mortem*
CPMR	*Calendar of the Plea and Memorandum Rolls of the City of London*
CPR	*Calendar of the Patent Rolls*
CUL	Cambridge University Library
DIMEV	*The Digital Index of Middle English Verse*, ed. by Linne R. Mooney et al.
EETS	Early English Text Society
es	extra series
IMEP	*Index of Middle English Prose*
IPMEP	*Index of Printed Middle English Prose*
IMEV	*The Index of Middle English Verse*, ed. by Carleton Brown and R. H. Robbins (New York: Index Society, 1943)
Jolliffe	P. S. Jolliffe, *A Checklist of Middle English Prose Writings of Spiritual Guidance* (Toronto: Pontifical Institute of Mediaeval Studies, 1974)
JRL	Manchester, John Rylands Library
LALME	*A Linguistic Atlas of Late Mediaeval English*, ed. by A. McIntosh, M. L. Samuels, and M. Benskin, 4 vols. (Aberdeen: University of Aberdeen Press, 1986)
LPFD	*Letters and Papers Foreign and Domestic*
LMA	London Metropolitan Archives
MED	*Middle English Dictionary*
NIMEV	*New Index of Middle English Verse*, ed. by Julia Boffey and A. S. G. Edwards (London: British Library Press, 2005)
NRO	Norfolk Record Office

List of Abbreviations

os	original series
ss	supplementary series
STC	*A Short-Title Catalogue of Books Printed in England, Scotland and Ireland, and of English Books Printed Abroad, 1475–1640*, first compiled by A. W. Pollard and G. R. Redgrave, 2nd edn revised and enlarged by W. A. Jackson, F. S. Ferguson, Katharine F. Pantzer, et al., 3 vols. (London: Bibliographical Society, 1976–91)
Supplement	*Supplement to the Index of Middle English Verse*, ed. by Rossell Hope Robbins and John L. Cutler (Lexington, KY: University of Kentucky Press, 1965)
TNA	The National Archives
VCH	*Victoria History of the Counties of England*
WAM	Westminster Abbey Muniments

Note on Transcription Policy

In citations from manuscript sources I have reproduced scribal spelling but have silently expanded abbreviations and added modern punctuation, capitalization, and word division to aid comprehension.

Introduction

The present study investigates the reception of late medieval literary texts, exploring and interpreting the evidence that reveals how they were read, by whom, and when. Its particular focus is a group of fifteenth-century manuscripts owned by a single English family in the sixteenth century. The twenty or so individual works contained within these eight manuscripts are largely, though not entirely, of a devotional nature, and so a special point of interest is the apparent disjunction between the contents of these texts, the products of a wholly Catholic age, and the considerably more complex religious environment in which their sixteenth-century readers found themselves, especially after the 1530s. More generally attention is paid to the various ways in which these early modern readers used their old medieval books – as a repository for family records; as a place where other texts of a favourite or important nature might be inscribed; as a source of practical information when preparing household remedies; and as a professional manual for the practising lawyer. All of these activities indicate that these manuscripts enjoyed a great deal of use in the sixteenth century, despite being much older than their owners. These manuscripts were not yet collectors' items, to be valued for their antique or rare nature rather than for their contents, and to be kept carefully, as curiosities; instead they were still treated as sources of reading material and stores of knowledge. Despite the inexorable rise of the printed book following the introduction of printing in England and a flood of imported books from the Continent, in the sixteenth century the manuscript remained a viable and desirable format in which to encounter the written word.

In general much more attention has been devoted to uncovering information about the production of medieval manuscripts than to considering how they and their textual contents may have been used. This has been especially true in recent years due to significant advances in the study of medieval scribes and their outputs. The idea that professional scribes, such as those employed at the chancery, might have been responsible for producing non-official works by moonlighting had long been mooted, but the identification of particular instances where this actually happened has emerged only recently. The rewards of looking in other places for the scribes who wrote literary texts were demonstrated by Carter Revard, whose detailed researches amongst documents localizable to early fourteenth-century Ludlow uncovered a much fuller picture of the work of the main scribe of the important trilingual miscellany, BL MS Harley 2253. This scribe, though still nameless, is now known to have been responsible for three manuscripts and forty-one legal writs, with the latter documents furnishing a profile of a man who flourished as a professional legal scribe in the Ludlow area from at least December 1314 to April 1349.[1] In short, we now know a lot more about the scribe of the Harley lyrics than we did before. Linne Mooney has followed a similar approach in the context of late fourteenth- and early fifteenth-century London and has argued that clerks who held major bureaucratic offices at the Guildhall were the copyists of some of the earliest manuscripts of works by Middle English authors such as Geoffrey Chaucer, John Gower, and William Langland.[2]

Even before these great steps forward in understanding patterns of late medieval scribal activity, more scholarly attention had always been directed towards the matter of manuscript production, as opposed to reception, perhaps because aspects of manuscript production are more naturally aligned with the business of textual criticism. Traditional methodologies of editing that sought to draw up a family tree for the existing witnesses of a text, and to establish a line of textual descent that could point the way back to their single common ancestor or 'Ur-text', relied on a particular aspect of production – scribal errors – as their guiding light. Close attention to shared textual errors could reveal affinities between existing witnesses and could also help the editor to recover the text's original readings. This emphasis on determining the original form of a text (and sometimes thereby identifying its author) linked naturally to an interest in any evidence as to where a text had been copied, and by whom, and at whose request. The publication of *A Linguistic Atlas of Late Mediaeval English* raised hopes that the locations where later Middle English texts had

---

[1] Revard, 'Scribe and Provenance', and see further the discussion by Fein, 'Literary Scribes'.
[2] See Mooney and Stubbs, *Scribes and the City*.

been copied could be determined; in fact this was never what its editors had promised, but the 'fit' technique did at least help to reveal where the scribes themselves had come from in linguistic terms. Following the principle that apples do not fall very far from the tree, this offered a useful advance in knowledge about manuscript production.[3] Matters of reception have generally been discussed less materially and in ways which focus on individual texts: in the tracing of the influence of one text on another; in charting the use of sources; and in the spread of ideas and philosophies. These are profitable lines of enquiry because medieval literature was deeply engaged in the matter of citation and allusion. As dwarfs on the shoulders of giants, contemporary authors sought to situate themselves within an authoritative tradition of writing by quoting and acknowledging greater writers who had preceded them, and identifying such influences is part of the work of the modern editor. Yet all of this relates more to where a text or texts *came from*, and rather less to where texts *went to* once they had been authored and copied; still less interest has been shown in the matter of identifying who actually read them. In fact the format of the critical edition leaves little scope for a full discussion of matters relating to either production or reception. The extended introduction that traditionally prefaces the edited text usually describes in detail only the manuscript which has been selected to form the base text of the edition. The characteristics of its scribal hand are described, and more information given about the scribe and any other manuscripts associated with him, but in this framework there is room to accommodate only fairly minimal discussion. Names of owners and a sketch of manuscript provenance typically appear in this section, but evidence of marginalia and the operation of later hands within the manuscript will be mentioned, if at all, in the notes to the text, where there is no opportunity for an extensive analysis of these characteristics of readerly engagement, textual reception, and the material use of the book.

An important overview of book production and reception is offered by the third volume of *The Cambridge History of the Book in Britain*, and no fewer than fifteen essays are marshalled under the heading 'Reading and Use of Books'.[4] Most of the contributions here seek to place emphasis on identifying overall trends, and usage is organized into broad groups (scholars, professionals, and

---

[3] McIntosh, Samuels, and Benskin, *LALME*, I.23–28; for a critique of its methodology see Burton, 'On the Current State of Middle English Dialectology', and the response by Benskin, 'In Reply to Dr Burton'.

[4] Hellinga and Trapp (eds.), *The Cambridge History of the Book in Britain, III: 1400–1557*.

lay readers), which means that the discussions are necessarily light in detail, and cannot pay much attention to examining the practice of individual readers. A more recent volume of essays published in 2011, *The Production of Books in England 1350–1500*, surveyed existing scholarship on later medieval manuscript production with individual essays by a range of contributors offering sustained focus on the different elements and phases of production required to produce the manuscript book.[5] The collection sought to build upon the work of an earlier and extremely influential volume of essays in the same subject field, *Book Production and Publishing in Britain 1375–1475* published in 1989, aiming to update the positions taken there and to augment the findings of its contributors.[6] Yet one major difference between the two essay collections is that whilst the earlier volume covered both production and reception, the latter focusses exclusively on production. In the 1989 collection seven of the fifteen essays discussed texts and their reception, with four of these included under the heading 'Patrons, Buyers and Owners', and several of the essays that examined production were predominantly interested in content rather than the process of assembly. Conversely in the 2011 collection seven of the thirteen chapters treat aspects of the production process in considerable detail, and the emphasis of the whole collection is firmly fixed on the methods, circumstances, and economy of manuscript production. There is no equivalent amongst the essays of the later volume to the detailed investigations into the users of books made by Kate Harris and Carol Meale in the earlier collection. This seems like a surprising omission since, after general advances in the subject over a period of more than two decades, there is surely more to say about the reception and use of medieval manuscripts. Given the continued work of many scholars including, to name only a few, Julia Boffey, Mary Erler, Ann Hutchison, Carol Meale, and Anne Sutton, and the perennial interest in the ownership and readership of manuscripts evident from ongoing publications in journals such as the *Journal of the Early Book Society*, *The Library*, and *The Book Collector*, a companion volume to *The Production of Books in England* that focussed instead on book *reception* might justifiably be imagined. Indeed, the editors Alexandra Gillespie and Daniel Wakelin do note that although the use of books is not the focus of the essays they present, 'the collection points up the importance of readers, libraries and provenance study', yet to date no equivalent collective study of

---

[5] Gillespie and Wakelin (eds.), *The Production of Books in England 1350–1500*.
[6] Griffiths and Pearsall (eds.), *Book Production and Publishing in Britain*.

Introduction

manuscript reception has been undertaken.[7] Further, Ralph Hanna has characterized this field of study as 'fragmented', observing that the main outlet for codicological work remains the article rather than the monograph.[8]

In splitting the codicological treatment of manuscripts into the separate fields of production and reception, there is a danger of forcing an artificial division upon the subject, since the two processes are inextricably linked; to focus too narrowly on one aspect or the other is to risk distorting and misinterpreting the true picture. The first readers of a text were also the scribes who copied it, meaning that every act of production was simultaneously an act of reception. The ways in which a text may be received cannot be controlled by its author, and to depend solely on reader responses is also to depend on evidence which is likely to be both incomplete and unreliable. As Raluca Radulescu has observed, the issues of production and reception are inseparable in that 'the unravelling of the back-processes of book production, and then the forward-processes ... of circulation and consumption' constitute significant stages in scholarly attempts to understand medieval texts.[9] The codicologist must therefore be Janus-like, and also able to piece together very different types of evidence. In practice, as the comments of Gillespie and Wakelin acknowledge, studies of manuscript production find it hard to ignore entirely evidence that relates to readership and ownership; similarly, a study primarily focussed on reception will not want to disregard interesting aspects of the production process that reveal themselves during the course of detailed examination. Accordingly, the present study will on occasion draw attention to features that relate to production, notwithstanding its primary concern with the afterlife of the texts and manuscripts that are its subject.

The paucity of similarly extended studies of the reception of medieval texts is undoubtedly linked to the sheer difficulty involved in this type of research. The evidence for the use of books, and for the reading of the texts within them, is hard to uncover, define, and interpret; sometimes, indeed, there may be little evidence to find.[10] The medieval manuscript is an object that carries information about its own production in its very fabric, on every leaf, and in every written letter; this is true of all manuscripts, but the same is not true in terms of

---

[7] Gillespie and Wakelin (eds.), *The Production of Books in England 1350–1500*, p. 11.
[8] Hanna, 'Analytical Survey', p. 245.
[9] Connolly and Radulescu (eds.), *Insular Books*, p. 16.
[10] For an articulation of some of these challenges see Boffey, 'Reading in London in 1501', pp. 51–61.

reception. Manuscripts may survive in pristine condition, left clean and unmarked by their well-behaved consumers, so we cannot rely on finding evidence of reception in every manuscript in the same way that we can be certain that there will be evidence of production. Evidence of reception, in codicological terms, consists of signs of ownership, marginal or other annotation, and damage. Inscribed names in margins and on endleaves do not necessarily constitute proof of ownership; they do, however, usually indicate some form of contact between book and user. Signs of ownership, which might include the inscription of names, owners' marks or book stamps, and library pressmarks, denote possession and sometimes location. Yet possession does not necessarily imply readership: we all have books that we own but have never read. Library books in particular may have been physically present in a collection or a community, but it is not easy to know which members of that community (if any), and at what times, actually borrowed or read the book, or what proportion of a book they may have read (or how they read it – from cover to cover, or more selectively – and with what attention).[11] Damage such as accumulated dirt or wear from rubbing or kissing can reveal much about the use of particular parts of a manuscript, and may often lead to insights into practices and rituals in which the book played a role (in devotional contexts, for example), as the recent work of Kate Rudy has shown, but such damage cannot show who handled the book.[12] Even annotation, the seam of gold that every researcher interested in reception wishes to discover, is not an unproblematic area. For a start the scripts used for the addition of comments and other reader responses are liable to be less practised, more casual, and thus hard to decipher. Such additions had to be fitted into whatever blank space was available, usually in the margins of a text, in the gutter, and in the spaces between lines; this paucity of writing space often led to the squashing, compressing, and abbreviating of comments. Material added to the margins was also liable to be partially lost to trimming if a manuscript was rebound, or – before the present day – removed by chemical substances in efforts to clean up the volume's appearance. Furthermore, annotations tend to present themselves in a jumble, having often been made over time, by different readers, or by a single reader on successive occasions. This may be apparent from the presence

---

[11] Though a great deal more is now known about the contents of medieval libraries through the publication of successive volumes in the Corpus of British Medieval Library Catalogues series.
[12] Rudy, 'Dirty Books'.

of different scripts and different hues of ink within the leaves of the same manuscript, with some sections more copiously annotated than others. Such layers of annotation are very hard to disentangle and to interpret. Even harder to deal with are various other non-verbal types of additions to the text such as underlining or the addition of pointing hands (manicules) in the margins. Whilst the immediate purpose of such additions in drawing attention to a particular section of the text is clear, attributing such markings to any particular reader may be difficult, unless the overall evidence is very coherent (for example, in a manuscript where only one reader using the same type of ink seems to have been active). If such marks appear on their own, without other surrounding comments, or without the helpful context of a known owner or at least a known era of use, they may prove impossible to interpret further, since in the absence of other evidence how can we possibly tell who underlined a text or when this took place? (The 'why' may be easier to work out.) Assembling a narrative of reception can thus involve skating out over thin ice. There is a rich corpus of evidence here, but one which is challenging to interpret, and assembling that material into a coherent scholarly argument is another challenge altogether.

Another reason that the reception of medieval texts and manuscripts has received less attention than it deserves is that a large part of the evidence for reception tends to be post-medieval in date, and so does not fall within the main purview of the medievalists who edit and criticize the texts. Here we meet a stubborn division in the subject between the medieval period and the Renaissance. There is a wealth of evidence for the reception of medieval texts in the sixteenth century which has largely been ignored, or at least not thoroughly investigated, because specialists in late medieval literature tend to be reluctant to venture forwards, either because they do not feel confident in dealing with a later historical context, or because they are unable to read sixteenth-century secretary script. This is not to suggest that there has been no attention at all to this area. The sixteenth-century afterlife of *Piers Plowman* in particular has attracted considerable interest, with studies of owners and readers of individual manuscripts and of the annotations in early printed copies.[13] This has forced a reassessment of the poem's doctrinal appeal in this

---

[13] See Schaap, 'From Professional to Private Readership'; Horobin, 'Stephan Batman and His Manuscripts of *Piers Plowman*'; Kelen, *Langland's Early Modern Identities*; Griffiths, 'Editorial Glossing and Reader Resistance'.

period, as evidence has emerged of the continued existence of a Catholic *Piers Plowman* alongside the Protestant Piers believed to be beloved by reformists.[14] Research on Chaucer's manuscripts remains preoccupied with issues of scribal production and the establishment of the poet's reputation in the fifteenth and sixteenth centuries, but there has been some investigation of readers' annotations in printed copies of Chaucer's poetry, and a recent study of John Walton's translation of *De Consolatione Philosophiae* analyses how it was read in both manuscript and printed form.[15] By and large these studies have been conducted by medievalists since sixteenth-century specialists are not generally interested in the medieval texts that are at the root of this issue, preferring instead to concentrate on works written in their own period of interest. Yet knowing what texts were read, and having a good sense of what texts were available for reading at any given point, is important not least because reading has a potential influence on writing, and Tudor cultural dependence on medieval literary texts is generally acknowledged.[16] Dates of publication (routinely available post-printing) only tell us when something was produced; when that work was read, and widely read, and became influential, is a more fluid, shadowy phenomenon that cannot be easily dated beyond its starting point. Books, once written, remain in circulation, and might influence thinking and opinion long after their own day might be thought to have ended.

It is also rare to be able to identify a suitable corpus of evidence that will support a sustained interpretation. The late medieval manuscripts collected and annotated by John Stow, along with his own works and handwritten copies, constitute a body of material that would repay more detailed investigation than it has yet received, but Stow's cramped handwriting is a major deterrent to would-be researchers.[17] There are the major sixteenth- and seventeenth-century collections assembled by men such as Matthew Parker (1504–75) and Robert Cotton (1571–1631), but in these cases there are the problems of scale and scope, with too much material to assimilate adequately, and where in any case it is clear that we are dealing with bibliophiles whose main interests lay in gathering

---

[14] Warner, *The Myth of Piers Plowman*, Chapter 4 (especially pp. 84–86).

[15] Wiggins, 'What Did Renaissance Readers Write in their Printed Copies of Chaucer?'; Edwards, 'Reading John Walton's Boethius in the Fifteenth and Sixteenth Centuries'.

[16] For a recent and wide-ranging account of this influence see Kelen (ed.), *Renaissance Retrospections*.

[17] Useful insights into Stow's importance are offered by the essays in Gadd and Gillespie (eds.), *John Stow*.

Introduction

significant numbers of books rather than purely in reading.[18] At the other end of the spectrum a more typical situation involves the single manuscript and a handful of inscribed names. Sometimes it is not possible to make much of those names, as for example in the case of the Auchinleck manuscript, the famous fourteenth-century collection of English verse romances and other texts, which has amongst its leaves many inscribed names, none of which has ever been identified.[19] And even when historical candidates can be more or less certainly identified as the makers of inscriptions there may simply not be enough recoverable biographical information to supply a robust context. High-status owners such as royal or aristocratic figures and their books have been better documented not just because of a historic tendency to value such figures more highly, but because their lives are more fully recorded and their reading easier to contextualize. Royal owners whose books have been much investigated include Richard III and Henry VIII.[20] The literate activities of upper-class secular women such as Margaret of York, Duchess of Burgundy, and Lady Margaret Beaufort have also received attention.[21] Amongst the ranks of professed female religious the community of nuns at Syon has attracted the most scholarly interest.[22] Lower down the social scale there have been some collective studies of reading communities, particularly female networks of book ownership and traffic, and especially involving urban mercantile classes.[23] A rare full-length individual study of a single female owner and her manuscript is Alexandra Barratt's account of Anne Bulkeley.[24] Most attention has been given to personal notebooks or miscellanies, especially those connected with owner-reader-producers such as Robert Thornton, Robert Reynes, Humphrey Newton, and John Hanson.[25] An alternative approach, focussing on text-type

---

[18] For studies of Cotton and his collections see Tite, *The Manuscript Library of Sir Robert Cotton*, and Wright, *Sir Robert Cotton as Collector*.

[19] Edinburgh, National Library of Scotland, MS Advocates' 19.2.1.

[20] See Sutton and Visser-Fuchs, *The Hours of Richard III* and *Richard III's Books*, and Carley, *The Libraries of Henry VIII*.

[21] Weightman, *Margaret of York, Duchess of Burgundy*, especially pp. 204–13; Jones and Underwood, *The King's Mother*, especially pp. 171–201.

[22] de Hamel, *Syon Abbey*, and Jones and Walsham (eds.), *Syon Abbey and its Books*.

[23] Meale, '... alle the bokes that I haue'; Erler, *Women, Reading, and Piety*; Boffey, 'Some London Women Readers'.

[24] Barratt, *Anne Bulkeley and her Book*.

[25] See Fein, 'Literary Scribes'; Meale, 'Amateur Book Production'; Youngs, *Humphrey Newton (1466–1536)*; May and Marotti, *Ink, Stink Bait, Revenge, and Queen Elizabeth*.

rather than book owner, is that taken by Eamon Duffy in his study of the use of books of hours and prayer-books in England in the late medieval and early modern periods; one of these books of hours, Cambridge University Library, MS Ii.6.2, is examined afresh and in greater detail in the present volume.[26] And a recent collection of essays edited by Mary Flannery and Carrie Griffin that considers where and how reading took place in later medieval England interprets that chronological era generously and includes contributions that investigate both medieval and Tudor texts and their readers.[27] Studies of early modern readers have generally been more numerous: indeed, this is a subject area recently described as 'in danger of drowning in the diversity of case studies'.[28] Individual readers who have received sustained attention include John Dee (1527–1609), Gabriel Harvey (1552/3–1631), and William Drake (1606–69).[29] There have also been significant overviews of early modern reading practices, based largely on the study of handwritten additions to printed books, and including consideration of printed marginalia as well.[30] However, annotations made by early modern readers in the leaves of medieval manuscripts have not yet attracted significant attention.

The present study seeks to chart and understand the afterlife of medieval texts by investigating their reception at a particular time and in a particular location through an examination of the evidence for the ownership and use of surviving manuscript copies. It covers ground that is cognate with Mary Erler's recent account of reading and writing during the Dissolution, but takes a longer chronological view and considers the impact of the Henrician reformation and subsequent reforms on lay rather than religious readers.[31] It makes a case study of the books of two generations of an English family who spent their adult lives under Tudor rule; eight manuscripts that contain more than twenty individual texts (in full form or extracts) may certainly be associated with this family. Whilst the codices themselves date from the fifteenth century, some of the texts within them originated in the late fourteenth century. Yet

---

[26] See Duffy, *Marking the Hours*, and Chapters 5 and 6 below.

[27] Flannery and Griffin, *Spaces for Reading*.

[28] Cambers, 'Readers' Marks and Religious Practice', p. 230.

[29] Sherman, *John Dee*; Jardine and Grafton '"Studied for Action"'; Sharpe, *Reading Revolutions*; and see also Cambers's study of Lady Margaret Hoby cited in the previous note.

[30] Key works include Jackson, *Marginalia*, Sherman, *Used Books*, and Slights, *Managing Readers*.

[31] Erler, *Reading and Writing During the Dissolution*.

Introduction

despite the old age of both the texts and the manuscripts that preserve them, the evidence for the reading of these books belongs to the period 1470–1585, a long century which spans the reigns of Edward IV, Edward V, Richard III, Henry VII, Henry VIII, Edward VI, Mary Tudor, and the first decades of Elizabeth I's reign. Members of the Roberts family who owned and read these books were located at Willesden and Neasden in Middlesex where their properties were clustered, and in London, where their professional affiliations were to the Inns of Court. This was not a noble family; instead these were gentry, whose fortunes were increasing during this period. The physical proximity of the family's property to the capital and their professional interests there mean that unusually they may be regarded as simultaneously metropolitan and provincial, and their legal activities reveal that these two categories were in any case much less distinct than might be supposed. Julia Boffey has drawn attention to the rich range of reading available in London in the early sixteenth century, and through a number of significant studies has highlighted the intersections of textual production and transmission, and of manuscript and print, in what she terms the 'interpenetration of different forms of book production'.[32] A similar point about 'interpenetration' might be made about the readers of those books who are generally designated as 'London readers', but who were in fact much more protean than that label implies. Such readers were mobile, not fixed, and to pin their activities to the capital belies the complex networks of personal and business affiliations that existed between London and its surrounding counties (and beyond) in the fifteenth and sixteenth centuries.[33] The capital's networks were dependent on, and reached out to, a wide provincial orbit, a fact that has been somewhat obscured by much excellent research into the city's records and the structures of its civic bureaucracy, including the activities of fraternities, guilds, and livery companies.[34] Such urban bodies offered important forums for merchants and members of the professional classes, but because many of those men had been drawn into London by their work (and in the case of lawyers, for their training), they continued to retain equally important links with their original provincial communities in terms of family, property, and landholdings,

---

[32] Boffey, 'London Books', p. 427; see also Boffey, *Manuscript and Print*.

[33] For some examples of such interpenetrating networks see Connolly, 'Late Medieval Books of Hours'.

[34] Important studies that have enhanced understanding of later medieval London include Barron, *London in the Later Middle Ages*, and Barron and Sutton (eds.), *Medieval London Widows*.

social connections and personal friendships. These parallel but more disparate influences on members of the late medieval and early modern gentry have not yet been intensively studied. The process of doing so is laborious: it requires a nuanced interpretation of very many documentary sources that are typically housed in different repositories, and even the initial process of locating the relevant surviving records may necessitate a great deal of painstaking research; the further work of identifying individual subjects and disentangling them from other similarly named contemporaries or relatives, in order to trace their activities and connections with other individuals whose identities must also be established, is timeconsuming and sometimes unproductive. Small wonder that members of this important stratum of English society remain under-known – and yet, there is much *to* know about such individuals; the recovery of more information about such men (because they are, by and large, men) will enhance understanding of late medieval and early modern readers and reading practices, and, in turn, of the patterns of circulation of medieval texts and the longevity of those works.

The present account of the Roberts family constructs a narrative of these later readers' interests in their old books. It makes a detailed investigation of their annotations, comments, and other markings, and also, on occasion, of places where they left no marks. An attempt is made to understand various losses and absences from their manuscripts, as well as to interpret readerly additions. Each chapter of this study after the first is structured around a particular manuscript or particular aspects of several manuscripts; to set the context for these discussions Chapter 1 treats matters of ancestry and locality. As middle-ranking gentry, the lives and achievements of members of the Roberts family are not generally accessible from published histories in the same way as those of their higher-ranking social contemporaries: theirs were not lives of distinction or significance that merit recording in the *Oxford Dictionary of National Biography*. Nevertheless there is much information to be recovered about the lives of members of the gentry through careful analysis of the contemporary records of local and national government, and by searches for surviving documents that relate to individual legal and property transactions.[35] From such research it is possible to construct profiles for these little-known Tudor gentlemen and thereby to flesh out their biographies. Such an approach is necessary not just to gain a firm knowledge of

---

[35] For a similar study of the Staffordshire owner-compiler of a sixteenth-century miscellany, see Youngs, 'Entertainment Networks'; on the evolution of gentry culture and its diversity see Radulescu and Truelove, *Gentry Culture*.

Introduction

the personal identities of these book owners but also to develop a nuanced understanding of the interests, aptitudes, and motivations that governed their reading of medieval texts. Accordingly in Chapter 1 the Roberts family background in the fourteenth and fifteenth centuries is sketched in as much detail as it has been possible to uncover, before the focus narrows to concentrate on Thomas Roberts (1470–1542) and his immediate personal life, marriages, and children. The family's land-holdings in Middlesex are described using detail from family history to demonstrate how their lands and properties gradually accrued to build up a substantial estate. Their longstanding connection with the church at Willesden, a late medieval centre of pilgrimage, and their participation in local society are also considered. Other, seemingly unconnected, families of the same name flourished throughout the period, and disentangling these from the Robertses of Middlesex has entailed weighing evidence drawn from later genealogies, wills, and other documentary sources; this information is summarized in Appendix IV.

In the second chapter Thomas Roberts's career at the Inner Temple and the range of connections open to him there are explored. One of his work books, a copy of the *Registrum Brevium*, survives in BL Harley 1859; the original contents of that manuscript and its added items are examined in detail. It was common practice amongst lawyers to lend and bequeath books, and evidence that Thomas may have been given this book by a colleague is considered. Other annotations show that his son Edmund Roberts (1520–85) used the same book even though details of his status as a lawyer cannot be verified. Thomas Roberts's work in local government and public life are also charted, with a view to constructing a fuller profile of him as a reader and uncovering his network of contacts and associates. Discussions of the books and libraries of legal practitioners tend to focus on the presence of law books, and overviews of the reading habits of lawyers assume that members of this group were narrowly interested in works connected with their own profession. Thus Alain Wijffels comments: 'To judge by a few examples, common lawyers' libraries, during this period, seem to have eschewed civilian literature.'[36] Yet the example of Thomas Roberts paints a rather different picture of a man who read considerable amounts of vernacular devotional literature. Chapter 3 considers other texts that he read, all works of English devotional prose and most, in their

---

[36] Hellinga and Trapp (eds.), *The Cambridge History of the Book in Britain, III: 1400–1557*, p. 408.

own day, inherently and unproblematically Catholic. In the period in which Thomas may be assumed to have read these texts – perhaps from the 1480s until his death in 1542 – these works assumed changing hues of orthodoxy depending on the prevailing political climate. This chapter makes a detailed appraisal of the various works contained in two manuscripts: BL Harley 2322, a copy of the *Pore Caitif* that has lollard elements, and Cambridge MA, University of Harvard, Houghton Library, MS Richardson 22, a collection of meditative devotional works and prayers directed towards Mary and Christ. The *Pore Caitif* is a substantial work that lacks a critical edition, and consequently the nature of this popular medieval compilation and the contents of its individual tracts are not well known to modern scholars. Most of the separate texts which were assembled in MS Richardson 22 seem to have had a limited circulation in the Middle Ages and are equally unknown today. The contents of these two manuscripts are therefore described in detail in Chapter 3, to allow an appreciation of what information and instruction Thomas Roberts might have found when he turned to these books. Once this has been established, the different nature of the evidence of reception in these two manuscripts, one heavily annotated and the other conspicuously clean, is examined and linked to the possible implications of reading these works in an age which was socially and politically very different from their era of origin (and set to become more so).

Chapter 4 continues to explore the ways in which Thomas Roberts may have acquired his books. He had professional connections with various religious houses and undoubtedly profited from their dissolution as did other men of his generation and social standing. The question of whether Thomas may have acquired any of his books in this way is considered and, in the absence of any concrete evidence for such acquisition, the textual contents of particular manuscripts are examined for indications of religious origin. Attention in this chapter is directed to the Roberts copy of Nicholas Love's *Mirror of the Blessed Life of Jesus Christ* in Manchester, JRL English 98, a deluxe manuscript that seems too splendid to have been originally made for the family. A reader has discreetly noted many passages in this manuscript, using lines and marks rather than comments; the problems of dating and attributing such markings are addressed, as are the difficulties of interpreting other evidence of ownership. This manuscript came to rest in the marriage family of Thomas's eldest daughter, Dorothy, whose brother-in-law, Edmund Horde, was the last prior of Hinton charterhouse. This intriguing connection between a manuscript of Love's *Mirror* and a member of the Carthusian order is highlighted, and other

Introduction

books owned by Edmund Horde and the extended Horde family are briefly noted.

The fifth chapter explores the very different uses to which old books could be put in the early modern period. These include keeping records of important events, and adding notes of births, deaths, marriages, and property interests, either to original blank leaves or to new leaves added for precisely this purpose. Eventually this function becomes the dominant use of these old books, which by the seventeenth century seem to have been primarily locations of safekeeping and remembrance. Various manuscripts are cited briefly in this regard. The more extensive practical use to which Thomas put his manuscript collection of medieval recipes is investigated in more detail. It is clear that the therapeutic knowledge contained in BodL Rawlinson C. 299, a fifteenth-century collection of medical recipes, was very much valued by its sixteenth-century owner who indexed its contents and added other contemporary recipes to what was thus a growing household manual. Finally, taking a different slant on the notion of use, this chapter also looks at the family's two books of hours, both of the prescribed use of Sarum. Both were owned by Thomas Roberts and one was passed down to his son Edmund; however, both also contain the obits of individuals who cannot be linked to the family, suggesting that these were second-hand books even in the sixteenth century. Edmund's use of CUL Ii.6.2 is treated in more detail in the following chapter, where close attention is paid to the prayers and other items that he added to its leaves. This final full-length chapter returns to a sustained consideration of the reading of later medieval texts in the early modern age, this time examining Edmund Roberts's experience of reading devotional English writings during the very different reigns of Mary Tudor and Elizabeth I; its particular focus is a manuscript that Edmund, and not his father, seems to have acquired, BodL Rawlinson C. 894, a collection of shorter devotional texts and extracts written in Middle English prose.

Implicit throughout this study is the question of cultural influence, and specifically how the reading experiences of these Tudor gentlemen were shaped by the social and political changes that beset sixteenth-century England. Their responses to the medieval texts that they read illuminate some of their preoccupations as young men, husbands, and fathers, as heads of households and men of work, and as men of social standing and holders of civic office. Above all – since most of the texts in these old manuscript books are devotional in nature – the annotations made by Thomas and Edmund reveal how seriously they tried to live good Christian lives. In a period of rapid and sometimes unpredictable religious change it cannot have been at all easy to discern the true path to salvation: in this Thomas, and even more so Edmund, experienced religion quite differently from their medieval ancestors. One might imagine that these men's responses to these instrinsically Catholic old books would clearly demonstrate their own personal religious views, but in fact this is far from true and the conclusion to this study tries to suggest why such a lack of clarity may have been inevitable. At the same time the underlying narrative of the present book seeks to unravel how Thomas Roberts – a man involved at local level first with upholding and then with dismantling the fabric of medieval monasticism – might have regarded the Henrician Reformation; it also aims to discover Edmund Roberts's position as he lived through the Henrician reforms, the radical Protestantism of the Edwardian regime, the Catholic volte-face of Mary's reign, and the return to Protestantism under Elizabeth.

Information contained in the opening leaves of BodL Rawlinson C. 894 allows us to trace several later generations of the Roberts family and their social connections in the sixteenth and early seventeenth centuries, down to the latest datable record, which relates to the death of Eleanor Aty Roberts in 1678. This was also the period when the Roberts estate was in decline: in 1698 their main property passed to another branch of the family, and in the early eighteenth century the estate was broken up and sold. There is evidence that at least some of their manuscripts had already passed out of family hands by this point. The few manuscripts that we can still connect with the family must be only the remnants of a larger personal library which would also have included printed books, even though none are known to survive. As a point of comparison the late fifteenth-century lawyer Thomas Kebell had at least thirty-three books, and half a century later Henry, Lord Stafford (1501–63) had a collection of 300 books, though he was much wealthier and of greater social rank.[37] The material evidence for the ongoing life of these eight manuscripts is noted in a postscript to this study's main chapters. This charts the subsequent history of the manuscripts in terms of their passage through the hands of various owners, their exchange by sale, and their entry into public repositories; no attempt is made to identify evidence of readership in this later phase of their existence. These are

---

[37] Ives, *The Common Lawyers*; Anderson, 'The Books and Interests of Henry, Lord Stafford', pp. 87–114.

Introduction

no longer private family books. Their presence in research libraries and, in some cases, their transformation into digital artefacts, has opened these manuscripts to a global audience, and to a readership far wider than could ever have possibly been imagined by their medieval producers. The leisure and access that we now enjoy (wherever and whenever) in reading their contents from screen rather than page will lead to the creation of new reading communities for the texts that they contain. In this situation it is much easier for new generations of scholars to peruse these old medieval texts in depth, and to move beyond the mere cataloguing of detail to a more nuanced consideration of content. Digital availability may also lead to the discovery of new connections, both in terms of production (in the matching of scribal hands and artistic styles), but also in reception (in the tricky recognition of annotating hands or the presence of non-verbal signs and markings in other manuscripts). Reception is a more open-ended process than production, even though production can continue or be resumed after a pause. Reception is in fact potentially endless: it is naturally ongoing, meaning that the possibility of drawing a line and claiming that a work's reception has ended is ever receding. The reading of medieval texts, and defining when such reading in a meaningful sense may have ceased; the other 'uses' of such books and their changing nature over time; and the definition of a readership that stretches beyond the circumstances of the works' original creation: these are questions that this study seeks to articulate and address, but the full story of these manuscripts is one that cannot yet be told.

1

Family Matters: The Roberts Family of Willesden

The main chronological focus of this book is the period between 1470 and 1585, a century which spans the reigns of seven monarchs (Edward IV, Richard III, Henry VII, Henry VIII, Edward VI, Mary Tudor, and Elizabeth), or ten, if the brief interval in 1470–71 when Henry VI was restored, and the even briefer reigns of Edward V and Lady Jane Grey, are also included. In terms of the individual readers and book owners whom this study investigates, that long century also encompasses the lives of a father, Thomas Roberts (1470–1542), and his son, Edmund Roberts (1520–85). Thomas and Edmund were members of the Roberts family whose main property holdings were in and around Neasden and Willesden in the county of Middlesex (see Map 1). Thomas was a lawyer whose practice was in the London parish of St Clement Danes; to different degrees both men were active in public life, and were assigned a variety of roles in local government and administration. Their careers and activities may be traced through the public record, from which a rich picture of their social and civic associations may be derived. A variety of documentary sources, including wills and records of property transactions, testifies to the steady rise in the family's fortunes during the sixteenth century, a period during which they increased their personal wealth through favour, business transactions, and judicious marriage alliances. These sources offer much information about family history and the Middlesex land base that underpinned their prosperity, and a close reading of these documents also provides insight into their extensive network of personal connections within the locality; this network sustained Thomas Roberts and his sons through a period of political instability and uncertainty. Before considering these men as readers, this chapter will situate them as family men, in terms of both their ancestry and their descendants, and as members of a closely interwoven local community.

Family Matters: The Roberts Family of Willesden

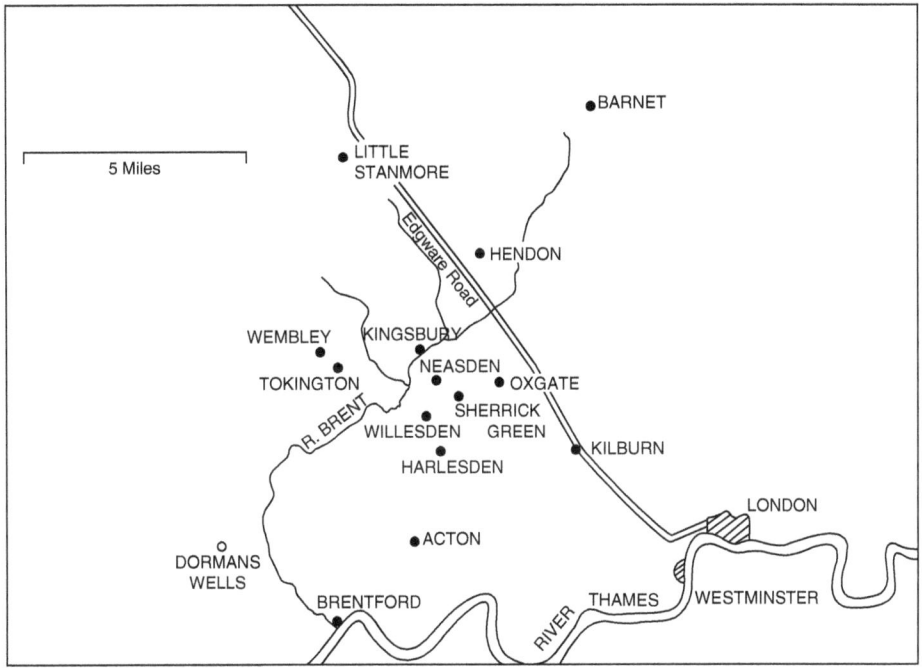

Map 1 Map of Willesden and Neasden.

THE FAMILY SEAT AND SOME FAMILY HISTORY

The groundwork for the family's Tudor aggrandizement had been laid during the two previous centuries by the steady acquisition of parcels of land and the patient rationalization of property holdings. The nucleus of the family seat, Neasden House, which by the mid seventeenth century was the largest house in Willesden, was a collection of seven tenements on Bower Lane which ran east from Neasden and then south to Sherrick Green.[1] Members of the Roberts family had long possessed property in this area. A confirmation of a transaction between John Le Mileward of Willesden and John de Middleton, citizen of London, in the reign of Edward I (1272–1307) describes some of the lands involved (a field called Thorncroft and lands in Brentcroft and Sheeproad) as adjacent to lands owned by Thomas Roberd, a witness to the charter.[2] Other

---

[1] For records relating to these properties see LMA, CLC/313/L/H/002/MS25122/383 (Taylors); TNA, E 40/6875; E 40/11588; E 40/11844 (Hales); E 40/11648; E 40/12065; LMA, CLC/313/L/H/002/MS25122/1354 (Bucklands).
[2] TNA, E 40/11648; the exact date of this document is obscured.

contemporary documents confirming John de Middleton's land holdings in the area mention William Roberd either as the owner of nearby properties (lands at Sherrick, southeast of Neasden, and Sheeproad) or as a witness.[3] A later transfer of Neasden lands to John de Middleton during the reign of Edward II lists John Roberd as a witness.[4] The exact relationship between Thomas, William, and John Roberd cannot be determined, but other records from the late fourteenth and early fifteenth centuries suggest that the family had multiple branches: for example, a petition of 1394 mentions Richard Robard and Ralph Robard with John Kynge the elder, 'all of Willesdoun'; a guarantee of surety of 1406 lists a Thomas Roberd amongst other Middlesex men; and a quitclaim of 1421 given at Paddington was witnessed by Richard Robert, John Roberd, and William Robert.[5] Ralph Roberts held Taylors cottage in Neasden, and made a grant of it in 1393 to his son, Thomas, to whose widow it was later assigned in 1411/12.[6] In 1424 and 1425 John Roberts consolidated his lands at Sheeproad by exchange with Robert Curson, clerk, one of the largest landowners in Willesden.[7] The first of these documents styles John Roberts as 'Seniorem de Willesdon', indicating that there were two John Robertses at this date; although it might be simplest to assume that these were father and son, that is by no means the only possible formulation that would account for identically named older and younger men within the same family. The John Roberts 'gentilman' mentioned in the gift of goods and chattels made by John Careley of Willesden in 1468 must have been the younger of these men.[8] This John Roberts is described in a note in one of the family's books as holding lands *infra Manorum de Nesdon* ('within the manor of Neasden'), and as having died in 1476, a date confirmed by a document of 1480 that describes

---

[3] TNA E/40/6874 (Sherrick), E 40/7893 (Sheeproad); listed as a witness in TNA, E 40/6806, E 40/7892, and E 40/6800.

[4] TNA, E 40/12065, dated 1325.

[5] Respectively, *CCR Richard II, 1392–96*, p. 199; *CCR Henry IV*, 3 (1405–9), p. 152; *CCR Henry V*, 2 (1419–22), p. 138. An indenture of 1438 mentions lands belonging to William Robert in the vicinity of East Bedfont, see *CCR Henry VI*, 3 (1435–41), p. 182.

[6] As noted in BL, MS Stowe 862, f. 45^r: 'All that I find of this, is, a grant of it by Ralph Roberts to his son Thomas 16 Ricardi secundi, 1393, and an assignment of it to the widow of the said Thomas, among other lands etc. by certain trustees, 13 Henry 4ti.' This Thomas Roberts was probably the Thomas Roberd recorded in 1406 in a memorandum of mainprise for John Lyn, chaplain, see *CCR Henry IV*, 3 (1405–9), p. 152.

[7] TNA, E 40/7644, E 40/10379.

[8] WAM, 17021; *CCR Edward IV*, 2 (15 Edward IV), p. 424 (no. 1521).

him as 'nuper of Willesden' and 'Gentilman iam defuncto': this John Roberts was Thomas Roberts's father.[9]

By 1510 Thomas Roberts held five houses in Neasden village, plus numerous crofts and open-field land from Neasden prebend.[10] Thomas continued to enlarge the family estate, acquiring other property held from Neasden and Chambers prebends and holding leases of various estates. These included lands that he held for a decade on behalf of the heirs of Thomas Frowyk, and others that he managed on behalf of John Page, the son of William Page of Harlesden.[11] In a complex tangle of legal transactions, Thomas Roberts also leased other lands that had formerly belonged to William Page and which had since been alienated to Westminster Abbey.[12] For much of the sixteenth century, Westminster Abbey leased its Neasden estate to successive members of the Roberts family: firstly to Thomas from *circa* 1516–39, then later to John *circa* 1553–56, and then to Edmund (1566–69).[13] The estate continued to be leased to later generations of the family until it was broken up and sold in the mid nineteenth century.[14]

The full extent of Thomas Roberts's disposable property can be seen from his will of 1542, which left the bulk of his estate to his eldest son and heir, Michael, but also parcelled out other properties amongst his other children.[15] Edmund was bequeathed three tenements in Harlesden, named 'Robertes Crofte', 'Dorans', and 'Panyermane', all of which were rented out and being farmed at the time. Other tenements in Harlesden (Downes and Brays), and some properties in Willesden, again all currently rented and farmed, were left to Thomas's youngest son John, along with the manor of Fosters in Acton. Thomas's daughter Anne, who was married to Thomas Smythson, was given a tenement in Tothill Street in Westminster, next door to the Swan

---

[9] BodL Rawlinson C. 299, f. 1ʳ; WAM, 17022; see the section titled 'Father and Son: John Roberts (d. 1476 and Thomas Roberts (1470–1542)'.

[10] *VCH*, p. 217.

[11] TNA, E 210/10147; BodL MS D.D. All Souls c 124/85a; TNA, C 1/349/1; C 1/349/2; C 1/349/3; C 1/767/20. See further discussion in Chapter 2, section titled 'Thomas Roberts at the Inns of Court'.

[12] WAM, 17026; *CPR* Henry VII 1494–1509, p. 517.

[13] WAM, 4680, 4697, 4706, and TNA, SC 6/HENVIII/2415, m. 16; WAM, 33185 and *CPR Philip and Mary*, 3 (1555–57), p. 352; WAM, 33187.

[14] See the discussion in *VCH*, p. 216.

[15] LMA, DL/C/356.

(presumably a tavern). The only unmarried daughter, Alice, was bequeathed nine tenements in Pety France in Westminster.

Thomas Roberts's predecessors had lived in a house on the east side of Neasden Lane, called Lyttel's or Barnhaw, but he rebuilt or greatly enlarged the property in this vicinity that his ancestor John Roberts had acquired from John Atte Wood.[16] Improvements to this property, now called 'Catt at Woodes', were continued by Thomas's son Michael, who refers in his will of 1544 to his 'mansyon and dwelling house in Neasdon'. The will's description of this property, though no doubt characterized by the inclusive formulae habitually used in law, evokes an extensive estate which consisted of 'gardeyns, orchardes, pounds, ffysshinges, yardes, doofehouse, banksides, meddowes, woodes, underwoodes, hedgerowes'.[17] This house formed the family's main residence in the sixteenth and seventeenth centuries. After Michael's death the manor or prebend of Neasden was leased for thirty years to Ursula, his widow, to whom Michael left the estate for her lifetime, stipulations that caused conflict between her and his brother Edmund.[18] Ursula was also to have tenements in St Albans which might have been part of her dowry, since they are not mentioned in Thomas's will of two years before. Michael reiterated that property at Fosters in Acton and some tenements in Harlesden were to go to his brother John, and a tenement in Tothill Street in Westminster to his sister Anne and her husband Thomas Smythson, as directed by their father's will two years previously; a tenement and garden plot in the parish of St Clements in London was left to his brother Edmund, and another tenement in Tothill Street went to a priest named John Busshop.[19]

The family estate was further extended by Edmund Roberts, who purchased Middletons manor from Richard Barley in 1563.[20] This property, which consisted of five houses, land, and rents, in Willesden and Hendon, greatly increased the Neasden estate. Edmund also leased the manor or prebend of Harlesden in 1576 for a period of twenty-one years, a lease that was continued by both his son and

---

[16] BL, MS Stowe 862, ff. 42^v–43^r.

[17] TNA, PROB 11/30/205.

[18] See further discussion in Chapter 5, section titled 'The Use of Sarum: Cambridge University Library, MS Ii.6.7 and Cambridge University Library, MS Ii.6.2'.

[19] John Busshop was probably the John Bishop who a little while later became vicar of Willesden (from 24 January 1546 to 1552).

[20] TNA, CP 25/2/171/5ELIZITrin.

grandson.[21] Edmund's son Francis Roberts bought Oxgate manor in 1587, along with other properties; when he died in 1632 he was said to be seised of thirty-four messuages and 1,654 acres in Willesden, a manor and land in Acton, a small estate in Kingsbury, and other estates in Lincolnshire.[22] Unlike his father and grandfather, who had both made marriages with women from families with London connections, Francis Roberts married more locally: his wife, Mary Barne or Barnes, was the daughter of John Barnes of Willesden, esquire. The match may indicate that the status of the Roberts family had risen amongst the Middlesex gentry, and marriage within this more local context gave rise to the possibility of consolidating the family estates, a process that was continued after Francis's death by his grandson and heir William (Francis's eldest son, Barne, predeceased him in 1610). William Roberts married Eleanor Aty, the daughter of Robert Aty of Kilburn Priory. Through this marriage William added considerably to the family estate, which he further augmented by buying up ecclesiastical properties during the Civil War and managing to retain them at the Restoration. William Roberts demolished the medieval cottages that surrounded Catewodes and converted their sites and Bower Lane into gardens and orchards for his house, by then renamed Neasden House, 'and the orchards & gardens adjoyning were lands belonging to divers small cottages which were pulled down in ye memory of some yet living, by Sir William Roberts Knight, about ye year 1656, and ye grounds enclosed with brick walls, at a great expence'. The eighteenth-century writer of this account added a symbol before 'living' to direct the reader to a list of names in the right margin (John Plomer, William Harman, George Cook, Nicholas).[23] By 1666 Neasden House was assessed on twenty-one hearths and was the largest house in Willesden.[24] However, after the death of Sir William Roberts in 1662 the Roberts estate began to contract. His son and grandson, both also named William, had to sell properties in order to clear their debts, and this process continued in the early part of the eighteenth century when the estate passed into the hands of a different branch of the family.[25]

---

[21] *VCH*, p, 212.

[22] His will is TNA, PROB 11/160/635; for the inquisition post mortem see TNA, C 142/482/65. The Lincolnshire estates may indicate inheritance through a family connection with the Robertses of that county.

[23] BL, MS Stowe 862, f. 40^r; a diagram on f. 39^v shows the layout of the properties.

[24] TNA, E 179/232/32 f. 26; see Davies, Ferguson et al., *London and Middlesex 1666 Hearth Tax*, ii.1623.

[25] *VCH*, pp. 217–18.

FATHER AND SON: JOHN ROBERTS (D. 1476) AND THOMAS ROBERTS (1470–1542)

The Thomas Roberts who is one of the two main subjects of this study was born in September 1470 during the turbulent tenth year of Edward IV's reign. A record of his birth is inscribed at the beginning of one of the family's books, BodL Rawlinson C. 299, a collection of medical recipes and other practical texts. On f. 1^r is a note recording the date of the Battle of Barnet in 1471, when the Yorkists defeated the Lancastrians: *Bellum de Barnetfeld fuit in die Pasche xiiij die Apriles littera dominicalis F anno domini millesimo ccccłxxi anno regnis rex Edwardi quarti xj* (see Figure 1).[26] This statement takes up just over three lines, and the fourth line has been completed with the words: 'Thomas Robertʒ then xxx wekes olde'. The addition is written in different ink and by a different hand, and comparison with a surviving copy of Thomas's signature shows that this was undoubtedly Thomas's own hand.[27] One of the ways in which individuals reckoned their ages in the pre-modern period was by reference to memorable historical events, and the Battle of Barnet must have resonated with particular local significance for Thomas since Barnet itself lay not far north of Neasden where the Roberts family lived.

Further records on the same leaf reveal that Thomas's father John died in 1476 when his son was only six years old: *Johannes Robertʒ pater dicti Thome Robertʒ coroner Middlesex obijt xj die Septembre anno domini millesimo ccccłxxvj & anno xvj R E iiij^{ti}*, and specify that Thomas was recognized as his father's heir two years later: *Ad curiam tentam apud Nesdon in parochia de Willesden anno xviij R E iiij^{ti} compertum fuit per homagium curia predicta quod predictus Thomas Robertʒ fuit filius & heres predicti Johannis Robertʒ ad omnia terra & tenementa dicti Johannis infra Manerium de Nesdon et quod dictus Thomas tunc fuit etatis viij^{to} an annorum* ('At the court held at Neasden in the parish of Willesden in the eighteenth year of the reign of King Edward IV, it was proved through homage to the aforesaid court that the aforesaid Thomas Roberts was the son and heir of the aforesaid

---

[26] An English version of this historical record is given later in the volume, on f. 51^r, there written in black ink by a rough hand that is perhaps Thomas Roberts's: 'Barnetfeld was the xiiij day of Aprill beyng Ester day the yere of our lord a ml ccccłxxj & a° xj R E iiij^{ti}.'

[27] Thomas's signature survives on a certificate of assessment for John Harman in Pynnor, 14 January 6 Henry VIII (1515), see *LP Addenda* Henry VIII, p. 36. Comparison of the two reveals that the capitals 'T' and 'R', and lower case 'h' and 'b', are identical. The document is accessible via *State Papers Online*.

Family Matters: The Roberts Family of Willesden

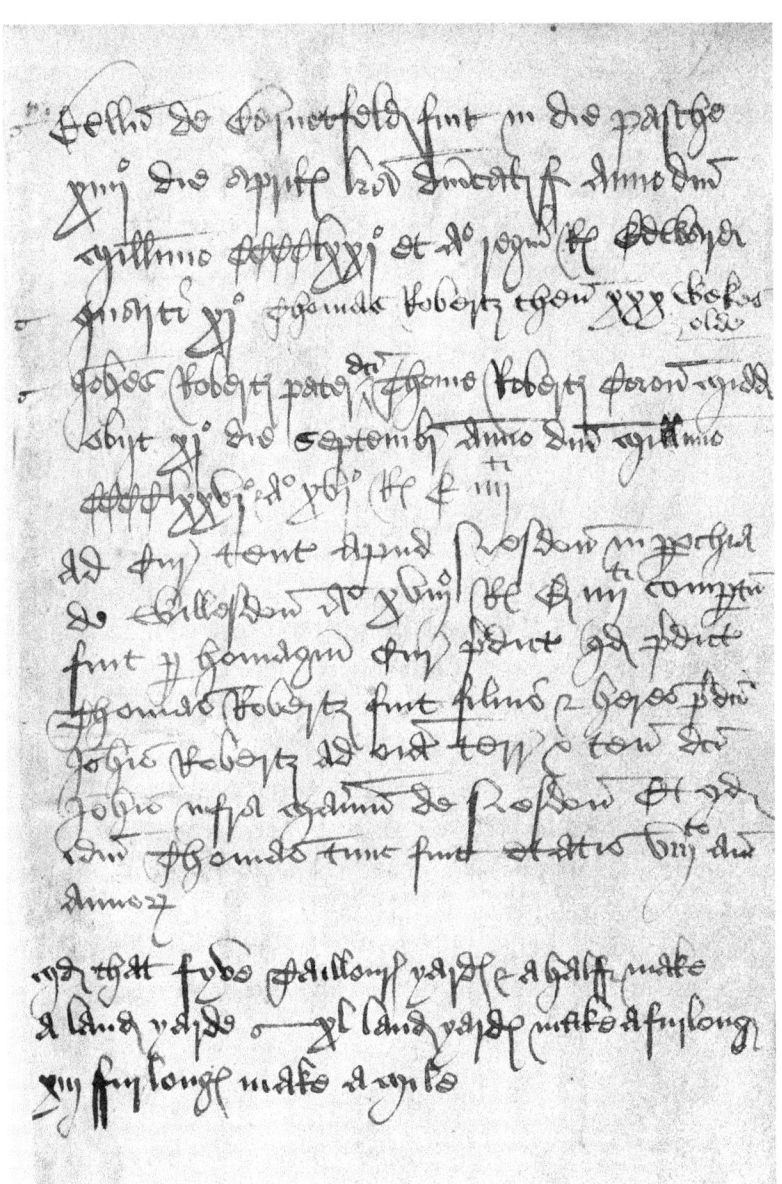

Figure 1 Oxford, Bodleian Library, MS Rawlinson C. 299, f. 1ʳ. Note of Battle of Barnet and Thomas Roberts's birth. Reproduced by permission of the Bodleian Libraries, the University of Oxford.

John Roberts, to all the lands and tenements of the said John within the manor of Neasden, and which said Thomas at that time was eight years of age'). John Roberts is named in, and was sometimes a witness to, a number of Middlesex property transactions in the 1460s.[28] The latest of these, which dates from 1468, styles him as 'gentilman': John Careley, 'husbondman' of Willesden, made a gift and confirmation by charter with warranty of all his lands and tenements, rents, reversions and services, meadows, woods, and pastures in Willesden, to three other Willesden men: John Roberts 'gentilman', Roger Frende 'yoman', and John Halle, 'husbondman'.[29] In a previous transaction from 1466 which involved George Adyf, vicar of St Dunstan in the West, and John Ball, chaplain, who were the grantors of a demise of property in Middlesex to Anne Cristede, John Roberts appears as a witness, along with John Carley, John Hall, Roger Frene (probably the same as Roger Frende), and John Twyforde the elder (later one of the witnesses to the 1468 transaction).[30] Similarly, John Roberts had also been a witness to the quitclaim of lands in Acton, Yellyng, and Fulham made by Beda Hede of Kyngesbury to Thomas Frowyk and others in 1462.[31] Yet John Roberts evidently had interests and connections in London as well as in Middlesex, because he is named very precisely ('John Robert of Nesedon in Willesden parish co. Middlesex') in a gift of goods and chattels made on 1 April 1470 by William Hulet or Hewlot, citizen and 'butcher' of London; the other citizens mentioned in the same transaction are Thomas Pernell and Thomas Alderton, both 'bochers', and a 'bruer', Robert Michell, along with William Bolton, rector of the parish church of St Nicholas in the Shambles, within Newgate.[32] William Hewlot repeated this gift of goods and chattels on 15 October 1474, this time naming as the recipients Thomas Parnyll, butcher of London, and Peter Hyll, notary of London, as well as John Roberts.[33]

The name 'John Roberts' occurs in several other mid fifteenth-century Middlesex records, but it is not easy to be sure that these references always

---

[28] WAM, 17019, 17020, 17021.

[29] WAM, 17021, *CCR Edward IV*, 2 (1468–76), p. 424 (no. 1521); given at Willesden 1 November 1468 and witnessed by John Twyford the elder, Robert Twyford, John Downe, John Twyford the younger, and David Wasse.

[30] *CCR Edward IV*, 1 (1461–68), p. 399; given at Willesden 5 December 1466. Anne, the wife of John Cristede, was the daughter of Henry Boys and Alice his wife, herself daughter of Agnes Guybon of London who had enfeoffed the property to Adyf and Ball, along with William Barnevile and John Hardy, now deceased.

[31] *CCR Edward IV*, 1 (1461–68), pp. 136–37. The other recipients were William Eston and Richard Bernes; the other witnesses were William Bernevyle, Ivo Chalkhyll, John Erlyche, John Veyser the elder, John Veyser the younger, and Thomas Lutton.

[32] *CCR Edward IV*, 2 (1468–76), p. 126 (no. 495).

[33] *CCR Edward IV*, 2 (1468–76), pp. 362–63 (no. 1306).

signify the man who was Thomas Roberts's father. Whilst some references clearly designate other men who happened to have the same name (such as the John Robert mentioned in a recognizance of 1452 who is described as a miller of Langford, near Harmondsworth), most probably do relate to the Willesden family.[34] For example, a John Robert was a witness in 1448 to a charter with warranty of all the lands, rents, and so on in Paddington made by the widow Margaret Hille to Thomas Wesynham and others.[35] A similar transaction made in 1450 by William Dorset to Lettice, widow of Robert Frampton, and others, involving lands in Paddington, Westbourne, Kensington, and Knightsbridge, also lists a 'John Robart' amongst the witnesses, and the location suggests that this was probably a member of the Willesden family.[36] The John Robert who witnessed the transfer of lands in Neasden in 1454 from John atte Hall to John Careley is clearly the same person mentioned in the other documented transactions that involve the same parties.[37] A grant of land by John Roberts to John Gloucester in 1449 offers some significant detail about family history; John Roberts stated that: *dicta tria crofta iure hereditario post decessum Thome Roberd de Wyllesden housbondman patris mei michi descendebant* ('the said three crofts descended to me lawfully by inheritance after the death of my father Thomas Roberts of Willesden, husbandman').[38] This indicates that the name of Thomas Roberts's grandfather was also Thomas, but it does not seem that this was the Thomas who was the son of Ralph Roberts because the later eighteenth-century account of the family's properties explicitly states that the name of Thomas Roberts's great-grandfather was John.[39] It is quite possible that Ralph Roberts had another son named John: some earlier fifteenth-century references to John Roberts of Willesden dating from 1419 (failing to appear to answer a charge of trespass) and the mid 1420s (land transfers) attest to a John Roberts who flourished at the appropriate time, and as we have seen one of these documents uses the style 'Johannem Robard Seniorem de Willesdon', indicating that there was more than one man with

---

[34] *CCR Henry VI*, 5 (1447–54), pp. 334–35.
[35] *CCR Henry VI*, 5 (1447–54), p. 93.
[36] *CCR Henry VI*, 5 (1447–54), p. 191. See also the reference to William Roberd of Westbourne 'husbondman' in the parish of Paddington in 1437, *CPR 1436–41*, p. 103.
[37] WAM, 17018.
[38] TNA, E 40/7253; John Roberts's small round seal, with a design of a five-pointed flower, survives on this charter.
[39] BL, Stowe 862, f. 42ᵛ; ff. 38r–59r of this manuscript comprise transcripts of a sixteenth-century rental and other material relating to the manor and prebend of Neasden.

that name in the 1420s.⁴⁰ The Roberts family was extensive, and the skeleton family tree that has been tentatively established to show Thomas Roberts's ancestry (see *Table 1*) offers no insight into the likely existence of many other siblings in each generation. It also seems that Thomas Roberts did not stand in the main line of succession. His great-grandfather John Roberts was described as having 'had his dwelling house in some other part of Neasden, adjoining to the ground called Littlecroft (as per cartam) where his descendants also inhabited, till Thomas Roberts, who was bred to ye law, & got a good estate, removed to Catewodes upon the death of his aunt ...'.⁴¹ The name of this aunt is not given, and the published pedigrees for Middlesex offer no help on this point, but she was probably a widow who had been allowed to remain in the property for her lifetime.⁴²

Table 1 Family tree: Suggested patrilineage of Thomas Roberts of Willesden.

SUGGESTED PATRILINEAGE OF THOMAS ROBERTS OF WILLESDEN

```
           Ralph Roberts      Johanna
           fl.1365–95         (dead by 1395)
                  |_____|
                        |
           ┌────────────┴────────────┐
    Thomas Roberts            John Roberts Senior
    (dead by 1411)            fl.1424
    m. ?
    fl.1411
                              Thomas Roberts
                              (dead by 1449)
                                    |
                       ┌────────────┴────────────┐
                 (elder brother)           John Roberts
                 m.???                     d.1476
                                                 |
                                          THOMAS ROBERTS
                                          1470–1542
```

Some other aspects of Thomas Roberts's immediate family remain unclear, in that I have not been able to establish the names of his mother or any of his

---

⁴⁰ *CPR* 1416–22, p. 222; TNA, E 40/7644; E 40/10379.

⁴¹ BL, MS Stowe 862, ff. 42ᵛ–43ʳ.

⁴² The pedigree published by Armytage (ed.), *Middlesex Pedigrees*, begins with Thomas Roberts (p. 165); that published by Grigson, 'Pedigree of Roberts', begins with John Roberts, purchaser of property from John Attewode, and indicates two generations (without Christian names) between him and Thomas Roberts. Both pedigrees have various inaccuracies.

siblings. In his will of 1542 he mentions 'my brother William Browne and Alice his wif and Beatrice Bodley, widowe', but although the tag 'my brother' must mean brother-in-law, the interpretation of this relationship seems to have been broader in this period than it would be now. Beatrice Bodley was certainly not Thomas's blood sister, as might have been assumed from this reference. Beatrice was the widow of William Bodley, grocer, who had died in 1540, and her maiden name was Sadler, indicating that her blood relation was not to Thomas Roberts himself but to his third wife, Katherine Sadler. Beatrice, who died in 1558, was Katherine's sister, and given the close conjunction of their names in Thomas's will, Alice may have been a third Sadler sister.[43] I have not yet succeeded in identifying William Browne, and the name is a common one; several prominent Londoners of this name occur too early to be the individual mentioned here.[44] Possibly the William Browne who was an alderman and who was married to Alice, the grand-daughter of Alice Bryce, might be the right person. Thomas Roberts's will also mentions William Newland and Alyce his wife without specifying any family relationship; they are the very first named recipients of bequests and they are left gifts of clothing, which would seem to bespeak a personal connection. They are also named in Michael's will of 1544 where they are bequeathed the tenement with an orchard called Bucklands (where they were living) for the term of their lives; William Newland had been the tenant of this property since at least 1535.[45]

Thomas himself was married three times, though there is very little information about his first wife, Margaret Fyncham, who died in 1505 (see *Table 2*). Her name is not mentioned in any of the family records found in the Robertses' personal books, perhaps because those are essentially records of births, and there was no surviving issue from this marriage.[46] A small commemorative brass at St Mary's, Willesden, with an inscription which is now mutilated, states: 'Pray for the soulle

---

[43] Sutton, 'Lady Joan Bradbury', p. 212, n. 12. William Bodley's will is TNA, PROB 11/28/311; Beatrice's will is TNA, PROB 11/42A/149. See Chapter 4, section titled 'Approved Reading: Manchester, John Rylands Library, MS English 98', for a discussion of books owned by them.'

[44] Barron, *London in the Middle Ages*, p. 347: a William Browne, mercer, was sheriff of London in 1491–92, mayor 1507–8, and died in 1508; another William Browne, mercer, was sheriff in 1504–5, mayor 1513–14, and died 3 June 1514; both died too early to be the William Browne named in Thomas Roberts's will.

[45] BL, MS Stowe 862, f. 46ʳ.

[46] For the book owned by Thomas and Margaret see Chapter 4, section titled 'Augmentations' (on the ownership inscription), and fuller discussion of its textual contents in Chapter 3, section titled 'Orthodox Reading: University of Harvard, Houghton Library, MS Richardson 22'.

of Margaret Roberte late [...] the daughter of Robert Fyncham Esquyer wh[...] xxiii day of august ye yere of o Lord MDV on whose [...]'.[47] The brass has been moved several times, only reaching its present position on the north side of the chancel when the church was restored in 1964; previously it was recorded as lying 'near altar' in 1783, and in the floor of the nave in 1839.[48] It was seen at a much earlier date by the heralds who compiled the collection of epitaphs and arms in what is now British Library, MS Lansdowne 874; on a visit to the parish church of Willesden in 1595 they drew sketches of the shields on Edmund Roberts's brass and made briefer notes of other memorials, including this one pertaining to 'Margrett d. to Robt Fyncham esq wyff to Thos Robertes obijt 1505'.[49]

Table 2 Family tree: The wives and children of Thomas Roberts.

THE WIVES AND CHILDREN OF THOMAS ROBERTS

John Roberts b.1476	Robert Fyncham	Humphrey Adam d.1507	Roger Sadler

THOMAS ROBERTS — **Margaret Fyncham**
b.1470   d.1505
d.1542

— Anna Adam   Henry

            — Katherine Sadler   Beatrice   John

| Dorothy b.1508 | Anna b.1509 | Alice b.1511 | Michael b.1519 d.1544 | Edmund b.1520 | John b.1531 |

The name 'Fyncham' (or 'Fincham') derives from Norfolk where a settlement of the same name lies in the west of the county, midway between Downham Market and Swaffham. In the fifteenth century Simeon Fyncham

---

[47] Valentine, 'The Roberts Family of Willesden', pp. 183–86, citing BodL Rawlinson B. 389b.
[48] Wadsworth, *The Church of St Mary, Willesden*, pp. 29–31.
[49] BL, MS Lansdowne 874, f. 78ᵛ.

(1388–1458) was the most substantial landholder there, and despite being described as 'an obscure person' who never held public office, he has been shown to have operated within an extensive network of friends and local associates.[50] The career of his son John demonstrates a rise in local prominence similar to that experienced by contemporary members of the Roberts family, and no doubt characteristic of gentry fortunes during this period. John Fyncham was justice of the peace for Norfolk from 1453, and is recorded as an apprentice of the law from 1456, though his name does not appear amongst the records of Lincoln's Inn, the inn favoured by most Norfolk lawyers.[51] He was a trustee of Sir Roger Townshend (c. 1435–93), having previously been a feoffee of Roger's father, John Townshend (d. 1466), and was also receiver to Anthony Woodville.[52] John Fyncham died in 1496 and was probably the owner of the copy of the *Nova Statuta Angliae* which is now in Norwich Castle Museum.[53] He was perhaps related to Thomas Fyncham, the prominent Suffolk office and land holder whose will is dated 1517, and to the later John Fyncham who was assessed at 100 marks in the Tudor subsidy of Norfolk in the 1520s.[54] This John Fyncham was probably the man of that name who died in 1541; his obit, and those of his wife and daughter, both named Ela, are recorded in the calendar of the so-called Fyncham Book of Hours, London, Victoria and Albert Museum, MS Reid 44.[55] Women with this surname occur as the prioresses of nearby female monastic houses. At the Benedictine house of Blackborough, a few miles north of Fyncham, the prioress from 1508–14 was Margaret or Margerie Fyncham, daughter of the John Fyncham who died in 1496.[56] At the Gilbertine priory of Shouldham, which was even closer to

---

[50] These networks have been traced by Maddern, ' "Best Trusted Friends" '.

[51] Baker, *Readers and Readings*, p. 13. Baker notes that where fifteenth-century apprentices of the law cannot be located to particular inns they were probably, by elimination, of the Temple (p. 11).

[52] See Moreton, *The Townshends and their World*, p. 25, p. 54.

[53] Norwich Castle Museum, MS 158.926/4g.1, a collection of statutes from the reigns of Edward III–Henry VI, in French and Latin, with the inscription *Constat Iohanni Fyncham* on f. 371^r; see Ker, *Medieval Manuscripts in British Libraries*, iii.519–20. His will is TNA, PROB 11/11/9, partly transcribed by Blyth, *Historical Notices*, pp. 155–57.

[54] Thomas Fyncham's will is TNA, PROB 11/19/56; see Oliva, *The Convent and the Community*, p. 54. For John Fyncham see Moreton, *The Townshends and their World*, p. 204.

[55] Described by Watson, *Western Illuminated Manuscripts*, i.225–35.

[56] Oliva, *The Convent and the Community*, p. 56, though not recorded in Smith and London, *The Heads of Religious Houses*, pp. 626–27; the genealogical details are recorded by Blyth, *Historical Notices*, p. 115.

Fyncham, the prioress at the dissolution in 1538 was Elizabeth Fyncham. She had apparently been prioress for eight years and was granted a pension of £5; she died in 1561.[57] The only Robert Fyncham I have been able to locate amongst Norfolk records is the Robert Fyncham of Westwynch (nine miles north of Fyncham) who is named in two charters of July 1489.[58] It is possible that he was the same man who, having moved to London, was admitted in 1495 as a lay member to the Fraternity of St Nicholas, the brotherhood of the parish clerks; the clerks had their own hall in Bishopsgate and a chantry priest and altar in the Guildhall Chapel. This fraternity was at the heart of civic life, with numerous aldermen and their wives amongst its membership, along with many other middle-ranking Londoners.[59]

Even though at first glance a marriage with the daughter of a Norfolk family might seem unlikely for the Middlesex-based Thomas Roberts, it should be remembered that his working environment at the Inns of Court and Chancery necessarily brought him into proximity with lawyers from all parts of the country, giving him access to a circle of connections which reached far beyond London and Middlesex. In this respect it is relevant to note that John Fyncham of Fyncham, who died in 1541, named John Spelman as one of his executors.[60] In fact, the range of personal contacts offered by the Inns of Court, and their potential for matchmaking, is amply demonstrated by Thomas's next marriage. His second wife was Anne, daughter of Humphrey Adam. Anne's parentage is mentioned briefly in the list of the birthdates of the three children that she bore to Thomas (recorded in JRL English 98) where her father is identified as 'Humfridi Adam generosi' ('gentleman'). Humphrey Adam was a lawyer at Lyon's Inn, one of the Inns of Chancery which, like Clement's Inn, was associated with the Inner Temple.[61] There is no official record of his membership of Lyon's Inn – though there are few surviving domestic records for any of the Inns of Chancery – but he bequeathed money (6s 8d) to the fellowship at Lyon's Inn. When he made his will in October 1507, Humphrey Adam directed that sums of money were to be distributed to poor households within the parish of St Clements without Temple Bar (which was also Thomas Roberts's parish

---

[57] Oliva, *The Convent and the Community*, pp. 190–92. LPFD Henry VIII, 14.i.600 (31 Henry VIII, no. 1355); Smith and London, *The Heads of Religious Houses*, p. 606.
[58] NRO, Hare 1853 192x6 (15 July 1489), Hare 936 190x3 (16 July 1489).
[59] See James and James, *The Bede Roll of the Fraternity of St Nicholas*, I, xxvi–xxvii and 165.
[60] As noted by Blyth, *Historical Notices*, p. 161.
[61] Baker, *Readers and Readings*, pp. 207–9.

in London, see Map 2), as well as amongst the poor of St Giles in the Field and the poor of Ashill in Norfolk.[62] Furthermore, he left money for a *placebo* and *dirige* to be said at Ashill, and instructed that the parson and churchwardens there were to pray for members of his family; Ashill, lying southeast of Swaffham, was evidently Humphrey Adam's parish of origin and he retained a house there (its 'stuff' is mentioned in the will), even though his legal business was based in London. Humphrey appointed his brother Nicholas Adam and Thomas Roberts as his executors; aside from a few individual bequests of jewellery and household items to his brother and his wife, to his sister, and to the family of his goddaughter, most of the arrangements concern Humphrey's children, Henry and Anne, who are to share the residue of his estate equally, as their own property. Thomas Roberts is specifically remembered with the gift of 'a ryng of fyn gold, with a scripture within: "I thanke God of all", my register at Lyons Inn, my bible and my ij portuous' (portable breviaries), and with the sum of four marcs for his trouble in acting as executor; two servants of Thomas Roberts are also remembered. Yet at no point is Thomas styled 'my son' (meaning 'son-in-law'), as might be expected, nor is Anne referred to here as 'Anne Roberts'. From this it would seem that when Humphrey made his will on 4 October 1507, Thomas and Anne were not yet married, but the date of birth of their first child, Dorothy, in August 1508, means that their marriage must have taken place within the last months of 1507. One wonders whether this was a marriage which had been planned by Anne's father before his death (the will was proved on 12 December 1507), or whether Thomas took advantage of his role as executor to benefit from Anne's inheritance.

FATHER AND SONS: THOMAS ROBERTS (1470–1542), MICHAEL ROBERTS (1519–44), AND EDMUND ROBERTS (1520–85)

By Anne, Thomas had three daughters: Dorothy, born 11 August 1508; Anna, born 20 September 1509; and Alice, born 7 March 1511 (see *Table 2*). After Anne's death Thomas took a third wife, Katherine, daughter of Roger Sadler,

---

[62] TNA, PROB 11/15/637. It might be noted that Thomas Roberts's remedy book, BodL Rawlinson C. 299, was produced in Norfolk, see Chapter 5, section titled 'A Book of Practical Use: Bodleian Library, MS Rawlinson C. 299'.

a draper who lived in the parish of St Mary Abchurch.[63] Good relations between the two families are indicated by Thomas Roberts's instruction in his will of 1542 that 'my brother John Sadler' should have 'the rule and guydyng' of his youngest son, John Roberts, until he came of age. Two years later, Michael Roberts appointed his uncle John Sadler as one of the overseers of his will and left him a gift of money. Michael refers to John as an alderman, indicating that this was the John Sadler, draper, who served as alderman in the city of London from October 1542 to April 1546.[64] By Katherine Sadler, Thomas had three sons: Michael, born on St Michael's day (25 September), 1519; Edmund, born on St Edmund's day (20 November), 1520; and John, born 22 December 1531. The births of these children and the names of their mothers are carefully recorded at the back of the family's copy of Nicholas Love's *Mirror of the Blessed Life of Jesus Christ*.[65] Similar lists of the names of the children and their birthdates are also recorded on blank leaves in two of the family's books of hours. There are some small variations in the information given in the three lists, but collectively they provide a clear picture of Thomas's offspring. It is also clear that many more children had failed to survive to adulthood, with statements in both books of hours to this effect: 'Thomas Robertes had by Godes will in all xxiiij childern'; 'T Robertes hath in all xxiiij chyldern wherof xviij ben decesed'.[66]

After Thomas Roberts's own death in 1542, the administration of his estate was granted to his eldest son, Michael, in the short-lived court of the Bishop of Westminster.[67] In his will Thomas left gold rings to his married daughters Dorothy and Anne, and to their husbands, and also to his brother-in-law John Sadler and his wife, Gresill (Griselda), his brother-in-law William Browne and his wife Alice, and his wife's sister, Beatrice Bodley. The rings were 'tokens of remembrance', with Thomas explaining: 'if my power of substance were better I woold geue them better'. Dorothy was left no property, and Anne was

---

[63] His will dated 18 February 1527 was proved on 6 November 1529 in the Commissary Court of London, see Fitch, *Index to Testamentary Records*, ii.230. It is unclear whether Roger Sadler shared any connection with Ralph Sadler (1507–87), who was MP for various counties including Middlesex in 1539, and whose fortunes flourished under Cromwell.

[64] Beaven, *The Aldermen of the City of London*, p. 110.

[65] JRL English 98, f. 137^v. See Chapter 4, section titled 'After the Dissolution: the Hordes of Ewell'.

[66] CUL Ii.6.2, f. 33^r and Ii.6.7, f. 132^r, see Chapter 5, section titled 'A Matter of Record'. Some of the eighteen dead children might have been from his first marriage to Margaret.

[67] LMA, DL/C/355, f. 22.

bequeathed a single tenement in Westminster. The more important provision was for Thomas's unmarried children, Alice, Edmund, and John, who were 'to haue, houlde, use and occupie peacably' the various premises which he bequeathed to each of them. Alice Roberts was left plate and household stuff to the value of fifty pounds as well as nine tenements in Westminster. Edmund was left some household stuff and three tenements in Harlesden, all currently rented and farmed. John was left other tenements in Harlesden and Willesden, a property called Frendes, and the manor of Fosters in Acton, all of which were currently rented and farmed. At the time of his father's death, John Roberts was only eleven years old, and he was still far from his majority when his brother Michael Roberts died two years later, a fact which is reflected in the regranting of these bequests in Michael's will.[68] Michael also confirmed the bequest of the tenement to his sister Anne Smythson and her husband, but other lands and tenements which Thomas Roberts had willed to his unmarried daughter, Alice, and her heirs in fee simple were granted by Michael in 1544 to John Busshop, priest, presumably signifying that Alice had since died. Michael left his tenement and garden plot in St Clement's parish to his brother Edmund.

Michael Roberts died when he was only twenty-five years old; he was married, but had no children, and his will makes generous provision for his widow, Ursula. She was to be allowed to inhabit their dwelling house in Neasden ('Catt at Woodes') for the rest of her natural life, and she was also assigned a number of other properties including the tenement called Bucklands (after the decease of William Newland and his wife), the tenement and lands called Fyndons, another house with lands currently occupied by Richard Turnour of Hendon, and tenements in St Albans. Poignantly Michael also allows for the possibility that Ursula might be pregnant, negating his other bequests in this instance, and instructing that the child is to be brought up by Ursula and her father, Anthony Huse.[69] In the event there was no child, and Ursula subsequently married Benjamin Gonson, treasurer of the navy; she and Benjamin had fourteen children together, five of whom were still alive when he made his will in 1594.[70]

Michael's position as head of the Roberts family was taken over by his younger brother Edmund, who would have been aged twenty-four in 1544.

---

[68] For Michael Roberts's will and inquisition post mortem see TNA, PROB 11/30/205, C 142/75/9, and WARD 7/2/151.

[69] See Chapter 2, section titled 'Thomas Roberts at the Inns of Court'.

[70] Records of the births for 1547–69 are in BL, MS Additional 15857, f. 153^{r-v}. Gonson's will is BL, MS Additional 74210.

Table 3 Family tree: The children and grandchildren of Edmund Roberts.

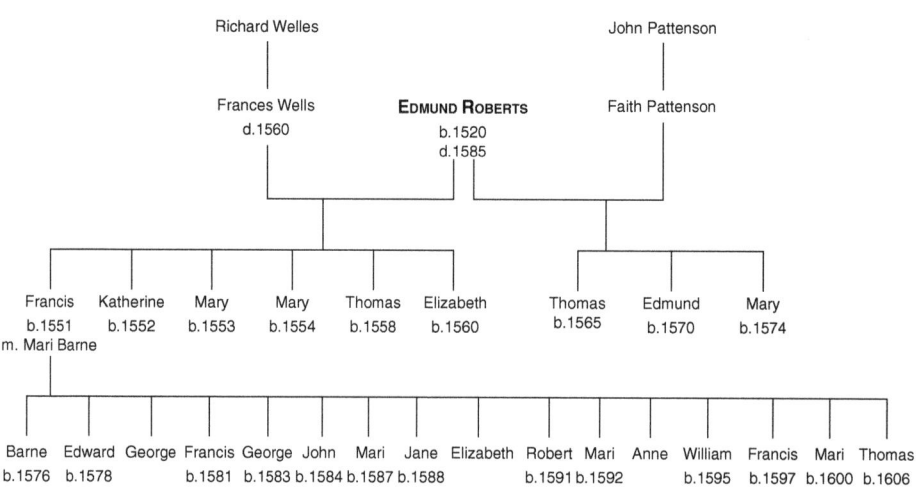

Edmund's first wife was Frances Welles, daughter of Richard Welles of Ware who had been a clerk in Henry VIII's Chancery.[71] Edmund and Frances were married on Candlemas Day (2 February) 1549 at Royston in Hertfordshire, and they seem to have been living in this location when their first child, Francis, was born on 8 February 1551, since he was christened at Royston and Sir Robert Chester, who held Royston manor, was one of his godfathers (see *Table 3*).[72] By the time their second child, Katherine, was born on 30 June 1552, they appear to have returned to Middlesex because although one of Katherine's godmothers was Lady Katherine Chester, the baby was christened at Willesden. Edmund's widowed sister-in-law, Ursula, had remarried by this point, ending her entitlement to remain in the family home which by law now reverted to Michael's next heir. Various records suggest that there was some dispute in the late 1540s over properties. In one action Ursula and Edmund Roberts stood together to resist a suit brought by Henry Kyng, reviving a case brought by Nicholas Kyng against Thomas Roberts and his wife Katherine, for lands in Harrow, Northolt and Hornsey, and Nuthows; but in another Ursula and

---

[71] For his will of 1539 (proved 1540) see TNA, PROB 11/28/25.
[72] The births of Edmund's children are recorded, with details of their godparents, in BodL Rawlinson C. 894, ff. iv^v–vi^v. A briefer list is given in CUL Ii.6.2, f. 109^v.

her second husband Benjamin Gonson acted against Edmund regarding lands in Northolt, Roxeth, Kilburn, Willesden, and St Albans.[73]

Edmund had four more children by Frances Welles: Mary, born 8 December 1553; another Mary 'the younger', born 10 February 1554; Thomas, born 30 July 1558; and Elizabeth born 12 June 1560. When Frances died on 20 July 1560, Edmund recorded that she 'lefte iiij chylldeyne alyue'; in the list of births in BodL Rawlinson C. 894 the entries for the second Mary and Thomas have been crossed through, suggesting that these were the children who had predeceased their mother.[74] Frances and all her children are commemorated on Edmund's memorial brass at Willesden (see further below), but it is likely that a separate brass was commissioned for her in 1560, and this may have been the brass now located on the south side of the chancel of St Mary's and identified only as 'Lady Unknown'.[75] Three years later, in June 1563, Edmund married Faith Pattenson who was the only daughter and heir of John Pattenson, deceased, formerly gentleman of London, and one of the yeomen of the customs house there, presumably the Woolwharf, just west of the Tower, where wool was weighed and customed for export.[76] In recording his marriage to Faith in BodL Rawlinson C. 894, Edmund wrote that she was 'at hallow tyd after xviij yeer of ayge as dothe apere in the churche at St Steues in collman street', that is, that she was more than eighteen years old in November, and that the proof of this (presumably her baptismal record) was preserved at St Stephen's in Colman Street.[77] John Pattenson is mentioned in a grant of February 1545 as having tenure of a property in the parish of St Michael, Basinghawe, which was in the same general area, and his inquisition post mortem of 1561 records other properties in the locality.[78]

Edmund had three children by Faith: Thomas, born 18 January 1565; Edmund, born 21 July 1570; and Mary, born 29 June 1574. Edmund himself carefully recorded the occasions of these children's births in an extended family records section at the front of BodL Rawlinson C. 894; he gives details of the

---

[73] TNA, C/1/1137/35–37 and C/1/531/57; TNA, C/1/1223/29.

[74] f. v^r and f. v^v.

[75] Torre, 'An Unrecorded Lady at Willesden', 284–86; Valentine, 'The Roberts Family of Willesden', 185.

[76] For Pattenson's inquisition post mortem of 1561 see Fry, *Abstracts of Inquisitions Post Mortem*, pp. 222–23.

[77] f. vi^r.

[78] *LPFD, Henry VIII*, 20.124 (36 Henry VIII, no. 282 grant 19).

date and time of day of their births, their christenings, and the names of their godparents. Similar birth records were maintained by his son Francis, and by subsequent members of the family until the late seventeenth century, preserving a great deal of information about the family's history; in general the records contained in the Roberts family books give more accurate information than the pedigree recorded by Richard Mundy.[79] Dates of deaths are more sparsely recorded, except in the case of infant mortality, and the note of Edmund's own death in 1585 is given not in this volume, but in his book of hours, CUL Ii.6.2.

THE ROBERTS FAMILY AND ST MARY'S, WILLESDEN

The long-standing connection between the Roberts family and Willesden may still be seen today in the fabric of the parish church of St Mary where the chancel preserves a number of memorials to sixteenth- and seventeenth-century members of the family. In front of the high altar is a line of six ledger stones set into the floor. The fifth in the line commemorates Sir William Roberts, Baronet (1638–87) and his wife Sarah (1658–86), and the fourth commemorates his nephew, another William Roberts (1673–1700) and his infant son, yet another William, who lived only for a few months in 1700. The second in the line is a memorial to the baronet's niece, Mary Roberts Hawkins (1679–1726). In front of this line of six stones is another stone, placed prominently in the centre of the chancel; this commemorates Sir William Roberts, second and last Baronet and the son of William and Sarah, who died in 1698. An earlier generation of the family is also represented in the chancel, where there are dark alabaster wall memorials to Francis Roberts (1551–1631) and to his father-in-law John Barne who died in 1615. Francis's wife, Mary, who died in 1623, has her own memorial ledger stone set as the sixth in the sequence before the altar. Another wall memorial commemorates Richard Franklyn (died 1615), whose second wife was Fraunces Roberts, daughter of Francis and Mary. In the sixteenth century the preference seems to have been for memorial brasses rather than stones or plaques. Of the six brasses which are set into the floor of the chancel, four relate to the Roberts family. The finest is that of Edmund Roberts (1520–85) and his two wives (see Figure 2); another, described only as 'the lady

---

[79] BL, MS Harley 1551, f. 124[r].

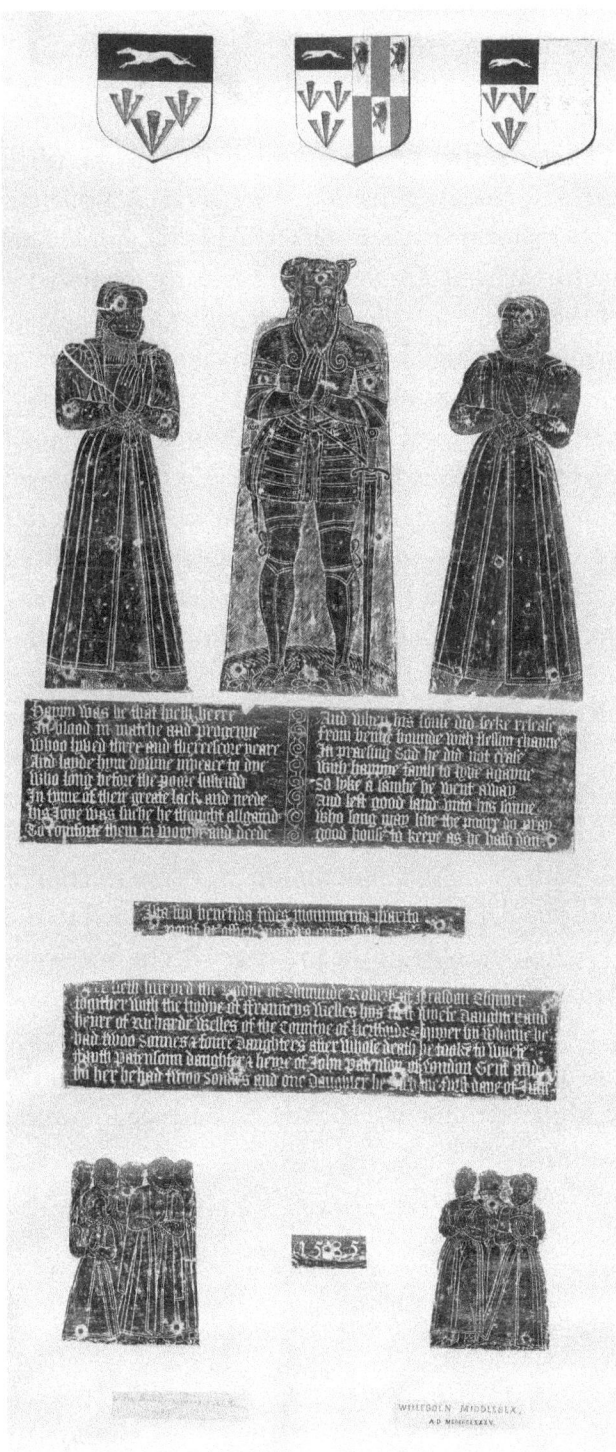

Figure 2 Tomb brass of Edmund Roberts in St Mary's Willesden; rubbing, from London, British Library, MS Additional 32490, CC. 31. Reproduced by permission. © The British Library Board.

unknown' because of its lack of an inscription, was probably an earlier memorial to Edmund's first wife which became redundant after she was commemorated on his.[80] There is also a brass showing Jane Barne (died 1609) and one of her daughters; her daughter Mary was Francis Roberts's wife. Finally, the earliest Roberts memorial is a brass dated 1505 commemorating Margaret Roberts, the first wife of Thomas. Another early memorial is now set into the exterior of the south wall where a stone tablet with the date 152* commemorates the untimely death of the fiancé of a daughter of Thomas Roberts.

The church of St Mary at Willesden was extensively restored in the nineteenth century. In 1852 the nave was extended westwards, and in 1872 the north aisle, vestry, and organ chamber were added; the south porch was rebuilt at this time, and in 1916 the south chapel was restored.[81] These renovations destroyed much of its medieval character and caused the removal or relocation of many tombs and memorials, but fortunately several early nineteenth-century descriptions survive which give an impression of the church's previous appearance. The antiquary Sir Stephen Richard Glynne (1807–74) visited Willesden in the late 1830s and made notes on the church's fabric, including some of the memorials relating to the Roberts family. He recorded that: 'In the nave there is a brass to Margaret Roberts and in the chancel some others bearing the dates 1505 and 1609 – one with a long verse inscription . . . In the exterior of the south wall is a tablet with the date 152* to one who was betrothed to the daughter of Thos. Roberts Esq. but died before the marriage.'[82] The brass with the long verse inscription is that of Edmund Roberts, and the one dated 1609 is that of Jane Barne. These two brasses are still more or less where Glynne observed them, but the brass of Margaret Roberts has been relocated to the north side of the chancel.[83] More revealing is a slightly earlier account of the

---

[80] This explanation was suggested by Valentine, 'The Roberts Family of Willesden', 185. The brasses are listed by Stephenson, *A List of Monumental Brasses in the British Isles*, p. 317.

[81] For details, with a plan of the church and photograph of the exterior, see Royal Commission on Historical Monuments, *An Inventory of the Historical Monuments in Middlesex*, pp. 132–34 and *plate* 178. See also www.stmarywillesden.org.uk/.

[82] Cited by Wadsworth, *The Church of St Mary, Willesden*, pp. 23–24. Glynne's notes on churches, in 106 volumes, are kept at Gladstone's Library, Hawarden, and accessible via Flintshire Record Office.

[83] The brasses were moved from the centre of the chancel to their present positions at the sides (for protection) in 1964.

church which was published in *Gentleman's Magazine* in 1825.[84] The correspondent notes the survival of the Roberts family pew:

> About twenty years ago the Church was new pewed, with one or two exceptions; the repairers having carefully preserved the pew opposite the reading-desk, on the door of which are carved the arms of Roberts, – a family, which, though now extinct, was once of some consequence in this sequestered village.

He also records details of the decoration in the south chapel, noting that:

> ... in the windows are the arms and quarterings of the family of Roberts, as follow. In the South window are these six coats: I. Argent, six pheons Sable, on a chief of the second a greyhound of the first gorged Or. II. quarterly of six; 1, 3 and 5, Argent a demi-griffin Sable, crowned with an eastern crown Or. 2, 4, and 6, Gules. III. Azure three leopards' heads caboshed Argent, langued Gules. IV. Argent, a chevron between three Cornish choughs. V. Gules, a chevron Ermine, between three lions rampant Argent. VI. as I. *Crest*, on a wreath, Argent and Sable, a greyhound Argent, gorged Gules. *Motto*, Nec cursus veloci – Nec victoria forti. In the East window of this chapel the arms of Roberts impaling, Argent, a demy-griffin Sable, crowned as before Or.

This is a valuable account because all traces of this heraldic glass have now completely disappeared: new stained glass was installed throughout the church in the mid Victorian period and parts of these windows have since been lost to vandalism or to enemy action during the Second World War.

The south chapel was built in the sixteenth century and originally dedicated to St Katherine of Alexandria, replacing a chantry altar to that saint which had stood at the east end of the south aisle since the fourteenth century: in 1350 Ralph Fairsire left in trust lands and property in the city of London to provide monies for a chantry priest to perform mass before the altar of the Blessed Katherine.[85] The heraldry in the windows suggests that aspects of the chapel's construction were financed by the Roberts family: the six shields described above are, respectively, those of Roberts (1 and 6), Welles (the family of

---

[84] A letter dated 7 October 1825 and signed 'I.T.S.', pp. 423–24. An earlier account by Lysons, *The Environs of London*, iii.611–24, gives fewer details.

[85] See the later reference to this apparently unauthorized bequest in *CCR Richard II, 1392–96*, p. 200.

Edmund Roberts's first wife), Barnes (the family of Francis Roberts wife), Brooke, and the last is as yet unidentified. Yet despite this blazonry the Roberts family do not seem to have used the chapel as a mausoleum. Although their various tombstones and brasses in the church have been disturbed and relocated over the years, a note in one of their books of hours records the precise position of Edmund Roberts's grave: 'Anno Domini 1585 the first daye of June departed owght off this lyff Edmund Robartes esquier and lyeth buryed in the upper end off the chawnsell in Willsden churche and lyved lxiij yeres vij monethes and ix dayes.'[86] Only the richest and most important laypeople could aspire to burial within this area of the church.[87] Edmund's older brother Michael was buried in the London parish of St Clement Danes beside their father who had willed to be buried in either place, depending on where he died; although both men left gifts of money to the church at Willesden, this was to the high altar rather than to St Katherine's altar in the side chapel. Those bequests probably indicate a residual devotion to the shrine of Our Lady of Willesden which was located within the chancel, even though by the time these men made their wills the shrine had been dismantled and the image destroyed.[88] In the lifetime of Thomas Roberts the shrine was a well-established and prominent centre of local pilgrimage; a pilgrim badge that depicts the Virgin and Child within a crescent moon may have been the token associated with visiting it.[89] It was listed as a popular pilgrimage destination by the dramatist John Heywood, along with other London locations associated with Mary: the palmer in *The Four P.P.* (1520) had been 'At Crome, at Wylsdome, and at Muswell ... And at Our Lady that standeth in the oke'.[90] The shrine was conveniently located eight miles from London and seems to have appealed particularly to women, including those of high rank: Henry VII's queen Elizabeth of York arranged for a pilgrim to make an offering on her behalf there in 1503, though by contrast the lollard Elizabeth Sampson derided the image as 'a burnt arse elf and a burnt arse stock'.[91]

---

[86] CUL Ii.6.2, f. 109ʳ.
[87] Daniell, *Death and Burial*, p. 98.
[88] The modern statue of the Virgin is housed in the south chapel, now called the Shrine Chapel.
[89] Spencer, *Pilgrim Souvenirs*, pp. 149–52, notes that 320 such badges have been recovered.
[90] Line 48 and line 50, Axton and Happé (eds.), *The Plays of John Heywood*, p. 113.
[91] Cited by Brigden (1989), p. 94.

Family Matters: The Roberts Family of Willesden

The Roberts family's long association with St Mary's church goes back to at least the fourteenth century. An indulgence issued on 1 February 1395 by Nicholas, suffragan bishop of Salisbury, mentions Ralph Roberts and Johanna his deceased wife, in conjunction with 'the church of the Blessed Mary of Willesden in the diocese of London':

> Universis sancte matris ecclesie filijs ad quos presentes littere pervenerint Nicholaus miseracione divina Christopolitanus Episcopus ac Sarum diocese sede episcopali ibidem vacante suffraganeus sufficienter deputatus Salutem in domino sempiternam obsequium pium et deo gratum tociens impendere opin(i)amur quociens allectivis indulgentiarum muneribus mentes fidelium ad opera pietatis propencius excitamus de dei igitur omnipotentis misericordia et beate marie matris domini(s) patrone nostre necnon beatorum apostolorum petri et pauli omniumque civium supernorum meritis et precibus confidentes omnibus Christianis vere penitentibus et contritis quorum diocesani habeant nostram indulgenciam ratam habuerint et acceptam qui ad sustentacionem seu relevamen fabrice ecclesie beate marie de Willesdon' London' diocese aliqua de bonis suis sibi a deo collatis donaverint legaverint procuraverint seu quovismodo assignaverint subsidia caritatis vel qui pro salubri statu Radulphi Roberdes de Willesdon' predict' dum vixit et pro anima sua cum ex hac luce migraverit et presertim pro anima nobilis mulieris Johanne quondam uxoris eiusdem Radulphi Roberdes defuncte et pro animabus liberorum eorundem ac omnibus fidelium defunctorum orationem dominicam cum salutacione evangelica dixerint mente pia quocienscumque quandocumque aliquod premissorum devote fecerint de iniunctis sibi penitenciis quadraginta dies indulgencie misericorditer in domino concedimus per presentes in cuius rei testimonium presentes has sigilli episcopatus nostri appensione fecimus comuniri dat' Sarum primo die mensis februarii anno domini millesimo CCC nonagesimo quinto.[92]

(To all the sons of our holy mother church to whom this letter shall have come, Nicholas by divine mercy bishop of Christopolis and duly appointed suffragan of Sarum, the episcopal see there being vacant, sends eternal greetings in the Lord. We do believe that it is our bounden duty, meet and pleasing to God to bestow indulgence as

---

[92] Text and translation printed by Keen, 'Documentary Evidence', 37–40 (p. 40).

often as we rouse the minds of the faithful more readily to works of piety by the incentive of granting indulgences; in consequence of the mercy of Almighty God and of the Blessed Mary, mother of Our Lord and our patron and putting our trust in the merits and prayers of the blessed apostles Peter and Paul and of all the citizens above, to all Christians that be truly penitent and contrite, whose diocesan bishops are in possession of our indulgence and hold it as ratified and accepted, and who have donated, bequeathed or made available towards the upkeep or repair of the fabric of the church of Blessed Mary of Willesden in the Diocese of London some part of the wealth bestowed upon them by God or in some way have allocated charitable contributions or who for the well-being of Ralph Roberdes of Willesden aforesaid while he lives and for his soul after he departed this life and especially for the soul of the gentle lady Johanna deceased, formerly wife of the same Ralph Roberdes and for the souls of the children of the same and all the faithful departed, have piously recited Our Father and Hail Mary for each several occasion they have done anything of the aforesaid devoutly, we do grant in the Lord of our mercy forty days of indulgence by this letter, in testimony to which we have caused the present letter to be ratified by the application of the seal of our episcopate. Given at Sarum 1st February in the year of our Lord, 1395.)

The indulgence offered a period of forty days' remission to penitent Christians who had made pious actions of some kind: these included the giving or bequeathing of money for the upkeep or repair of the fabric of St Mary's church; charitable contributions of some type; and, significantly, the offering of prayers for the souls of Ralph and Johanna and their children. The end of the indulgence makes clear that forty days' remission may be gained 'for each several occasion' that any one of these pious acts takes place. To be named in this way, as the direct beneficiary of prayers offered by the masses, Ralph Roberts must have been an important donor to the church and a figure of considerable standing in the local community. His dates of birth and death are not known, but his name may be traced in the public record between 1365–94. He is mentioned as a witness to a charter in 1365, and in a quitclaim and a writ in the 1390s.[93] He was also named in a grant of pavage in 1389, which was an

---

[93] *CCR Edward III, 1364–68*, p. 190; *CCR Richard II, 1389–92*, p. 293; *CCR Richard II, 1392–96*, pp. 199–200, 217.

attempt to improve the condition of the Edgware Road (or the London way, as it was then known), the most important road in Willesden.[94] More generally, his name occurs many times in deeds relating to property at Neasden, later copies of which survive in BL, MS Stowe 862, the eighteenth-century compilation which drew upon Thomas Roberts's collection of legal records and papers.[95] The preservation of the indulgence may also be attributed to Thomas Roberts because the only copy of it survives at the back of his legal handbook, *Registrum Brevium*, where it was added by his hand on an originally blank leaf.[96] Thomas transcribed this indulgence at least a century after it was issued, probably because of its continuing significance to him. As their descendant, Thomas was specially obligated to pray for the souls of Ralph and Johanna, and by doing so he would gain the forty days' remission; but, simultaneously, Thomas was also the beneficiary of those prayers which were offered for Ralph and his children, if 'children' is understood more figuratively to imply subsequent generations of the family.

Despite his prominence within the Willesden community at the close of the fourteenth century, there is no memorial to Ralph Roberts in the church there. The finest surviving memorial is that of his descendant, Edmund Roberts, whose aforementioned commemorative brass – now set into the floor on the south side of the chancel at St Mary's – shows him flanked by his two wives and his nine children. Above his head is a shield with the arms of the Roberts family, and above the heads of his wives are shields which combine the Roberts arms with the Welles arms and Pattenson arms, respectively. Beneath the figures is a rhyming inscription that consists of two eight-line stanzas:

> Happy was he that lyeth heere
> In blood in match and progenye,
> Whoo lyved three and threescore yeare
> And layde hym down in peace to dye;
> Who long before the poore susteind   5
> In tyme of their greate lack and need,
> His Joye was such he thought all gaine
> To comfort them in worde and deede.

---

[94] *CPR Richard II, 1388–92*, p. 123.
[95] BL, MS Stowe 862, ff. 38ʳ–59ʳ.
[96] BL, MS Harley 1859, f. 218ᵛ. See Figure 3 in Chapter 2.

> And when his soule did seek release
> From being bounde with flesshy chayne, 10
> In praesing God he did not cease
> With happye fayth to lyve agayne;
> So lyk a lambe he went away
> And left good land unto his sonne,
> Who long may live the poore do pray 15
> Good house to keepe as he hath don!

The pun in line 12 on the name of Edmund's second wife, Faith, is continued in a separate inscription of two lines of Latin: *Ista suo benefida fides monumenta marito ponit ut officii pignora certa suo*, which when translated reads: 'The ever faithful Fayth sets up this monument to her husband as a sure pledge of her devotion.'[97]

The emphasis in the inscription on Edmund's attentiveness to good works, particularly for the poor, need not be taken as indicative of reformed religious standing: poor relief was a pressing social issue in Elizabethan England, and charitable almsgiving was encouraged, even though it represented a continuity of a medieval devotional practice that promised rewards for the soul after death. Eamon Duffy describes Edmund as a 'conforming protestant', without making clear whether the 'conforming' is to be understood as a sincere alignment with the new religion or as a mere toe-ing of the line.[98] This book will suggest that the latter is more likely. This is implicit in Duffy's other observation that Edmund evidently made much use of the prayers that had been added to the family's medieval book of hours, prayers that were 'very Catholic indeed'.[99] If Edmund had indeed been a sincerely conforming protestant by the end of his life, one might expect to see at least some reflection of that reformed religious sensibility in his choice of reading and his use of books. The following chapters will consider those books that are known to have been in the family's hands in the sixteenth century and which were variously used by Edmund Roberts and his father. In each case the traces that these readers left within these books will be examined for indications of the nature of their beliefs, and for evidence of

---

[97] Translation taken from Wadsworth, *The Church of St Mary, Willesden*, p. 34. There is a rubbing of Edmund's brass in BL, MS Additional 32490, CC. 31 (see Figure 2).
[98] Duffy, *Marking the Hours*, p. 89.
[99] Duffy, *Marking the Hours*, p. 96.

their religious conformity, or otherwise, during a period in which it cannot always have been clear what measure of conformity might be expected next. Not all of the books themselves are of a religious nature, and the discussion begins with one of a different type, *Registrum Brevium*, a legal textbook, intended as a book of reference and an important store of legal knowledge for the late medieval lawyer. After some consideration of Thomas Roberts's activities as a lawyer, his affiliation to the Inns of Court, and the advantages that this environment afforded, Chapter 2 will explore the varied uses to which he put his copy of *Registrum Brevium*.

2

Private Faces in Public Places

THOMAS ROBERTS AT THE INNS OF COURT

The length of association of the Roberts family with Willesden, and the extent of their property holdings there by the seventeenth century, may mistakenly give the impression that theirs was always a country gentry family of substantial means and status. In reality, it seems that the fortunes of the family followed an upward curve during the sixteenth century, and that prior to this their wealth and social standing may have been more modest. Although Thomas Roberts's father, John Roberts, is styled 'gentilman' in some records, earlier and collateral branches of the family in the fifteenth century may have lacked this status, and might also have been located in the city where there were more opportunities.[1] Thomas himself had a residence and business in London, despite his property acquisitions in Neasden, and his marriages were not to women from the ranks of the Middlesex gentry but to women whose families had London connections. He may have felt a closer affiliation to London than he did to his properties in Neasden, and it would be easier to understand this if other family connections with the city could be uncovered.

By profession Thomas Roberts was a lawyer, conducting his business from premises in the parish of St Clement Danes in London, close to Temple Bar (see Map 2). His copy of the legal textbook *Registrum Brevium* in BL Harley 1859 contains records of his admission to the Inns of Court. A memorandum at the back of the volume reads: *Thomas Robertȝ de Willesdoun Gent admissus est in societatem hospicij vocatus Clementis Inne* ('Thomas Roberts of Willesden, gentleman, was admitted to the fellowship of the inn called Clement's Inn'),

---

[1] TNA, E 40/7253 (dated 1449) describes both John Roberts and his father Thomas Roberts as 'housbondman' (farmer or tenant farmer).

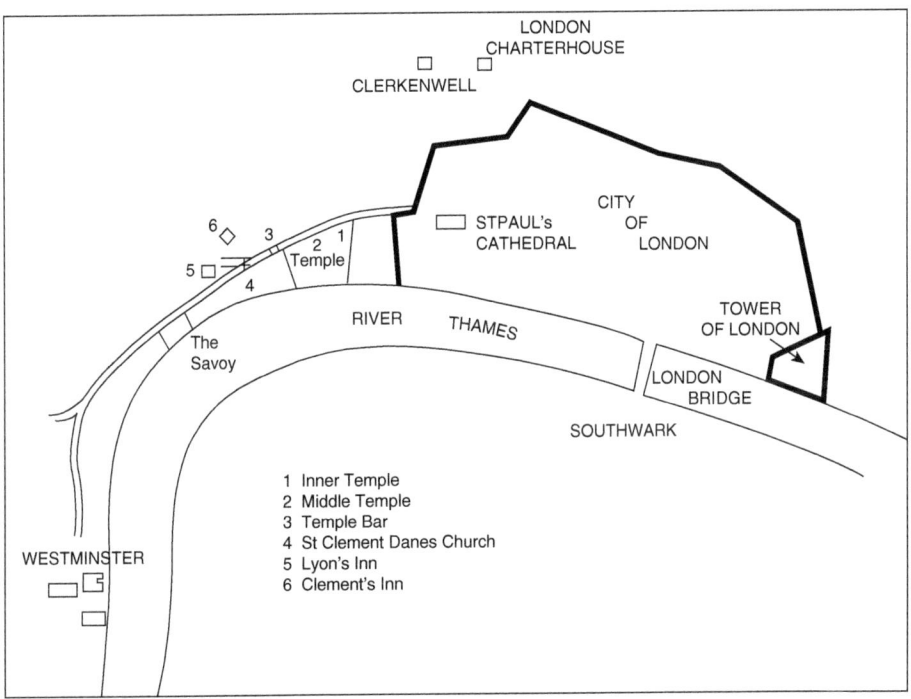

Map 2 Map of the parish of St Clement Danes, London.

and gives the date as *in crastino animarum anno Regis Henrici septum decimo*, that is 3 November 1494 (see Figure 3).² The memorandum goes on to say that Thomas remained part of that fellowship until 1 August in the fourteenth year of Henry VIII's reign (that is, 1522) when *supradictus idem Thomas Robertʒ admissus est in societatem Interioris Templi* ('the aforesaid same Thomas Roberts was admitted to the fellowship of the Inner Temple'). The first statement refers to Thomas's admission as an apprentice of the law, and since Clement's Inn was one of the lesser inns associated with the Inner Temple his subsequent progression there is not surprising. His admission to the Inner Temple was sponsored by John Baldwyn, gentleman, who was the treasurer, and John Pakyngton, gentleman, another member with whom Thomas served on a number of commissions in the 1520s and 1530s.³ At the front of BL Harley

---

² BL, MS Harley 1859, f. 218ᵛ.

³ John Baldwin was reader at the Inner Temple in 1516 and 1524, and treasurer 1521–23; he died 1545. John Pakington was a bencher at the Inner Temple in 1517 and reader in 1520 and 1528; he was treasurer 1528–33 and died 1551. For both, see Baker, *Readers and Readings*, p. 76, Baker, 'Baldwin, Sir John', and Baker, 'Packington, Sir John'.

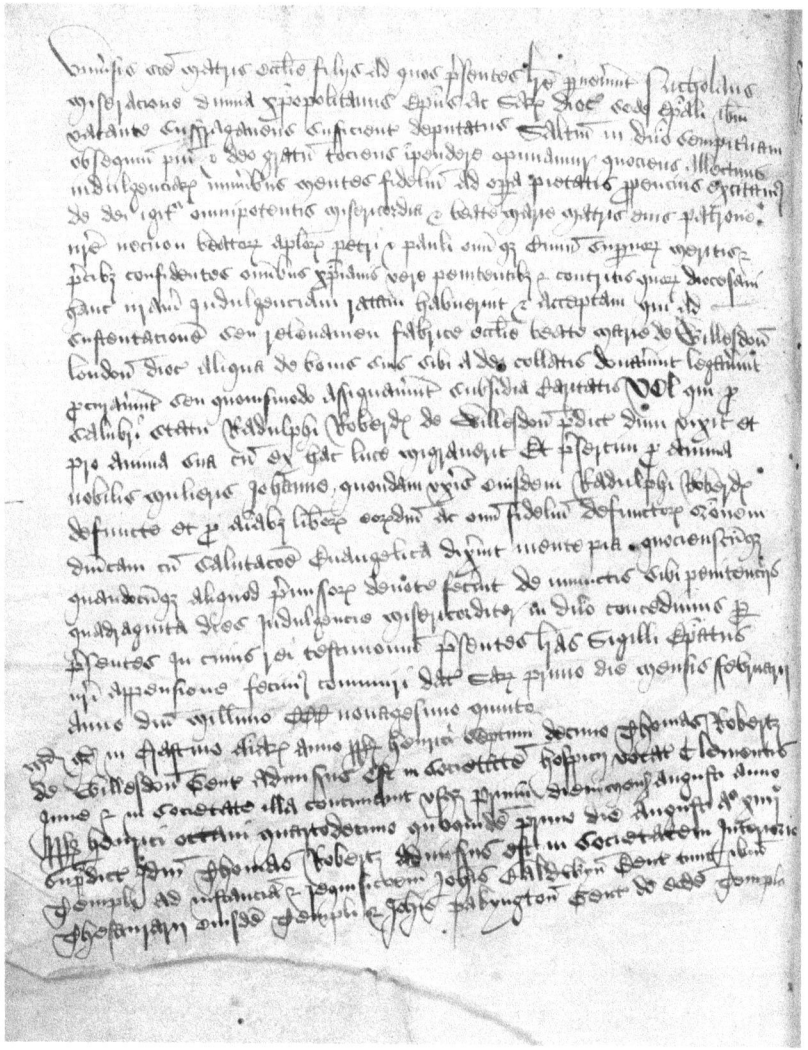

Figure 3 London, British Library, MS Harley 1859, f. 218ᵛ. Memorandum of Thomas Roberts's admission to the Inner Temple; copy of the indulgence naming Ralph and Johanna Roberts. Reproduced by permission. © The British Library Board.

1859, on a flyleaf preceding the start of the *Registrum Brevium*, is a copy of the oath taken by serjeants at law:

> Ye shall swere that well & truly ye shall serue the kynges people as one of the sergeantes at the lawe – and ye shall truly counsell theym that ye

shal be reteyned with after your connyng – and ye shall nat deferre tracte or delay their causes willyngly for covetous of money or other thyng that may turne you to profyte – and ye shall geve attendaunce acordyngly as God helpe you & his seyntes.

This addition was made by Thomas Roberts's hand, though there is no evidence to confirm that he actually attained the office of serjeant (see Figure 4).[4]

Day-to-day legal work such as conveyancing and notarizing must have involved Thomas Roberts in much writing. One document by his own hand that has survived is an indenture that he drew up on 13 January 1522 between Sir Thomas Cheyne and his wife Dame Frideswide and Nicholas Neweton, gentleman (see Figure 5). Dame Frideswide was the daughter of Thomas Frowyk, and she had been aged nine when her father died in 1506.[5] Thomas Roberts was one of four executors authorized by Frowyk's will to hold his lands for a decade after his death, and in this document Thomas Roberts mentions lands that he holds of Thomas Cheyne and his wife 'to ferme'. This, and his action in drawing up the document, suggests a close relationship of trust and service as the family's attorney over a period of almost twenty years. Yet other documents reveal less harmonious associations. A set of complaints and responses related to Thomas Roberts's administration of lands for the heir of William Page of Harlesden details a dispute, in which Thomas was accused of taking the lands of Page's wife Margaret for his own use and profit and starting a wrongful action of trespass; a particular grievance was that 'the seid Thomas Robertes wrongfully kepith from your supliant chartours and munimentes' concerning the relevant properties.[6] Some of the rhetoric is probably no more than legal posturing, but there can be no doubt that Thomas Roberts gained financial advantage from his activities as a lawyer.

Membership in the London legal community also provided Thomas with ample opportunity for social advancement. At least one of his wives was the daughter of a fellow lawyer, and the advantageous marriages made by two of his children depended upon connections made in legal contexts. Thomas's first attempt to find a lawyer husband for his eldest daughter Dorothy came to nothing; she was betrothed sometime in the 1520s, but the match never took

---

[4] On the order of serjeants at law see Baker, *The Order of Serjeants at Law*.
[5] See section titled 'On Commission: Thomas Roberts and His Associates' below.
[6] TNA, C 1/349/1, and see also C 1/349/2, C 1/349/3, and C 1/767/20.

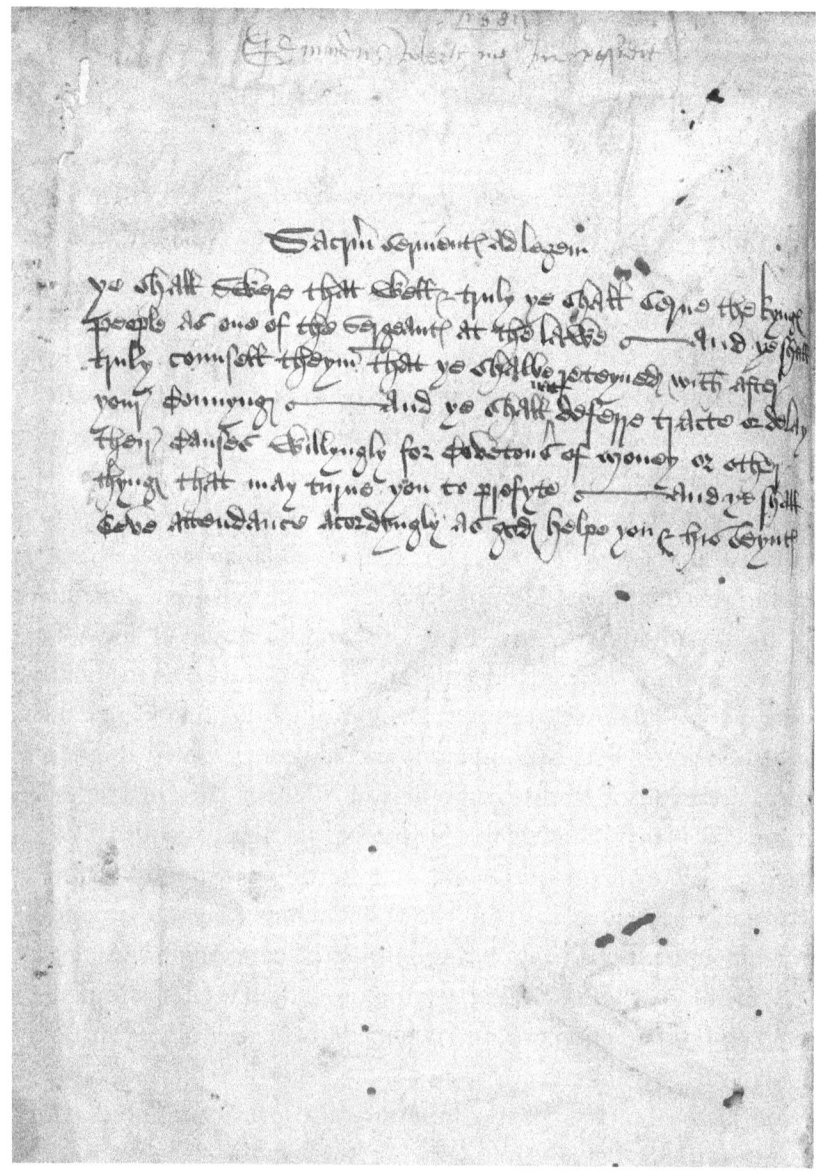

Figure 4 London, British Library, MS Harley 1859, f. *1ᵛ. Inscription by Edmund Roberts; copy of sergeant's oath in the hand of Thomas Roberts. Reproduced by permission. © The British Library Board.

place because the groom died before the wedding. Evidence of this unhappy outcome is recorded in a damaged inscription at St Mary's Willesden, where a tablet on the exterior of the south wall reads:

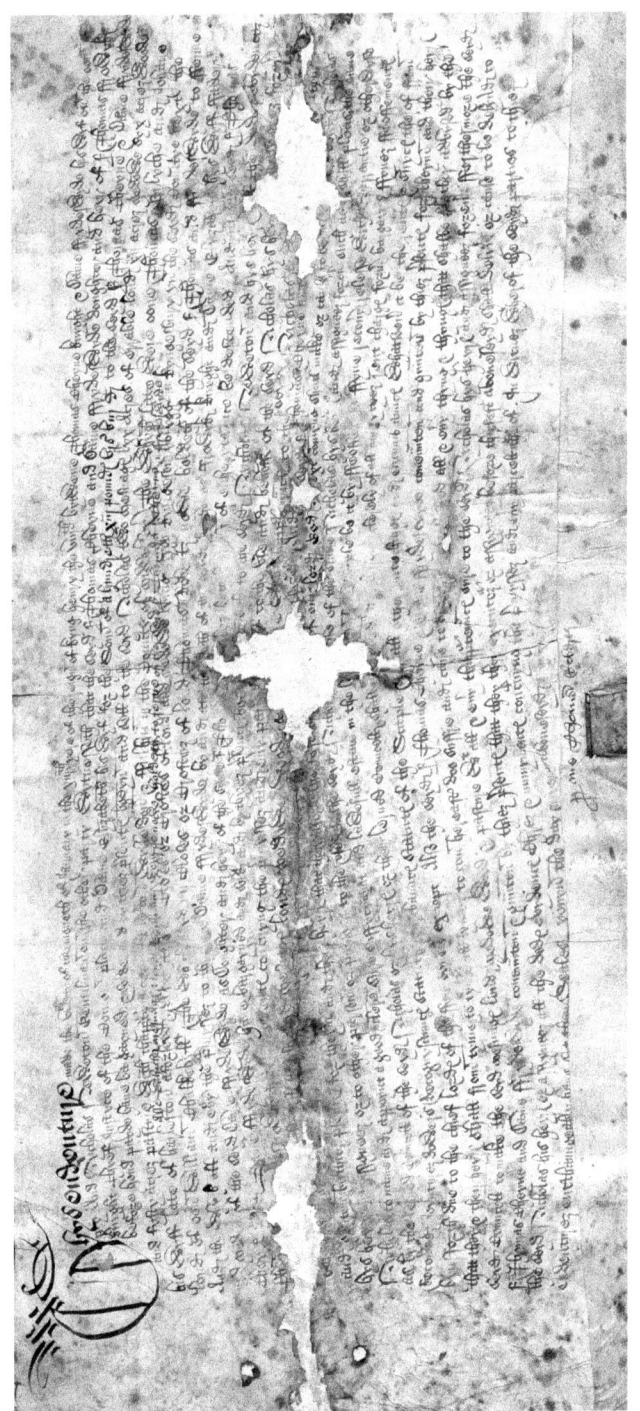

Figure 5 TNA, E 210/10147. Indenture written by the hand of Thomas Roberts. Reproduced by permission of the National Archives.

Table 4 Family tree: The children and grandchildren of Dorothy Roberts and Alan Horde

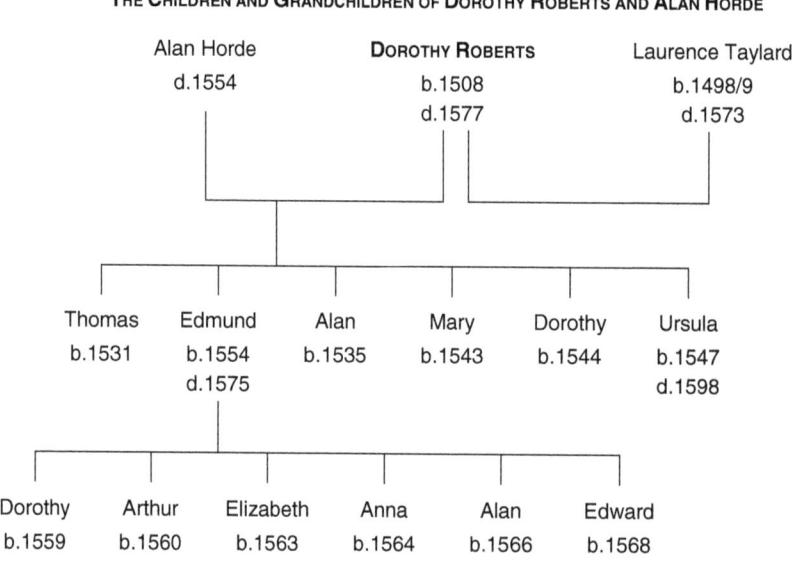

[...] [...] [... *iuris* ...] [...] *qui desponsatus fuit* [...*theae*] *Roberts filiae Thoma[s]* [...*s*] *armigeri et obiit ante* [...]*salia* [....*o*] *die* [...]*ebris* [...] *domini millesimo quingen* [...] *vicesimo* [....] *et hic* [...*us*] *est cui deus sit propicius amen.*[7]

However, within a few years Dorothy was married to Alan Horde, a member of the Middle Temple. The marriage must have occurred by early 1531 at the latest since their first surviving child, named Thomas after his grandfather, was born on All Saints Day (1 November) of that year (see Table 4). If the record of the admission to the Middle Temple on 4 July 1511 of a junior by the name of Hord relates to Alan Horde, as seems likely, then Alan must have been rather older than Dorothy; in 1531 she would have been twenty-four but he must have been in his late thirties at least. This junior is noted as having later achieved the rank

---

[7] That is: '[...] [...] [.... lawyer ...] [...] who was promised in marriage to [Dorothy] Roberts daughter of Thomas [Roberts] esquire and died before [the nuptials] on the ... day of [...] in the year of our Lord one thousand five hundred and twenty [...] and this [...] to whom God be favourable, Amen.'

of bencher, and by 1553 Alan was indeed occupying a chamber as bencher.[8] The family record in JRL English 98 notes six children born to Dorothy and Alan, three boys (Thomas, Edmund, and Alan) and three girls (Mary, Dorothy, and Ursula), but as with the various lists of Thomas Roberts's own children the convention seems to have been to list only the names of those children who survived infancy.[9] A gap in the dates between 1535 and 1543 indicates that some births went unrecorded, and this fits with the different evidence of Dorothy's monumental brass in Ewell church where ten, not six, children are listed (there are two more sons, William and John, and two more daughters, Katherine and Elizabeth).[10] At least one son, Edmund Horde, was admitted to the same inn as his father (in May 1552), and their eldest son Thomas may have been a member there also; there is a Thomas Hoorde who was admitted to the Middle Temple sometime between February 1524–25 and February 1550–51 (the exact date is unclear because the volume of records for this period is missing).[11] Alan Horde had property at Ewell, in Surrey, but his family was from Bridgnorth in Shropshire. One of his nephews, Francis, the third son of his brother Richard, was also a Middle Temple lawyer, admitted on 6 August 1555.[12] And the George Hord who was admitted on 9 October 1560 and called on 16 June 1575 may also have been a relative.[13]

Thomas Roberts's son and heir Michael was unmarried at the time of Thomas's death in 1542, but his marriage to Ursula Huse may have already been planned and must have taken place within the next two years. Ursula was the daughter of Antony Huse or Hussey (1496/7–1560), who was not a barrister but a notary and proctor. His career had prospered during the reign of Henry

---

[8] Alan Horde was admitted on 4 July 1511, see Sturgess, *Register of Admissions*, i.7. Dorothy's second husband, Sir Lawrence Taylard (1498/9–1573) of Diddington, Huntingtonshire, was also a lawyer at the Middle Temple, admitted in 1520, see Bindoff, *The History of Parliament*, iii.427–28.

[9] See further discussion of such lists of births in Chapter 5, section titled 'A Matter of Record'.

[10] As recorded in *VCH Surrey* III, 282, and see also the Hoord pedigree given in Bannerman, *The Visitations of the County of Surrey*, pp. 222–23. See Chapter 4, section titled 'After the Dissolution: the Hordes of Ewell'.

[11] 31 May 1552, see Sturgess, *Register of Admissions*, i.20; for Thomas Hoorde see i.15.

[12] Sturgess, *Register of Admissions*, i.21. The connection between the two branches of the family is evident from a legal record of 1541 (18 March) which notes a recognisance of Alan Hoorde, of London, for the appearance of John, son and heir of Ric. Hoorde, of co. Salop, see *LPFD Henry VIII* 16.298 (no. 632).

[13] Sturgess, *Register of Admissions*, i.25.

VIII to the extent that by 1539 he was judge of the admiralty court and chief registrar to the archbishop of Canterbury, Thomas Cranmer.[14] Hussey owned a large house in Paternoster Row and held lands in Essex which had come to him from his wife, Catherine Webbe; his own family originally came from Sussex. His sister Margaret was married to Thomas Goodman, an Essex landowner and London mercer, who was appointed as the overseer of Michael Roberts's will and remembered with a gift of money.[15] Hussey was named as coexecutor of the will, along with his daughter, and appointed as guardian of any unborn child; he and his wife both received money gifts. Also amongst the witnesses was Matthew Huse, probably a brother of Ursula's.

Thomas Roberts's youngest son, John, was admitted to the Middle Temple in 1560.[16] There is no record of John's elder sibling Edmund Roberts having been admitted to any of the Inns of Court, nor is there any firm proof that he chose to follow their father in the legal profession; this lack of evidence may simply be due to an unfortunate gap in the records of admissions for the relevant period.[17] Certainly Edmund participated in the types of public service usually performed by those with legal training, serving on various commissions and acting as justice of the peace in the 1550s, a position that required at least some legal background. Many of his friends and associates seem to have been from legal circles, and it is worth noting that Edmund's choice of godfather for his eldest daughter, Katherine, who was born in 1552, was 'master Johan Armyster master of the temple and lord of Nesdon': the designation 'Master of the Temple' denotes the senior clergyman at the Temple church.[18] Collectively these are indications that Edmund maintained connections in these legal environs, whether or not he himself was a lawyer. Furthermore, Edmund's inscription of ownership occurs twice in the copy of the standard legal textbook, *Registrum Brevium*, that his father Thomas had owned, suggesting – at the very least – an interest in reading law books.[19]

---

[14] See Baker, *Readers and Readings*, p. 152; Bindoff, *The History of Parliament*, ii. 420–21; MacCulloch, *Thomas Cranmer*, pp. 608–9. Hussey's will is TNA, PROB 11/43/569.

[15] TNA, PROB 11/30/205.

[16] 24 May 1560, 'John Roberts, third son of Thomas R., of Wilsden, Middlesex, esq., decd.', see Sturgess, *Register of Admissions*, i. 25.

[17] See above.

[18] As recorded in BodL, Rawlinson C. 894, f. iv^v. For more details of Edmund's career and associates see the Conclusion.

[19] See section titled 'A Lawyer's Book: British Library, MS Harley 1859' later in this chapter.

In the next generation three of Edmund's grandsons, Barne Roberts (1576–1610), Robert Roberts (1591–1636), and James Roberts (b. 1597), were admitted to Gray's Inn, as was one of his great-grandsons, the son of Barne, William Roberts (1604–62). Another later member of the Willesden family, Richard Roberts, gentleman, was admitted to the Inner Temple in 1664.[20] He may have been the owner of BL Harley 2729, an eleventh-century manuscript that contains works of Roman history and military strategy (Eutropius, *Breviarium historiae Romanae*, and Julius Frontinus, *Stratagemata*) and which bears the name 'Ric. Robertz' in two places written by a seventeenth-century hand.[21] There are also other cases where it is not clear whether lawyers with the name 'Roberts' belonged to the Middlesex family or not: one such is the John Roberts who was admitted to the Middle Temple in 1518–19.[22] Confusingly, the Robertses of Bristol and the Robertses of Little Braxted, Essex, also had connections with the Middle Temple, as is demonstrated by the admissions of John Roberttes, son and heir of John Roberts of Bristol, gentleman, in February 1571–72, and Thomas Robertes of Little Braxted on 29 June 1592.[23] Another late sixteenth-century record of the admission of 'John Robartes, late of Staple Inn, gent.' to the Middle Temple, could relate to any of these families.[24]

Later generations of the Roberts family were also university men. There is no evidence that Thomas Roberts or any of his sons attended either of the English universities, but from the time of Francis Roberts (1551–1631) the family developed a connection with Cambridge. Francis Roberts matriculated at Peterhouse in 1568, and four of his sons also attended Cambridge: Barne Roberts matriculated at Christ's College in 1595–96; Robert Roberts matriculated at Peterhouse in 1609, and graduated BA in 1612–13 and MA in 1616; James Roberts matriculated at Peterhouse in 1614, and his brother Thomas Roberts (b. 1606) at the same college in 1626. Subsequently Barne's sons William and Richard also went to Cambridge: William Roberts matriculated

---

[20] 18 May 1664, see Inner Temple Admission Database, www.innertemple.org.uk/archive/itad/detail.asp?id=4652.

[21] The name occurs on f. 109ᵛ and f. 110ʳ, the latter cancelled. A sample leaf (f. 34ᵛ) of this manuscript may be seen at http://www.bl.uk/catalogues/illuminatedmanuscripts/ILLUMIN.ASP?Size=mid&IllID=25453.

[22] 4 February 1518–19, see Sturgess, *Register of Admissions*, i.10.

[23] Sturgess, *Register of Admissions*, i.35, 65. For details of these families see Appendix V below.

[24] 13 May 1580, Sturgess, *Register of Admissions*, i.46.

at Queen's College in 1622 and then migrated to Emmanuel; Richard Roberts matriculated at Emmanuel in 1625, achieving the BA in 1628–29 and the MA in 1632.[25]

ON COMMISSION: THOMAS ROBERTS AND HIS ASSOCIATES

One aspect which distinguishes the career of Thomas Roberts from those of his forebears is the extent of his involvement in public life. As a lawyer his name naturally occurs in the public record; the earliest mention that I have been able to trace occurs in 1501 when Thomas was named in a release and quitclaim from George Shordyche, the son and heir of Robert Shordyche and his wife Margaret.[26] The quitclaim is dated 7 April 16 Henry VII (1501), and was acknowledged on 8 May. It relates principally to the manor of Southall in Middlesex, and to rents in Northcote, Hese, and Harrow. These properties, which are all located west of Willesden, had lately been recovered by Thomas Roberts and William Mordaunt, John Scotte, and Stephen Fryssheney, for the use of Edward Cheseman and his heirs.[27] Edward Cheseman, a lawyer of Gray's Inn and an officer of King's Bench, was the cofferer and keeper of the Wardrobe of the Household to Henry VII. Through his friendship with the widow Joan Luyt, Cheseman acquired control of the chapel dedicated to the Virgin and All Angels at Brentford in 1497, a foundation whose fraternity included many lawyers and royal officials.[28] In the Middlesex pedigrees collected by Richard Mundy, his family is referred to as 'Cheesman of Dormans Well' because their chief property was at Dormer's Wells, near Southall.[29] The pedigree records two younger brothers for Edward: John and Robert, both described as having lands in Lewisham, and gives his heirs as a son Robert and five daughters. Thomas Roberts served on a number of Middlesex commissions with members of this family: once with John Cheseman in 1524, and several times between

---

[25] For details see Venn and Venn, *Alumni Cantabrigiensis*, pp. 464–67.
[26] *CCR Henry VII*, 2.15 (16 Henry VII, no. 44); cf. the earlier conjunction of John Shordyche and John Roberts as witnesses to a grant of lands in 1450, *CCR Henry VI*, 5.191–92 (28 Henry VI).
[27] William Mordaunt was a bencher at the Middle Temple before 1500 and treasurer 1506–8, see Sturgess, *Register of Admissions*, i.2; John Scott or Skott(e), gentleman, held lands in Harrow; Stephen Fryssheney, clerk, is reported as deceased by 1501.
[28] See Sutton and Visser-Fuchs, 'The Cult of Angels', pp. 244–45.
[29] Armytage, *Middlesex Pedigrees*, p. 47.

1523 and 1540 with Edward's son Robert. His closest connection, though, may have been with Edward himself, since he was named as one of the executors of his will.[30] Thomas Roberts was involved in another quitclaim in 1505, again relating to lands in Middlesex (in Harlesden, Willesden, and Fulham), held by Sir Thomas Frowyk, second son of the Sir Thomas Frowyk who compiled a short historical chronicle in the early 1480s.[31] Frowyk, who died on 7 October 1506, had extensive property holdings in Middlesex, including lands in Neasden and Oxgate manor (which was later owned by Thomas's grandson, Francis).[32] As a close neighbour with local interests, it is not surprising to find Thomas Roberts listed in this transaction, but he knew Frowyk from legal circles as well: Frowyk was a member of the Inner Temple who had been appointed as serjeant at law in 1501, and as chief justice of common pleas in 1502; subsequently Thomas Roberts served as executor to both Thomas Frowyk and his brother Henry.[33]

Thomas Roberts's first official appointment seems to have been as one of the coroners for Middlesex, an office that he held from at least 1508.[34] A range of other county-based commissions followed. In August 1513 Thomas Roberts was one of four commissioners appointed, along with Sir Richard Cholmeley, Thomas Jakys, and Nicolas Bowne, to seize the property of any Scotsmen living in the county; the commission, which was repeated for other English counties, was a response to openly hostile moves on the Scottish border by James IV during Henry VIII's absence in France.[35] Thomas Jakes (Jakys) had been named with Thomas Roberts in the quitclaim pertaining to Thomas Frowyk in 1505. Another of the same name, Robert Jakes, along with his wife Maud, is mentioned in the 1501 quitclaim, suggesting that these were members of a closely-knit Middlesex circle with related property interests. Both Cholmeley and Bowne (or Boone) were amongst those named with Thomas Roberts in the 1516 Commission of Sewers 'for the district extending from the town of Ware up to the river Thames along the banks thereof', that is, covering

---

[30] He is described as Edward Cheseman's executor (along with William Bonde) in a pardon and release of 20 March 1517, see *LPFD Henry VIII*, 2.ii.973 (8 Henry VII, no. 3035). For Cheseman's will written 10 August 1509, proved 14 November 1510 see TNA, PROB 11/16/292.

[31] Sutton and Visser-Fuchs, 'The Making of a Minor London chronicle'.

[32] *CIPM* 2nd series, III.III–15 (20–24, Henry VII, no. 195).

[33] See Baker, *Readers and Readings*, p. 69; Doe, 'Frowyk, Sir Thomas'; and TNA, PROB 11/15/285. Henry Frowyk's will, proved 15 November 1505, is TNA, PROB 11/14/771.

[34] *CPR Henry VII vol. ii: 1494–1509*, p. 564.

[35] *LPFD Henry VIII*, 2nd ed., 1.ii.996 (5 Henry VIII, no. 2222, grant 16).

not just Middlesex but also Essex and Hertfordshire.[36] In this much larger commission, which lists twenty-six men drawn from very different ranks (beginning with the dukes of Norfolk and Surrey), there can be much less of an assumption that the individuals involved shared social ties, though one of the more junior-ranking men named here, John Kyrton or Kirkton, who also appears in other commissions with Thomas Roberts in the 1520s, probably did belong to the same social circle. According to the pedigrees, Kyrton's second wife Ann was the widow of John Leek of Edmonton, and both Kyrton's son William and daughter Margaret married into this family as well; Margaret's husband, Jasper Leek, son of John, appears in commissions with Thomas Roberts in the late 1530s.[37] Another relatively low-ranking member of the 1516 Commission of Sewers, Richard Lyster, probably knew Thomas from the Inns of Court since he was presumably the Richard Lyster, son of John Lyster of Wakefield, Yorkshire, who was admitted to the Middle Temple prior to 7 July 1501 and who was a bencher in 1515 and treasurer 1522–24.[38]

Although there is no formal record of Thomas Roberts's appointment as a subsidy commissioner for Middlesex before 1523, the survival of a certificate of assessment for John Harman of Pynnore (Pinner) for the subsidy granted in the fifth year of Henry VIII's reign (1514) suggests that he had already been working in this capacity for some time. The certificate is dated 14 January 1515 and is signed and sealed by Thomas Goodere and Thomas Roberts, described as 'commissioners in Middlesex'.[39] Thomas Goodere was also involved in the 1505 quitclaim of Thomas Frowyk's lands in Willesden, and a Francis Goodere, presumably a member of the same family, features alongside Thomas Roberts in a number of commissions in the late 1530s.[40] In both 1523 and 1524, Thomas Roberts was named in the subsidy commission along with other men from the middle ranks of the Middlesex gentry. Altogether the commission for 1523 consisted of fourteen men: Roberts, Sir Thomas Nevill, Sir Thomas More, Sir John Daunce, John Neudegate, John Spilman, Henry Frowike, John Kyrton, Robert Wroth, Robert Elryngton, John Pakynton, Robert Cheseman, Richard

---

[36] *LPFD Henry VIII*, 2.ii.646 (8 Henry VIII, no. 2138).
[37] Armytage, *Middlesex Pedigrees*, pp. 106–7 and pp. 12–14.
[38] See Sturgess, *Register of Admissions*, i.2.
[39] *LPFD Henry VIII Addenda* p. 36 (no. 124).
[40] They were probably members of the Goodere family of Hadley, Middlesex, for which see Armytage, *Middlesex Pedigrees*, pp. 23–24.

Hawkys, and John Palmer.⁴¹ A more detailed account of the division of districts for the 1524 subsidy shows that the particular district that Thomas Roberts was assigned to was the Hundred of Gore, comprising Hendon, Edgware, Stanmer Magna and Parva, Kyngsbury, Pinner, Harrow, Roysey (Roxeth), Sudbery, Wembley, Aperton, and Harrow Wylde; this included areas where he had financial interests, though his own lands at Willesden lay within the Hundred of Osulstone.⁴²

Leaving aside the three highest ranking individuals and John Spelman (or Spilman), serjeant-at-law, later Sir John Spelman and judge of the King's Bench, some brief consideration of the remaining group of ten men named in these commissions provides an insight into the existence and operation of social networks in Middlesex in the first quarter of the sixteenth century. Only Richard Hawkys may not immediately be placed as a member of a Middlesex family. The Neudegate (Newdigate, Newdigatt) family were associated with Harfield, the Kyrton family with Edmonton, the Wroths with Enfield, the Elryngtons with Hackney, the Pakyngtons with Edgworth and Little Stanmore, the Chesemans with Dormer's Well, and the Palmers with Kentish Town.⁴³ The Frowike (Frowyk) family had their seat at the 'Old Fold', and had properties in Finchley, Willesden, and Gunnersbury, as well as in London and Kent.⁴⁴ As holders of lands and properties within neighbouring areas, these families naturally shared a range of local interests which, not surprisingly, they tended to consolidate through marriage arrangements, a practice which resulted in a complex web of inter-family relations. This discussion can scarcely do justice to the extent of these connections, but one or two such marital links might pertinently be noted here. John Palmer's wife Eleanor, who was the widow of Edward Taylor of Hadley, was also one of the daughters of Edward Cheseman.⁴⁵ Robert Wroth's mother, Margaret, was

---

⁴¹ *LPFD Henry VIII*, 3.ii.1361 (15 Henry VIII, no. 3282). The list given for the 1524 subsidy is identical, except that it names John rather than Robert Cheseman, and adds Roger Cholmeley, see *LPFD Henry VIII*, 4.i.232–33 (16 Henry VIII, no. 547).

⁴² *LPFD Henry VIII*, 4.i.421–22 (16 Henry VIII, no. 969). Thomas had interests as a steward in Stanmer Parva and Wembley.

⁴³ For fuller information see Armytage, *Middlesex Pedigrees* under the pedigrees listed for each family.

⁴⁴ See Armytage, *Middlesex Pedigrees*, pp. 88–90. Note that Thomas Roberts was named in 1519 in a grant of livery of lands relating to Henry, son and heir of Henry Frowik, *LPFD Henry VIII*, 3.i.172 (11 Henry VIII, no. 492, grant 19).

⁴⁵ See Armytage, *Middlesex Pedigrees*, p. 44.

a daughter of the Newdigate family, and his wife was the widow of Thomas Goodere.[46] Clearly the men who were selected to perform administrative tasks at county level were connected by more than just regional property interests. Even John Spelman, whose own family came from Narborough in Norfolk, may be counted as a member of this Middlesex network since he married Elizabeth, daughter of Henry Frowike (Frowyk) and niece of Thomas.[47]

A more select group of these middle-ranking Middlesex men, consisting of Newdigate, Wrothe, Kyrton, Hawkes, and Thomas Roberts, was commissioned to collect the subsidy (to fund the war with France) in Middlesex in 1523, with Sir John Daunce (given as 'Dauncey' but doubtless the same), this time in association with different senior men: the lord of St John's (at this date Sir Thomas Docwra), Sir Thomas Lovell, and Sir Richard Broke.[48] With the possible exception of John Kyrton, who was almost certainly John Kyrketon of Edelmeton (i.e. Edmonton), Middlesex, with lands also in Essex, Leicester, and Surrey, these Middlesex men were also figures that Thomas Roberts would have naturally encountered in city legal circles.[49] John Newdigate of Lincoln's Inn was serjeant at law 1510–28.[50] Robert Wrothe (died 1535) was reader at Staple Inn *circa* 1520.[51] Richard Hawkes was filazer of the King's Bench, mentioned in Lincoln's Inn in 1530.[52] Amongst the senior men, Richard Broke (died 1529) was reader at Gray's Inn, and Thomas Lovell was reader at Lincoln's Inn.[53] Lovell was a very senior figure indeed, having been chancellor of the Exchequer

---

[46] See Armytage, *Middlesex Pedigrees*, p. 17.

[47] See Armytage, *Middlesex Pedigrees*, pp. 88–89, and for further information about Spelman who was a reader at Gray's Inn, see Baker, *Readers and Readings*, p. 30 and Baker, 'Spelman, Sir John'. Spelman also owned a collection of yearbooks, BL Additional 37659, which previously belonged to Thomas Frowyk and Thomas Jakes, see the next section of this chapter.

[48] *LPFD Henry VIII*, 3.ii.1457 (15 Henry VIII, no. 3504). For Lovell see Gunn, 'Lovell, Sir Thomas'.

[49] Kyrton's will of 1529 is TNA, PROB 11/23/246. The name 'Kyrton', perhaps the same, occurs on f. 44ʳ of BL Lansdowne 465, a fifteenth-century collection of legal readings.

[50] See Baker, *The Order of Serjeants at Law*, p. 528, with a reproduction of his brass at Harefield church as plate 5. This John Newdigate was evidently older than Thomas Roberts, having been admitted to Lincoln's Inn in 1483.

[51] Baker, *Readers and Readings*, p. 215.

[52] Baker, *Readers and Readings*, p. 6; the filazer or filacer was an officer of the superior courts at Westminster who filed original writs and issued processes.

[53] Baker, *Readers and Readings*, pp. 27 and 109 respectively, and see also Baker 'Broke, Sir Richard'.

1485–1516 and treasurer of the royal household 1486–1509; he was also a knight of the Garter. When he died in 1524, his funeral at the priory of Halliwell was a large-scale event attended by many liveried mourners, amongst them Thomas Roberts, Wrothe, Kyrton, and Hawkes.[54]

Later the same year, Thomas Roberts was amongst those appointed to conduct privy searches into properties in London. This appointment, renewed the following year, and also in 1528, pertained to 'Kilborne and Wilsdon', which he was to cover with one other man, initially with Nicholas Jenyns of London, latterly with Henry Lodisman.[55] Another document suggests that Thomas's role was more extensive, and lists his name and Cheseman's in conjunction with other areas to be searched: Islington, St John's Street and Clerkenwell; Tothill Street and St Stephen's; and the district from Temple Bar to Charing Cross.[56] Overall, between thirty and forty-five men were assigned to these searches, which were to be made all on one date, starting at midnight; suspects were to be committed and interrogated, and weapons and gambling equipment were to be removed from inns and other suspicious houses and openly burned.[57]

In the summer of 1531 Thomas Roberts was granted an exemption from being made escheator of Kent, Middlesex, or any other county. Two similar grants, one of 18 June and the second of 5 July, repeat this exemption, the first styling him as 'Thomas Robertz of London', the second as 'Thos. Roberts, of Willesden, Middx., gentleman, *alias* of London'.[58] The following year Thomas Roberts's name occurs for the first time in the Commission of the Peace for Middlesex.[59] The list of thirty men includes some familiar associates with whom he had served on previous subsidy commissions: John Pakyngton, Robert Wrothe, Robert Elryngton, Robert Cheseman, and John Palmer; the John Newdigate now mentioned was either the son or grandson of the previously mentioned John. Amongst the rest, many were men from the London legal milieu: John Denysell and Roger Cholmeley, serjeants at law, were both of

---

[54] *LPFD Henry VIII*, 4.i.149–55 (16 Henry VIII, no. 366).
[55] *LPFD Henry VIII Addenda*, pp. 139–40 (no. 430); *LPFD Henry VIII*, 4.i.473 (16 Henry VIII no. 1082); *LPFD Henry VIII Addenda*, pp. 202–203 (no. 609).
[56] *LPFD Henry VIII Addenda*, pp. 140–41 (nos. 431–32).
[57] *LPFD Henry VIII Addenda*, p. 203 (no. 609).
[58] *LPFD Henry VIII*, 5.149 and 174 (23 Henry VIII, no. 318 grant 25, and no. 364 grant 10).
[59] *LPFD Henry VIII*, 5.704 (24 Henry VIII, no. 1694). Thomas Roberts also served on the Commission of the Peace in 1537, 1539, and 1540, see *LPFD Henry VIII*, 12.ii.353–4 (29 Henry VIII, no. 1008, grant 31) and note 65 below.

Lincoln's Inn, as was John Skewes; John Hales was from Gray's Inn, Henry White from the Inner Temple, and John Brown from the Middle Temple (though the last is a common name for which there are several possible contenders).[60]

Also at about this time a Thomas Roberts was named in a number of records relating to a land transaction near Waltham. The lands in question lay near to Copped Hall, northeast of Waltham Abbey. A letter from Christopher Hales, the attorney-general, to Thomas Cromwell, dated 26 October 1532 reports: 'Mr Riche and I are at a point with Roberts the auditor for his lands which were Mrs Lubbyshed's near Copthall. Roberts and Ryche behaved well, but the former would not part with the land except to the King. We have promised him 220l., which he gave for it. He says it is worth 400 marks.'[61] A few months later, in February 1533, a warrant was issued to Cromwell to pay Thomas Roberts £200 for these lands, and in March a note of the payment, via Richard Riche, appears in Cromwell's accounts.[62] A final record three years later in 1536 which summarizes Cromwell's administration mentions this land transaction again, detailing 'the manor and park of Coppydhall; certain lands from Thos. Robertts, the auditor, lying beside Waltham'.[63] Although land-holdings in Essex seem remote from his usual sphere of property interests, the designation 'auditor' would seem to indicate that this is indeed Thomas Roberts of Willesden. In a Commission of 1535 (the Tenths of Spiritualities), Thomas Roberts was listed with sixteen others to make enquiries in London; five of the men, Roberts included, are designated as auditors: the others were John Bugon, Thomas Myldemay, Thomas Burgon, and John Notte. It might be noted that the Thomas Roberts listed in the commission of the same date for Kent is *not* styled auditor.[64]

Thomas Roberts's name continues to appear in various grants and commissions relating to Middlesex in the late 1530s and early 1540s. Most of these appointments were of a routine nature, in line with the type of public service which was expected of the middle-ranking gentry. In July 1539 Thomas was

---

[60] See Baker, *Readers and Readings*, passim.
[61] *LPFD Henry VIII*, 5.619 (24 Henry VIII, no. 1470).
[62] *LPFD Henry VIII*, 6.78 and p. 102 (24 Henry VIII, no. 170 and no. 228).
[63] *LPFD Henry VIII*, 10.513 (28 Henry VIII, no. 1231). See also later reference to this land and Thomas Roberts's former ownership of it in *CPR Philip and Mary* 2 (1554–55), p. 262 and *CPR Elizabeth* 3 (1563–66), p. 90 (no. 396).
[64] *LPFD Henry VIII*, 8.49 (26 Henry VIII no. 149, grant 42).

named in the Commission of the Peace for Middlesex along with thirty-eight other men, and the following summer he was listed with very much the same company in the commissions of Peace and Oyer and Terminer for Middlesex.[65] Another smaller commission was given to four of the men from this group in November 1540 when Thomas Roberts, Robert Cheseman, Francis Goodyer, and Thomas Wrothe were charged with enquiring into the lunacy of Nicholas Wethers.[66] Thomas Roberts was also named in a commission of gaol delivery for Newgate gaol in London; his name occurs in this regard in a grant of November 1542, along with twenty-two other men, seven of whom had previously been associated with him.[67] This seems to have been his last assignment, and it is also the last recorded mention of him during his lifetime; he died less than two months later on 1 January 1542 (that is, 1543 according to modern dating), and was buried in his London parish church of St Clement Danes. His eldest son Michael succeeded him as head of the family, and seems to have been poised to follow him in a life of public service as well, taking up an appointment as escheator for Middlesex a few months later.[68] In the event this promising career was cut short by Michael's own sudden death in 1544, aged just 25, which left Edmund Roberts, aged 24, and his much younger brother John, aged 13, as Thomas's only surviving sons.

Thomas's name continues to appear posthumously in public records of the next few years, often in connection with property, as in the grant of 1545 to Hugh Losse and his wife Agnes which named Thomas, amongst others, as the holder of properties in Edgeworth (Edgware) and Stanmore Parva.[69] In the previous year, when the king needed to muster troops for the war against France, only two Middlesex men were named as being required to provide foot soldiers for the vanguard: Jasper Fesaunt, who was to send three men, and Thomas Roberts, who was to send two. It seems that the clerks responsible for compiling the muster had not realized that Thomas Roberts was dead, but details for paying the soldiers' wages at Calais on 9 June correctly record

---

[65] *LPFD Henry VIII*, 14.i.585 (31 Henry VIII, no. 1354, grant 11); *LPFD Henry VIII*, 15.407 (32 Henry VIII, no. 831, grant 47b), see note 59 above.
[66] *LPFD Henry VIII*, 16.141 (32 Henry VIII, no. 305, grant 33).
[67] *LPFD Henry VIII*, 17.633 (34 Henry VIII, no. 1154, grant 24).
[68] *LPFD Henry VIII*, 18.i.242 (35 Henry VIII, no. 449, grant 59).
[69] *LPFD Henry VIII*, 20.ii.327 (37 Henry VIII, no. 707 grant 44); see also *LPFD Henry VIII*, 21.ii.162 (38 Henry VIII, no. 332, grant 61).

Michael Roberts's name instead.[70] The period after Michael's death seems to have been one in which members of the Roberts family did not enjoy much public prominence. The youngest son, John Roberts, was still a minor under the 'rule and guyding' of his mother's brother, John Sadler, as stipulated by his father's will.[71] Edmund, now head of the family aged twenty-four, was scarcely at an age to attract much notice; by comparison, his father's long career in public service only seems to have begun as he approached his late thirties. Certainly there seems to be no mention of Edmund in public service during the final years of Henry VIII's reign and throughout that of Edward VI, though this might also be an indication that Edmund's religious preferences did not sit well with the staunchly Protestant regime of this decade. He did become more visible after the accession of Mary Tudor in 1553; from that point, for the next few years at least, Edmund's career followed the pattern of his father's, with a regular stream of public commissions at county level. In November 1553 Edmund was named among those commissioned with surveying the sewers (that is, walls, streams, ditches, etc.) 'from Saynt Kateryns to Stratford and all the sewers within the lymittes of Stratford and Hackney within the Countie of Middlesex'.[72] His name appears again in the Commission of Sewers the following year, with many of the same group of men, this time also including his relative John Sadler.[73] In February 1554 Edmund was appointed to the Commission of the Peace for Middlesex and was justice of the peace for the county in 1555.[74] In both years he served alongside many men who were lawyers: Sir John Baker, Sir Robert Broke, Sir Humfrey Browne, Robert Chidleye, Sir Roger Cholmley, William Cordell, Edward Griffin, Sir Nicholas Hare, John Newdigate, William Roper, John Southcote, Sir William Stanford, and Anthony Stapleton. Similarly, in September 1557, when Mary needed to raise funds for war against the French and the Scots, Edmund was named as one of the commissioners for the loan in Middlesex, along with Sir Roger Cholmley, John Newdigate, and Robert Chidleye.[75] These various public commissions during Mary Tudor's reign suggest that,

---

[70] *LPFD Henry VIII*, 19.i.158 (35 Henry VIII, no. 274) and 19.i.412 (36 Henry VIII, no. 655).
[71] LMA, DL/C/356.
[72] *CPR Philip and Mary*, 1 (1553–54), pp. 35–37.
[73] *CPR Philip and Mary*, 2 (1554–55), pp. 107–108.
[74] *CPR Philip and Mary*, 1 (1553–54), pp. 21–22; *Calendar of State Papers, Domestic Series, Mary I*, pp. 80–91 (p. 85), no. 160.
[75] *Calendar of State Papers, Domestic Series, Mary I*, pp. 295–97, no. 656.

like his father, Edmund had probably had legal training, though a gap in the surviving records of admission at Middle Temple between 1524 and 1551 makes it difficult to be sure of this. Certainly Edmund's public service brought various rewards. For example, in December of 1555 he was granted the office of a keeper of Waltham Forest, previously allocated by Henry VIII to one Richard Johnson. This office brought with it wages of 8*d.* a day, payable for life, and was granted to Edmund 'in consideration of his service'.[76]

Initially these patterns of activity seem to have continued under Elizabeth I. In October 1559 and again in July 1560 Edmund was named as part of a commission to survey the possessions of the bishopric of London (the bishopric had been declared void and its possessions taken by the Crown). The other men named include familiar associates John Newdigate and Thomas Elrington, and also William Paten of Stoke Nuyngton, John Hales of Totnam Hiecrosse, and Thomas Persye of Islington.[77] In terms of county commissions, however, this seems to be the final mention of Edmund Roberts, and for the last two decades of his life he seems not to have sought, or been favoured with, public service. As with his father there is the problem of potential confusion with other men of the same name; several records refer to Edmund Roberts, merchant, a member of the Kentish Roberts family.[78] The only later reference I can find to the correct Edmund Roberts is in two licences to alienate lands granted in 1575 to James Altham and John Barne; the lands are in Hertford and Kent, respectively, and the other named recipients, Thomas Altham and Emmanuel Wolley, were friends or associates of his.[79]

A LAWYER'S BOOK: BRITISH LIBRARY, MS HARLEY 1859

As a legal practitioner Thomas Roberts would have required access to books as part of his day-to-day professional activities. Medieval common lawyers needed

---

[76] *CPR Philip and Mary*, 3 (1555–57), p. 169.

[77] *CPR Elizabeth*, 1 (1558–60), p. 30 and p. 422.

[78] See, for example, *CPR Elizabeth*, 4 (1566–69), p. 274, no. 1589: 'Edmund Robertes of the County of Kent, merchant'. The Edmund Roberts whose name is mentioned in a letter written on behalf of Queen Elizabeth to William IV, Landgrave of Hesse-Cassel on 10 March 1567/8, in connection with a complaint raised against him by Adolph Zenck, is likely to be this merchant rather than Edmund Roberts of Willesden; see BL Royal 13 B. I, f. 216 and the catalogue description at www.searcharchives.bl.uk.

[79] *CPR Elizabeth*, 7 (1575–78), pp. 425–26, nos 2834–35.

close knowledge of the texts of parliamentary statutes and of the writs that were issued by the royal Chancery and by the central law-courts. Access to such texts was provided partly on an institutional basis: the Inns of Court had developed dedicated library rooms by the end of the fifteenth century, and there are various records of the bequests of books to these libraries by members during the late fifteenth and sixteenth centuries.[80] The Inner Temple received one such bequest from Thomas Jakes, a senior clerk, in 1513.[81] Jakes left instructions that his wife should deliver 'to the company of the Inner temple my fayer Boke of the newe statutes wryten and lymed and my greate Boke of Entres'. It is clear from Jakes's will and the wills of other lawyers that men in this profession built up their own personal collections of books. The Norfolk lawyer Sir Roger Townshend, who died in 1493, owned more than forty books, at least half of which were legal volumes.[82] Thomas Kebell (c. 1439–1500), serjeant-at-law and squire of Humberstone in Leicestershire, had at least thirty-three books, both manuscript and print, which are listed in some detail in the inventory of his goods. Kebell's will specified several bequests of books, including a large number to his son who was to have 'all my bookes of Scripture, of Lawe, of Cronicles or stories, and alle other my bookes in latyn, Frenssh or Englissh'.[83] Typically lawyers passed on their books both to institutional libraries and to fellow lawyers, but as so often with books bequests tell only half a story. Thomas Jakes had himself inherited books from Sir Thomas Frowyk, whose executor he had been in 1506, but the books are not mentioned in Frowyk's will; instead they came to Jakes indirectly after his marriage to Frowyk's widow, Elizabeth. In Jakes's own will of 20 January 1513, he specified that the two books which were to be given to the Inner Temple were volumes that had previously belonged to 'my Singuler good lord Frowykes', and that they were 'there to remayne in the librarie to thentent they shuld the better remember my seid good lord'. Jakes also stipulated that five associates were each to choose 'euery of them a boke of lawe' from his collection, or to have twenty shillings instead if

---

[80] See Ramsay and Willoughby, *Hospitals, Towns, and the Professions*, pp. 130–33.

[81] See Ramsay and Willoughby, *Hospitals, Towns, and the Professions*, pp. 145–47. Jakes's will is TNA, PROB 11/18/47, f. 12^v.

[82] Moreton, 'The "Library" of a Late Fifteenth-Century Lawyer', makes a study of Townshend's library; for a fuller study of the family see Moreton, *The Townshends and their World*.

[83] Ives, *The Common Lawyers*, p. 426; for Kebell's will and inventory of goods see pp. 425–47.

they preferred (giving some indication of the perceived worth of the volumes in question). These five associates were John Fowler, Richard Bellamy, John Chauncy, Robert Hawkes, and Thomas Roberts. Thomas Roberts and Richard Bellamy, here specified also as Jakes's executors, had both been named in Frowyk's inquisition post-mortem of 1506, and Roberts had also recently served with Jakes on a commission in 1513 to investigate the property of Scots living in Middlesex.[84]

It is possible that BL Harley 1859 might have been the book which Thomas Roberts chose from the collection assembled by Jakes, but there are no signs of this in the manuscript itself; aside from numerous additions of the name 'Roberts' there are no other names to help identify any earlier owners.[85] It is equally possible that Thomas Roberts acquired some other book from Jakes, perhaps one which no longer survives, or one which is not now traceable to either owner. Some other extant law books have been identified as having belonged to Jakes, comprising three yearbook collections and a terrier (a survey of lands).[86] He also owned two non-legal books: the first is a collection of Latin works including the *Speculum stultorum* by Nigel Witeker (or Wireker), a *Vita S. Eustachii*, and a *Catalogus eruditorum Thome Becket*; the second is a volume of vernacular poetry and prose that contains *Piers Plowman* and Mandeville's *Travels*.[87] The survival of these latter two volumes is a useful reminder that lawyers did not restrict themselves to legal reading. Thomas Roberts's own collection amply demonstrates this, as does another book bequest in which he is mentioned, that made by Humphrey Adam in 1507. Adam left his brother, Nicholas: 'all my books, rolls, estates, and muniments touching the king's chancery and also a register being in his keeping', which suggests that Nicholas

---

[84] *CIPM* 2nd series, III. 111–15 (20–24 Henry VII, no. 195); *LPFD Henry VIII*, 2nd ed., I. ii.996 (5 Henry VIII, no. 2222, grant 16). See earlier section in this chapter titled 'On Commission: Thomas Roberts and His Associates'.

[85] As suggested by Ramsay and Willoughby, *Hospitals, Towns, and the Professions*, p. 145, following Putnam, *Early Treatises*, p. 182 n. 5, but see below for an alternative suggestion.

[86] See the discussion by Ramsay and Willoughby, *Hospitals, Towns, and the Professions*, p. 146. The three yearbook collections are now BL MSS Hargrave 210, Additional 37657, and Additional 37659 (see www.searcharchives.bl.uk for brief descriptions). The terrier is now Sheffield Archives, Jackson Collection, JC/14/17 (formerly JC/ 901); a catalogue description is available through www.calmview.eu/SheffieldArchives/.

[87] The first of these is now BL Arundel 23; a list of its contents is given at www.searcharchives.bl.uk; another brief discussion is given in Ward and Herbert (1883–1910), ii.695. The second is CUL Ff.5.35, for which see Hardwick and Luard, *A Catalogue of Manuscripts*, ii.495–96 and Doyle, 'Remarks on Surviving Manuscripts', p. 45.

was also a lawyer. Adam wanted Roberts to have 'my bible and my ij portuous', that is, religious rather than legal books, though he also bequeathed to Roberts 'my register at Lyons Inn', which may be a more precise reference to BL Harley 1859.[88] Lawyers might also acquire books in other ways, including as pledges for security: a faded and now only partially legible inscription at the back of BL Harley 2322 seems to indicate that it had been subject to such an exchange at some point.[89] Purchase was also a convenient option, especially for law texts which were readily available from the Fleet Street press of Richard Pynson.[90] In fact, until 1502 Pynson's shop had been located in St Clement Danes, and his request to be buried at the church there beside his first wife rather than by his second at St Dunstan in the West reveals that he maintained connections with the parish where Thomas Roberts would have been one of his neighbours.

Nevertheless, the only legal book that can now be connected with Thomas Roberts is a manuscript. BL Harley 1859 is a medium-sized volume of 219 folios on parchment, measuring 270 mm x 192 mm. Its text is laid out in single columns with a written space which measures 200 mm x 125 mm, and was professionally produced, with alternating red and blue paraphs and with integral marginal glosses marked with colour in a similar fashion. The text begins on f. 2^r: *Ricardus dei gracia Rex Anglie et Francie* . . ., with a historiated initial 'R', nine lines in depth, depicting a seated king; the initial is decorated in blue, purple and gold, with the same colours also used in the sprays of the three-quarters 'bracket' border on this leaf.[91] At the bottom right-hand corner the border ends in a scroll, on which is written: 'Morys Stafford Me fecit'; in this inscription the initial letters of 'Morys' and 'Me' are in blue and the remainder in gold. Morys (Maurice) Stafford was probably the name of the illuminator rather than the scribe, and is not recorded elsewhere to my knowledge. The main part of the volume (ff. 2^r–217^r) consists of a copy of *Registrum Brevium*, the Latin register of precedents of writs and forms of action which formed the staple source of knowledge for any common lawyer. The text is

---

[88] Sturgess, *Register of Admissions*, p. 12 notes that Nicholas Adams, perhaps the same, was admitted to the Middle Temple sometime between 1524–25 and 1550–51.

[89] f. 153^v: *Johannes . . . petit securitam pecis de . . . Johannes . . . iustum mortis* . . . . Thomas Roberts's ownership inscription on the facing leaf is written over an erasure.

[90] Neville-Sington, 'Pynson, Richard'.

[91] See Scott, *Later Gothic Manuscripts*, i.65 note 4, and 78 note 66, and also the online catalogue entry for this manuscript, with a facsimile of f. 2^r, at www.bl.uk/catalogues/illuminatedmanuscripts/record.asp?MSID=3577&CollID=8&NStart=1859

written by one hand throughout, but there are signs that the book may have been prepared as two volumes. The codex is made up throughout of gatherings of eight leaves, except in the case of the twenty-first and twenty-fifth gatherings which are of ten leaves, and the twenty-seventh (and final) gathering which is of four leaves. Catchwords are mostly present throughout, and where they are not (as on ff. 57^v, 81^v, 89^v, 97^v, 105^v, 113^v), it is probably because they have been lost to trimming (as on ff. 65^v and 73^v, where only traces of the catchwords now remain). There are three sets of quire numbers, each signed a-h: the first runs through the third to the tenth gatherings (the first two gatherings have none); the second runs through the eleventh to the eighteenth gatherings; and the third runs through the nineteenth to the twenty-sixth gatherings (the final gathering of four has no signatures). At the juncture of the second and third sets of signatures, the catchword on f. 153^v matches the beginning of the next leaf and the text continues unbroken. By contrast, there is an obvious break at the juncture of the first and second sets of signatures at f. 81^v; here the text finishes on f. 81^v, while f. 82^r has been left blank, with copying beginning again on f. 82^v. It is possible that f. 82^r was purposely left blank so that it might serve as a cover, though its clean appearance suggests that it never actually functioned in this way.

The distribution of inscriptions of the Roberts name throughout the manuscript also suggests that the codex did not consist of a single bound book in the sixteenth century. Various forms of the family name, 'Robertes', or less frequently, 'Robertȝ' and 'Robtes', occur a dozen times throughout, often at the beginning of quires (as on ff. 50^r and 74^r), or on the second leaf of a gathering (as on ff. 51^r and 83^r), and at the ends of quires (as at ff. 25^r and 105^r), or on the penultimate leaf of the gathering (as on ff. 170^r and 186^r); the name also occurs on ff. 1^r, 47^r, 151^r and 156^r. These repeated additions of the family name, which are always placed in the top right-hand corner of a recto leaf, seem designed to ensure that there could be no dispute about the ownership of quires which were loosely bound or perhaps not bound at all. In some other places there are fuller inscriptions. Thomas Roberts's possession of the volume is declared on f. 2^r: *Thome Robertz pertinet*, and again on f. 129^r: *Robertes T pertinet per*. There is also a small parchment label pasted in at the bottom of f. 219^v which reads *Constat T Robertȝ*; this might formerly have been used on an outer cover, or even on another book. Thomas's son Edmund eventually inherited this book or books, seemingly coming by its two halves at different points. On f. 82^r he wrote

Edmondʒ Robertʒ me Jure possidet 1555 ('Edmund Roberts lawfully owns me'); he wrote the same formula of words but with the date '1582' on f. 1*ᵛ.

Aside from the repeated inscriptions of the family name and other statements of ownership, there are few other additions to the main part of BL Harley 1859. The text of the *Registrum Brevium* was already furnished with a series of marginal glosses which provided the means for the reader to navigate the volume easily, removing the need for individual users to devise their own apparatus. There are one or two places where running headers have been replicated or expanded (for example on ff. 118ʳ and 129ʳ), but there is nothing in this volume to compare with Thomas Roberts's treatment of his collection of medical recipes (BodL MS Rawlinson C. 299), where he added page numbers and marginal headings keyed to an index of its contents.[92] Thomas undoubtedly consulted the key legal text of the *Registrum Brevium* in his professional capacity, but he has left few obvious traces of his use; exceptionally, some marginal headings have been rewritten more prominently, as on f. 111ʳ⁻ᵛ where marginal headings set low on the page (*de Curia claudendi* and *quod permittat*) have been replicated in the top margins as Thomas Roberts marked out sections of particular interest. There are also one or two additions throughout the text in different shades of ink, as on f. 105ʳ where the text ends midway down the page and the last line and a half, which gives reference to similar material to be found *in tercio folio sequente ad talia signa* ('on the third folio following, by such marks'), are written in a slightly darker ink, with the script carefully formed to resemble that of the preceding text. This section has been marked with two rough crosses in the right margin, and equivalent markers are to be found in the left margin of f. 107ᵛ where the last three lines of text are also an addition, extending below the text-frame, again written in a darker ink. The style of writing is not recognizably that of either Thomas or Edmund.

Other additions of herbal and medical material have been made on ff. 117ʳ⁻ᵛ in what seems to have been an originally blank space between two legal texts. Here the legal text *De herede rapto et abducto* (on abducted heirs), which began on f. 116ᵛ, ends at the top of f. 117ʳ; the next legal item, *De forisfactum maritagum* ('Writ of forfeiture of marriage'), begins on f. 118ʳ, and close examination shows that the space between them was originally left blank.[93]

---

[92] See further discussion in Chapter 5, section titled 'A Book of Practical Use: Bodleian Library, MS Rawlinson C. 299'.

[93] Both texts begin with the same type of large initial 'R', 4 lines high.

The material that now fills this gap consists of two items. The first, in Latin, was seemingly written by the original scribe using a slightly darker shade of ink. Red and blue ink has been used to mark out paragraphs and marginal headings here in just the same way as in the rest of the manuscript, so this text blends in very inconspicuously with its surroundings. A blue manicule in the left margin alerts us to the start of a new text: *Allium ventrem turbat stomacum siccat situii amonet & corpori* . . .. Thereafter there are various entries beginning *Allia vina venus* . . ., *Ista nocent oculis* . . ., *Absinthium est herba* . . ., *Crocus est erba* . . ., and marginal headings (*Safron, Finiculis, Rosa*), indicating that this is a herbal. Some of the later entries on f. 117^v are recipes (*Pro dolore capite* . . ., *Pro dente dolore* . . .), and the final five lines of the text give a list of days that are inauspicious for bloodletting. This herbal and medical Latin material is followed by another addition at the foot of f. 117^v, in a different script that again tries to conform to the appearance of the text's main hand. The addition begins in Latin, *In nomine patris & filii & spiritus sancti*, with the tail of the initial 'I' extending out into the margin, matching the appearance of the beginning of the previous entry; as a consequence this added material blends in almost invisibly with the original, disguising the presence of another non-legal piece whose Latin *incipit* quickly gives way to English:

> *In nomine patris & filii & spiritus sancti amen.*
> Seint Iorge þat ys our lady kny3th
> & seruyt hir both day & ny3t,
> þis worme þat springit out of þe bond,
> fel ne fle3 let hym brec non,
> God & Seint Iorge & Seint Ione,
> strewe þis wykyt wrme.
> Þe nam of God & Seint Iorge & of Ione,
> 3er be3 ix vormes:
> from ix to viij, from viij to vij, from vij to vj, from vj to
>   fyue, from fyue to fowr to iij to ij to j.
> Amen, pur charite.

This text is laid out in the manuscript as continuous prose, but its English opening lines form a couplet that seems to echo the opening of another set of verses, 'Seynt Iorge our Lady kny3th / He walked day, he walked ny3th', that survives in BodL MS Rawlinson C. 506 and which was printed in the sixteenth century.⁹⁴ Despite the similarity of their opening lines, however, the two texts then develop quite differently: that in the Rawlinson manuscript is a charm against nightmare, whereas the present formula is to be invoked against worms. It features the technique of diminishment or counting down as the means to remove the affliction, and resembles a number of other similar Middle English charms, many of which were prescribed to cure the farcy in horses.⁹⁵

These additions on ff. 117ʳ⁻ᵛ cannot be ascribed to Thomas or Edmund Roberts; the hands that contributed them were older and, in the case of the first, may have been that of the original scribe. Such care has been taken to disguise these additions that they easily pass undetected by the casual reader, whose sense of the manuscript as an anthology of legal texts remains undisturbed. The presence of this herbal and medical material in a collection of legal texts probably did not perturb the sixteenth-century users of BL Harley 1859. Indeed, judging by additions that Thomas Roberts made elsewhere in his books, it is clear that this type of practical text was highly valued by him, and much consulted.

There are also various additions on the flyleaves at the beginning and end of BL Harley 1859, some of which have been discussed already, but for clarity they are listed together here. At the beginning of the volume, the former parchment pastedown (f. 1*ʳ) is blank except for the number '15/11E' which has been written in the middle towards the top part of the page. The verso (f. 1*ᵛ) has Edmund Roberts's inscription and the date 1582 set in the top centre in light brown ink, and beneath this is the serjeant's oath written in black ink. At the very top of f. 1ʳ are two lines of Latin aphorisms: *Quid loqueris & vbi de quo cui quomodo & quando* ('Of whom you speak, to whom you speak, and how, and when, and where') – *Acta probant homines non verba genus neque vestes* ('Men reveal themselves through their actions, not words, and through their nature, not their clothing') – *Si tibi tua non sufficient confirma te tuis* ('If it is not sufficient to strengthen your . . .'); and at the top right-hand corner is the family name 'Robertes', followed by two lines in English about measuring distances. This reads: 'v Tailloures yardes & a half make a lande yarde – xl lande yardes

---

⁹⁴ ff. 297ʳ⁻ᵛ, edited by Robbins, *Secular Lyrics*, p. 61; *NIMEV* 2903; *DIMEV* 4601 also notes printed witnesses in Thomas Blundeville, *The fower chiefyst offices belongyng to horsemanshippe*, 1566 and *c.* 1570, *STC* 3152 and 3153.

⁹⁵ Various other charms against worms are recorded by Keiser, 'Works of Science and Information', p. 3879; on this type of text see Hunt, *Popular Medicine*, p. 81, p. 83, and p. 357 (note 81).

[lande yardes *canc.*] make a furlong – xiij furlonges make a myle'; a 'tailloures yarde' comprises thirty-six or thirty-seven inches, that is the distance of a yard as customarily measured by a tailor.[96] The same text occurs in another of Thomas Roberts's books, the medical anthology BodL Rawlinson C. 299, where it has again been added to an early leaf.[97] At first sight this might seem to suggest a possible connection with the tailoring trade, but the conversion from tailors' yards to land yards, and further into furlongs and miles, was no doubt a mnemonic text which would be useful to anyone whose occupation involved measuring; it need not bespeak a particular affiliation to the tailor's craft. Any transactions which related to the transfer of properties would require such knowledge, and the text may have had a particular currency amongst lawyers. The additions on f. 1^r were probably made at different times, but they are by the same hand – that of Thomas Roberts, who was also responsible for various added items at the back of the book. The verso of f. 1 has been ruled but left blank, and before the text commences on f. 2^r there are another two ruled leaves, also blank and not foliated.

At the end of the volume, after the close of the main text on f. 217, there is an unfoliated parchment leaf and then two further parchment leaves, ff. 218–219. The additions on these leaves are all by the hand of Thomas Roberts. The memorandum of his admission to the Inner Temple on f. 218^v fits with the volume's other legal contents, but the other additions he made at the back of the book are of a more religious character. Above the memorandum is the copy of the 1395 indulgence to Ralph and Johanna Roberts that has already been discussed in Chapter 1. An indulgence is arguably both legal and religious in nature, but the other Latin text that follows on f. 219^{r-v} is distinctly theological. This piece, approximately 400 words in length, is attributed to St John the Evangelist and is initially cast in dialogue form with John questioning Christ about what will happen at the end of the world: *Johannes Euangelista interrogauit dominum de fine mundi. Respondit eius dominus: Sol vertet in tenebras & luna in sanguinem & de arboribus stillabit . . . .*[98] This indication of interest in

---

[96] *MED*, yerd n.(2), 6. (b) taillour(es) yerd. Although *MED* states that eight furlongs make a mile, xiij (13) is the reading here.

[97] f. 1^r.

[98] Another copy of this text occurs in BL, MS Royal 17 B. XVII, a fourteenth-century manuscript that contains the *Lay Folk's Mass Book* and various short theological works in prose and verse, in both Latin and English. Various pieces, including this one, were edited by Horstman, *Yorkshire Writers*, see ii.63–64.

eschatology underlines the fact that Thomas Roberts's reading interests extended beyond the law, and in fact his other surviving books were predominantly religious, including service books and also volumes whose function was primarily to provide material for private devotional reading. The next two chapters will consider the range of medieval devotional texts in English that was available in the Roberts household, as evidenced by just three surviving volumes, and will explore what can be deduced about Thomas's responses to those works.

3

Devotional Reading in the Reigns of Henry VII and Henry VIII

A GOOD REDERE AND A DEVOWTE: WHAT THOMAS READ

With the exception of two volumes, one legal and one medical, all of the fifteenth-century manuscripts that can now be identified as having been connected with the Roberts family are religious manuscripts. Two of these are books of hours, a type of book widely owned by members of all classes in the later Middle Ages, and one which remained popular well into the sixteenth century, to judge from the number of printed *horae* produced during this period.[1] This type of book was used in private devotions, and its contents might be augmented by personally chosen prayers, as is the case in one of the Roberts copies; its use, whether privately or publicly at a church service, constituted a fulfilment of the duty of Christian observance. To develop a deeper understanding of Christian teachings, readers needed different books: at the most basic level these were manuals of instruction that taught the essential elements (sins, virtues, works of mercy, and so on), in ways that might be easily memorized. Once these foundations were laid, the 'good redere' might move on to a large variety of texts of religious instruction written in the vernacular, including prayers, meditations, and imaginative works of a more literary nature whose function nevertheless remained didactic and devotional.[2] Four of the Roberts manuscripts contain Middle English religious texts of these types. Whilst one of these, BodL Rawlinson C. 894, a collection of short texts and extracts from English devotional texts, may have been acquired by Edmund

---

[1] For some statistics see Erler 'Devotional Literature', pp. 505–6.

[2] The quotation that heads this section is from the *Wise Book of Philosophy and Astronomy*, see the edition by Griffin, *The Middle English Wise Book*, p. 13, line 228.

Roberts, the other three appear to have been in the possession of the family for longer.[3] It is rarely possible to be sure at which points the Robertses obtained their books, still less who in the family may have been reading them at any given time. There are, however, clear indications that three of their manuscripts passed through the hands of Thomas Roberts and then into the hands of his children. This chapter attempts to recover a sense of the devotional reading that was available to Thomas in the first few decades of the Tudor regime and, where possible, to chart his responses to the texts that he read. Yet such an approach cannot confine itself to indications of active reading. Close attention to the contents of the texts in these manuscripts, regardless of whether those texts were annotated, offers insights into what Thomas and other members of his household could choose to read. Some of these texts are well-known, others less so, and some (judging by extant copies) were widely disseminated in full or in extracted forms, whilst others seem to have had a more limited circulation; but collectively they demonstrate that early Tudor spirituality, as practised by individual gentry through personal devotional reading, was strongly medieval in nature.

The best known of these texts, Nicholas Love's *Mirror of the Blessed Life of Jesus Christ*, will be discussed in the next chapter; the focus of the present chapter is on two other volumes from Thomas Roberts's library, BL Harley 2322 and University of Harvard, Houghton Library, MS Richardson 22. These two manuscripts offer rather different examples of the later medieval devotional compilation: BL Harley 2322 contains a single work, the *Pore Caitif*, that is itself a compilation of short tracts drawn from devotional and pastoral sources; Harvard Richardson 22 contains a variety of texts of different origins, ranging from substantial works in prose to shorter verse texts, and including some prayers. The label 'devotional compilation', though codicologically applicable to both manuscripts, misleadingly suggests a homogeneity in contents and, by extension, use. Conversely, as is revealed by the close analysis of their multiple texts, the intrinsic nature of the two collections is very different, and the experience of reading their texts would have been equally so. As will be demonstrated below, Harvard Richardson 22 contains many elements that suggest a strong devotion to Mary and a steadfastly orthodox belief in her powers of intercession. By contrast, the *Pore Caitif* acquired a certain whiff of lollardy. Though generally now regarded as entirely orthodox in origin, the text

---

[3] This manuscript is discussed in Chapter 6 below.

was long attributed to John Wycliffe and his followers. As M. Teresa Brady has shown, a small number of its manuscript copies do contain interpolations sympathetic to lollard concerns; BL Harley 2322 belongs to this particular group. What Thomas Roberts and other members of his family made of those lollard elements, in particular the short text, 'Answeris to hem þat seien þat we schulde not speke of holy writt', in the dramatically changing religious context of the 1530s and subsequent decades, will be explored below.[4]

'COUNSEYLOUR OF WRECCHIS': READING BRITISH LIBRARY, MS HARLEY 2322

BL Harley 2322 was produced in England in the first half of the fifteenth century.[5] It is a small, pocket-sized volume of 159 folios on parchment, measuring 150 mm x 100 mm, written in black ink by a single hand.[6] The manuscript was professionally made: it has been pricked and ruled, and the text is laid out in a single column with generous margins (the text space is 95 mm x 65 mm); the regular gatherings of eight have quire numbers (running a–t) and catchwords, and the latter have been distinguished with box lines and minimal decoration in red.[7] The beginnings of major sections (the Pater Noster, Ave, Creed, and Decalogue) are marked with gold initials which are four lines high on a background of pink and blue with white geometrical decoration; other initials are usually two lines high, in blue, with red tracery that extends up and down the margin; *incipits* and *explicits* are in red. Whilst it is by no means a lavish production, this devotional manuscript is nevertheless an attractive small book, carefully prepared and finished at some cost, and was likely to have been a valued volume in the Roberts family's library.

Thomas Roberts's possession of this book is apparent from statements to that effect placed at both the beginning and the end of the manuscript. On f. ii[r]

---

[4] BL, MS Harley 2322, ff. 87–88. See Brady, 'Lollard Interpolations and Omissions', pp. 183–203.

[5] See the online catalogue entry for this manuscript, with a facsimile of f. 18[r], at www.bl.uk/catalogues/illuminatedmanuscripts/record.asp?MSID=7349&ColIID=8&NStart=2322.

[6] The manuscript has three parchment flyleaves at the beginning, then 152 numbered folios followed by four more parchment leaves, the first two of which are unnumbered, and a paper flyleaf.

[7] Here and throughout in the context of manuscript production I use the term 'professional' to denote expert preparation by a trained scribe, not to imply any form of commercial book production.

is the inscription: *Constat Thome Robertz*, and at the back of the book, on f. 154^r, this format is extended and repeated: *Iste liber constat Thome Robert*, there written over an existing and now illegible inscription that was set within a scroll.[8] Further down this leaf is another erased inscription which reads faintly *Quem librum . . .*, below which in black ink is written *Thome Robertz pertinet*, and then below that, also in black ink: *Iste liber dico constat Puero generoso / Si quis queratur Thomas Robertz nominatur* ('I say this book belongs to a gentle boy; if anyone asks his name is Thomas Roberts'), which suggests that Thomas had this book in his youth. A faded inscription on the opposite leaf seems to indicate that the book had been pledged, not necessarily to Thomas but he was clearly concerned to proclaim his rightful ownership.[9] There are a further eight places throughout the volume where Thomas set his characteristic 'Robertz' inscription, usually at the very top right corner of recto leaves (as on ff. 1^r, 4^r, 18^r, 115^r), and once at the top left corner of a verso leaf (f. 88^v), but sometimes lower down in the margin alongside the point where a new text begins (as on ff. 23^r, 37^v, and 39^r), see Figure 6.

In fact in all of these instances Thomas was marking the start of a new text, and in these instances his inscription seems primarily to signal interest in content rather than ownership: none of these places except the first coincides with the start of a new quire, so the driving concern cannot have been to mark the possession of a series of unbound gatherings. Beyond this persistent inscribing of his name, Thomas added other annotations throughout, largely it seems driven by a concern to quantify the exact scope of the volume's contents. At the start of almost every text is a marginal note of how many leaves that text occupies: for example, the treatise on the Pater Noster which begins on f. 4^r has the note 'xiiij lefes' in the top margin; the next text, on the Ave, on f. 18^r has the note 'v lefes', and so on.[10] Sometimes assessing how much space a text occupied was not an easy task, especially when a work was short: Thomas described the prologue to the Decalogue on f. 38^r as taking up 'a lefe & demi' (one and a half leaves), and the short tract on temptation on f. 95^v as occupying 'a lefe and more'. These calculations of how much space each text

---

[8] The final 'z' of Thomas's surname has been lost due to the trimming of the volume.

[9] See Chapter 2, section titled 'A Lawyer's Book: British Library, MS Harley 1859'.

[10] These marginal notes of quantity appear in all but three instances: the prologue to the Pater Noster on f. 1^r; the Decalogue on f. 39^r, though in this instance the length of each of the Ten Commandments is individually quantified; and the second tract on the Decalogue on f. 85^r.

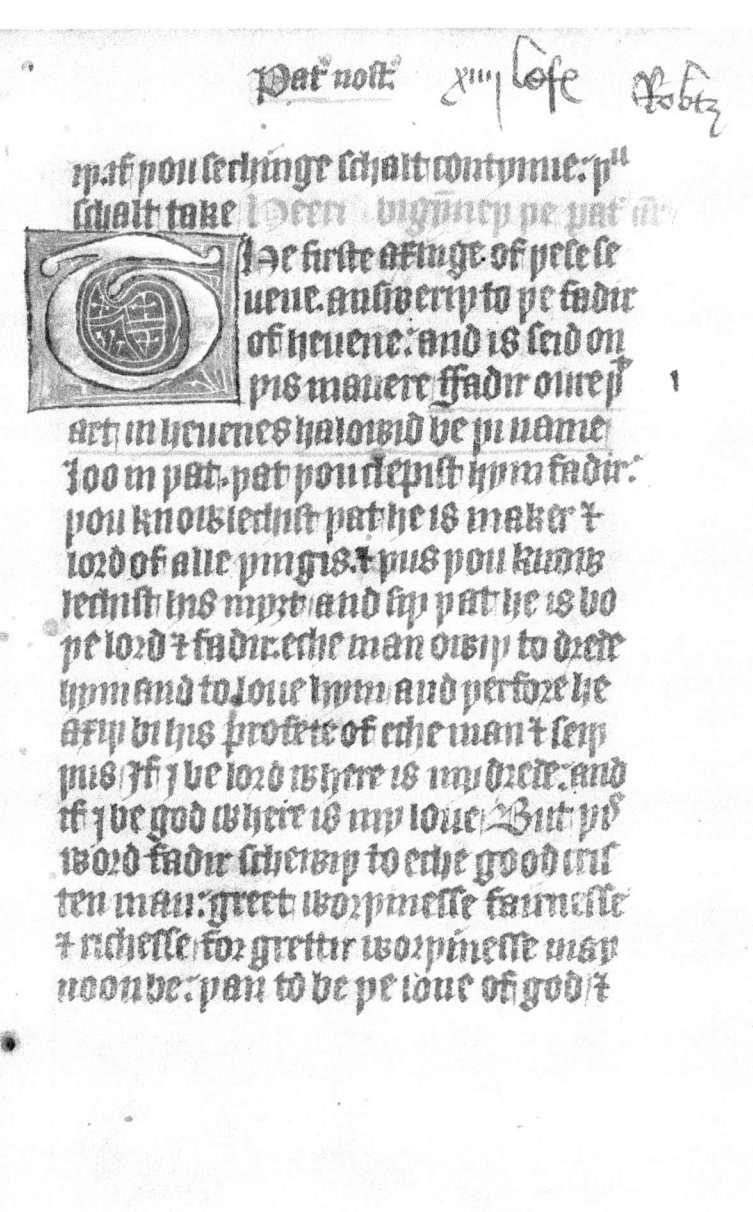

Figure 6 London, British Library, MS Harley 2322, f. 4ʳ. Roberts ownership inscription at top right corner. Reproduced by permission. © The British Library Board.

occupied were then transferred to a table of contents on f. i^v where Thomas listed the titles of all the individual treatises:

> A prolog conteynyng iij lefes
> the pater noster conteynyng xiiij lefes
> the aue mary conteynyng v lefes
> the credo conteynyng xiiij lefes

and so on through twenty separate entries. In some instances he either changed his mind or made an error at the point of transfer, since there are some discrepancies in the totals: the text 'Vertues paciens' ('Virtuous patience') is described on f. 92^r as taking up three leaves, but recorded as four leaves in the list of contents; conversely the text 'Aunswers of holy writte' is described on f. 87^r as taking up two leaves, but in the contents list as only one. The motivation that lay behind this quantifying of textual space is not easy to discern, but it seems rooted in a desire to make the volume's contents easier to negotiate. In this instance Thomas counts the leaves but does not number them, and whilst he transfers the headings of each text to the list of contents he does not also replicate those headings in the margins of the texts themselves. His treatment of the textual contents of one of his other books, BodL Rawlinson C. 299, was considerably more sophisticated, with items there numerically keyed to an index at the back of the volume, and it may be that his efforts to calibrate BL Harley 2322 represent a preliminary attempt at designing this type of apparatus.[11] Some other marginal annotations will be considered further below as evidence of Thomas's engagement with particular texts, but collectively his inscriptions within this volume demonstrate a detailed awareness of its contents and a level of response that can only be inferred in the case of his other devotional books. Yet it is difficult to assess the motivation that lay behind Thomas's willingness to write in this book. Did the impulse to write arise from a deep interest in the ideas of its texts? And was this driven by his own needs if he used the volume as a boy, or by a need to make the contents accessible to other readers such as his wives or children? It may also be that the more humble format of this manuscript encouraged an interactive response; certainly his treatment of its texts is closer to the way in which he engaged with the contents

---

[11] For his treatment of BodL Rawlinson C. 299, see Chapter 5, section titled 'A Book of Practical Use: Bodleian Library, MS Rawlinson C. 299'.

of his remedy book, BodL Rawlinson C. 299, than to his respectful handling of his copies of Love's *Mirror* and the Pseudo-Augustinian *Soliloquies*.

BL Harley 2322 contains a copy of the popular late fourteenth-century manual of doctrine and devotion known as the *Pore Caitif*. This was a compendium of vernacular religious instruction that drew on a wide variety of scriptural, patristic, and didactic sources; it was designed for lay readers and circulated widely, judging from the large number of surviving manuscripts.[12] Although these show some variation in content and organization, it seems that the *Pore Caitif* was intended to consist of a prologue and fourteen tracts. The first three of these, on the Creed, the Decalogue, and the Pater Noster, are of substantial length (especially the treatment of the Decalogue). These are followed by ten shorter tracts: 'The Counsel of Christ'; 'Of Virtuous Patience'; 'Of Temptation'; 'The Charter of Our Heavenly Heritage'; 'The Horse or Armour of Heaven'; 'The Name of Jesus'; 'The Desire of Jesus'; 'Of Meekness'; 'Of Man's Will'; and 'Of Active Life and Contemplative Life'; after which the work concludes with a final, more lengthy piece, 'The Mirror of Chastity'.[13] Thomas Roberts's copy of the *Pore Caitif* contains all of these individual elements with the exception of the work's brief introductory prologue which is omitted, yet the list of 'the contentes of this boke' which Thomas wrote on f. i^v enumerates twenty, not fourteen, items and reveals some differences in the ordering of the tracts as well:

>A prolog
>the pater noster
>the aue mary
>the credo
>a prolog
>x hestes
>x hestes

---

[12] The text survives in thirty-two complete or originally complete copies and twenty-four sets of extracts and fragments; for details see Lagorio and Sargent, 'English Mystical Writings', pp. 3135–36 and 3470–71. See also Simpson, *IMEP* 7, p. 5, recording one further copy in Durham University Library, MS Additional 754. Some further fragments (parts of the tracts on the Pater Noster and the Decalogue), sold at Sotheby's, 2 October 2008, lot 4810, but not identified there, are now Takamiya MS 110; I thank A. S. G. Edwards for giving me this information.

[13] This ordering of contents was worked out by Brady, 'The Pore Caitif', and is generally accepted.

> Aunswers of holy writte
> Councell of Crist
> Vertues paciens
> Tempacioun
> Chartre of heven
> Armure of heven
> Name of Ihesu
> loue of Ihesu
> verry mekenesse
> Effecte of wille
> Actyeff lyfe & contemplatyfe lyfe
> Mirour of chastyte
> Virgynete

The difference in the total number of contents may be partly explained by Thomas's habit of listing constituent parts of individual tracts as separate items. Thus, for example, the first entry on the list, 'A prolog', is merely the prologue to the tract on the Pater Noster which follows and not a separate work. Similarly Thomas records the tract on the Decalogue as consisting of a prologue and two texts (both referred to as 'x hestes'), whereas in fact the whole tract is made up of a prologue, the explanation of the Ten Commandments, and an epilogue. Thomas also misunderstood the nature of the compilation's final tract, 'Mirour of chastyte'. Despite the fact that the scribe had marked each of its five chapters in the margins, Thomas took its first chapter as the whole work, only three leaves long, and then marked the beginning of its second chapter as the start of another work on virginity, quantified as fifteen leaves, under which he wrote 'v chaptours' (f. 137^r), even though from this point onwards there were only four more. However, once these anomalies are accounted for it is apparent that Thomas's copy of the *Pore Caitif* still contains two additional texts: the first a tract on the Ave (ff. 18^r–23^r); the second the text 'Aunswers of holy writte' (ff. 87^r–88^r).[14]

The ordering of material in this copy of the *Pore Caitif* also differs from the compilation's usual arrangement in that the first text here offers an explanation, not of the Creed, but of the Pater Noster. This defies the logical progression of the *Pore Caitif*, articulated in its overall prologue by its compiler, as one that proceeds from the foundation of faith, 'cristen mannes

---

[14] See further discussion of these two texts below.

bileeue'.[15] Since the primary statement of Christian faith is enshrined within the Apostle's Creed, the *Pore Caitif* placed this tract first, and because faith alone is insufficient, the Ten Commandments ('in whiche þe charitable werkis ben conteyned') are outlined next; only after these two aspects of doctrine have been assimilated is any advice given on prayer. The compiler is quite clear that this is an appropriate ordering:

> And for it is hard to purchace ouȝt of god in preier til to man verili bileeue & lyue aftir his heestis, as he seiþ himsilf in þe gospel – 'wherto seien ȝe to me lord, lord, & doen not þilke þingis þat I seie?' – þerfore, folowinge aftir þe heestis, he þenkiþ with þe help & mercy of god, to shewe shortli þe preier þat ihesu crist tauȝte hise disciplis, þat is þe pater noster . . .

Conversely the version of the *Pore Caitif* that Thomas Roberts owned privileged prayer above everything else, placing the tract on the Pater Noster first, ahead of instruction on belief and good works. This is no doubt why in this copy the work's usual overall prologue was omitted, since its articulation of the compilation's logical structure was effectively rendered redundant by this change in the ordering of its constituent parts.

This different arrangement of the usual ordering of its tracts may be atypical of the *Pore Caitif*, but it meant in fact that Thomas's devotional reader more closely resembled the format of many other fifteenth-century devotional manuals that had been produced with the lay reader in mind.[16] A comparison might be drawn with the different set of short texts laid out in JRL English 85, there introduced by a prologue which states: 'This litil copilacioun bigynneþ wiþ preier, and folowinge next is bileeue, and aftir þat ben þe comaundementis of God . . .'.[17] Very many such devotional anthologies were in circulation in the fifteenth century: they frequently began with the alphabet and then provided the texts of the Lord's prayer, the Ave Maria, the Creed, and the blessing. Once these fundamental elements had been covered, other basic elements of Christian instruction might be introduced, with expositions of the Ten Commandments and the enumeration of concepts such as the sins, works of

---

[15] The prologue to the *Pore Caitif* is not found in BL, MS Harley 2322; the quotations in this paragraph are taken from the edition by Brady, 'The Pore Caitif', pp. 1–2.

[16] BodL Additional B. 66, which is related to BL Harley 2322, also adopts this ordering of texts.

[17] For a discussion of this group of manuscripts see Connolly, 'Books for the "helpe of euery persoone þat þenkiþ to be saued"', 170–81.

mercy, virtues, wits, and so on.[18] In this typical scheme the Ave features as a key devotion, second only to the Pater Noster. In BL Harley 2322, where the reordering of the texts on the Pater Noster, Creed, and Decalogue has already aligned this version of the *Pore Caitif* with the intention of other similar works of basic instruction, the inclusion of a text on the Ave straight after that which discusses the Pater Noster seems a logical development, even if the actual content of that text provokes some difficulties, as will be discussed further below.

BL Harley 2322 opens with the prologue to the tract on the Pater Noster. This describes the Pater Noster as 'þe praier ful of witt and of helþe', and schematizes its seven petitions as relating to the Trinity (the first three) and to the profit and help of mankind (the other four). Much justification of individual points is provided by quoting the Bible, principally the gospels, but also St Paul and the psalms, and patristic authorities; the original scribe has provided biblical references in the margin but does not locate the quotations from the Fathers. The prologue also outlines eight conditions that need to be met if man's prayer is to be heard, seeking to place the reader in the proper frame of mind for devotional observance. The text itself then offers a detailed explanation of the clauses of the prayer, paralleling its seven petitions with two other groups of seven, the deadly sins (pride, envy, wrath, gluttony, covetousness, sloth, and lechery), and the gifts of the Holy Ghost (wisdom, understanding, counsel, strength, knowledge, pity, and dread). Thomas Roberts marked the prayer's individual clauses by setting small Roman numerals in the margins alongside. This further emphasis was unnecessary because these sentences were already underlined with red ink, as were the words of the Ave and the individual clauses of the Creed.[19] Though not the same shade as the red ink that supplies the decorative tracery to the blue capitals, this red ink is an original feature rather than a later addition. It was used to underline and highlight letters in the running headers, to underline the marginal citations, and for corrections throughout the manuscript. Thomas numbered the clauses of the Creed, adding small Roman numerals to the margins as he did in the Pater Noster, with the exception of the first clause on f. 25^v which he labels as 'first'. Within this text he also picked out some other aspects, noting especially those points where lists of features were already enumerated within the text, adding

---

[18] See the discussion of this type of volume by Connolly, 'Compiling the Book', pp. 134–39.
[19] On f. 18^r and ff. 23^r–37^v respectively.

marginal numerals to emphasize this, as for example on f. 27^v where he added the numbers i–iv to the description of the four parts of the cross of penance, and on ff. 35^v–36^r where he added the numbers i–iii alongside the description of the three divisions of the church. This persistent numbering has the effect of making particular sections easier to retrieve, and is also evidence that Thomas read these texts with some degree of attention. The level of engagement seems equivalent to a student's reading of a textbook, highlighter pen in hand, and accords with the supposition that Thomas used this book during his youth.

This simpler form of reading is even more apparent from Thomas's interactions with the next text, which lists and discusses the Ten Commandments. Here Thomas has added marginal numbers again, and key words which summarize each commandment: 'one god', 'no othes', 'holy day', and so on, to all but the tenth commandment (f. 83^v), perhaps because it was so similar to the ninth.[20] Yet there was really no need to draw further attention to the start of each separate commandment, which was already typically marked by enlarged initial capitals, in blue with red tracery, usually two lines high but sometimes larger. On the recto leaves there are also running headers, in black, underlined with red, that indicate which commandment is currently being discussed. Further, in almost all cases the beginnings of the commandments had been made highly visible by red ink, used both to distinguish each numbered rubric ('þe .v heeste', or more briefly 'vi he.', 'vii hest'), and to underline the words of the commandment itself. Sometimes that red underlining is extensive, as at the beginning of the list where the explanation of the first commandment replicates the text of Exodus 20.1–6; here twenty lines in total were underlined.[21] The intention seems to have been to emphasize quotations from the Bible, since the underlining carefully avoids any words or phrases not found there. The selective underlining of words in the statement of the sixth commandment demonstrates this point: 'In þe sixte heeste god *forfendiþ* al manere of *leccherie*' (Vulgate: *Non moechaberis*).[22] Similarly the eighth commandment reads: '... god *forfendiþ* eche man & womman *to bere any fals witnesse aȝens her euen cristen*' (Vulgate: *Non loqueris contra proximum tuum falsum testimonium*).[23] In the account of the fifth commandment which 'forfendiþ al manere wrongful

---

[20] ff. 39^r, 46^v, and 52^r.

[21] ff. 39^{r-v}; Trivedi, '"Trewe techyng and false heritikys"', p. 139, notes a similar use of red ink in other associated manuscripts of the *Pore Caitif*.

[22] f. 67^r.

[23] f. 75^v.

mansleinge', the word 'wrongful' is carefully not underlined, remaining closer to the simpler sense that *all* homicide is wrong (Vulgate: *Non occides*). Thomas seems to have been alert to this distinction, and has preserved it in his own marginal version 'slee no man', by underlining the word 'no' (see Figure 7).[24] The overall effect of his marginal notes is to provide a rapid mnemonic of the Decalogue: 'one god; no othes; holy day; worship fadir & mother; slee no man; do no lecherie; do no theft; no false witnes; desire no maner Goodes'; perhaps inscribing this was originally part of the process of learning the commandments by heart. Certainly in the original presentation of this text there was already sufficient guidance for the reader to negotiate the work successfully, and Thomas's contributions do not add much of value: his marginal numbers replicate metatextual features that were already present, and his key words merely repeat terms already used in the text rather than expanding upon them.

In the text of the Creed, however, Thomas went further. Beneath the marginal numbers that he added he also inscribed the equivalent Latin version of each clause. So alongside the first statement of the Creed ('I bileue in God fadir almy3ty maker of heuene & of erþe'), on f. 25^v, Thomas wrote '*credo in deum patrem*' (see Figure 8); on f. 26^v, alongside the second statement ('I bileue in Ihesu criste goddis oonly sone oure lord'), he wrote '*et in Ihesum cristum*', and so on, continuing to translate the individual clauses until the end of the text.[25] The result is the provision of a translation of the text of the Creed, given in the vernacular in the *Pore Caitif*, back into Latin. Did Thomas do this – as a schoolboy – to practice his own Latin or to learn his catechism, or did he at a later stage provide the Latin text to help his children or his wives? Possibly he was merely augmenting the text for himself: normally the tract on the Creed includes only the English words of the prayer, but a small number of manuscripts give the Latin words within the text as well, and there are other manuscripts where the Latin appears in the margins; if Thomas had seen another such copy he might have been moved to emend his own.[26] Of course, Thomas's

---

[24] f. 61^v.

[25] Thus, in the margins of ff. 25^v–37^v Thomas provides most of the Latin text: *credo in deum patrem ... et in Ihesum cristum ... qui conceptus ... passus sub pontio ... descend* [sic] *ad inferna ... ascendit ad celos ... inde venturus est iudicare ... credo in spiritum sanctum ... sanctam ecclesiam ... remissionem peccatorum carnis ressurrectionem ... vitam eternam.*

[26] Trivedi, ' "Trewe techyng and false heritikys" ', p. 139, records the inclusion of Latin within the tract on the Creed in six manuscripts of the *Pore Caitif*; Hill, 'Pedagogy, Devotion, and Marginalia', p. 202, notes at least two manuscripts where the scribes provided the Latin text of the articles in the margins.

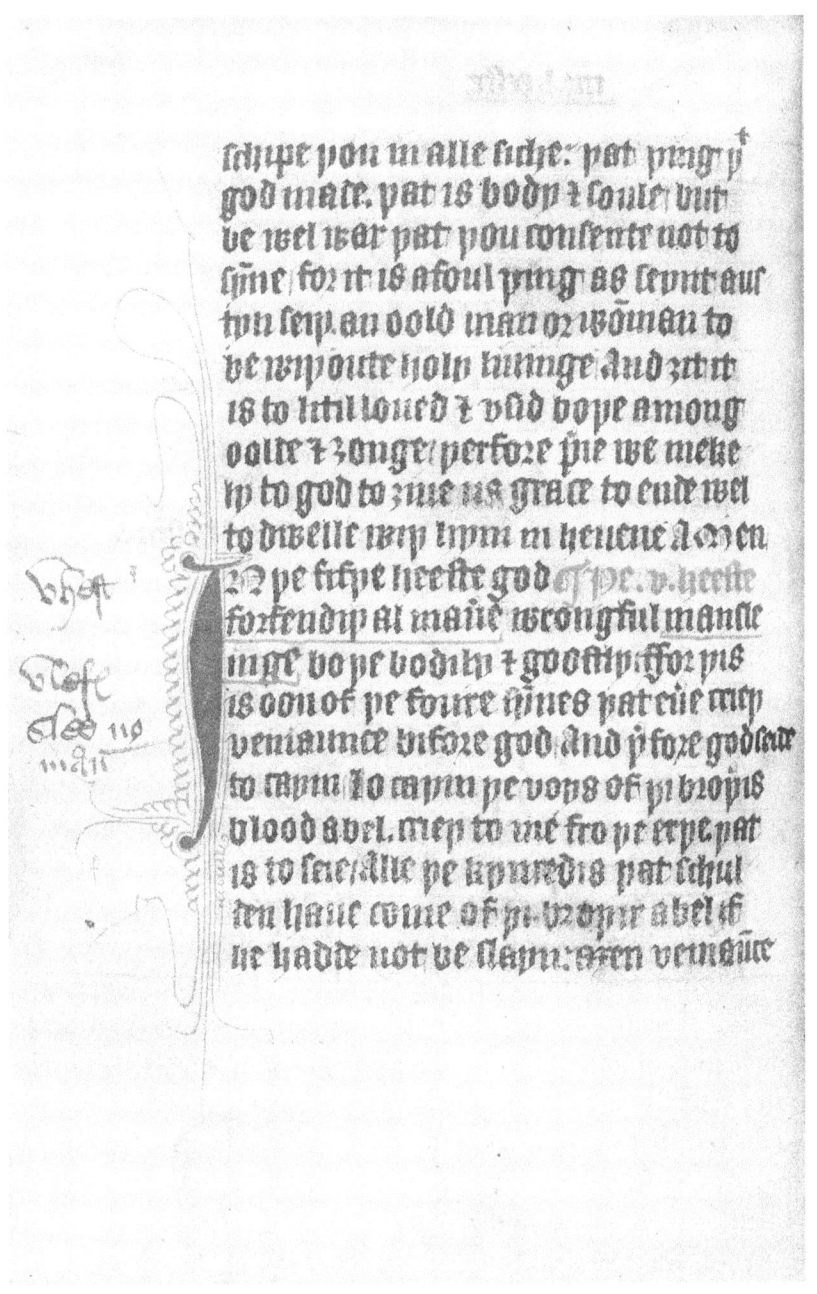

Figure 7 London, British Library, MS Harley 2322, f. 61ᵛ. Thomas Roberts's annotations in the text of the Ten Commandments (part of the *Pore Caitif*). Reproduced by permission. © The British Library Board.

use of this book need not have been confined to one particular period of his life, and his reading of its texts in his own youth does not preclude the possibility of returning to it later as a teaching manual. The sections that seem to have attracted his keenest attention are the Pater Noster, Creed, and Decalogue, which were precisely the elements of faith that the Injunctions of 1536 stipulated must be taught to children.[27] If Thomas had wished to comply with the spirit of these injunctions, then the *Pore Caitif* would have been an eminently suitable compilation to use with his youngest children such as John, born in 1531.

Although Thomas's annotations continue throughout the remainder of the manuscript, his interaction with the series of shorter tracts that makes up the rest of the *Pore Caitif* seems to have been less intense in that, whilst he continues to calculate the length of the tracts, he does not comment on their contents. This lack of annotation makes it impossible to know how closely Thomas read these texts or in what regard he held them. Some indication of interest may be inferred from the fact that he wrote his name at the start of two of them: at the beginning of 'The Counsel of Christ' on f. 88^v, and at the top right corner of f. 115^r, the leaf on which 'The Name of Jesus' begins, since where he inscribes his name in this way elsewhere in the volume it is almost always in connection with those texts that he annotated more closely. Signs of wear and rubbing on certain leaves may also indicate which of these texts Thomas (or other readers) turned to more frequently: 'On Temptation' definitely has the appearance of being rather well-thumbed, as do certain openings of 'The Charter of Our Heavenly Heritage', and some individual leaves towards the end of the volume's final text, 'The Mirror of Chastity'.[28] In the final chapter of the latter, a marginal mark that resembles a lower-case 'a' with a loop draws attention to the names of four of the five female virgin saints mentioned in the text. These four were easy to pick out, since each was already preceded by a red paraph mark; the one that was not, Lucie (f. 147^v), is missed by the annotator as well.

Thomas would certainly have found material amongst these shorter tracts that chimed in with what he could read in his other books, and in particular with the contents of Harvard Richardson 22.[29] The allegorical content of 'The

---

[27] Hill, 'Pedagogy, Devotion, and Marginalia', p. 194, finds that the Decalogue was the section of the *Pore Caitif* that also attracted most attention from fifteenth-century readers.
[28] Respectively ff. 95^v–96^r; ff. 99^v–100^r and 101^v–02^r; and ff. 148^r, 149^v.
[29] See the next section of this chapter.

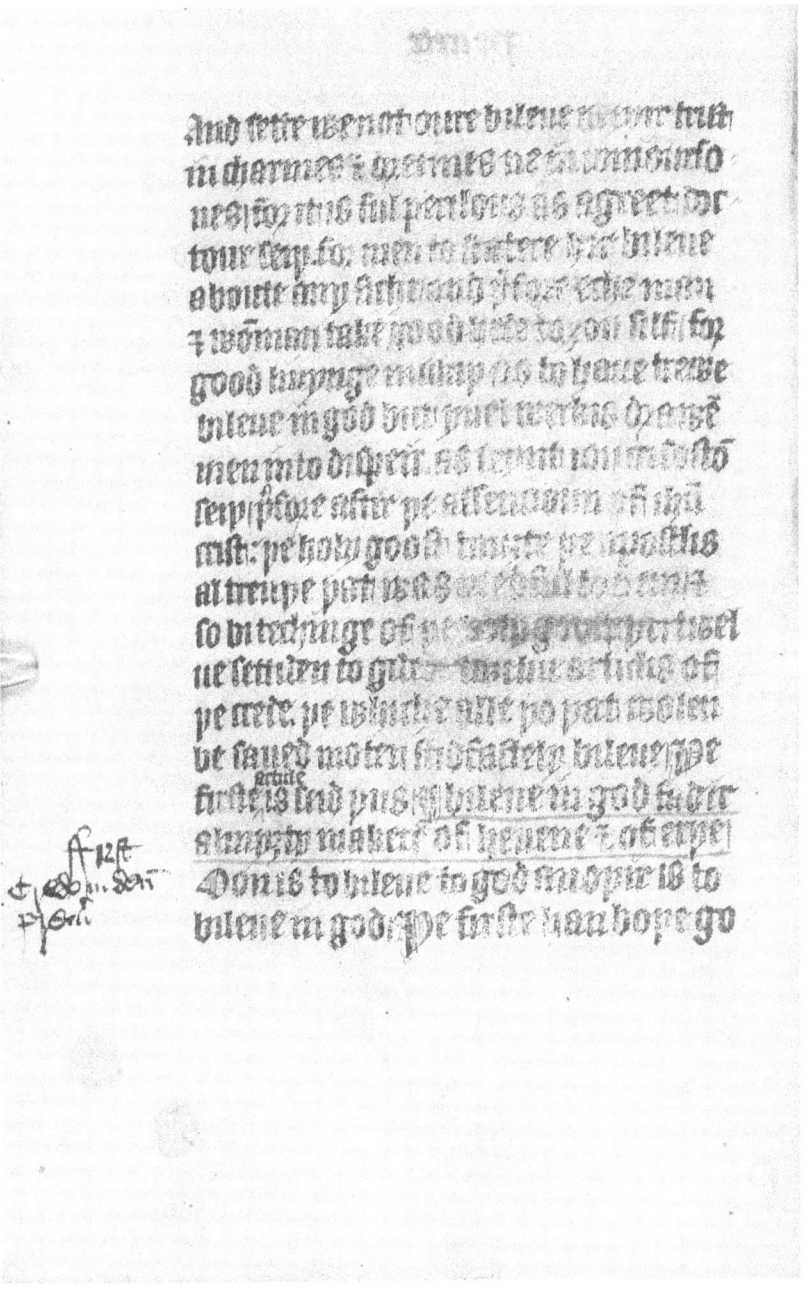

Figure 8 London, British Library, MS Harley 2322, f. 25ᵛ. Thomas Roberts's Latin annotations in the text of the Creed (part of the *Pore Caitif*). Reproduced by permission. © The British Library Board.

Charter of Our Heavenly Heritage' tract, with its extended metaphor that equates the different aspects of the legal document (parchment, letters, seals, and laces) with the suffering of Christ, closely resembles the content offered by the Charters of Christ. The mystical content of the 'Desire of Jesus' tract, derived from Richard Rolle's *Emendatio Vitae* and *Form of Living*, was similar to ideas of the sweetness of Christ's love expressed in the verses of 'A songe of loue to owre lorde Ihesu Christe', and the short tract on 'The Name of Jesus' might have recalled to Thomas the final verses of the long English poetic devotion addressed to the Virgin with its concluding focus on the holy name.[30] Similarly, if Edmund Roberts looked at BL Harley 2322 (though there is no indication that he did), the allegorical tract 'The Horse or Armour of Heaven' would undoubtedly have reminded him of the very similar work to which it is related, *A Tretyse of Gostly Batayle*, which he had in his own devotional anthology, BodL Rawlinson C. 894.[31] And as well as reading material, the shorter tracts of the *Pore Caitif* also provided the texts of various prayers, meaning that Thomas did not need to look to his books of hours or elsewhere when he wanted to pray. For example, before giving an exposition of the three degrees of love, the opening section of 'The Desire of Jesus' offers a set of prayers addressed to God, Christ, and the Holy Ghost; and the last part of 'The Name of Jesus' apostrophizes the holy name:

> O þou good name. O þou swete name. O þou glorious name. O heelful name. O desireful name. Wickid spirits moun not anoie þere, where þei holden þe name of Ihesu, either in mynde to loue Ihesu, I soughte and euere þe more I wexe parfijt in his love, so myche þe name of hym sauerde swete to me. Þerfore blessid be þe name of of [*sic*] Ihesu, into þe worldis of worldis amen.[32]

The process of reading the compilation's longer texts also naturally led the reader into prayer and meditation; for example, the explanation of the fifth clause of the Pater Noster concludes with a description of Christ's sufferings and an encouragement to respond with a prayer whose words closely echo those of the clause itself: 'And þus seie we þese wordis: Blessid fadir forʒiue us as we

---

[30] For the *Pore Caitif*'s incorporation of material from Rolle see Brady, 'Rolle and the Pattern of Tracts' and Brady 'The Seynt and His Boke'.

[31] See further Chapter 6, section titled 'þou shalt moch profett in redyng: what Edmund read'.

[32] f. 119ʳ. The prayers in 'The Desire of Jesus' are on ff. 119ʳ–20ʳ.

forʒiuen; and haue mercy on us. Amen'.³³ The explications of the Pater Noster, Ave, and Creed also contain the words of those key prayers, which are easily discerned in this manuscript thanks to the scribe's consistent use of red underlining. This aspect might have made the book suitable for the elementary instruction of children or other household members, and although there is little indication that it was used in this way, a few scattered annotations of a very basic nature suggest some traces of this type of reading.³⁴

Previous critical attention to the copy of the *Pore Caitif* preserved in BL Harley 2322 has largely focussed on the theological heterodoxy of its contents.³⁵ This manuscript and others have long been labelled 'lollard-interpolated', that is, having certain insertions and/or omissions of material that relate to important lollard concerns including images, oaths, the composition of the Creed, confession, preaching, and persecution. These differences are clearly summarized by Brady, who contends that in these manuscripts the standard version of the *Pore Caitif* was manipulated, with the tracts on the Creed and the Decalogue most affected.³⁶ Recently it has been argued that this group of lollard-interpolated manuscripts might in fact represent the original form of the *Pore Caitif*, and that the text was subsequently cleaned up and made into orthodox reading.³⁷ Whichever of these views of the text's origins may be correct, and we might heed Fiona Somerset's caution that 'much more needs to be said about the *Pore Caitif*'s lollard affiliations',³⁸ it is striking to note that, according to the evidence that Brady presents, the texts of BL Harley 2322 show fewer differences compared to their equivalents in the other manuscripts of the heterodox group. The aspects that are different in BL Harley 2322 include the excision of the apostles' names from the Creed, as lollard thinking denied the popular legend that the individual clauses of the Creed might be associated with different apostles.³⁹ Lollards also questioned the need for confession to a

---

³³ ff. 13ᵛ–14ʳ.
³⁴ For instance, on f. 29ʳ the abbreviated form 'apo' in the text has been completed to 'apostolis' by a larger, rougher hand, and in the margin of f. 143ᵛ the same word is again written out roughly in full.
³⁵ See Rice, 'Reformist Devotional Reading'.
³⁶ See Brady, 'Lollard Interpolations and Omissions'; a list of the twelve lollard manuscripts is given on p. 185.
³⁷ See Trivedi, '"Trewe techyng and false heritikys"'; there is a helpful summary of the opposite views in Rice, 'Reformist Devotional Reading', pp. 178–79.
³⁸ Somerset, *Feeling Like Saints*, p. 39, n. 32.
³⁹ See Brady, 'The Apostles and the Creed'.

priest, which is reflected here by the advice urging 'trewe knowlechinge to God' instead.[40] Similarly, in the commentary on the first commandment, passages on the legitimate use of images do not appear. Yet various other points are left untouched. One such is the admonition in the eighth commandment against making false oaths, which most of the lollard manuscripts truncate, but which BL Harley 2322 replicates in full. Another is the advice on the duty of preaching contained in the commentary on the fifth commandment, which several of the other manuscripts extend with additional quotations, but which here is left unexpanded. Collectively these aspects indicate a textual response that transcends a simple binary divide between orthodox and heterodox, and which supports an emerging understanding that expressions of late medieval dissent were complex and multi-layered.[41]

The most obvious signs of the heterodox nature of the copy of the *Pore Caitif* in BL Harley 2322 lie in the inclusion of two texts which did not properly belong in the compilation at all. These are the commentary on the Ave Maria that follows that on the Pater Noster, and the short piece that defends the discussion and preaching of the gospel which lies between the longer tracts and those that the prologue to the *Pore Caitif* describes as 'summe short sentencis'.[42] Even if Thomas Roberts did not know that these texts were interlopers in the compilation, he would at least have noticed their contents. The presence of a text that explicates the meaning of the Ave and furnishes the words of the prayer seems unremarkable in this devotional context, and similar material may be found in Thomas's other books, notably in Harvard Richardson 22 with its long poetic devotion to Mary built around the prayer's Latin text.[43] Yet whilst that poem works through the words of the devotion to construct a straightforward celebration of Mary's virtues, the content of the commentary offered in BL Harley 2322 develops rather differently, dwelling on many aspects of sin.[44] The text argues that men and women should learn from Mary's example by emulating her virtues and by keeping God's commandments. This advice is

---

[40] f. 28^v.

[41] See, for example, Hornbeck, *What is a Lollard?* and (particularly with respect to images), Gayk, *Image, Text, and Religious Reform*.

[42] Cited from Brady, 'The Pore Caitif', p. 2.

[43] See the next section of this chapter.

[44] The text of the Ave is on ff. 18^r–23^r. Five other copies are known, see Rand, *IMEP* XX, p. 61 [18], where this manuscript is not listed. Matthew, *The English Works of Wyclif*, pp. 203–8 prints the text from Cambridge, Corpus Christi College, MS 296; this is different in several respects from the version preserved here.

directed to both sexes, but to 'genteil wymmen' above all, and several points are made about women's behaviour in particular, such as their misplaced concern with outward appearances and the propensity for such displays to lead men into sin.[45] The sins that are to be avoided are mentioned repeatedly, and much detail is offered about specific activities that may give rise to sin, such as 'to lyue in riot of daunsinge and oþir unleeful pleies aȝens resoun'.[46] There is also much emphasis on sins connected with speech: lying, boasting, and swearing, especially 'sweringe bi þe membris of crist'.[47] The text several times condemns theatrical performance, criticizing those 'who can pleie a pagent of þe deuel', and the 'cursid japis' beloved by fools that take place at Christmas and other festivals.[48] A distrust of religious plays was a typical lollard concern, but the references to dramatic performances may have resonated with the adult Thomas Roberts for a different reason since his London environment at the Inns of Court was frequently the location for plays, masques, and revels.[49] Throughout, the author paints a picture of leisured gentry life that contains numerous sinful distractions, with too much attention paid to 'þe roten body' and too little to the immortal soul: 'for sumtyme curtesie & gentrie was holy liuinge; but now it is turned into harlotrie of synne'.[50] Whilst there is some passing criticism of the priests who permit such sin – they are 'cursid of god', the main emphasis is placed on individual personal responsibility, and especially on the head of the household.[51] It is for each man to maintain order amongst his family and servants and to instruct his subordinates in the ways of proper living: 'eche man teche his meyne to kepe þe heestis of god'.[52] When the text returns, in its later stages, to the example of Mary, it lauds her as the antidote to Eve, and sets her clearly above the other saints in a hierarchy of grace. The emulation of Mary's life is encouraged, particularly in the keeping of seven virtues: 'feiþ hope & charitee mekenesse chastitee soburnesse and

---

[45] f. 18^v.

[46] f. 19^r.

[47] f. 20^r.

[48] f. 20^r.

[49] Details of the myriad types of entertainment available at the Inns are documented by Nelson and Elliott, *The Inns of Court*, vol. I. Winston, *Lawyers at Play*, p. 177, summarizes the complex conventions associated with the Christmas revels.

[50] Quoted from f. 20^v and f. 19^v, respectively.

[51] f. 21^r.

[52] f. 21^v.

brennynge desir of riʒtwisnesse'.⁵³ Yet even whilst promoting devotion to Mary, and prescribing the use of the Ave – in particular the habit of repeating the 'twey deuout wordis' (the names of Mary and Jesus) – at the end of this prayer, the author is decidedly equivocal about any specific rewards that might be gained from this practice:

> But cristen men of her deuocioun seien þese twey wordis 'Marie' and 'Iesu' and þese ben twey deuout wordis. And summen seien þat popis graunted greet pardoun to seie þese wordis; but houeuere it be of pardoun þis addinge herto is trewe, for þe gospel telliþ to up þese twey names and þei stiren to deuocioun.⁵⁴

One wonders how Thomas Roberts would have interpreted this comment. Would he have read this as an outright condemnation of the granting of pardons, or a subtle refusal to pass judgment on that practice? Beyond adding his monogram at the top right corner of f. 18ʳ and noting that the piece amounted to 'v lefes', he did not contribute any further annotations to the commentary on the Ave, leaving few clues about his response to this text. But that response must have been qualified at least by his own participation in the culture of indulgences and pardons. His book of hours, CUL MS Ii.6.2, contains memoranda that note various pardons and concessions including those granted by Urban V for reciting the Ave, and by Urban IV and John XXII for saying the name of Jesus at the end of the prayer, that is, the very arrangement commented on here.⁵⁵

In this commentary on the Ave, scriptural authority clearly trumps the papal stamp of approval, and a characteristic of this text is a strong emphasis on the scriptural authority which lay behind the prayer. At the start, after providing the text of the Ave in English, the commentary makes a careful distinction between its two sentences, explaining that the first was voiced by the Angel Gabriel, and the second by Elizabeth, but it nevertheless stresses that both sentences occur in Luke's gospel and are therefore to be regarded as authoritative. This insistence on the central importance of Holy Writ is the topic of the second non-canonical text included in Thomas Roberts's copy of the *Pore Caitif*, a short polemical rebuttal, 'Answeris to hem þat seien þat we schulde not

---

⁵³ f. 22ᵛ.
⁵⁴ ff. 18ʳ⁻ᵛ.
⁵⁵ Discussed further in Chapter 6, section titled 'I youse thys prayer well every daye: howe Edmund Roberts said his prayers'. See also Peikola, '"And after all, myn Aue-Maria"'.

speke of holy writt'. There are two other copies of this text, which seems not to have been printed, but it is short enough to reproduce here:

> First wite eche man þat charitee is þe principal part of holy writ and if any part of holy writ be taken fro us þanne a part of cha-[f. 87ᵛ]-ritee is taken fro us. For Seynt Poul seiþ if we kepen charitee we fulfillen al þe lawe. God is charitee and if we schulen not speke of holy writ we moun not speke of God neiþer of charitee. Also Poul seiþ if any man knowiþ not holy writ he schal be unknowen. And if we moun not speke of holy writ we moun not blesse God neiþer men, neiþir we moun not speke of heuene neiþir of erþe ne of helle, ne of no creature þat euere God made. For holy writ spekiþ of alle þe werkis of God. And whanne Ihesu Crist was here on erþe he wolde not lette þe fend to speke of holy writ, as þe gospel telliþ in þe firste sunday of Lente, ne noon oþere synneris, but he tauȝte it hymsilf to alle men goode & yuele. For we knowen not good from yuel but bi wisdom [f. 88ʳ] of holy writ. And þerfore God [seiþ *canc.*] cursiþ in his lawe alle men þat bowen awey her eeris from it, and blessiþ alle men þat heren it and kepen it iustly. And so as erþely men demen hem to be acursid þat letten þe testament of a deed man, so alle heuenly men demen hem to be acursid þat letten þe testament of Ihesu Crist. And his testament is þe holy gospel þat he comaundide to be prechid to alle creaturis. And he ordeynede foure holy men to write þis testament, þat is Matheu Mark Luk and Jon. And he þat lettiþ þis testament to be knowen to þe puple holdiþ wiþ þe fend aȝens Ihesu Crist and is cursid of God. *Explicit.*[56]

In its defence of the preaching of scripture, and in particular of the gospels, the tract's reformist credentials are very clear: universal access to the word of God, a central tenet of lollardy, is what is demanded. Some of the terminology is very characteristic of lollard writing: the term 'letten' in particular stands out in this regard.[57] Whether Thomas Roberts's ear would have been attuned to the subtleties of such vocabulary is unknowable, and again he has left no evidence of interaction with this text that might reveal his opinion of it – though its

---

[56] ff. 87ʳ–88ʳ. This text also appears in CUL Ii.6.26, ff. 40ᵛ–41ᵛ, and incompletely in BodL Additional B. 66 ff. 90ʳ⁻ᵛ; it was edited from the Cambridge manuscript by Hunt, 'An edition of tracts', ii.310–12.

[57] See Peikola, 'Congregation of the Elect', pp. 188–92.

warning about obstructing the will of a dead man would surely have struck a chord with him as a lawyer.

There is much in these two texts that coheres with lollard preoccupations: a distrust of religious plays, a condemnation of unworthy priests, an emphasis on the responsibilities of the individual Christian, and an insistence on the centrality of the preaching of God's word. There is also here much general advice for proper behaviour and clean living, mixed in with a certain amount of antifeminist diatribe, and an interesting refusal to condemn outright the granting of pardons. Trying to establish Thomas Roberts's reaction to this mixture of ideas is very difficult, and we must allow that in reading and re-reading the book over many years as boy and man, his responses would not necessarily have remained static. Whether he could have been aware that his copy of the *Pore Caitif* was one that contained lollard elements is not at all apparent. The work was never printed, and although it enjoyed a wide manuscript circulation, especially in London, there cannot have been many other copies readily available for Thomas to consult, even if he had thought to do so.[58] Without some means of comparison, how would an early modern reader have been able to assess the authenticity of a text and judge how far it adhered to, or deviated from, what its author had originally intended? In the case of the *Pore Caitif* many of the differences between the versions now labelled orthodox and heterodox lie in material which was either omitted or truncated (alternatively added and expanded, depending on which version is believed to have been the original), forms of alteration which cannot have been easy for a pre-modern reader to spot. Detecting substitutions cannot have been a straightforward exercise either. For example, it has been noted that in the tract on the Decalogue the heterodox manuscripts consistently use a different translation for the English text of the commandments.[59] This results in a range of subtle variations between the two traditions, but it does not give rise to any substantial differences in meaning or interpretation. In such instances, could Thomas have been aware that the version of the commandments that he had in his copy was different from the version that some other copies of the *Pore Caitif* contained?

---

[58] The only part of the *Pore Caitif* that was printed in the sixteenth century was a variant version of the tract, 'The Charter of Our Heavenly Heritage'; this was printed as *A Good Tretys of a Notable Chartour of Pardoun of Oure Lorde Ihesu Crist* by R. Lant (*STC* 19187), in ?1542, so almost certainly not during Thomas Roberts's lifetime; see *IPMEP* 166.

[59] See Trivedi, '"Trewe techyng and false heritikys"', pp. 140–41.

An even more fundamental question might be raised about Thomas's knowledge of what he was reading. Other manuscripts of the *Pore Caitif* use the term 'pore caitif' in the *incipits* or *explicits* that identify the text, following the hint about authorship given in the work's prologue which states that the treatise was 'compiled of a pore caitif & nedi of goostli help of al cristen peple'.[60] BL Harley 2322 does not include the prologue, and its final *explicit* identifies the text differently as 'þis blessid tretis þat is counseylour of wrecchis' (f. 152ʳ). Given that his copy nowhere uses the title or term 'pore caitif', would Thomas Roberts even have known that this book *was* the *Pore Caitif*? This is a point of some importance. The *Pore Caitif* had long been connected with John Wycliffe, despite the fact that it actually contained very little that could be labelled peculiarly Wycliffite, at least in the majority of its manuscript copies. This association was formalized by John Bale who catalogued the text under Wycliffe's name in 1559, giving it the title *Confessionem derelicti pauperis*.[61] This was after Thomas Roberts's time, but it seems reasonable to suppose that Bale's identification was based on existing popular assumptions, and that the *Pore Caitif* was a work linked with lollardy and with reformist thinking in the earlier decades of the sixteenth century. Of course, if Thomas Roberts did not recognize that his 'tretis þat is counceylour of wrecchis' was the *Pore Caitif*, then he may well not have made any such connection about the supposed origins of its contents. As Fiona Somerset has noted, largely in relation to the fifteenth century but the point holds true for the first half of the sixteenth century as well, readers did not always know what they had in their hands, and would only have recognized lollard texts if they were 'attuned to the specific idiom and polemical talking points' of them.[62] Certainly, if Thomas Roberts regarded this material as Wycliffite he has left no indication of his opinion of it. In this instance he has marked the volume more thoroughly than some of his other books, allowing us to be confident in supposing that he read this compilation from start to finish even though he seems to have responded more fully to some parts.[63] Perhaps most revealing is that he was happy to set his mark of ownership in many places through the whole volume, evidently fearing no reprisals

---

[60] Cited from Brady, 'The Pore Caitif', p. 1.
[61] John Bale, *Scriptorum illustrium Maioris Bryttannie ... catalogus* (Basle, 1559).
[62] Somerset, 'Censorship', p. 244.
[63] Hill, 'Pedagogy, Devotion, and Marginalia', notes a general lack of annotation in manuscripts of the *Pore Caitif*, though the focus of this analysis is on the text's reception in the fifteenth century rather than later.

from his possession of it; if this text was in any sense 'hot property' in any of the periods in which he read it (potentially from the 1480s to the end of the 1530s) Thomas Roberts either did not know, or did not care.

ORTHODOX READING: UNIVERSITY OF HARVARD, HOUGHTON LIBRARY, MS RICHARDSON 22

University of Harvard, Houghton Library, MS Richardson 22 was produced in England in the first quarter of the fifteenth century.[64] It consists of ninety folios and is generously sized, measuring 245 mm x 166 mm, on good quality parchment, written by two hands, the first a bastard Anglicana, and the second (responsible only for the final item) a more informal Anglicana hand.[65] The text layout is mostly in double columns, with single column format used in the middle of the manuscript for three items. Overall the manuscript bears all the hallmarks of professional production: it has been pricked and ruled; there are traces of quire signatures in various places; and there are catchwords at the bottom right corner of the last leaf of most gatherings. Light box lines have been drawn around each catchword, which is thus attached to the furthermost right vertical line of the page ruling.[66] The manuscript is handsomely decorated with painted and burnished gold initials with sprays. The first text has lost its opening chapters, but the three-quarters bracket border used at the start of the second text gives an indication of the type of decoration that was probably present, since the decorative programme is fairly consistent throughout. As well as the larger initial capitals, four lines in depth, with sprays, that are used at the start of each new text, the longer texts mark the start of each chapter with similar but slightly smaller initials, and less formal divisions with alternating red and blue paraphs; the shorter texts use red and blue capitals with decorative tracery of the other colour, as does the final, less decoratively splendid, text in

---

[64] For a brief description see Voigts, 'A Handlist of Middle English', 56–60. The manuscript is fully digitized at http://nrs.harvard.edu/urn-3:FCHL.HOUGH:1260236; I have relied on these images for my analysis and have not seen the manuscript at first hand.

[65] The change in hands occurs at f. 89^v. Voigts, 'A Handlist of Middle English', 56, states that the first hand uses textura for the Latin prayer on ff. 69^r–71^r, but I do not see this difference.

[66] Due to trimming the prick marks are more visible on some leaves than others; for a good example see f. 67^r. For quire signatures see f. 11^r 'b iiij', f. 33^r 'e iii', f. 34^r 'e iiij', f. 39^r 'f', f. 41^r 'f iij', f. 42^r 'f iiij', f. 47^r 'g j', 48^r 'g ii', f. 49^r 'g iiij', f. 55r 'h j', f. 56r 'h ij', f. 57r 'h iij', f. 58r 'h iii-'; f. 65r 'I iij', f. 66r ' I iii-', f. 73^r 'k'. Catchwords are present at the ends of the first nine gatherings (ff. 7^v, 15^v, 22^v, 30^v, 38^v, 46^v, 54^v, 62^v, 70^v), though that on f. 22^v is almost cropped away.

the manuscript. Red ink is used throughout to distinguish Latin, except in the case of the Latin prayer on ff. 69ʳ–71ʳ where, exceptionally, the Latin text is written in black ink, but its extensive English rubric, now erased, was in red.

Although the manuscript has been nicely decorated and rubrication has been supplied throughout, there are gaps in the illustrative programme and at least three spaces where the expected illustrations were never supplied. These represent a failure or interruption at the volume's production stage, but the manuscript is incomplete in other ways too. It now consists of ninety-two leaves (the modern pencil folio numbers go only to ninety because in two places leaves were missed and left unnumbered), but the volume was originally somewhat larger, though perhaps not by much.[67] The first text now starts incompletely in its fourth chapter, indicating that probably an entire quire has been lost from the beginning of the manuscript, and the last text in the volume is also incomplete, breaking off abruptly at the foot of f. 90ᵛ; assuming regular quires of eight this means the loss of at least four more leaves. These losses might have happened at any point before the volume was bound, and could easily have been accidental since the parts of the book affected are those areas that are most vulnerable. Yet the date of the binding, which is late sixteenth century, indicates that these losses must have already occurred by that point at least, and perhaps earlier.[68] The losses may still have been accidental, but there is also the possibility of deliberate damage. It seems rather coincidental that the other most deluxe Roberts manuscript, JRL English 98, has also lost leaves at the beginning – the place most likely to carry information about ownership. Was there a purposeful attempt to disguise information about former provenance in these two instances?

Other traces of evidence suggest attempts to conceal or alter the volume's true nature. On the blank flyleaf which faces what is now the first leaf of the text are tiny fragments of printed text.[69] These adhere to the surface of the parchment in several places within a rectangular area that measures approximately 121 mm x 65 mm, indicating that a piece of paper of at least this size was once pasted in here. The fragments are too small and damaged to decipher actual words, but the letters are clearly in mirror-writing, and upside down, and the

---

[67] The unnumbered leaves lie between ff. 3–4 and ff. 17–18.
[68] The catalogue describes the binding as late sixteenth-century English brown calf, blind-stamped with a crowned Tudor rose, http://lms01.harvard.edu/exlibris/aleph/a20_1/tmp/usmo14723926.txt.
[69] This is now flyleaf 6.

language looks more like Latin than English. These are the remnants of whatever text was on the reverse of the paste-in, which I assume was most likely a woodcut of a holy image, perhaps a pilgrim souvenir, or an indulgence text, now removed. Another kind of removal is evident on ff. 68ᵛ–69ʳ where the long English rubric to the following Latin prayer has been carefully erased. I suspect, though I cannot prove, since the erased text resists modern technological attempts to restore it and remains stubbornly illegible, that the English rubric promised the reward of a certain number of days remission from purgatory provided that the following Latin prayer was recited for the correct number of times. Such promises would cause offence to a certain kind of reader – not to Thomas or Edmund, judging by their annotations in other volumes, but possibly to a member of a later generation of the family – and might prompt the expunging of such material. Yet there has been no systematic attempt to purge the volume of Catholic sentiment: the long devotion to Mary, on ff. 78ʳ–82ᵛ, for example, has been left untouched, which suggests that the contents of the volume as a whole were not intrinsically unpalatable to its readers. Protestant interference is usually the most likely reason to account for such removals, but religious fervour is not the only possible cause, and political astuteness may have played a role here. The 1530s was a decade of tumultuous social change, focussed on religion and religious practices, driven by Henry VIII's desire for a divorce and his need to circumvent papal authority. On the one hand there were campaigns against Protestant heresies and the possession of banned books; on the other there was the systematic dismantling of outward manifestations of devotion with the taking down of roods and the suppression of shrines, chantries, and monastic houses.[70] In the Roberts books of hours the feast days of St Thomas Becket have been dutifully deleted, in accordance with the decree of 1538; perhaps the various deletions to Harvard Richardson 22 stemmed from a similar desire to show conformity to the prevailing political regime, regardless of Thomas's own religious preferences.

Compared with most of the other manuscripts owned by members of the Roberts family, Harvard Richardson 22 seems conspicuously clean. The name 'Robertz' is inscribed in red at the top of the front flyleaf, but one wonders why it never appears at the top of individual folios as it does in BL Harley 2322 and Harley 1859, or why Thomas refrained from inserting his monogram in the

---

[70] On the complexities of religious affiliations during this period see Marshall, *Religious Identities*.

decorated borders in the way that he added it to the borders of JRL MS English 98.[71] Blank flyleaves and blank spaces at the ends of texts have not been filled up in this manuscript in the way that they have in other Roberts family books, and no texts of an incidental nature – prayers, recipes, memoranda – have been added to the volume's original contents. Although there is persistent marginal annotation in many of the texts, it is of modern origin: these pencil annotations are the work of the manuscript's last private owner, W. K. Richardson.[72] With very few exceptions there are almost no annotations that seem contemporary with Thomas or other members of his family. We therefore have little particular insight into the family's use of this volume, but an examination of its contents can at least develop a deeper understanding of what range and type of material was available in the Roberts household in the sixteenth century for private devotional reading.

The first text in the volume is a Middle English translation of the pseudo-Augustinian *Soliloquiorum animae ad deum*. This compilation of extracts from various works, including Augustine's *Confessions* and Hugh of Saint Victor's *De arrha animae*, was widely disseminated in its Latin form during the later Middle Ages, and subsequently translated into many vernaculars; versions in both Latin and English were printed from the sixteenth century.[73] It should not be confused with Augustine's genuine *Soliloquies*, and was not in fact by Augustine at all, though it was attributed to him and circulated under his name. The text consists of a set of theologically complex and highly emotional meditations that privilege notions of the interior spiritual life, and seek to develop both self-knowledge and knowledge of God through personal affective devotion. Much stress is placed on the wretchedness of the individual and his/her unworthiness when estranged from God: 'I was nouht & I am nouht and to nouht I am brouht' (f. 1^r), and on the need to resist one's enemies and the temptations of the devil. Each chapter contains several direct addresses to God, many of which could be used as discrete prayers; a system of alternating red and blue paraph marks, combined with the decorated initials that distinguish the beginnings of chapters, allows different sections of the text to be easily located and used in this way. A tiny cross in the left margin of f. 2^r seems to mark the

---

[71] See further discussion in Chapter 4, section titled 'Augmentations'.
[72] See, for example, the comments in the margins of ff. 6^r, 12^v and 13^r; there are many others.
[73] ff. 1–52^r. For the Latin text see *PL* 40:883–98. See Sturges, 'A Middle English Version', 74, and for a summary of the text's contents and some selections from the text see Sturges, 'The Middle English Pseudo-Augustinian *Soliloquies*'.

start of one particular request, 'Lord Ihesu make myn enemyes agast, defend me & deliuer me owte of þe bondes of þes fendes ...', and another similar cross in the right margin marks the start of another: 'Soþe it is goode Lord ...'. This type of mark occurs again on f. 3ᵛ, in the right margin alongside 'From whenis cam me þis bounete ...'. It is hard to tell what vintage these marks might be; they are very small and faint. A clearer addition occurs on the verso of the unnumbered leaf that stands between ff. 3–4. Here a sixteenth-century hand, probably that of Thomas Roberts, has written *nota seynt Austyn* in the left margin, alongside the sentence: 'And þis is he þat ys myn glorie & my uerey joye in whom I reioyse me'. These additions are exceptional; for the most part the text is free from readers' annotations, except those added by its modern owner.

Only one other copy of the Middle English *Soliloquiorum animae ad deum* exists, in BL Cotton Titus C. xix, ff. 3–92. This copy preserves the first three chapters that are missing from Harvard Richardson 22, but offers a slightly different version of the whole text in that what appears as the last (thirty-third) chapter of the text in Richardson is moved forward and augmented so that it serves as a proper prologue to the translation.[74] Other passages of commentary added by the translator are omitted from the copy in the Titus manuscript, either because of the particular nature of their contents, or perhaps because the compiler of that manuscript recognized them as digressions from the original text. The most substantial interpolated passages occur in chapter 27 (ff. 28ᵛ–35ʳ), where the translator takes up the topics of free will and predestination, and chapter 30 (ff. 37ʳ–45ʳ), where he discusses images, the Eucharist, Scripture, and the priesthood; his purpose seems to have been to guard against possible Wycliffite interpretations of the pseudo-Augustinian text by offering a more orthodox reading of his own.[75] This concern to combat erroneous interpretation reveals the orthodox beliefs of the early fifteenth-century translator of the text; to a later fifteenth- and early sixteenth-century reader such as Thomas Roberts, there was nothing remarkable about these sentiments. The firm pronouncement that all who believe in Christ and his words 'byleue verreyly in þe sacrament of þe awter' would do nothing to disturb his own understanding of devotional duty and observance.[76] We do not know (since there is

---

[74] For an edition of the prologue see Wogan-Browne et al., *The Idea of the Vernacular*, pp. 224–29.
[75] This is discussed in detail by Sturges, 'Anti-Wycliffite Commentary'.
[76] ff. 42ᵛ–43ʳ.

no evidence) whether Thomas favoured the translation of the Bible into the vernacular, but there is nothing to encourage that here – quite the opposite in fact, as the important role of the clergy as correct interpreters of God's word is underlined: 'Therfor whan any creature haþ suche conseytes or dowtys in redynge of scriptures or by ymagynacions or temptatioun þey schuld anone take counsayle of clerkys & do by here doctrinis'.[77] Most of all, a man whose properties lay in close proximity to a Marian shrine that was the centre of local pilgrimage would find no difficulty with the statement that 'ymages are nat goddys but figuris imade to þe likenes of god & of owre lady & of seyntys', nor with being told that such images were to be revered 'wiþ trewe loue & feyþ'.[78] Yet over time these statements must have gradually taken on a rather different significance. Although 'known men' (lollards) and heretics of all kinds were investigated and prosecuted during the first decades of the sixteenth century, other voices such as John Colet's were speaking out against the worship of images, and the desire to read the scripture in the vernacular was gaining wider support. By the time that Henry VIII broke with Rome in 1534 the reformers were a significant force at court, images were already being taken down, and within a few years Henry had given approval to license Miles Coverdale's translation of the Bible.[79] Within a short space of time, what had been devotion had become superstition, and veneration had turned into idolatry. It is perhaps not surprising then that nothing draws attention to these passages in the manuscript. As time had passed, what had once been thoroughly orthodox had now become suspect and out of step with current political thinking (and this would become even more true in the lifetime of Edmund Roberts); faced with such change, readerly silence was perhaps the best course to follow.

The second text in the manuscript is also a translation. This is *A Tretyse of þe Stodye of Wysdome þat Men Clepen Benjamin*, the Middle English version of Richard of Saint Victor's *Benjamin Minor*.[80] Richard of St Victor, who died in 1173, was one of the major decisive influences in shaping the thought of medieval European writers on mystical theology. He was an Augustinian canon professed at the Abbey of St Victor near to Paris, and he was profoundly influenced there by the work of Hugh of St Victor. Richard's extensive Latin

---

[77] f. 43^r.
[78] f. 42^v.
[79] For an overview see Brigden, *London and the Reformation*.
[80] On ff. 52^v–68^v. For an edition of the text see Hodgson, *The Cloud of Unknowing*, pp. 129–45.

writings include two classic texts on mysticism, one shorter (*Benjamin Minor*), and one later and longer (*Benjamin Major*); these works became authoritative textbooks in monastic libraries. The Middle English version of *Benjamin Minor* gives a coherent synopsis of the Latin original, following the shape of the story and the main interpretations, but many of the eighty-seven chapters of the original Latin are omitted, and only a few short chapters are translated closely. Richard's text uses the Old Testament story of Jacob and his wives, Leah and Rachel, their handmaidens, and their children (found in Genesis 29–35) as a framework to show the interrelationship of the human faculties in their labour towards contemplative prayer. Leah and Rachel are construed allegorically as representations of affection and reason, and their respective servants Zelfa and Bala as sensuality and imagination; the thirteen children that they produced between them are allegorized as different virtues, each of which is allocated its proper place in a hierarchy that aligns sensuality as the subordinate of affection and imagination as the subordinate of reason. The culmination of the story is the birth of Benjamin (who represents contemplation) and the death of Rachel (reason) in childbirth. The explicit identification of Jacob with God is an innovation in the Middle English text, as is its Christocentric conclusion.

There are twelve other fifteenth-century manuscripts of *Benjamin Minor*, and the work was printed by Henry Pepwell in 1521, indicating that the text enjoyed some popularity in the early sixteenth century.[81] In most manuscripts the first section of the text contains a diagram, similar to a family tree, in which the relations of the children to their mothers, and the virtues represented by each child, are laid out schematically. This diagram deftly visualizes the text's allegorical structure, and is an aid to understanding that must also have functioned as a mnemonic to medieval readers. In Harvard Richardson 22 the diagram is introduced on f. 53ᵛ: 'And þe names of þese children & þese vertues schal ben knowen be þis figure þat folwiþ here after. In schewynge.', but there was not room to accommodate it in the remaining space on this leaf.[82] Instead the diagram is copied on the facing page (f. 54ʳ), with the names of the mothers and children written in black ink with red initials, and their allegorical meanings written in red ink, preceded by blue paraphs; exceptionally the names of Dyna (given as 'Byna') and Benjamin are written only in black ink. Although

---

[81] *IPMEP* 4; Pepwell's edition is *STC* 20972. The manuscripts are listed by Lagorio and Sargent, 'English Mystical Writings', p. 3428.

[82] The remaining thirteen lines of column b are left blank.

the alternation of blue and red is not quite regular, to the casual eye, this resembles little more than a list of contents; the scribe has continued to follow the two-column layout ruled on the page and the only diagrammatic feature is a series of irregularly drawn brackets and lines in brown ink. The figure is unfinished but was presumably intended to resemble a tree of Jesse with Jacob the progenitor lying at the bottom and his progeny growing upwards from Lya and Zelpha to the left and Rachel and Bala to the right.[83]

These two previous texts are written in prose, but the next item is the first of five English texts that are all in verse. First come two eight-line stanzas on the seven works of mercy, bodily and ghostly:

> The seuyn dedis of mercy
> I wole do as God vs bede:
> þursty nakyd & hungry,
> ȝeue hem drynke cloþe & fede;
> Uisite prisoneris & syke þat lye,
> & helpe hem þat haþ nede;
> to pouer folke hold herbagery;
> to byri þe dede ys charite dede.
>
> Gouerne hym þat is unwise;
> cownsayle þe redeles nyht & day.
> Chastise folis þat wole be nys;
> Forȝȝeue þy dettis þat may nat [pay].[84]
> Conforte hem in sorwe þat lyes,
> & for þyne enemye to God þou pray;
> Cherische þe sinful to turne from vy[se],
> & wisse hem in to þe riht way.[85]

---

[83] Hodgson, *Deonise Hid Diuinite*, p. 15, describes the diagram in Harvard Richardson 22 as 'wholly confused', and gives a summary of the diagrams in the other manuscripts; that offered in British Library, MS Harley 674, f. 112ʳ, is much clearer, and she reproduces this as the frontispiece.

[84] I cannot read the final word from the digital image because it disappears into the gutter; but the sense and the rhyme scheme indicate that this must be the reading; similarly the penultimate line, where Voigts, 'A Handlist of Middle English', gives 'vyse'.

[85] f. 68ᵛ. *NIMEV* 3459 (but the text does not extend onto f. 69ʳ as stated there); *DIMEV* 5459.2.

A knowledge of the works of mercy constitutes one of the elements of the Christian faith, along with the virtues, sins, sacraments, and gifts of the Holy Ghost, and there are very many short texts in both prose and verse which seek to enumerate and exemplify these basic and central concepts. The simple verses given here spell out succinctly and in a form that might easily be memorized the duty incumbent on the individual Christian to act in a charitable manner to other men, ministering to the needs of others whether those needs be physical or spiritual. Such texts frequently occur in manuals of instruction, a neglected category amongst medieval manuscripts, and there are likely to be many more examples that are as yet unidentified. Robert Raymo's survey of this area notes several verse versions including one which is the same as that given here and, interestingly, this other copy, preserved in San Marino, Huntington Library, MS HM 127, also follows a copy of *Benjamin Minor*.[86]

The next item in Harvard Richardson 22 has been almost entirely erased. It began on the line immediately below the conclusion of the verses on the works of mercy, and the initial capital 'S' in blue ink with red tracery remains undamaged. The rest of the text seems to have been written entirely in red ink; it occupied the remaining seven lines of the second column of f. 68ᵛ, and the whole of the first column and the first six lines of the second column on f. 69ʳ (see Figure 9). Comparison with script on the surrounding leaves suggests that the erased text was probably about 175 words long. What was this text and why was it erased? The erasure was clearly deliberate, rather than the accidental product of the repeated touching or kissing that devotional items (usually pictures) could attract.[87] The process of erasure was also carried out very carefully; none of the text of the Latin prayer that begins midway down the second column of f. 69ʳ has been lost, nor has the decoration that extends down the central margin from its opening initial 'D' been damaged in any way.

With some difficulty the opening words may be deciphered, and more could probably be recovered with ultraviolet light.[88] The *incipit* reads: 'Seint austyn made þis orisoun & who s. . . day seyþ it . . . xix. dayes . . .'. Although various Middle English texts have similar opening words – devotions attributed to St

---

[86] f. 62ᵛ. See Raymo, 'Works of Religious and Philosophical Instruction', p. 2290 and p. 2517.

[87] Rudy, 'Dirty Books', has alerted us to the possibility of such devout damage, but this was not the cause here.

[88] I have worked only from the digital images available at http://pds.lib.harvard.edu/pds/view/8166619.

Figure 9 Cambridge, MA, Harvard University, Houghton Library, MS Richardson 22, f. 69ʳ. Erased English rubric to Latin prayer.

Augustine are fairly common – all the ones that I am aware of would be too long to fit the space allocated here, though we must allow for the possibility that what was copied might have been an extract of a longer work.[89] The fact that it was all written in red ink suggests that it was both an indulgence and also an extended rubric for the text that follows, a Latin prose prayer to Jesus that begins: *Dulcissime domine ihesu christe, qui de sinu patris omnipotentis missus es in mundum relaxare peccata . . . .*[90] This very common prayer, which appears in many fifteenth- and sixteenth-century manuscripts, was often attributed to St Augustine, partly because a much older prayer with a very similar *incipit* was traditionally associated with him.[91] The prayer has been connected with Richard III, and even referred to as 'Richard III's prayer', because it is found amongst items added to his personal book of hours, but the prayer's origins were older and it is found in late fourteenth-century manuscripts from across Europe.[92] Some copies of this popular prayer were prefaced by a rubric that promised certain benefits to the suppliant if various conditions were met: as well as having a contrite heart, the suppliant must be without mortal sin; the prayer should be said whilst kneeling; and it should be repeated on thirty (sometimes thirty-three) consecutive days. If these stipulations are followed then the prayer will have the power to wash away sins and to save souls from purgatory.[93] In the sixteenth century, the usual title that occurred with this prayer was 'A prayer in affliction', indicating that this was a text suitable for use by those in distress or danger. The benefits that were promised from its correct recitation outraged later Protestant readers, who regarded these kinds of devotional practices as too closely associated with spells and magic. Neither Thomas Roberts nor his son Edmund are likely to have been offended by these sentiments – indeed, in his book of hours Edmund signed his name alongside an English devotion that made similar promises – so the person responsible for

---

[89] See, for example, the meditation 'Seynt Austyn þe hooly doctour techiȝt þorwȝ declaracioun of holy writt . . . ', listed by Jolliffe, *A Check-List*, I.32; or the translation of *De Contemptu Mundi*: 'Seynt Austyn saithe Iffe þou sey this ys an hard world I may not dispice the world and loue mischieffe . . . ', listed by Jolliffe, *A Check-List*, I.20; there are several others.

[90] For other examples of red indulgences in BL MSS Additional 37787 and Harley 2445 see Scase, 'John Northwood's Miscellany Revisited', p. 115.

[91] The prayer that begins: *Domine Ihesu Christe qui in hunc mundum propter nos peccatores de sinu patris advenisti . . .*; see further discussion of this connection in Sutton and Visser-Fuchs, *The Hours of Richard III*, p. 68.

[92] See Sutton and Visser-Fuchs, *The Hours of Richard III*, pp. 67–78.

[93] Sutton and Visser-Fuchs, *The Hours of Richard III*, pp. 68–69 cite various examples.

erasing the text on ff. 68ᵛ–69ʳ is likely to have been a later member of the family, or a subsequent owner. It might be noted that the copy of the prayer in Richard III's book of hours, London, Lambeth Palace Library, MS 474, lacks its opening lines and any associated rubric because the leaf which preceded this text is now missing from the manuscript; this loss may have been purely accidental, but equally it might also have been a deliberate removal prompted by Protestant sensibilities.[94]

In Harvard Richardson 22 the Latin prayer to Jesus is copied on ff. 69ʳ–71ʳ and is about 800 words in length.[95] Addressed to Christ, the oration begins by referring to Christ's work on earth: he came to forgive sins, ransom the afflicted, free those in prison, comfort those in grief, minister to the contrite in heart, heal the sick, and console the penitent. These opening lines effectively summarize the works of mercy, both bodily and spiritual, that were expected of every Christian, and which were listed in English in poetic form in the preceding text on f. 68ᵛ. After acknowledging many benefits that Christ brings to humankind, the prayer then draws a series of comparisons using key figures from the Old and New Testaments: for example, Christ mitigates the anger that our enemies have towards us, in the same way that the anger that Esau felt towards his brother Jacob was mitigated. This series of examples cites the most familiar personalities of the Old Testament: Joseph, Noah, Moses, David, Susanna, Judith, Jonah, and a smaller selection from the New Testament: Peter, Paul, John the Evangelist; the account of these biblical deliverances, and the recitation of the names of the famous individuals involved, reads like a series of powerful incantations, along with the repeated requests for protection: *libera et custodi nos; ita nos domine liberare digneris; ita nos domine defendere et liberare*.[96] In the next section of the prayer the major events in Christ's life are alluded to, and protection is requested in the name of Christ's incarnation, nativity, circumcision, and suffering at the Passion. A further section of the prayer relates the seven words that Christ spoke from the cross.[97] The supplicant is then reminded of everything that Christ did for mankind: his descent

---

[94] An alternative explanation is suggested earlier in this section, see above.

[95] Sutton and Visser-Fuchs, *The Hours of Richard III*, pp. 76–78 transcribe and translate the version in London, Lambeth Palace Library, MS 474 which this copy closely resembles, except for the personalizations made for Richard himself.

[96] ff. 69ᵛ–70ʳ.

[97] One of Christ's statements, his words to the thief (*hodie mecum eris in paradiso*) is omitted.

into hell, his ascension, and his anticipated second coming at the day of judgment. The prayer concludes with a reminder of the hidden nature of divine wisdom, and a final expression of praise and gratitude.

The natural progression of the prayer leads the reader or reciter towards a focus on Christ's passion, with a remembrance of both the words and the emblems associated with the event. In some copies more detail is included about the *arma Christi* – the implements used to torture Christ; here reference is confined to the crown of thorns, the bitter drink, and the cross itself. Another small difference between this and other copies of the prayer is the incorporation of two references to Mary. The first of these occurs amongst the listing of the events of Christ's life, where the mention of his incarnation is extended to read *per sanctam incarnacionem quam de uirgine gloriosa recepisti sicut uerus hominem* ('by his holy incarnation which was accepted by the glorious Virgin as if he were a real man'). The second occurs immediately after the reference to Christ's second coming: *et orationes gloriose virginis marie matris tue*. These references to Mary may be no more than natural elaborations in a prayer addressed to her son, but they also anticipate the long Marian poem that is copied later in the manuscript; otherwise the focus of this collection of devotional texts, from this point until the end of the section copied by the first scribe (f. 89^v), is predominantly on Christ himself.

The topic of Christ's crucifixion and man's redemption is addressed more directly in the next text in the manuscript, an English poem that begins, 'Now witeþ alle þat been here / And after schal be leue & dere', and which is known as the *Short Charter of Christ*.[98] This work, which consists of thirty-four lines in English rhyming couplets, imagines the body of the crucified Christ as a legal charter given by Christ himself. The speaking voice is Christ's own, and in the first few lines he succinctly summarizes his own incarnation and crucifixion:

> That Y Ihesu Christ of Nazareth
> For þe loue of man suffryd deeth
> Uppon þe crosse, wiþ woundes fyue
> Whiles I was man on erþe alyue.   (lines 3–6)

---

[98] ff. 71^v–72^r; *NIMEV* 4184 records a total of twenty-four copies; *DIMEV* 6769 and 6768. For an edition of the text, though not from this manuscript, see Spalding, *The Middle English Charters of Christ*, pp. 4–16; see also the more recent discussions by Steiner, *Documentary Culture* and Ashe, 'The "Short Charter of Christ" '.

This brief exposition is followed by details of what is being given by the charter: 'heuyn blisse wiþowte endynge' (line 9), to whom: all those who are repentant, and the 'rente' (line 15) that is expected in return:

> Kepe I nomore for alle myne smerte
> But þe loue of man, wiþ alle his herte,
> And þat þow be in ful charite
> And loue þyne neschebore as I do þe. (lines 11–14)

As is usual in a charter, there are witnesses to the contract, here specified as the events surrounding the crucifixion (the loss of daylight; the earthquake; the tearing of the veil in the temple; the dead rising from their tombs) and those who were present at the time (Mary and John, 'and oþer þat were þer many one', line 28). The contract is finally validated by the process of sealing and dating: Christ's 'owne seele' is used, further specified as the wound in his side, 'ʒouyn at kaluarye / þe first day of grete mercye' (lines 33–34).

The legalistic English terms used in the poem: 'rente' (line 15); 'chief lorde of þe fee' (line 16); and the repetition of 'witnesse', 'witnessiþ', and 'in witnesse of' in the later stages (lines 21–29) would have been reassuringly familiar to medieval and early modern readers since such language was very much part of the official fabric of contemporary society. The Latin phrases that occur in this copy of the poem would have been similarly recognizable.[99] The text borrows the phraseology of medieval charters, beginning with the protocol *Sciant presentes et futuri*, making a general address to all present, but also providing opportunities for particular readers to insert their own names at the prompts *nomen et cognomen* (after the opening Latin address, and after line 2). Other Latin phrases, always distinguished in red ink, are interspersed throughout the English text, and these denote the main sections of the charter: the giving clause, *dedi concessi*; the expected return or *reddendo* clause, *redditus warantiʒatio*; the list of witnesses, *hijs testibus* and so on. These Latin phrases would have been commonly familiar, since if members of medieval and early modern society encountered any written document at all in their working lives it would have been the charter. For Thomas Roberts, the legal imagery and terminology of this text would have held an even greater resonance and appeal

---

[99] Not all copies of the poem include the Latin elements: see for example the plain and wholly English version in BodL Ashmole 189, ff. 109ʳ–110ʳ, and similarly the version in BodL Ashmole 61, f. 106ʳ which has a Latin heading, *Testamentum dominum*, but no other Latin in its text.

since, as a lawyer, he would have handled such documents on a daily basis. With his lawyer's eye for detail he must have noticed that the charter, in fact, lacks its authenticating seal. After the dating clause that concludes the text, the final Latin rubric reads: *Sigillum Carte domini nostri Ihesu Christi*. An overgenerous word space, equivalent to about eight letters, has been carefully left between *Sigillum* and *Carte*, indicating that the seal with its image of Christ's side-wound should have been placed (probably drawn) here. The following line has been left blank to accommodate this, and in the line below that, in the rubric to the next text which follows, another over-sized word space (this time equivalent to only four letters) has been left after the opening words of 'Here begynniþ' and before continuing with the next words 'a song of loue', so that when the drawing of the seal above was supplied it could be finished off with an authentic trailing seal tag. Yet no drawing of the seal was ever supplied, perhaps for the same reason that prevented the completion of the diagram in *Benjamin Minor*.

In its lack of a seal the *Short Charter* is incomplete, and there is another indication that this work might not have been entirely finished in the way that the commissioner of the manuscript had originally intended. The preceding item, the Latin prayer *Dulcissime domine Ihesu Christe*, ends on f. 71^r, in the ninth line ruled on that leaf. The rest of that leaf was ruled but not written upon, yet the heading that belongs to the *Short Charter of Christ, Carta redempcionis* is written on the very bottom line. This is an odd place to find the heading to a text. That it is a heading, and not some kind of placement indicator like a catchword, is clear from both its elaborate format – it is written in red with a blue capital 'C' surrounded by red tracery – and its position, at the bottom of a recto leaf which is also the first leaf of a new quire. One wonders why the scribe did not just start the *Short Charter* on f. 71^r where there was ample room to accommodate about one third of the text. Possibly he preferred to place it on a double-page opening instead, for maximum visual impact, and it is true that the text fits almost perfectly on ff. 71^v–72^r, where it takes up all but the final four ruled lines of f. 72^r. Indeed, if the heading had been placed at the top of f. 71^v, and the seal actually drawn in at the bottom of f. 72^r, the text could have neatly occupied all of the space on this double-page spread. Why then was the heading *Carta redempcionis* placed separately on the last line of the previous leaf? Although it is not possible to be certain of the reason, the blank space left on f. 71^r and the positioning of the heading at the very bottom of that leaf might indicate another way in which this text was left incomplete. At least one other copy of the *Short Charter* was illustrated: the version in BL, Additional MS 37049, shows an image of the crucified Christ upon which a picture of a sealed charter containing the text of the *Short Charter* has been superimposed.[100] Perhaps in Harvard Richardson 22, space was left on f. 71ʳ to accommodate a similar picture, not least because such an image would relate both to the *Short Charter* and to the preceding prayer whose later sections (copied on the facing f. 70ᵛ) dwell on the sufferings of Christ.

The manuscript's Christological focus continues with the next item, a long poem composed of seventy monorhyming quatrains with the title 'A songe of loue to owre lorde Ihesu Christe'.[101] The poem begins:

> Ihesu most swettest of any þynge,
> To loue ȝow I haue gret longyng;
> þerfore I byseche ȝow, heuyn kynge,
> Make me of ȝowre loue to haue felinge. (lines 1–4)

Almost all of the quatrains begin with an address to Jesus, usually by the direct articulation of his name, occasionally incorporated into an apostrophe such as 'Blissful Ihesu', 'Merciable Ihesu', 'O sweet Ihesu'.[102] The opening initial of each quatrain is an enlarged capital, one line high, alternately in blue and red with tracery of the opposite colour. This regular alternation of colour has been the usual practice adopted by the rubricator throughout the manuscript, but in this text because the decorated initial is so frequently the letter 'I' the pattern appears to be more insistent than usual, and the effect is to make the page visibly participate in the repetitive rumination being encouraged by the words of the text. As a whole, this lengthy series of verses is a meditation that ruminates on the sweetness of Christ's love, a remembrance of his Passion, and a recognition of how indebted man is to Christ. These ideas are explored more than once, sometimes with a deeper focus on the events of the Passion as, for example, in stanzas 15–20 which draw a mental picture of the crucifixion with Mary at the foot of the cross, and which refer to Christ's wounds and the words that he spoke:

---

[100] f. 23ʳ; the image may be viewed at: www.bl.uk/manuscripts/Viewer.aspx?ref=add_ms_37049_fs001r.

[101] ff. 72ʳ–78ʳ; *NIMEV* 1732.5; *DIMEV* 2876.

[102] Only two stanzas break this pattern: stanza 30, which continues the thought from the previous verse and is implicitly addressed to Christ, who is the 'þe' of line 120; and stanza 28, which is addressed to Mary.

> Ihesu I owe to loue ȝow, þat are so free.
> For þat schewiþ me wel, þe crosse of tree,
> þe corowne of þornys, þe naylys þree,
> þe spere þat percyd, ȝoure herte for me.
>
> Ihesu of ȝoure loue ys sooþ to kennynge,
> ȝoure armys arne spradde, to mannys clippynge;
> ȝoure syde ys openyd, to loue schewynge;
> ȝowre hede bowiþ, to swete kyssynge.
>
> Ihesu ȝoure moder þat by ȝow dydde stande
> Tenderly wepte, and wrange her hande;
> ȝowre woundys wiþ ȝoure blood rennande,
> Made here herte sorwfull, and weymentande.

However, for the most part the thoughts expressed throughout the meditation are more abstract considerations of sin, contrition, and a repeated contrast between Christ's worthiness and man's wretchedness; eventually this is brought to a conclusion with thoughts of death and how the soul may attain bliss. This particular combination of verses occurs uniquely in this manuscript, but many of the stanzas closely resemble parts of another Middle English poem, 'Iesu suete is þe loue of þe / noþing so suete may be', a version of the hymn *Iesu dulcis memoria*.[103] The resemblances between the two are sometimes very close, extending over several stanzas; at other times the match is less complete, and may be detected in either the rhyming word or the poetic thought, but not both; some other stanzas do not match at all. This mixture might point to an independent translation of the same well-known Latin source, or to a more complex tissue of borrowings between different English versions of the hymn. The presence of the poem 'Iesu suete is þe loue of þe' in the early fourteenth-century anthology BL Harley 2253 indicates that the text enjoyed a long transmission, and there are other manuscript copies and also other poetic combinations of very similar material, but looking for direct associations and borrowings seems a fruitless task: the devotional ideas expressed are of a very conventional nature, and the choice of monoryhme would naturally generate similar lines and combinations of phrases.[104]

---

[103] *NIMEV* 1747; *DIMEV* 2899.
[104] See *NIMEV* 3236 and 3238; *DIMEV* 5075 and 5077.

This long prayer to Christ is followed by another English verse prayer, this time addressed to the Virgin. This begins on f. 78ʳ:

> Aue, quene of heuen, ladi of erþe welle of all bownte,
> Emperice of helle, & of mekenes þe souereynte,
> Ryht briht sterre schynynge of all fayrnes þe flour,
> Throw ȝow haue we grace counfort and socour.
> Gracious moder of Ihesu [f. 78ᵛ] maydyn meke & mylde,   5
> That by þe vertu of God conseyuyd & were wyþ childe.
> Whan pyte meuyd him to þat he dyd his wille,
> To take in ȝow humanite for mannys sowle schulde nat spylle
> This meruelous tydynges ȝe had from þat lord,
> Whan he sent ȝow to wyte his wille & his word,   10
> Bi Aungel Gabriel þat to ȝow sayde, Aue.

The prayer consists of 199 long lines, arranged in rhyming couplets which are grouped into stanzas of variable length; initially these are of five couplets, then six, then nine, six, or seven, according to no discernible pattern, though a regular feature is that each stanza concludes with a single short line or bob. There are fifteen such stanzas, each focussed on a word or phrase from the *Ave Maria*: *Aue Marya gracia plena dominus tecum benedicta tu in mulieribus et benedictus fructus ventris tui Ihesus Amen*. The words from the Latin prayer are set at the start and end of each stanza, and worked into the English text in the manner of an acrostic, so that the whole poem functions as a macaronic devotion structured around Gabriel's words to Mary. The *mise-en-page* draws attention to the acrostic: at the start of each stanza a blue initial with red tracery is used to distinguish the first use of the Latin word which is written in red ink, and red is used again when the word is repeated at the end of the stanza.[105] Thus by reading this English poem the reader might also learn the words of the Latin prayer and achieve a fuller understanding of the *Ave Maria* as a whole. The number fifteen resonates with the fifteen mysteries (five each of joyful, sorrowful, and glorious) associated with praying the rosary, and with the date of Mary's principal feast, the Assumption, on 15 August. In addition, the prayer articulates the whole range of Christian doctrine: Christ's incarnation through

---

[105] Two initial capitals were missed: the 'G' of 'Gracia', f. 78ᵛ, was left blank and has been supplied in brown ink; the 'T' of 'Tui', f. 81ᵛ, seems to have been gone over in brown ink – in this case red tracery has been supplied but not seemingly the blue of the capital.

Mary in order to redeem the sin of Adam; Christ's immaculate conception; and Christ's death on the cross, harrowing of hell, resurrection, and ascension. Mary is important, it is stressed, because of Christ, and she is deserving of worship because of her role as his mother; but she is also important as an intercessor, and in the later stages the speaker articulates this:

> Ladi I am a vicious and a synful creature,
> Ful of venemous vices wiþowte mesure.   160
> To ȝoure sone or to ȝow [f. 82ʳ] unworþi I am to praye,
> For wickyd menynges þat styryn in me al daye.
> But ȝit wiþ hope to ȝow I seche prayinge of ȝoure grace,
> That ȝe wole vowchesafe vertues me purchase.
> For Ihesu god, ȝoure sones loue, lady forȝyteþ me nat,   165
> But prayiþ for me as ȝe best know & wote,
> That I may haue forȝeuenesse of all myne synnys here,
> And in Ihesu mercyful grace to stonde so plenere.

The whole poem has been addressed to Mary, but in the thirteenth stanza (from line 153) the tone changes from merely descriptive and didactic to a direct and personal appeal for help. The penultimate stanza, focussed on the final word of the *Ave*, 'Jesus', allows that appeal to be shifted from Mary to Jesus, cleverly mirroring the movement of the poem which has been to encourage the reader to come to Christ via Mary. From line 171 onwards the address is to Christ, with an initial focus on the holy name:

> Ihesus ȝoure name ys to us boþ ioye & blysse,
> In owre dissese aȝenst all þe feendes malisse.
> Hit ys owre scheelde & strengþe oure comfort & socoure,
> For Ihesu ys as moche to saye as souerayne saueoure.   175
> Therfore Ihesu god, to ȝoure mercy holy I me bytake,
> Prayinge for ȝoure moderis loue þat ȝe me nat forsake.
> Sende me comfort & strengþe, in alle temptacioun
> And pacience mekely to suffer for ȝoure loue in tribulacioun.
> Alle wickyd styrynges & vayne dredes put away fro myne herte, 180
> Haue pite on me swete Ihesu for greetly myne paynys smerte.
> I am right syke & ful woo þerfor I putte me in to ȝoure cure,
> [f. 82ᵛ] Sende me lorde some salue þat may myne hele recoure
> For ȝoure gracious name Ihesu be to me, Ihesus Crist.

This poem is apparently unique.[106] There are many other Middle English poems that recall the events of the Annunciation, including a few that take the words of the *Ave Maria* as their particular inspiration. One such, the poem that begins 'Heil and holi ay be þi name', offers a similar acrostic, but in that instance the words used are from the English version of the *Ave*, and they are used only at the start of each stanza and not repeated at the end.[107]

The final verse text in the manuscript, and the last to be copied by the first scribe, is the *Long Charter of Christ*.[108] This constitutes a long address to mankind spoken directly in the voice of Christ, though the first-person narrator of the preceding prologue is human:

> Whoso wole ouer rede þis booke,
> And wiþ his gostly yȝe þere on loke,
> To oþer scole þar he nat wende,
> To saue his sowle fro þe feende.
> Than forto do as þis boke tellyþ,   5
> For holy writte forsooþ it spelliþ.
> Where for I pray ȝow for charite,
> ȝe þat þis book wole rede or see,
> Wiþ ȝoure herte & alle ȝoure mynde.
> Kepyþ derworþly þat ȝe here in fynde,   10
> And fulfilliþ it in dede,
> Þat ȝe schul now on þis boke rede.
> For now ȝe schul here anone rihte,
> ȝowre saueoure speke to ȝow as tyhte,
> Wordes of charite þat he haþ wrohte,   15
> Þat ȝe mow know in alle ȝoure þowhte.
> And who þis booke can understonde,
> Teche it forþ þorwe all þis londe,
> Until oþer þat þis boke haue nat sowen,
> To saue here sowlys riht as here owen.   20
> For ellis ȝe þat can & wole nat teche,

---

[106] *NIMEV* 454.5, but note that the total number of lines is 199 not 181; *DIMEV* 737.

[107] *NIMEV* 1024, *DIMEV* 1680; printed by Brown, *Religious Lyrics of the Fourteenth Century*, pp. 230–33. See also *NIMEV* 1062, *DIMEV* 1731.

[108] ff. 82ᵛ–89ᵛ; *NIMEV* 4154 where ten copies are recorded; *DIMEV* 6650. For an edition of the text see Spalding, *The Middle English Charters of Christ*, pp. 46–81, though this particular manuscript was unknown to her. See also Steiner, *Documentary Culture*.

> It is to drede of ful grete wreche
> For ellis ȝe schul nat wiþowte grete stryfe,
> Fram þis worlde passe in to þe londe of lyfe.
> Now I wolde bygynne to rede þeron,   25
> His pees he ȝeue us euerychone.

The prologue as a whole reads in a way which is reminiscent of the book curse – one expects to hear at any moment the request that the book be safely returned, and the anathema that will be the consequence for those who fail to meet this obligation. Subverting the usual formula, the prologue instead implicitly promises rewards from the reading of the following text, saying that the reader need go to no other school to save his soul from the fiend (lines 3–4).[109] Indeed, the benefits to be gained from the reading of the text are so great that there is an exhortation to proselytize and share this knowledge with others (lines 17–18) so that they too may be saved (lines 19–20). This direction is repeated later by Christ, and there are also warnings both here (lines 21–24) and later to those who fail to fulfil this responsibility. The authority of the text is emphasized by the reference to 'holy writte' (line 6), and the use of 'spelliþ' in the same line implies that this is specifically the gospel (godspell); further authorization is given with the assurance that the reader will hear Christ's own voice (line 14) speaking words that he 'wrohte' (line 15).[110] Throughout the text repeated use is made of formulas familiar from oral performance with injunctions to the reader to hear, hearken, and also look. The poem's didactic function is emphasized by Christ: 'Here wole I foure wordes ȝou teche / And to þe pepyll I pray ȝou hem preche' (lines 115–16). I take the 'four wordes' to be the Latin sentences, of which there are actually five, that are highlighted for the reader's attention in the manuscript by the use of rubrication.[111] The first: *Hoc facite in meam commemoracionem*, 'Do this in remembrance of me', is Christ's instruction to his disciples at the Last Supper, that they should continue to meet and break bread in fellowship after his death; these words would be familiar to the poem's audience from the liturgy where they were used in the Mass, as indeed they are still the invitation to partake in the sacraments in most denominations of the Christian faith. But just in case the words did not resonate, or were not properly

---

[109] Drogin, *Anathema!*, offers many examples of the medieval book curse.
[110] References to 'holy writ' are reiterated at the end of the poem, lines 407 and 411.
[111] A sixth Latin phrase that is picked out with red ink is the opening protocol to the charter, *Sciant presentes & futuri* (after line 180).

understood, the poet spells out: 'þese wordis towchiþ þe sacrament' (line 119), with the further explanation that:

> Hit semiþ many & is but oon,
> Hit semyþ brede & it is none,
> Hit quicke & semiþ dede,
> Hit is myne bodi in forme of brede. (lines 121–24)

Slight variations on these lines exist as independent quatrains in four manuscripts, and what Robbins describes as a 'favorite tag for doctrinal instruction' also features in a carol by James Ryman and in a sixteenth-century carol preserved in Richard Hill's anthology, Oxford, Balliol College, MS 354.[112] The second statement *Susciperunt me sicut leo paratus ad predam*, translated in the previous line (136): 'As a lyoun þat gooþ abowte his praye', is a quotation from Psalm 16:12. The third statement precedes Christ's reading of the charter: *O vos omnis qui transitis per uiam attendite & uidete si est dolor similis sicut dolor meus*, and is translated in the next few lines of verse:

> ȝe men þat goon here forþ by þe way,
> Biholde & see booþ nihte & day,
> And rediþ uppon þis parchemyn,
> ȝif any sorwe be so greete as myne. (lines 174–78)

This text is an adaptation of Lamentations 1:12, and is used in the liturgy of Holy Week, as part of the Tenebrae Responsories for Holy Saturday. The fourth statement is made during the description of the crucifixion:

> The selinge wex was dere ibowht:
> At myne herte rote it was isowht;
> All itemprid wiþ fine vermuloun,
> of myne rede blood þat ran a downe.
> *Factum est cor meum tanquam cera liquessens in
> medio ventris mei* (lines 232–34)

These lines are taken from Psalm 22:14. The fifth rubricated quotation repeats Christ's final words from the cross, *Consummatum est*, mentioned at line 343

---

[112] See *NIMEV* 1640, *DIMEV* 2754. Robbins, 'Popular Prayers', 344 notes that the lines appear as the second stanza of Ryman's carol 'This brede geveth eternall lyfe' (*NIMEV* 3583, *DIMEV* 5665), and in Hill's 'Man that in earth abides here' (*DIMEV* 3379).

and preceded by the statement: 'This worde I must nedis speke / And þan myne hert schal al to breke'. It is noticeable that in each instance the Latin is fully translated and explained for the reader; a literate readership is not assumed, suggesting that the original audience intended for the poem was an inclusive one of lay readers and perhaps the lesser-educated clergy including nuns.

Aside from the first introductory section, the poem is spoken in the voice of Christ. He narrates the story of his own incarnation, his immaculate conception by Mary, his temptation by the devil, the Last Supper, Judas's betrayal, the scourging at the pillar, and the crucifixion, descent into hell, and resurrection, all the time framing these events in the context of man's redemption. Details of Christ's life on earth are related in chunks in the poem, punctuated by reminders that all this has been done to atone for man's sin and to redeem mankind, Christ's rightful property, from the devil. Christ's speech begins with a reminder of his great love for man and man's inadequate response: 'Loke what loue I do to þe / and loke what loue that thow hast doon to me' (lines 29–30). Paradise has been lost through waywardness (line 31), and man has strayed: 'As a beest þat goþ on straye' (line 34). In response Christ explains that he has come to find his lost sheep and to restore man's inheritance of eternal life. The legalistic vocabulary that he uses casts the Christian message of redemption in terms of later medieval English property law: Christ speaks of eternal life as 'myne heritage þat is so free' (inheritable property), and – this term is used repeatedly – as a 'sesynge' (a possession in freehold) that he will give to man. In order to save man from the consequences of sin Christ will exchange himself: 'I wole ȝyfe myne lyfe aȝenst þe quede' (line 86), 'quede' literally meaning evil and wickedness (man's sin), but also in legal terms signifying a promise, legacy, or will (man's legacy, from sinfulness, is death, but through Christ this may be exchanged for man's *rightful* legacy of eternal life).

Christ promises to record this transaction in 'a charter of fefment' (line 75), as a permanent proof that can be produced as required. This familiar legal act of creating a written record leads into the conceit of Christ using his own body, not just as a substitute for man in dying on the cross, but also as the very material on which the record will be written:

> Parchemyn to fynde wist I none
> to make þyne charter aȝenst þyn fone,
> That wolde last wiþ owtyn ende.
> Herkenyþ now to myne wordis hende.

>   But as trew loue bad me do,
>   Myne owne skynne I toke þerto. (lines 93–98)

In contrast to the usual practice, it is not animal skin but human skin that will provide the parchment used for the charter; unlike the ephemerality of human skin, this will create a record that will last for ever – a permanence that stems from Christ's divinity and the everlasting nature of the Godhead, but this also constitutes an incidental comment on the durability of parchment and the expectation that such records or 'evidences' would last for a long time. Details of the transformation of skin into parchment are imagined through the suffering of Christ at the pillar where he is 'tuggyd & beten' and 'waschyn wiþ myne owne bloode', 'Straynid wel harde up on tre / As parchemyn owyþ for to be' (lines 156–57, 161–62). The pens that write the letters of the charter's text are the scourges with which Christ was beaten, and the number of letters is said to equate to the number of wounds on his body (believed to amount to 5,560).

Having described the physical process of making the charter, Christ now turns to its textual content, proposing to read its text and calling for attention from the audience several times before he does so. As with the *Short Charter* the opening, *Sciant presentes & futuri*, recalls the protocol with which actual charters begin, and what follows mimics the format of legal charters, naming first the donor (Christ, line 184), the donee (mankind, line 194), and what is given:

>   I made a sesinge whan I was borne,
>   To saue mankende þat was forlorne.   190
>   But wiþ myne charter here present
>   I made to mannys sowle a fefment.
>   That I haue grauntid & ȝyue
>   To mankynde wiþ me forto lyue
>   In myne kyngdome of heuyn blisse.   195
>   To haue & to holde wiþ owte mysse,
>   So in þis condicioun þat þow bekynde
>   And myne wonderful dedis þou haue in mynde.
>   Frely to haue & freli to holde.,
>   wiþ alle þe purtenaunce for to be bolde,   200
>   And in myne blisfull ioye euer to dwelle,
>   For þe rent þat I schal telle.
>   Myne heritage þat is so free,

> For homage or for fewte.
> No more wole I aske of þe 205
> But a foure leuyd gras ȝelde þou me.

The diction used in this section of the poem is insistently the language of the law, with terms such as 'sesynge', 'charter', 'fefment', 'condicioun', 'purtenaunce', 'rent', 'heritage', 'free', 'homage', 'fewte'.[113] English phrases shadow the correct Latin legal terminology used in the context of charters: 'I haue grauntid & ȝyue' (*dedi, concessi, confirmavi*); 'to haue and to holde' (*habendam et tenendam*). A condition is attached to the gift, and a rent is due from the recipient though only of the peppercorn type: a four-leaved clover is the token demanded, allowing an allegorical aside that explains the leaves to represent confession, contrition, repentance, and penance. The warranty clause follows, and an explanation of the fashioning of the five seals (from the nails and spear) and the sealing-wax (Christ's blood) used to authorize the document; the five seals are those of the Father, Son, God, Man, and Holy Ghost. Finally the witness clause (*testibus*) names five witnesses: the four evangelists and Christ's mother Mary. Then after a long section that focusses on the foot-of-the-cross scene, Christ revoices his own final words on the cross to indicate that the charter is finished: '*Consummatum est*, þis charter ys doon' (line 343). Immediately he is off to hell, 'þis charter to schew' (line 345), and other types of legal agreements and documents are invoked in the poem's closing stages. Christ makes one 'comonaunt' (covenant, line 349) with Satan in order to regain his 'catel' (property, line 351), and another with man (line 401) whereby man must follow Christ's teaching, as explained through the Pater Noster (line 403), and pay the rent specified earlier in order to be sure of his heavenly reward. Indeed, exhortations to fulfil the obligation of paying the rent occur insistently in the final thirty lines of the poem. Christ also leaves an 'endenture' (indenture, line 357) with man which is specified as the sacrament: 'in þe preestis honde myne flesche & bloode' (line 359). An indenture is a contract between two parties, often between a lord and his retainer; the document that records this consists of two copies written on a single sheet of parchment which was then cut in a zigzag fashion: each party retained one half, and was able to demonstrate proof of the agreement by reuniting the two. Richard Firth Green has argued for the continuity of later medieval written indentures of retinue and earlier oral trothplights of homage, citing

---

[113] For definitions of these terms see Alford, *Piers Plowman*.

Bracton's account of the original ceremony. In this respect it might be significant here that Christ defines the sacrament as lying 'in þe preestis honde', since Bracton's account has the tenant reciting the formula of homage whilst his hands were placed between the two hands of his lord.[114] Finally, Christ leaves with man a 'wel fayre signe' (line 365):

> A token of the cros þat I was on do,
> To bere wiþ þe whidur þou go,
> To saue þe euer fro þine foo.   (lines 366–68)

So universally recognizable is the cross as the symbol of the Christian faith, still carried in religious processions or worn as jewellery, that we may miss the legal inference here. In the Middle Ages tokens were frequently given or exchanged in the formalization of contracts; the practice continued into modern times, and survives in some contexts still, most commonly in the rituals attached to engagement and marriage. Medieval romance texts are filled with legal tokens, often invested with magical significance, that are exchanged as part of agreements or contracts, or that function as mnemonics or as objects of recognition. The token of the cross here is given with an instruction (that the recipient is to carry it everywhere), and it is also invested with special protective power. Christ also speaks of the coat of armour that he wears (line 377), 'the which I toke of þyne lyure', meaning that he has taken on human form (the livery of man). This apparel is now decorated with 'fine rosis reed', that is, the wounds that Christ has suffered; these function as a token of recognition: 'Whan I came agayne to þe / By þis cloþinge þow mayste know me' (line 385–86), just as Thomas knew Christ by his wounds; they are also as a reminder of the rent that is due to Christ, and those who do *not* keep them in mind and do not pay (line 388) will suffer the consequences of 'hyhe iustice' (line 391).

The presence of both the *Short Charter of Christ* and the *Long Charter of Christ* in the same manuscript may seem like an unnecessary duplication, but the two texts are actually quite different. Whilst the *Short Charter* has a sparse, legalistic style, the *Long Charter* is more elaborate and seeks to fulfil several objectives simultaneously. Laura Ashe has argued that the two texts should be regarded as distinct, and that to see the *Short Charter* as a shortened, tidied up version of the *Long Charter* is to misrepresent the relationship between the two poems.[115]

---

[114] See Green, *A Crisis of Truth*, p. 157.
[115] Ashe, 'The "Short Charter of Christ"'.

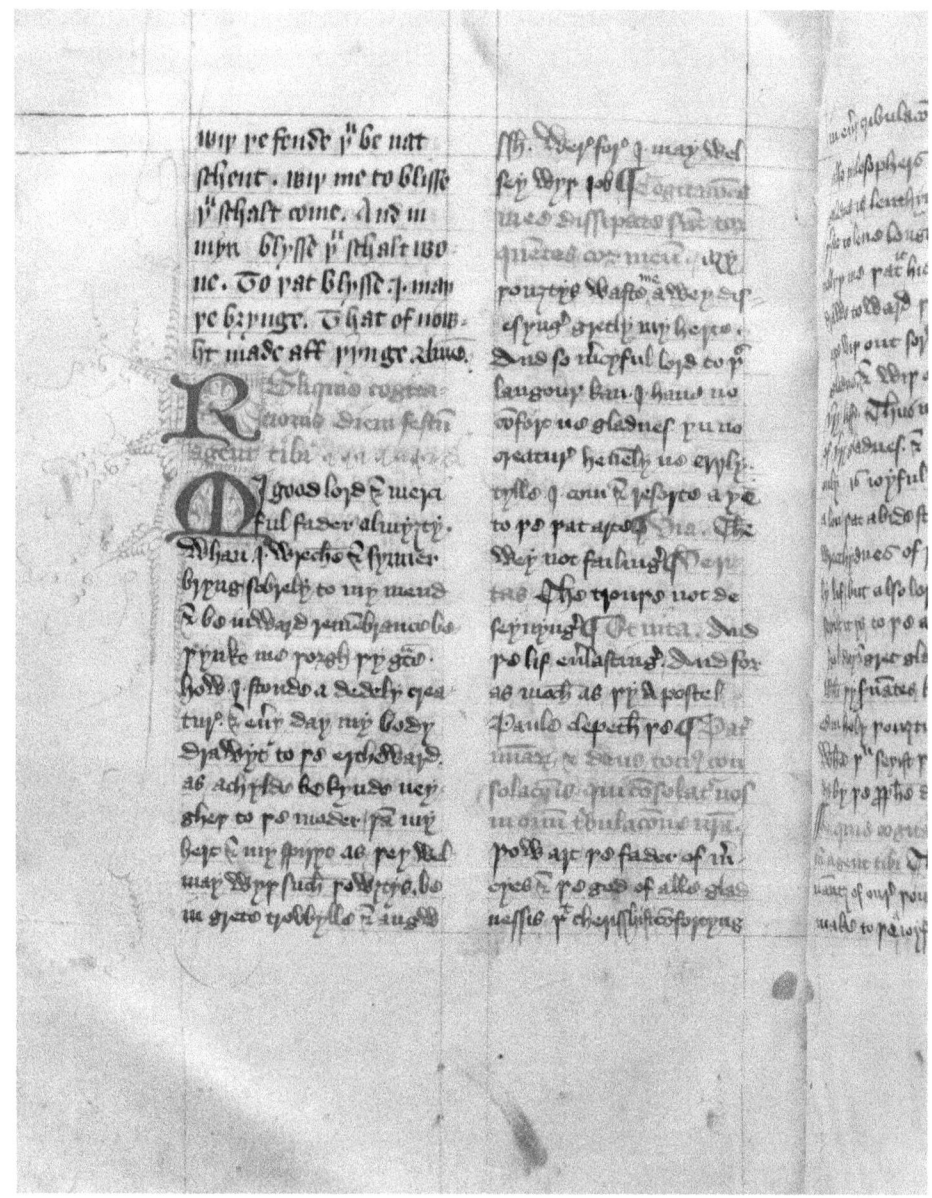

Figure 10 Cambridge, MA, Harvard University, Houghton Library, MS Richardson 22, f. 89ᵛ. End of Long Charter of Christ and start of final text, showing change of scribal hands.

Robert Raymo, whose classification groups both short and long charters together under the same heading, identifies three versions of the *Long Charter*; according to his scheme the poem included here is an early copy of the B-version, extant in ten manuscripts, mostly from the second half of the fifteenth century.[116] In terms of production, it has been suggested that these charter texts might have originated among the clerical dependents of a great estate, either ecclesiastical or secular.[117] Less seems to have been uncovered about reception: Raymo comments that the various forms of the text were widely popular from the mid fourteenth century onwards, though such might be inferred simply from the large number of extant manuscripts (more than forty). In the sixteenth century at least one other copy seems to have been owned by a lawyer: CUL MS Ee.2.15, whose other contents include eight sermons from John Mirk's *Festial*, Chaucer's *Man of Law's Tale*, and Lydgate's *Lives of St Edmund and St Fremund*, was owned by 'francis heyley', perhaps Francis Hawley of Buckland, Somerset, who was admitted to Middle Temple in 1565. That manuscript is made up of booklets which may have been sold separately, but it seems safe to assume that these were associated with each other by the mid sixteenth century.[118] A second copy, which follows the *Canterbury Tales* in CUL MS Ii.3.26, may also have circulated in a legal milieu. This manuscript has the inscription: 'Thys ys George towkars bowke lentt to hyme by George Herrollde surgentt the Fyrst day of Awgust Anno Domini 1558' (f. 239ᵛ). Although the term 'surgentt' need not necessarily imply sergeant-at-law (the office of serjeant of the royal household is another possibiity), and the name is not recorded by Baker, in 1544 a George Hairolde is recorded as the holder of a tenement very near to Middle Temple, suggesting proximity to legal circles at least.[119] The attraction of the text to lawyers seems self-evident. Of all the devotional texts in Harvard Richardson 22, the two charters of Christ are likely to have resonated most loudly with Thomas Roberts. Although he has left no trace of his engagement with them, his legal training would have made him a sophisticated reader of these texts, one who was capable of understanding fully the subtle implications of the legal conceits and diction employed by the poet.

The last text in the manuscript was written by a different, more cursive hand, though the text is still laid out professionally in double columns with coloured paraphs and rubrication (see Figure 10). The text is a Middle English prose

---

[116] Raymo, 'Works of Religious and Philosophical Instruction', pp. 2343–44 and 2548–50; to the nine manuscripts listed there may now be added a fragmentary copy in Canterbury Cathedral, MS Additional 46, see Boffey and Edwards, 'Unrecorded Middle English Verse Texts', 55–56.

[117] Green, *A Crisis of Truth*, p. 261.

[118] For a brief description see Powell, *John Mirk's Festial*, ii.565–67.

[119] *LPFD Henry VIII*, 19.ii.181 (36 Henry VIII).

meditation on human unworthiness that begins 'Mi good Lord & merciful fader almyȝty, whan I wreche & synner bryng sobrely to my mend & be inward remembrance beþynke me þorgh þy grace, how I stonde a dedly creature ...', and which has the rubric *Reliquie cogitationis diem festum agent tibi*.[120] Another meditation on the same theme exists in two copies, and in both those instances is paired with another, *Da nobis domine auxilium de tribulacione*.[121] It is not possible to tell whether this pairing was intended here, since at the bottom of f. 90^v the text breaks off incompletely at the words: 'I conceyue be þy grace þat þogh þu aske of me but þe remnauntes yit þu askyst of me þe beter parte. For nou', and the following leaves are lost. This rupture frustrates a fuller knowledge of this final text and the purpose for which it was added to the volume, whilst further obscuring our sense of the integrity of the codex as a whole.

Overall Harvard Richardson 22 seems to offer a series of absences – some arising from failures in the completion of its production cycle, others consisting of deliberate erasures, and still others resulting from depredations which might have been either intentional or accidental, or perhaps a combination of both. None of this is very helpful to an analysis of reception and use, and without any prompts such as annotations or marks to guide our interpretation we can only guess at Thomas Roberts's responses to the texts that he encountered in this book. Yet some aspects of this volume's multiple absences may themselves be telling. The lack of any Protestant-leaning comments or despoilations in the 'Aue, quene of heuen' devotion allows a confidence that Thomas placed value on these verses and might have used them in personal acts of worship in the same manner that he used the Marian prayers in his book of hours. The similar absence of any negative responses to the two Charters of Christ texts, both of which depict Christ communicating directly and personally with mankind, very much in the style of a dramatic monologue, suggests that Thomas was probably not disquieted by this type of performance and did not distrust religious plays. And ultimately the very preservation of this volume, damaged at points, but for the most part carefully preserved, demonstrates that its perceived worth to the family was as an approved source of devotional reading.

---

[120] ff. 89^v–90^v. The phrase is from Psalm 75 v. 10.

[121] In Oxford, Bodleian Library, MS Bodley 423, ff. 156^v–61^r and British Library, MS Arundel 197 ff. 64^r–70^r. Modernized versions of the two meditations are printed by Kirchberger, 'Veni Creator Spiritus' and 'Te Deum Laudamus', but neither corresponds with the version included here.

4

Out of the Cloister, Out of the Family

APPROVED READING: MANCHESTER, JOHN RYLANDS LIBRARY, MS ENGLISH 98

In 1532 Thomas More outlined a general programme of personal devotion that pious individuals might follow, recommending that they 'occupye them selfe besyde theyr other busynesse in prayour, good medytacyon, and redynge. . .'.[1] The specific works he suggested included Walter Hilton's *Scale of Perfection*, the *Imitation of Christ*, and Nicholas Love's *Mirror of the Blessed Life of Jesus Christ*, which were, he declared, 'suche englysshe bookes as moste may norysshe and encrease deuocyon'. By this time these were all old works. The *Scale of Perfection* was written in the late fourteenth century (Hilton died in 1396); the *Imitation of Christ*, commonly attributed to Thomas à Kempis (1379/80–1471), was probably written in the 1420s and was first translated into English in the mid fifteenth century; and Love's *Mirror* was approved for circulation by Archbishop Arundel in 1410. Hilton's and Love's works enjoyed a significant circulation in manuscript form if the numbers of surviving copies are any guide: there are forty-nine extant manuscripts of the English version of the *Scale of Perfection*, and sixty-one of the *Mirror*.[2] The earliest English translation of the *Imitation of Christ* is preserved in only four manuscripts, but the Latin text survives in twenty manuscripts of English origin and in vast numbers of copies from continental Europe.[3] These works were also widely available in print by

---

[1] More's comment occurs in *The Confutation of Tyndale's Answer*, see Schuster et al. (eds.), *The Complete Works of St Thomas More vol. VIII*, i.37.
[2] See Sargent, 'What Do the Numbers Mean?', p. 206.
[3] See Biggs, *The Imitation of Christ*, p. vii and pp. xxxv–xxxvi, and http://fama.irht.cnrs.fr/oeuvre/267495.

the time that More was writing. The *Scale of Perfection* had been printed by Wynkyn de Worde in 1494, by Julian Notary in 1507, and by de Worde again in 1525 (and would be issued again by de Worde in the following year).[4] William Atkynson's translation of the *Imitation of Christ*, commissioned by Lady Margaret Beaufort, had been printed by Richard Pynson in 1503/4 and again in 1517, and by Wynkyn de Worde in 1518/19 and again in 1528.[5] A different translation, *The Folowynge of Cryste*, attributed to Richard Whytford, was printed four times in 1531.[6] Love's *Mirror* had been printed twice by William Caxton (probably 1486 and 1490), twice by Richard Pynson (1494 and [1506]), and five times by Wynkyn de Worde between 1494 and 1530.[7]

Estimates of print runs for works produced from English presses during this period are hard to come by, but figures of between 300 and 500 copies have been tentatively suggested for various different types of books.[8] Even if the numbers of copies produced were somewhat lower in the case of the issues noted above, the cumulative effect of the successive printings of these works would have been to release a significant volume of texts onto the English market, especially in London, and More could quite reasonably assume that his contemporary devout readers would access the texts he had recommended in the form of recently printed editions. Old books do not just disappear, however, and there were plenty of manuscript copies of these works still in circulation. This is particularly apparent in relation to Love's *Mirror*. Early copies had been prepared for armigerous lay owners such as Joan, Countess of Kent (d. 1442) and Robert, Lord Willoughby d'Eresby (d. 1452), but later in the fifteenth century copies were owned by individuals such as Sir Peter Ardern, Chief Baron of the Exchequer (d. 1467), and various merchants and citizens of London and elsewhere.[9] One such was the grocer Richard Bodley, whose will of 1491 details several primers, a psalter, and some English books including one that contained the lives of Christ and St

---

[4] *IPMEP* 255: *STC* 14042, Part 1, *STC* 14043, Part 1, *STC* 14044, Part 1, *STC* 14045, Part 1.

[5] *IPMEP* 838: *STC* 23954.7, *STC* 23957, *STC* 23956, *STC* 23960 (Books 1–3 only).

[6] *IPMEP* 284: R. Wyer, *STC* 23961; T. Godfray, *STC* 23963; R. Redman, *STC* 23964 and 23964.3.

[7] *IPMEP* 553: *STC* 3259 and 3260; *STC* 3262 and 3263; *STC* 3261, 3264, 3265, 3266, and 3267.

[8] See Erler, 'Devotional Literature', p. 505, in respect of printed *horae*, and Baker, 'The Books of the Common Law', p. 427, in respect of law books.

[9] See Erler, 'Devotional Literature', pp. 517–18, and the more detailed account in Meale, '"oft siþis with grete deuotion"', pp. 19–46.

Katherine.¹⁰ This vernacular devotional volume is almost certainly identifiable as Cambridge, Corpus Christi College, MS 142.¹¹ Richard bequeathed it to his son, William Bodley, also a grocer, and the inscriptions at the end of the volume show that it was handled not just by William but by his first wife, Elizabeth (née Masset), and then by his second wife, Beatrice (née Sadler). Another book which seems likely to have been theirs is Edinburgh University Library, MS 39, a fifteenth-century book of hours of the use of Sarum which has a note of the birth of 'Franciscus Bodley' in 1532 on a front flyleaf; William and Beatrice's son, later a grocer and fishmonger, was indeed called Francis.¹² There are several points of interest to note here beyond the simple fact of the continued use of Love's text in manuscript form. One is the practice of handing down old books through generations of the same family; another is that those books may not necessarily have had their origins in the family that later came to possess them. The Bodleys' primer has an extensive list of birth records for the period 1451–74, but the names listed are the fourteen children of Thomas and Margaret Babham who lived in the parish of All Hallows Barking.¹³ There may have been a family connection between the Babhams and the Bodleys that is not now apparent, but the link between them might just as easily have stemmed from common business interests and membership of the same guild, since Thomas Babham was also a grocer and a contemporary of Richard Bodley.¹⁴ A further point of interest lies in the type of books and reading material evidenced here: the book of hours has additional hymns and prayers addressed to St Katherine, and the copy of the *Mirror* in Corpus 142 is accompanied by three saints' lives (Nicholas, Katherine, and Margaret), *A Tretyse of Gostly Batayle*, and forms of confession and excommunication. This selection broadly accords with the kinds of books and texts available in the Roberts family library, and is a reminder of how representative their surviving books are of the tastes and preoccupations of early sixteenth-

---

¹⁰ See TNA, PROB 11/9/28, and the discussion by Sutton, 'Lady Joan Bradbury', p. 212.

¹¹ For full details of its contents and ownership inscriptions see the online description at parkerweb.stanford.edu, but note that the website perpetuates M. R. James's misreading of Beatrice's surname as 'beuerley'.

¹² See the description in Borland, *A Descriptive Catalogue of the Western Medieval Manuscripts*, pp. 61–64.

¹³ Borland, *A Descriptive Catalogue of the Western Medieval Manuscripts*, provides a transcription on p. 333. See also Lacey, 'Margaret Croke', p. 146.

¹⁴ Thomas Babham's will, dated 11 October 1490, is TNA, PROB 11/8/491. See further discussion in Connolly, 'Late Medieval Books of Hours'.

century readers. This is brought into sharp focus when the links between the two families are more clearly perceived. William Bodley was not only an exact contemporary of Thomas Roberts, but was related to him through marriage: William's second wife Beatrice, daughter of the draper Roger Sadler, was the sister of Thomas's third wife, Katherine, meaning that the two men were brothers-in-law.[15] Beatrice Bodley was therefore Edmund Roberts's aunt, and Edmund and Francis Bodley were first cousins.

The presence of copies of Nicholas Love's *Mirror of the Blessed Life of Jesus Christ* in this clearly defined network of personal connections in London in the 1530s is not in itself surprising. The work had been designed for a mixed audience of religious and lay readers, and as time passed those lay readers had become both more numerous and less socially elevated. Thomas More's very recommendation of this text amongst other devotional works is a sign of its currency and availability in this period. Yet there is little indication that Thomas Roberts or other members of his family read Love's text with the close attention that More anticipated. Their copy of the text, now John Rylands Library, English 98, has few marks of readerly activity, and even the few that are present may not confidently be ascribed to the Robertses. Most strikingly, and in contrast to some of their other books, there are no marginal comments, very few pointers such as *nota*, and very little underlining of passages of text. Exceptionally in the account of the flight into Egypt (on f. 27^v), the name of the place has been underlined in the phrase 'þat londe that hiȝte lyermopolus'.[16] Similarly in the account of Christ's virtues (on f. 77^v) the key words 'prudence', 'strengthe', 'temperaunce', and 'riȝtwisnesse', have been underlined; in both these places red ink has been used in a rough manner of application that looks quite like the Robertses' style of annotation.[17] Possibly theirs too is the sketched design before the catchword on f. 14^v, which is an attempt to replicate a paraph with faint pen tracery in blue and brown ink; there are two other similar sketches in red with blue tracery in the left margins of f. 42^v and f. 45^v. Yet these are efforts to reproduce aspects of the manuscript's

---

[15] William Bodley died in 1540; for his will see TNA, PROB 11/28; for Beatrice's will of 1557 see TNA, PROB 11/42A.

[16] Quotations from the text in this chapter are from the manuscript, with equivalents noted in Sargent (ed.), *Nicholas Love*. This passage is from the Tuesday section, chapter 10, Sargent (ed.), *Nicholas Love*, p. 53, lines 31–32.

[17] Thursday, chapter 36, Sargent (ed.), *Nicholas Love*, p. 135, lines 30, 33, 38, and p. 136, line 6.

decorative design rather than marks to identify particular passages in the text, and moreover, these doodling-type additions might have been made by one person or several.

On the other hand, the manuscript does have a sustained series of marginal annotations which were evidently made by a single reader, at the same time, as part of a sustained reading of the text. A considerable number of passages have been marked for attention by the addition of faint vertical lines in light brown ink. These lines, which are straightish rather than wavy, are headed with a tiny lozenge and sometimes finished off at the bottom with ticks.[18] The first instances of these occur in the Proem. The first runs down the right side of the first column of text on f. 2^r and marks out the clause 'in parfite dispising of the worlde, in pacience, suffringe of aduersitees, & in encressynge in getynge of vertues'. The second is set alongside the second column of text, starting beneath the marginal rubric *Nota bene de martiribus*, and marking out the quotation from St Bernard and some following text:

> ... in that they setten al here herte and deuocioun in the passioun and the woundes of Crist. For what tyme the martir stant with al the body to rent, and neuerþeles he is joiful and glad in al his peyne, where trowest is thanne his soule and his herte? – sothely in the woundes of Iesu.[19]

More text in this section, extending the example of martyrs to confessors and virgins 'and alle þat lyuen riȝtwisly dispisinge þe worlde', is marked out overleaf on f. 2^v where the Proem's advice about how readers may get the maximum benefit out of 'the fruite of this booke' is also highlighted.

Marks of this type then occur regularly throughout the first half of the text.[20] They are present throughout the section for Monday, where they mark out many passages that relate to proper Christian behaviour, and in particular the need for virtues such as meekness and silence. In the second chapter, which describes Mary's youth, the highlighted passages stress her devotion, picking out the three precepts that she kept (following Matthew 22:37–39) and the seven petitions she made to God; in the following chapter, attention is again drawn to the example of Mary and the quality of meekness, and the need to

---

[18] I thank John Thompson for initially drawing these to my attention.
[19] Sargent (ed.), *Nicholas Love*, p. 11, lines 34–36 and p. 12, lines 13–18.
[20] The marks also occur on ff. 4^r, 6^{r-v}, 7^{r-v}, 8^v, 9^{r-v}, 10^{r-v}, 14^v, 15^v, 16^{r-v}, 17^r, 18^{r-v}, 21^r, 26^{r-v}, 27^r, 33^r, 34^r, 35^{r-v}, 36^r, 37^r, 38^{r-v}, 39^v, 41^r, 42^r, 45^{r-v}, 46^r, 47^{r-v}, 48^{r-v}, 49^{r-v}, 50^{r-v}, 51^{r-v}, 52^{r-v}.

resist the seven deadly sins. In the fifth chapter, which concerns Joseph's doubts about Mary, the marked sections concern the need to combat tribulation with patience, perseverance, silence, and a withdrawal from the distractions of the world; towards the end of this chapter, substantial passages that encourage a meditative focus on the suffering of Christ are also marked, reminding the reader that the 'wickid lyuynge of untrewe cristen men' was the cause of Christ's greatest pain. In the sixth chapter, attention is again drawn to meekness and penance, and above all to poverty. These ideas are drawn together in a final marked passage in the Monday section, at the end of the chapter on Christ's circumcision:

> This also goostly circumcisioun nedith to be in alle our bodily wittis as in seynge, herynge, touchinge, and othere þat is to seie þat we in alle þise shewe superfluite and kepe skarsete and namely in spekynge. For moche speche without fruyte is a grete vice and displesynge to God and god man, and token of an unstable and dissolute herte; as aȝeinwarde silence is a grete vertue, and for grete cause of goodnes ordeyned in religioun . . .[21]

In the Tuesday section, Love suggests that contemplation of the holy family's flight into Egypt should provoke compassion, and expounds various points from this including the need for patience and humility, and an understanding that persecution will be visited on those dear to Christ. These points are marked, as is the summary: 'thou þat sufferest here tribulacioun kepe therinne pacience, and loke not to haue hereof a pryuelege of hym that wolde not take it hymsilfe . . .'.[22] Nothing draws the reader's attention in the next two chapters, but remarks on the highest and hardest degree of perfection, whereby man is content to be 'dispisid and holde as foule vnworthy and abiecte', are noted in chapter 13; here the need for meekness is again stressed.[23] In the following chapter, which focusses on Christ's baptism, Love outlines three degrees of meekness and this is again the aspect that is marked in the manuscript. The concept of withdrawing from the world is taken up in the first chapter of the Wednesday section. Love includes here a long quotation from Bernard about how to achieve solitude of spirit, and almost all of this passage is marked for

---

[21] f. 21ʳ, Sargent (ed.), *Nicholas Love*, p. 43, lines 10–18.
[22] f. 27ʳ; Tuesday, chapter 10, Sargent (ed.), *Nicholas Love*, p. 53, lines 12–14.
[23] f. 33ʳ and f. 34ʳ; Sargent (ed.), *Nicholas Love*, p. 62, lines 6–8 and 10–17, and p. 63, lines 23–24.

special attention. A little later in this chapter, a long passage about eating and drinking has also been marked, as are the chapter's closing lines which advise a general meditation on Christ and his actions.[24] The need for patience is noted again in chapter 17, and points relating to poverty are marked in chapter 18 and the short chapter 19 (all of which is marked). These notions – meekness, patience in the face of adversity, and an eschewing of riches – are ones that this reader has consistently picked out throughout the preceding parts of the text. In the Wednesday section some other important aspects of Christian devotion are introduced, namely prayer, belief, and confession, and these chapters are the most heavily marked of all sections. In chapter 18 Love's counsel against private prayers 'for special mede' is particularly noted, and the long section that relates to the Pater Noster, the 'moste beste and effectuele praiere', is almost all marked out for attention (see Figure 11).[25] Two points about the power of true faith are marked in the short chapters 20 and 21: one relates to the vicarious redemption of baptised children through their godfathers' faith, and the other relates to healing. In chapter 22 the emphasis is on confession. The sections which tell the story of Mary Magdalene's conversion are marked, as are her own words of confession. A few other comments are picked out in the first part of this chapter, and then the whole of the later part concerning charity, confession, penance, and contrition is marked for attention.[26]

The same light brown ink used in these vertical lines has also occasionally been used to make other additions. One such is the faint *nota* written in the left margin of f. 8ᵛ, alongside a marked passage about the nature of the Trinity that emphasizes the meaning of Christ's incarnation: 'that the secunde person in trinite goddis sone of heuene came in to erþe'.[27] Another occurs in the left margin of f. 52ᵛ, alongside the text: 'we haue ensaumple & techinge what tyme we bene tempted to justifiynge of oure selfe'.[28] Similarly a small sign that resembles a lower-case 'a' (perhaps a late medieval form of the paragraphus serving here as a *nota* mark) occasionally occurs in conjunction with marked passages, as on f. 16ʳ alongside: 'if we wolde haue besily in mynde howe þat hiʒe

---

[24] ff. 38ʳ⁻ᵛ, 41ʳ, and 42ʳ; Sargent (ed.), *Nicholas Love*, p. 70, lines 17–18, 24–37, 40–42, p. 71, lines 1–3, p. 74, lines 19–30; and p. 76, lines 7–18.
[25] f. 47ʳ⁻ᵛ and 48ʳ; Sargent (ed.), *Nicholas Love*, p. 84, lines 32–40, p. 85, lines 2–41.
[26] See especially ff. 50ᵛ–52ʳ where almost all of the text has been marked for attention.
[27] Monday, chapter 3; see Sargent (ed.), *Nicholas Love*, p. 23, line 41.
[28] Wednesday, chapter 22; see Sargent (ed.), *Nicholas Love*, p. 93, line 37.

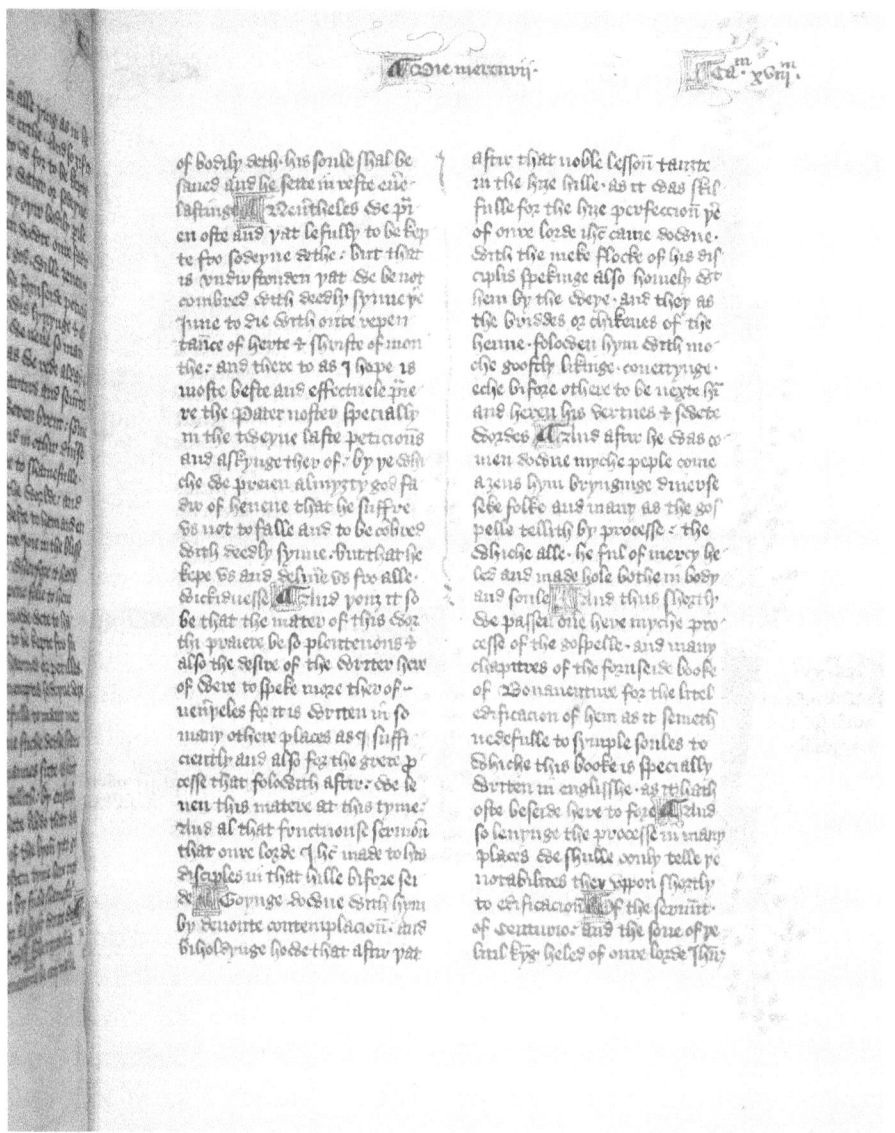

Figure 11 Manchester, John Rylands Library, MS English 98, f. 48ʳ. Nicholas Love, *Mirror of the Blessed Life of Jesus Christ*; marginal marks in the section that discusses the Pater Noster. Copyright of The University of Manchester, reproduced with permission.

lorde of so grete mageste so moche lowede hymselfe', and on f. 18ᵛ by 'Woo to ȝou riche men þat haue ȝoure comforte here'.[29] The same light brown ink has

[29] Respectively, Monday, chapter 5, Sargent (ed.), *Nicholas Love*, p. 35, lines 40–42, and chapter 6, Sargent (ed.), *Nicholas Love*, p. 39, lines 16–17.

been used on f. 10ʳ to mark the text 'þou shalt conceyue sa thi maidenhoode' with double forward slashes in the right margin, and on f. 33ʳ to underline the words 'and al þat we done as nouȝt to acounte'.³⁰ However, after the Wednesday section of the text all of these light brown annotations peter out; the Thursday section has some other marks, as noted above, but none of this style, and the remainder of the text has no annotations at all.³¹ It is impossible to say for certain that this series of marks was *not* made by a member of the Roberts family, but this discreet style of annotation is not apparent in any of their other books where additions tend to be made more overtly, disrupting the appearance of the original text in a way that does not happen here, and often accompanied by translations or transliterations of unfamiliar words.

It is possible that these annotations were made by another, earlier reader of the text. JRL English 98 was made in the early fifteenth century; the manuscript was therefore at least fifty years older than Thomas Roberts, but there are no indications of who might have owned it before him.³² This is largely because of damage to the beginning of the volume where the opening gathering of eight now lacks its first and second leaves, meaning that the most likely location for any statements of ownership or commission is now absent. This also means that the 'Attende' note is missing, and the text begins mid-way through the Proem, on what is now f. 1ʳ; this leaf is very dirty, and is scarred by a tear which has been mended.³³ The *Mirror* is the only work in the manuscript. It concludes with the 'Treatise on the Sacrament' and the Memorandum, with three further leaves that were originally blank; in total the manuscript consists of 140 folios. It is comparatively large, measuring 304 mm x 204 mm, with generous margins; the written space is 188 mm x 130 mm, and the text is laid out in two columns of thirty-five lines each. These aspects indicate that this parchment copy of Love's *Mirror* was designed as an expensive product. It is certainly the most splendid of the surviving books from the Robertses' library, and its attractive appearance may have encouraged more careful handling, deterring readers from adding

---

³⁰ Respectively, Monday, chapter 3, Sargent (ed.), *Nicholas Love*, p. 26, lines 3–4, and Tuesday, chapter 13, Sargent (ed.), *Nicholas Love*, p. 62, lines 19–20.

³¹ An exception is the red pencil mark in the right margin of f. 69ʳ, drawing attention to the citation of Walter Hilton in the text, Sargent (ed.), *Nicholas Love*, p. 122.

³² For descriptions of the manuscript see Tyson, 'Handlist', pp. 152–219; Ker, *MMBL*, iii.416; and Sargent (ed.), *Nicholas Love*, intro pp. 118–19. A full digital facsimile of the manuscript is available at: http://luna.manchester.ac.uk/luna/servlet/s/719p99.

³³ The text begins at the equivalent point to Sargent (ed.), *Nicholas Love*, p. 10, line 2 '& euery'.

conspicuous marginal annotations. In fact the manuscript now appears rather less splendid than it would have originally seemed. In common with several other copies of the text produced during the first quarter of the fifteenth century, JRL English 98 has rich decoration with a sequence of illuminated borders designed to distinguish the major divisions of the text. Only three of these illuminated borders now survive: on f. 26^r a bracket or three-quarters border marks the opening of the Tuesday section; on f. 37^v a column border (between the two columns of text) marks the opening of the Wednesday section; and on f. 56^r a bracket border marks the opening of the Thursday section.[34] At least three further illuminated borders were originally present: traces of similar bracket borders on leaves that are now missing from the volume may be detected as imprints or offsets on adjacent surviving leaves.[35] The first instance of this is perceptible on what is now f. 1^r, where the right margin shows faint signs of being pressed against the verso of a preceding (now missing) leaf which had decoration in its left margin; this missing border would have marked the opening of the Proem section of the text. Similarly, the missing leaf which stood between what are now ff. 90^v and 91^r had an illuminated bracket border on its verso to mark the opening of the Friday section, as may be surmised from the faint impression of this missing border in the right margin of f. 91^r.[36] Finally, where a leaf has been cut out between ff. 126^v and 127^r, it is clear from the faint imprint of decoration on the right margin of f. 127^r that the verso of the missing leaf had an illuminated bracket border which in this case marked the beginning of the 'Treatise of the Sacrament'.[37] Individual chapters begin with illuminated initial capitals that are three lines high, on a ground of blue and pink with white decoration and with sprays that extend up and down the margin, elaborated with green leaves and gold balls. An incomplete example may be seen on f. 76^v where the gold has been supplied

---

[34] Sargent (ed.), *Nicholas Love*, p. 100 gives a reproduction of f. 56^r (Plate 8).

[35] An example where this type of impression may be seen alongside its cause is present on ff. 2^v–3^r where the decorated capital 'A' and its tracery on f. 3^r has left an offset on f. 2^v.

[36] f. 90^v ends before the close of the Thursday section in chapter 39, 'And so whoso hath grace inwardly … ', corresponding to Sargent (ed.), *Nicholas Love*, p. 156, line 5; f. 91^r begins ' … the fairest the wisest and the most rightwys', corresponding to Sargent (ed.), *Nicholas Love*, p. 159, line 25, that is, in the third paragraph of the Friday section (chapter 40).

[37] f. 126^v ends ' … dide the comynge of þe holy … ', corresponding to Sargent (ed.), *Nicholas Love*, p. 219, line 32, that is mid-way through chapter 63; f. 127^r begins ' … haue mynde of we conceyuen in spirite … ', corresponding to Sargent (ed.), *Nicholas Love*, p. 224, line 1.

to a capital 'A', but no background colour has then been added. Paraphs are mostly in blue (sometimes gold) with decorative red penwork. Marginal notes are in red, and are distinguished by gold paraphs with blue decorative penwork tracery. Running headers are set above the central margin and are in red with gold paraphs and blue penwork; chapter numbers are also set as headers, at the top right corner of each page, and are in red with blue paraphs with red decorative tracery.

This expensive level of decoration places JRL English 98 quite high in the decorative hierarchy of later medieval English books. Kathleen Scott's survey of the decorated manuscripts of Love's *Mirror* ranks those with a sequence of borders in third place, below those with miniatures and those which have an initial decorated with the Holy Name monogram, but above those which have only one or two borders at the front of the text.[38] She finds that over one-fifth of all the surviving complete or originally complete copies of Love's *Mirror* had a sequence of borders, a level of decoration which she takes as evidence of more serious intervention by a patron, rather than indicative of normal shop design. Such patronage would seem to have been beyond the means of the Roberts family in the 1420s, the period to which Scott dates the production of JRL English 98. Although by the second half of the sixteenth century the Robertses were amongst the most substantial landowners in Middlesex, their fortunes had advanced only relatively recently, and previous generations could best be described as prosperous rather than wealthy. The loss of leaves at the start of the manuscript means that we cannot be wholly certain that the Roberts family did not instigate the production of JRL English 98, but it would seem more likely that their association with this deluxe volume came about at a later stage in its history. As well as all the usual ways of acquiring books – by purchase or commission, as hand-me-downs within the family, and as personal bequests from friends and colleagues – we must consider that in the 1530s some of the Roberts family's books might have originated from monastic libraries.

AUGMENTATIONS

As a lawyer and as a member of the Middlesex gentry, Thomas Roberts was naturally involved in the administration of local justice and in matters of secular government at county level. These roles would have provided him

---

[38] Scott, 'The Illustration and Decoration of Manuscripts', pp. 61–86.

with additional sources of income, supplementing his income from property and from his legal practice. He drew further income from his role as a steward for two religious houses. He was employed by the Augustinian canons of St Bartholomew's Priory in London to collect rents from their manor of Stanmore Parva (Stanmore the Less, or Little Stanmore, now called Whitchurch).[39] The priory had been endowed with lands in Stanmore Parva by Roger de Ramis shortly after its foundation in the twelfth century, and this original gift was augmented by several subsequent ones including some large grants during the fourteenth century; eventually the priory's holdings in Little Stanmore amounted to 957.5 acres, making this the largest of all its properties. In 1535 the total value of the property, including woods and perquisites, was £84 16s 11d; six years later, in 1541, this had risen to £97 19s 4d.[40] For managing the priory's property interests in Stanmore Parva, Thomas Roberts was paid an annual fee of £1.[41] He was employed in a similar capacity by the nuns of Kilburn Priory, a small house of Augustinian canonesses, or possibly Benedictine nuns, which was dependent on the abbey of St Peter at Westminster.[42] Amongst the nuns' holdings in Middlesex, which brought them an annual revenue of £11 10s in 1535, were properties in Oakington (Tokyngton in Harrow) that had been given to the priory by Ralph Tokyngton in 1246–47, and in Wembley; these were managed by Thomas Roberts, for which he received an annual stipend of 6s 8d.[43] Through his role as steward Thomas Roberts would have known key figures in each location, such as the rector and bailiff of Stanmore Parva (in 1535 these were John Deane and Henry Downer, respectively), and the auditor John Burgoyne (probably the same as John Bugon, with whom Thomas served on the Tenths of Spiritualities Commission in 1535).[44] At St Bartholomew's Priory he would have known the receiver well, and he would have also probably encountered the men who were stewards of properties in other areas. At Kilburn Thomas's main dealings would have been with the treasuress, whose name we do not know, but because this was a small house he was likely to have had contact with the prioress herself. Until 1528 (from at least 1525, and

---

[39] Webb, *The Records of St Bartholomew's Priory*, i.383.
[40] Webb, *The Records of St Bartholomew's Priory*, i.348–53 and 378–84.
[41] *Valor Ecclesiasticus Henry VIII*, i.408. The range of duties undertaken by lay administrators is outlined by Savine, *English Monasteries*, pp. 252–53.
[42] For a description see *VCH Middlesex* i.178–82.
[43] *Valor Ecclesiasticus Henry VIII*, i.432.
[44] Webb, *The Records of St Bartholomew's Priory*, i.383.

probably before this date), the prioress was Sybil Kirke; after she moved to become prioress at Stratford-at-Bow, the prioress of Kilburn was Anne Browne.[45] Thomas Roberts refers to a William Browne – 'my brother' (i.e., brother-in-law) – in his will, so it is possible that Anne Browne was a relative by marriage. Anne Browne was still the prioress at the time that Kilburn was dissolved, and she received a pension of £10, whilst at Stratford-at-Bow Sybil Kirke's pension was £15.[46]

With the demise of the monastic houses the role of steward disappeared, and with it a valuable source of personal income. Kilburn was one of the smaller houses, and accordingly it was suppressed in 1536; St Bartholomew's was dissolved in 1539.[47] Like other men who had fulfilled similar roles and who now suffered financial losses, Thomas Roberts received compensations, though it is difficult to find direct evidence of any grants of property or land.[48] It seems likely that he would have acquired those of the priory's lands at Stanmore Parva that were later granted in fee to Hugh Loss, esquire, because the grant of 1546 to Loss mentions 'all lands of Thos. Roberts'; Loss later served as justice of the peace for Middlesex alongside Thomas's son Edmund.[49] Thomas might have acquired lands and properties in Oakington or Wembley, and the manor of Fosters in Acton which he bequeathed to his youngest son John may originally have been a holding of the priory.[50] The site of Kilburn priory itself was first acquired by the Knights of St John, and afterwards in 1546 by the earl of Warwick.[51] However, direct grants of land or property were not the only ways in which the dissolution of the monastic houses benefitted the laity. Henry VIII's commissioners recorded movable property and its value, particularly the silver and plate and the fabric furnishings of the churches. The most costly and

---

[45] See Smith and London, *The Heads of Religious Houses*, pp. 659 and 695.

[46] For the prioresses' pensions see *LPFD Henry VIII*, 13.i.574 (30 Henry VIII, no. 1520).

[47] For the dissolution of Kilburn see *LPFD Henry VIII*, 10.515 (28 Henry VIII, no. 1238), and *LPFD Henry VIII*, 13.ii.503 (30 Henry VIII, no. 1196); for St Bartholomew's see Webb, *The Records of St Bartholomew's Priory*, i.253.

[48] For example, the lawyer Richard Bellamy was among the annuitants of St Helen's, Bishopsgate (noted by Paxton, 'The Nunneries of London', p. 288).

[49] In 1555, see Chapter 2, section titled 'On Commission: Thomas Roberts and his Associates'; for the grant to Loss see *LPFD Henry VIII*, 21.2.162 (38 Henry VIII, no. 332: 61).

[50] The manor of Acton, with its lands, rents, and services, is listed amongst the former holdings of St Bartholomew's Priory, see *List of the Lands of Dissolved Religious Houses*, ii.178.

[51] See *VCH Middlesex*, p. 181. Park, *The Topography and Natural History of Hampstead*, lists some subsequent owners and traces its descent through marriage into the hands of the Roberts family in the seventeenth century.

valuable items were removed for the king's use or disposition, and processed through the newly established Court of Augmentations, but as the dissolution gathered pace this process must have become increasingly selective with many movable items judged not worth the costs of transportation. Local administrative officials such as Thomas Roberts were ideally placed to receive such items, whether directly, as a reward for service or as a form of compensation for the loss of future earnings, or more indirectly when goods and chattels were sold off in situ.

Amongst the flood of monastic goods and chattels flowing out of the cloister and onto the secular market in the late 1530s were large numbers of books, especially service books, which were apparently little valued as royal spoils. These books met a variety of fates: some were taken away by departing religious, and many were acquired as part and parcel of the properties by their post-dissolution owners; unwanted books were then disposed of in various ways: some were sold as reading books, others simply as scrap paper.[52] Thomas Roberts certainly found himself in the right place at the right time to encounter and acquire books of such provenance, particularly at the smaller house of Kilburn where he had greater authority. Although we cannot link any of the Roberts family books with either of the two monastic houses where he was steward, the number of surviving volumes in each case is so small that we may be sure that we are seeing merely a fragment of the whole picture. St Bartholomew's Priory, where the scribe John Cok (*c.* 1392–1468) worked, must have possessed an extensive library, but Ker records a total of only nine surviving books: eight manuscripts and one printed volume.[53] One of the surviving manuscripts is the priory's foundation book; others are collections of theological writings, a bible, and a copy of the *Brut* in English. For Kilburn Ker lists nothing, and all that is known of its library comes from some remarks preserved in the inventories of Henry VIII's commissioners. At Kilburn they found two copies of *Legenda Aurea* in English, one a manuscript and one a printed book.[54] They also recorded 'two masbookes, one old writen, the oder in print, at xx d. . . . four processions in parchement, iiij s. and paper, x d. . . . two

---

[52] See the accounts given by Carley, 'The dispersal of the monastic libraries', and *The Libraries of King Henry VIII*, pp. xlii–xliii; and also essays included in Carley (ed.), *The Library on the Post-Dissolution Wandering of Books*.

[53] Ker, *Medieval Libraries of Great Britain*, p. 123 and Watson, *Supplement*, p. 47.

[54] Caxton's English translation of the *Legenda Aurea*, *c.* 1483, was subsequently printed by Wynkyn de Worde and Julian Notary, in a total of ten editions before 1530, see *IPMEP* 682.

Legendes, viij d, the one in parchement, and thoder in paper... two chestes with diverse bookes perteininge to the chirche, bookes of no value.'[55]

There is no direct proof that any of the books in the Roberts family library came from monastic houses, since none of the surviving volumes bears any monastic ex-libris or inscriptions that can be traced to members of religious orders. But it is certainly the case that several of their books were pre-owned. Some may have come into the family's hands through marriage, or via bequests, as in the case of the bible and 'ij portuous' (portable breviaries) willed to Thomas Roberts by fellow lawyer Humfrey Adam in 1507.[56] It would also be normal for older books to be handed down through successive generations of the family, and we can observe this practice continuing as Edmund Roberts inherited some of his father's books. There are various signs, however, that at least some of the Roberts family books were newly acquired in the late 1530s and early 1540s, and that these had probably come from sources outwith the family circle. Most tellingly, the repeated appearance of lists of the birth dates of Thomas Roberts's children in some of his books suggests that these were volumes that had *not* belonged to earlier generations of the family. In these lists the names of Thomas's own parents and any siblings are not included, and the records are inscribed en bloc rather than piecemeal, indicating their addition at a single point in time rather than as an ongoing narrative of family history.

In JRL English 98 the addition of the list of Thomas Roberts's children on f. 137^v is one indication that the book might have been a recent acquisition in the sixteenth century (see Figure 12).[57] Another such indication is the presence of the semi-monogrammatic 'Robertʒ' inscription in red ink in each of its decorated borders: on f. 26^r (Tuesday) 'Robertʒ' has been added to the bottom margin of the border, the last letter now appearing indistinctly because it has been written over a pinkish brown leaf; on f. 37^v (Wednesday) 'Robertʒ' has been added to the bottom border beneath the second column of text, with the 'R' and 'o' superimposed on each other; on f. 56^r (Thursday) 'Robtʒ' has been added to the bottom border beneath the first column of text. All three instances

---

[55] Dugdale, *Monasticon*, iii.425.
[56] See the discussion of Humphrey Adam's will in Chapter 1 above, section titled 'Father and Son: John Roberts (d. 1476) and Thomas Roberts (1470–1542)'; note also Thomas Jakes's bequest of a book to Thomas Roberts in 1513, discussed in Chapter 2 above, section titled 'A Lawyer's Book: British Library, MS Harley 1859.'
[57] See further discussion of this list in the following section of the present chapter.

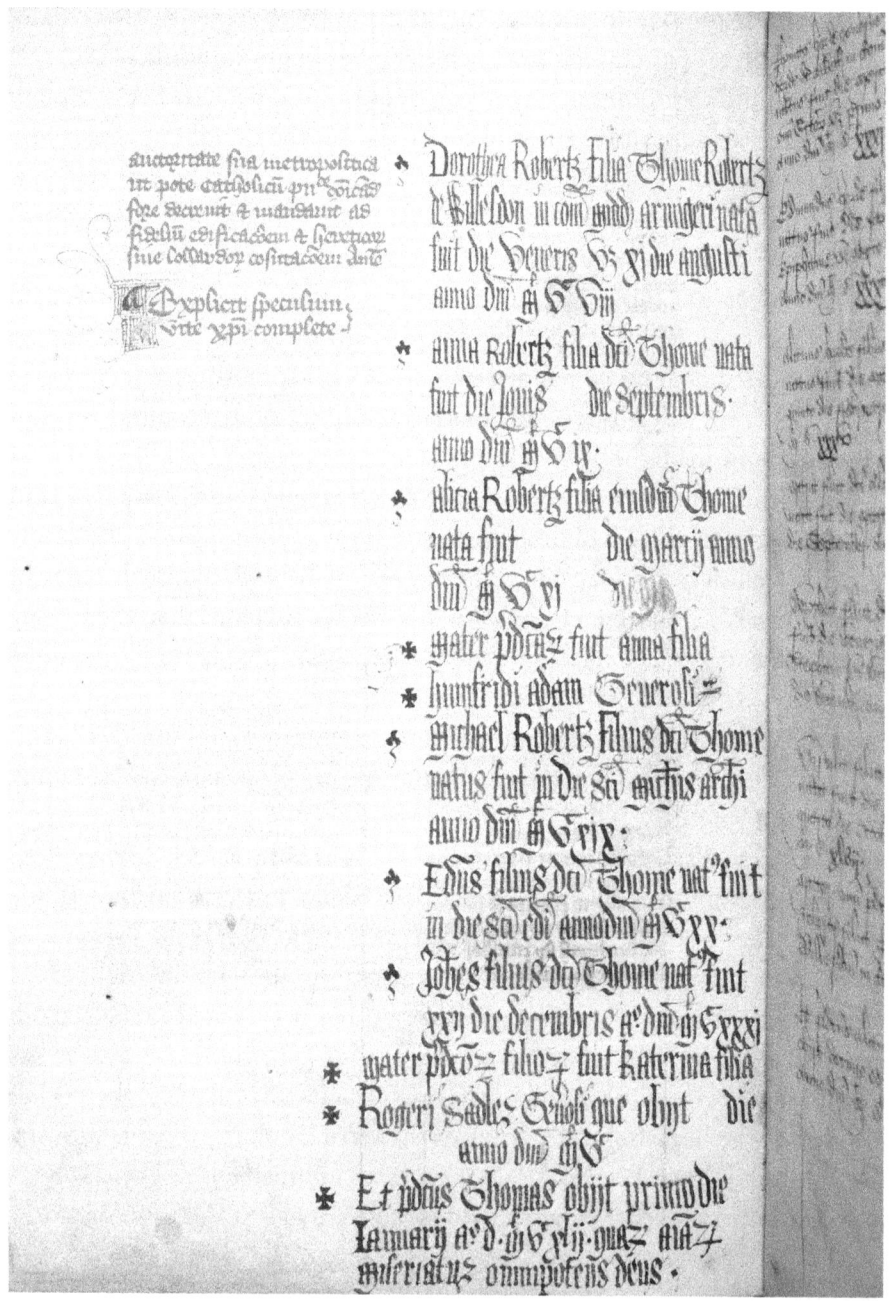

Figure 12 Manchester, John Rylands Library, MS English 98, f. 137ᵛ. Birth records of Thomas Roberts's children, and note of his death. Copyright of The University of Manchester, reproduced with permission.

are clearly additions, but each has been carefully worked in so as to cause minimal disruption to the decorative scheme. One further such addition of the monogram occurs on f. 3ʳ, at the start of the first chapter of the text and the opening of the Monday section. Here the marginal marker beside the second column of text, an abbreviated *Capitulum primum*, in red with a blue paraph, has the addition of 'Robertȝ' above and *die lun* below, in a slightly darker red, less carefully written.

The motivations for adding this device so frequently can only be guessed at. As well as the obvious declaration of present ownership which these marks convey, there may also have been an intention to deceive. The careful placement of the 'Robertȝ' monogram within rather than below the decorated borders mimics the presence of heraldic shields or other identifiers which were used in such locations to proclaim commission and ownership, and might be intended to give the impression that the book had been prepared for an earlier generation of the family. The underlying motivation for this could arise from simple personal pride, or from a desire to consolidate the present standing of the Roberts family (whose wealth and status were increasing in the sixteenth century), by exaggerating the position of their fifteenth-century forebears. A more straightforward motivation might have been security, and it is perhaps significant that the 'Robertȝ' monogram usually appears on decorated leaves.[58] We have no way of knowing when the missing leaves were taken from the manuscript, and although there is a tendency to assume that such mutilations occurred later, as a result of the unscrupulous practices of eighteenth- and nineteenth-century collectors of miniatures and illuminated initials, it is at least possible that the leaves were already missing when Thomas Roberts acquired the book, and that he added his monogram to the surviving three leaves with decorated borders to guard against further thefts. Alternatively Thomas might even have removed leaves from the manuscript himself. The missing leaves seem only to have contained text with decorated borders and not miniatures, as was the case in a few manuscripts of Love's *Mirror*, so the reason for their removal cannot be attributed to a desire to use holy images more directly in personal devotions or in public display.[59] Aside from accidental loss, surely the only reason for Thomas to inflict such damage on his own book

---

[58] The exception is f. 3ʳ, which does not have a decorated border, though the monogram is placed alongside a decorated capital.

[59] Scott, 'The Illustration and Decoration', pp. 63–67, notes that two copies contain miniatures, Edinburgh, National Library of Scotland, Advocates' MS 18.1.7 and New York,

would be in order to remove traces of the volume's provenance, and to deflect any accusations that he had come by it in some unscrupulous manner.

The textual contents of this and other of the Robertses' religious manuscripts are also suggestive of monastic origins, at least in terms of their original commission and production. The *Mirror* was a Carthusian product, written by Nicholas Love, prior of Mount Grace in Yorkshire, and one copy, CUL, MS Additional 6578, has a colophon which identifies it as the property of that house. Another, Glasgow University Library, MS Hunter 77 (T.3.15), has a note that it was copied by Stephen Dodesham at Sheen in 1474–75. Dodesham was also responsible for making two other copies of the text, though it should be remembered that he was a professional scribe before joining the order.[60] Three other manuscripts of the *Mirror* have been assumed to be of Carthusian origins on account of also containing Adam of Dryburgh's *De Instructione Anime*.[61] The evidence for the production of JRL English 98 is not at all clear. Whilst there has been some suggestion that the language shows characteristics of the South West Midlands, Kathleen Scott's analysis of the volume's decorative scheme indicates that it was illuminated in a metropolitan context.[62] Of course, the book might have been copied at a provincial location and then sent to London for decoration. Recently, however, Linne Mooney has tentatively identified the hand which copied JRL English 98 as that of the 'Selden Scribe', a metropolitan copyist who was responsible for a number of other manuscripts containing material by Lydgate (three copies of the *Troy Book*) and Hoccleve (two copies of the

---

Pierpont Morgan Library, MS M 648, and that CUL, MS Oo.7.45(i), which is a fragment of only five leaves, has spaces for miniatures which were never supplied.

[60] Oxford, BodL, MS Rawlinson A. 387B and Cambridge, Trinity College, MS B.15.16.

[61] These are Glasgow University Library, MS General 1130; Leeds Catholic Diocesan Archives, *Mirror* MS, and Yale University, Beinecke MS 535 (*olim* Colin Franklin); see Sargent, 'The Transmission by the English Carthusians', pp. 230–31, and Sargent (ed.), *Nicholas Love*, pp. intro 89–90.

[62] The manuscript was not assessed for *LALME*, but Malcolm Parkes comments that the manuscript was 'copied apparently in the South-West Midlands', see 'Punctuation in Copies', p. 57 note 31. Parkes was citing 'four slightly later copies of the β version of the text, whose dialect features indicate that they were copied in the Southern Province ... ' – the other manuscripts noted here are Princeton University Library, MS Kane 21; Yale University, Beinecke MS 324, copied apparently in the metropolitan area; and CUL, MS Ll.4.3. Scott, 'The Illustration and Decoration', p. 75, concludes that almost all the extant illuminated copies of the *Mirror* were decorated in London.

Regiment of Princes).⁶³ If this identification holds, then the balance of probability would seem to be that JRL English 98 was both copied and illuminated in London. The Selden scribe's profile of predominantly secular copying would seem to preclude a Carthusian identity, but in fact, as is apparent from the oeuvre of Stephen Dodesham, who was a commercial scribe before entering the order, scribes might have long and varied careers.⁶⁴ Similarly, a metropolitan provenance need not mean that the book did not travel since the Carthusians in particular were well known for their habit of lending books between different houses.⁶⁵ Although this text was approved by Archbishop Arundel and deemed suitable for the 'edification of the faithful and the confutation of heretics or lollards' (*ad fidelium edificacionem, & hereticorum siue lollardorum confutacionem*), it did not just circulate amongst a lay audience.⁶⁶ Evidence from wills shows that copies were given to nuns, and in the early sixteenth century one copy was owned by a priest, John Langrige.⁶⁷ The copy that was owned by Sibille de Felton, abbess of the Benedictine abbey of Barking in the first quarter of the fifteenth century, was still at the house at the time of the dissolution when it was in the hands of Margaret Scrope. When the abbey was suppressed, Margaret moved to the household of her sister, Lady Elizabeth Peche, and subsequently passed the book to one of her gentlewomen, Agnes Goldwell.⁶⁸ Another copy that may have moved from monastic to lay ownership at the same point is Takamiya MS 20, which has inscriptions of two women's names preceded by the honorific 'Domine', suggesting religious profession. This copy was owned by Sir John Gage of Firle Place in Sussex, who was a prominent courtier under Henry VIII and Mary Tudor, and who may have obtained the book at the dissolution.⁶⁹

---

⁶³ Linne Mooney and A. I. Doyle have identified five other manuscripts by this scribe: Oxford, BodL, MS Selden Supra 53; BodL, MS Rawlinson C. 446; BodL, MS Digby 230; Cambridge, Queen's College MS 12; and Bristol, Public Library, MS 8, see Mooney, 'A Scribe of Lydgate's *Troy Book*'.

⁶⁴ On Dodesham see Doyle 'Stephen Dodesham'.

⁶⁵ Several loan lists survive, see Doyle (ed.), *The Libraries of the Carthusians*.

⁶⁶ Sargent (ed.), *Nicholas Love*, p. 7.

⁶⁷ References given in Meale ' "oft siþis with grete deuotion" ', pp. 30–31, and p. 26, and Sargent (ed.), *Nicholas Love*, intro p. 134.

⁶⁸ References given in Meale, ' "oft siþis with grete deuotion" ', p. 34, and Sargent (ed.), *Nicholas Love*, intro p. 127.

⁶⁹ References given in Meale, ' "oft siþis with grete deuotion" ', pp. 28–29, and Sargent (ed.), *Nicholas Love*, intro pp. 126–28.

Two other volumes of English devotional prose in the Roberts library also have indications of early connections with monastic environments. In MS Harvard Richardson 22 the presence of the names 'Fyncham', in black ink, and 'Robertz', in red, written by different hands but placed closely together at the top of the front flyleaf, would seem to signify that this volume had belonged to the family of Thomas Roberts's first wife, Margaret Fyncham (or to Margaret herself), and that it came into the Robertses' library at the time of their marriage or perhaps when her father, Robert Fyncham, died.[70] The manuscript itself was much older than both Thomas and Margaret, having been produced in the first quarter of the fifteenth century, and so it must either have been handed down within the Fyncham family or acquired by them from earlier owners. As demonstrated in the previous chapter, this is a devotional anthology whose texts, a mixture of prose and verse, offered suitable religious instruction for readers with some measure of education. The volume's limited use of Latin – there is only one item written in Latin which is the prayer on ff. 69–71^v, and Latin is occasionally used in the rubrics – and the elementary level of religious instruction offered by its texts, mean that it would have been equally appropriate reading for members either of a lay household or of a community of nuns. Its first text, the Middle English translation of the pseudo-Augustinian *Soliloquiorum animae ad deum*, is addressed to an audience of sisters. The translator explains that he has prepared his work for this audience: 'Myne sustris for wham I haue to the worschip of God labowrid to englysch these meditaciouns...', and later indicates that the work was undertaken at their request: 'Thankyd be almyhti God, my gode sustren, I haue now parformyd ȝour desyre in englysshinge þese meditaciouns and confessions of Seint Austyn...'.[71] The text is acephalous, beginning in chapter four, due to the loss of leaves (probably an entire quire) from the beginning of the manuscript, which means that, as with JRL English 98, the most obvious place to find further information about the circumstances of its commission, translator, and original audience is also lacking. The only other extant copy of this English translation of the *Soliloquies* is directed towards a less specific readership, and its prologue has been constructed by combining material from Anselm's *Prayers*

---

[70] See discussion in Chapter 1, section titled 'Father and Son: John Roberts (d. 1476) and Thomas Roberts (1470–1542)'. De Ricci, *Census*, i.961 recorded the inscription as 'Robert Fyncham (?)' which has invited some fruitless searching for a single owner of that name.

[71] f. 30^v and f. 51^v, respectively. Sturges, 'Anti-Wycliffite Commentary', discusses the translation's intended audience.

and Meditations with sections from the epilogue to the text in MS Harvard Richardson 22.⁷²

The contents of the other English devotional anthology in the Roberts family library, BodL, MS Rawlinson C. 894, are more strongly indicative of monastic origins. The extract from Walter Hilton's *On the Mixed Life* in this volume begins unusually with a plural address to 'Breþerne and systerne' (as opposed to the usual 'broþer and syster').⁷³ Another text, 'The Twelve Degrees of Meekness', addresses itself several times to a 'brother', and the short text 'A good contemplacion for a prest or he go to masse' clearly envisages a clerical audience, though not necessarily an enclosed one.⁷⁴ The final text in BodL, MS Rawlinson C. 894, 'A lytil tretise ayence fleischly affeccyoneȝ & alle vnþrifti loves' addresses itself specifically to an audience of female religious, whilst acknowledging that a wider readership will find its contents beneficial.⁷⁵ The texts in this anthology closely duplicate those in BL, Royal 17 C. XVIII, leading to suggestions that both may have originally been prepared for a double religious community such as Syon.⁷⁶

Syon, the most prestigious Middlesex house, and one very much associated with learning, is the most obvious location for the production of such manuscripts, and must certainly be considered as a potential origin of books that were later absorbed into the Roberts family library. Syon was not too remote from the family's land holdings and sphere of interests, and at least one of Thomas's close acquaintances, John Newdigate, serjeant at law (d. 1528), had a daughter, Mary, who was enclosed there; another daughter, Joanna Newdigate, who married Robert Dormer of Ascott, was a notable benefactor of Syon.⁷⁷ Furthermore, Thomas Roberts's grand-daughter, Ursula Horde (1547–98),

---

⁷² The other version is found in BL, MS Cotton Titus C. XIX, ff. 3ʳ–92ʳ. For an edition of its prologue see Wogan-Browne et al., *The Idea of the Vernacular*, pp. 224–26.

⁷³ Six copies of this longer version are known, see Lagorio and Sargent, 'English Mystical Writings', pp. 3433–35. For further discussion of the manuscript's contents see Chapter 6, section titled 'Þou shalt moch profett in redyng: What Edmund Read'.

⁷⁴ Doyle, 'A Survey', ii.215, mistakenly records this copy of the 'Twelve Degrees' as addressed to a nun.

⁷⁵ f. 98ᵛ: 'also specially as it is written to women'; Jones, 'The Compilations of Two Late-Medieval Devotional Manuscripts', p. 88.

⁷⁶ Doyle, 'A Survey', ii.221; Jones, 'The Compilations of Two Late-Medieval Devotional Manuscripts', p. 88. *LALME* locates BodL Rawlinson C. 894 in Middlesex, LP 6480, grid reference 516 183.

⁷⁷ John Newdigate of Harfeld married Amphilis: their eleven children included the heir John; second son Sebastian, the Carthusian martyr who died in 1535; Mary, misrecorded as a

joined the Syon community in exile abroad, eventually becoming its prioress, which could suggest a longstanding connection with the house, though such a connection might equally have stemmed primarily from the influence of the Horde family.[78] During Thomas's own lifetime there is no evidence of any direct link between the Roberts family and Syon, and since there were other monastic communities where the male religious ministered to the female, it is worth reconsidering these as alternative locations for the production of BodL Rawlinson C. 894 and BL Royal 17 C. XVIII. Another example of this double arrangement existed between the Augustinian canons of Holy Trinity Priory in London and the canonesses of Clerkenwell and Halliwell, nunneries that were in the archdeaconry of London.[79] Close associates of Thomas Roberts had family connections with both these nunneries. Sybil Newdigate, another daughter of John Newdigate (d. 1528) and sister of Mary, was a nun at Halliwell and was elected as its last prioress in 1534; the following year a relative, John Newdigate, is recorded as under-steward, and in 1537 Sybil appointed her brother George (*generosus frater mei*) as the chief steward.[80] Elizabeth, daughter of Edward Cheseman, for whom Thomas had stood as executor, was a nun first at Halliwell and then at Kilburn.[81] Kilburn itself had a peculiar position as a priory of nuns dependent on an abbey of monks (St Peter's, Westminster), and this relationship might easily have involved the responsibility for supplying the nuns with books, meaning that it is at least possible that BodL Rawlinson C. 894 and BL Royal 17 C. XVIII might have been produced for there.[82] Thomas Roberts's own association with Kilburn through his role as its steward, and his social connections with families who had daughters enclosed there, also make this house a very feasible source for some of the books that came into his library.

nun at 'Lyon'; and Sybil who was a nun at Halliwell; see Armytage, *Middlesex Pedigrees*, p. 67 and Bainbridge, 'Syon Abbey'.

[78] See the next section of the present chapter.

[79] Further afield in Hertfordshire, a similar arrangement existed between St Albans and the nunneries at Sopwell and Markyate; these possibilities, along with the Minoresses, were all initially mentioned by Doyle, 'A Survey', ii.221, but only the notional connection with Syon has been explored further.

[80] *VCH Middlesex* i.177.

[81] According to Armytage, *Middlesex Pedigrees*, p. 47; Thomas is named in many commissions alongside Elizabeth's brother Robert. The Kilburn pension list is noted in *LPFD Henry VIII*, 13.i.574 (30 Henry VIII, no. 1520), but the calendar only records the name and amount allocated to the prioress.

[82] See *VCH Middlesex* i.178.

But the passage from religious to secular hands seems to have been less direct, or at least less immediate, in the case of BodL Rawlinson C. 894, since Thomas himself does not seem to have owned this book. Its possession by his son suggests that it was in fact Edmund who acquired it from the 'Wylliam harlowye' whose name is inscribed in both this manuscript and its congener.[83] Although the route of acquisition is not quite clear, demonstrable connections between the two families in the next generation make this seem the likeliest possibility. William Harlowe was buried on 3 October 1562 in the church of St Mary the Virgin, Aldermanbury; his daughter Elizabeth was married to Sir Martin Bowes, with whom Edmund had served on at least one public commission.[84] Their son, William Bowes, stood as godfather to William Roberts, son of Francis and grandson of Edmund, in 1595, and William Bowes's wife, of unknown Christian name, had been godmother to an elder sibling, Robert Roberts, a few years earlier; these relationships are noted amongst the extensive family records at the front of the manuscript.[85]

AFTER THE DISSOLUTION: THE HORDES OF EWELL

In JRL English 98 two sets of family records have been added at the back of the book. The first is a list of the children of Thomas Roberts, and the second is a list of the children and grandchildren of his daughter Dorothy. The simplest interpretation of these two sets of family records and the various additions of the Roberts monogram elsewhere in the manuscript is that JRL English 98 was acquired by Thomas Roberts at some point before his death in 1542, and that the book then came into the hands of his eldest daughter. Books were evidently handed down within the family, even though Thomas's will makes no mention of such bequests. Edmund Roberts inherited Thomas's book of hours and his copy of *Registrum Brevium*, and perhaps other books as well, but there are no signs that he ever handled JRL English 98. Thomas was certainly fond of his

---

[83] On f. 106ʳ; and in BL Royal 17 C. XVIII, in the form 'Wylliam horlow' (f. 81ʳ) and 'Harlywes' (f. 118ᵛ).

[84] Bannerman, *The Registers of St Mary the Virgin*, i.22; Jewers, 'Grants and Certificates of Arms', 270. This relationship was first uncovered by Morgan, 'A Critical Edition', i.33. Edmund Roberts and Martin Bowes were both part of the Commission of Sewers, December 1554, *CPR Philip and Mary*, 2 (1554–55), pp. 107–8.

[85] f. viiiʳ.

daughter and her marital family. His will remembered both Dorothy and her husband with gold rings, and his grandchild and godson Thomas Horde with twenty shillings; the lesser sum of six shillings and eight pence was to be given to every other child that Dorothy and Alan had (there were at least two others at the time of Thomas's death).[86] The book was subsequently retained within her marital family, the Hordes of Ewell in Surrey, passing from Dorothy to her second son Edmund (born 1534) and his descendants. This is only one possible interpretation of the book's movements, however, and should not be taken as fact. It is important to remember that the material evidence available to us in JRL English 98 is only partial; the removal of leaves from the beginning of the codex has potentially obscured other signs of ownership or commission which, if still present, might lead us to interpret the later additions to the manuscript rather differently.

The list of Thomas Roberts's children takes up the whole of the originally blank second column on f. 137^v, and was written by a single hand, apparently in a single stint. The script is formal and professional, of the type used for display, and typical of sixteenth-century legal records, but it is evidently not the hand of Thomas Roberts himself: its appearance differs from his usual script and, most tellingly, the final entry records the date of his death, on the first day of January 1542. This entry is marked with a small Maltese-style cross, as are four other names in the list: Thomas's second wife Anna and her father Humphrey Adam, and Thomas's third wife Katherine and her father Roger Sadler. Alongside the names of the six Roberts children is a different symbol, one resembling a trefoil or clover-leaf. These marks seem to be intended as distinctions between births (trefoils) and deaths (crosses), the trefoils perhaps also signifying that those family members so marked were all alive at the time that this list of family records was drawn up. If this interpretation is correct, it would pinpoint the date at which these records were added to between January 1542 when Thomas Roberts died and December 1544 when his heir, his eldest son Michael, also died.

The second run of records, on f. 138^r, gives details of the births of six children between 1531 and 1547 to Dorothy Roberts, Thomas's eldest daughter, and her first husband Alan Horde: the names listed are Thomas, Edmund, Alan, Mary,

---

[86] LMA, DL/C/356, f. 22; see further discussion of Thomas Roberts's will in Chapter 1, section titled 'Father and Sons: Thomas Roberts (1470–1542), Michael Roberts (1519–44), and Edmund Roberts (1520–85)'.

Dorothy, and Ursula. The death of Alan Horde on 16 August 1554 is also recorded, followed by a note of the births of the six children of Edmund Horde (Dorothy's grandchildren by her second son) between 1559 and 1568: these were Dorothy, Arthur, Elizabeth, Anna, Alan, and Edward (see Table 4).[87] These records, which are set out in two columns, mimicking the layout of the volume as a whole, were added at different points, by two different hands. The first hand was responsible for all of the entries in the first column and the first two in the second, that is, for recording all of the births of Dorothy's children and two of her grandchildren. However, only the two entries for the grandchildren were written in fully in the first instance; in all the earlier entries the year dates were originally left blank to be filled in later (this is apparent from differences in the colour of the ink). This suggests that the writer was confident of the information to be recorded in the entries for Dorothy and Arthur, born in 1559 and 1560 respectively, but needed to check the details of the rest – a strong indication that all these entries were made in or near to 1560. The remaining four entries in the second column (recording the births of Elizabeth, Anna, Alan, and the first part of Edward's) were added in one stint by a second, coarser hand using a darker ink. The same darker ink has supplied some of the missing dates in the earlier part of the list, completing the entries for the three sons of Alan Horde and also recording his death date. The final entry in the list, recording the birth of Edward in 1568, was written by this second hand but using two shades of ink; the lighter ink which was used to complete this entry has also been used to supply the year dates for the births of Alan's daughters in the earlier part of the list. Collectively these differences in script and ink suggest that the addition of the Horde family records on f. 138^r was not made until 1560 at least, and also not until the book was in the hands of Dorothy's son Edmund Horde (1534–75) and his children.

Edmund Horde was admitted to the Middle Temple in 1552.[88] A collection of yearbooks from the reign of Edward II, that records various cases and reports from the Common Bench, and which has the name 'Edmond Hord' in a very upright clear secretary hand on a flyleaf, was probably his.[89] Edmund might

---

[87] In the manuscript the year of Alan's death is actually given as 1553, but he made his will in January during the first year of Mary Tudor's reign (regnal year from 19 July 1553 to 5 July 1554) and probate was granted on 24 August 1554.

[88] See the discussion in Chapter 2, section titled 'Thomas Roberts at the Inns of Court'.

[89] BL Harley 1062, f. 1*^{v}. The form of the signature does not match that of his uncle, Edmund Horde, for whose books see below.

have been named for his uncles on either side of the family, his mother's half-brother Edmund Roberts, or his father's brother, Edmund Horde. The latter was probably his godfather, since uniquely amongst Dorothy's children Edmund was favoured with a bequest from this uncle of 'a salte of siluer with a couer'.[90] Edmund was buried with his mother in St Mary's church at Ewell. The position of their brass memorial, in the middle of the chancel, reflects the prominence of the Horde family in this Surrey community (see Figure 13).[91] Alan Horde's property holding there was extended by Edmund's purchase of Fitznell's manor in 1562, and a survey of the parish in 1577 records Elizabeth Horde (probably his widow) as the second largest landowner.[92] The connection with Ewell seems to have been a fairly recent one, however, probably not extending back before Alan's time. The family's main seat and origins were in Shropshire, where they had been pre-eminent landholders in Bridgnorth since the beginning of the fifteenth century. Two manuscripts that might be connected with members of this family are Shrewsbury School, MS 37, a twelfth-century copy of Juvenal's *Satires* inscribed with the name 'Richard Horde' by a fifteenth-century hand, which was given to the school in 1610 by a bookseller based in Bridgnorth; and BL Harley 3432, a copy of the *Orchard of Syon* which has the name 'George Horde' and several place names connected with Shropshire inscribed in its margins.[93] The family's main property, Horde Park, just north of Bridgnorth, was inherited by Thomas Horde, the eldest of five or six sons of John Horde. The other sons included Alan (Dorothy's husband), Edmund (the godfather to Dorothy's son Edmund), Robert, and Richard. There were evidently close connections between the brothers. Edmund and Robert were both named in Alan's will of 1553, and in 1541 Alan had to stand bail for his nephew John, Richard's son, who had been imprisoned for stealing plate from his old school at Eton. This John Horde and his younger

---

[90] Alan Horde's will of 1553 notes this bequest 'whiche my brother Docter Horde gaue hym', see further discussion below.

[91] The memorial was recorded at the visitation of 1634, see Bannerman, *The Visitations of the County of Surrey*, p. 52, and mentioned by Ellis, 'Pedigree of the Family of Hord', p. 39, just before the Victorian rebuilding of the church. Stephenson, *A List of Monumental Brasses in the British Isles*, pp. 486–87, lists the brasses at Ewell, and Stephenson, *A List of Monumental Brasses in Surrey* (1921), pp. 224–39, gives more detail about their relocation to the walls at the western end of the south aisle of the present church. There is a rubbing of Dorothy's brass in BL, MS Additional 32490, vol. LL13 (no. 3278), see www.bl.uk/catalogues/manuscripts.

[92] See *VCH Surrey* iii.278–84.

[93] Ker, *MMBL*, iv.324.

Out of the Cloister, Out of the Family

Figure 13 Tomb brass of Dorothy Horde in St Mary's, Ewell; rubbing, from London, British Library, MS Additional 32490, LL 13. Reproduced by permission. © The British Library Board.

brother Jerome may also have been lawyers; both were returned to parliament for Bridgnorth during Mary Tudor's reign.[94] Members of this extensive family held positions in the Church as well as in the legal profession. Towards the end of the fifteenth century the prioress of Brewood White Ladies, an Augustinian house in Shropshire, was an Elizabeth Horde, doubtless a member of this family.[95] A cousin of Alan Horde and his brothers, Maurice Glynn, was Archdeacon of Bangor in the early sixteenth century.[96] Most significantly, Alan's brother Edmund Horde was a member of the Carthusian order.

In 1529 Edmund Horde succeeded John Batmanson as prior of Hinton Charterhouse in Somerset.[97] A graduate of Oxford and fellow of All Souls, Edmund held various benefices in Oxfordshire and elsewhere which he vacated in 1520 in order to enter the Carthusian order.[98] However, his name does not occur amongst the list of monks at Hinton in 1521, and he was probably professed at another house, most likely London, since he was a proctor in the Court of Arches and was admitted to Doctors Commons in 1516.[99] A will of 1525 describes him as 'proctour of the Charterhouse near London', which probably means the London charterhouse but might conceivably signify Sheen.[100] Edmund Horde was well known and respected in the Carthusian order, and held considerable influence in the years immediately preceding the dissolution. At Hinton the monks assented to the Act of Supremacy and Succession in 1534, though Edmund's reluctant acceptance of Anne Boleyn as rightful queen of England aroused suspicion, making it necessary for him to write personally to the king in September of that year, professing his loyalty.[101] Despite this Edmund found Cromwell's directive that the clergy should preach the doctrine of the royal supremacy difficult to stomach, exposing him to further pressure to conform; Cromwell sent Sir Walter Hungerford to argue with him, after which Edmund wrote to Cromwell in March 1535 professing his obedience and offering his

---

[94] See Bindoff, *The History of Parliament*, ii.390–91.
[95] Smith and London, *The Heads of Religious Houses*, p. 628.
[96] Squibb, *Doctors Commons*, pp. 134–35.
[97] At this time Batmanson was appointed as prior of the London charterhouse, see Smith and London, *The Heads of Religious Houses*, iii.358.
[98] See *BRUO*, ii.961–62.
[99] See Squibb, *Doctors Commons*, p. 135.
[100] TNA, PROB 11/21/564, will of Maurice Glynn, 15 July 1525; he names 'my cosyne dan Edmond Hord' and Alan Hord as his executors.
[101] *LPFD Henry VIII*, 7.444 (26 Henry VIII, no. 1127).

services.¹⁰² In that year the Archbishop of York, Edward Lee, recommended Edmund to Cromwell as an arbitrator in the dispute with the London Carthusians. The London monks had continued to resist demands that they accept the Act of Supremacy and Succession, and some of them had openly expressed a desire to consult 'the prior of Hinton, Dr Howrde'.¹⁰³ Lee advised that Edmund was a figure 'whom all the religioun esteems for virtue and learning. . . . They will give him more credence, and rather apply their conscience to his judgment than to any other, although of greater learning . . .'.¹⁰⁴ More evidence of the respect and good-standing that Edmund enjoyed throughout the order is apparent from a letter sent to Cromwell in the following year from one of his agents who was then at Mount Grace. The writer advised that the northern Carthusians would follow Edmund's directive: 'If a commission were issued to Dr. Horde, one of their religion, and one joined with him, there would be no stop and all of that order in the North parts will be inclinable'.¹⁰⁵ However, it seems that Cromwell distrusted Edmund Horde because he did not choose to employ him.

Hinton's endowments were sufficiently large for the house to be unaffected by the first round of monastic closures in 1536. In January 1539 the king's commissioners John Tregonwell and William Petre arrived at Hinton, having just effected the surrender of Keynsham Abbey, a nearby house of Augustinian canons. As they reported to Cromwell, Edmund Horde resisted strongly, responding: 'thatt if the kinges maiestie wold take his howse so it procedyd nott of his voluntary surrender he was contentyd to obey butt otherwise he sayd his conscience woll nott suffer hym wyllingly to giue ouer the same . . .'; the other brothers were of the same mind, 'iij exceptyd whiche war conformable'.¹⁰⁶ When he learned of his brother's resistance, Alan Horde wrote to Edmund warning him that he risked causing the displeasure of the king and of the Lord Privy Seal, Thomas Cromwell. In response Edmund wrote back on 10 February 1539, promising that he would encourage his brethren to surrender the

---

¹⁰² *LPFD Henry VIII*, 8.158 (26 Henry VIII, no. 402).
¹⁰³ *LPFD Henry VIII*, 8.292 and 8.400 (27 Henry VIII, no. 778 and no. 1011), and 9.13 (27 Henry VIII, no. 49). For a copy of a letter from one of the monks, Andrew Boorde, to Edmund sent in May 1534 see *LPFD Henry VIII*, 7.283 (26 Henry VIII, no. 730); see also Boorde's letter to Cromwell, *LPFD Henry VIII*, 8.355 (27 Henry VIII, no. 901).
¹⁰⁴ Quoted from the calendared entry in *LPFD Henry VIII*, 8.400 (27 Henry VIII, no. 1011).
¹⁰⁵ *LPFD Henry VIII*, 11.37 (28 Henry VIII, no. 75).
¹⁰⁶ *LPFD Henry VIII*, 14.i.54 (30 Henry VIII, no. 145), see SP 1/142 f. 155, viewable through *State Papers Online*.

house. Edmund restates their devotion to their duty to God, and denies any cause that the house should be suppressed; but he also promises: 'I wyll endevere my selffe as muche as I maye to perswade my bretherne to a comfformyte in thys matere' because Alan has written of the displeasure of the king and the Lord Privy Seal, Thomas Cromwell, 'whoo euer hath byn my esspecialle good lorde & I truste yette wyll be'.[107] Seven weeks later, on 31 March 1539, Hinton was surrendered, with the deed signed by Edmund Horde and sixteen others.[108] Edmund Horde was granted a generous annuity of £44 and a cash gift of £11; there is no record of his pension being paid after 1542.[109]

Hinton and all its possessions were divided up, with various local landowners competing for the prize of the house itself. Sir Henry Longe, who had been sheriff of Wiltshire 1536–37, begged Cromwell for help in becoming 'farmer of the house of Henton'.[110] Sir Walter Hungerford, who had been appointed steward of the Hinton lands in 1536, requested that he might have 'in fee farm, for ever, the manors of Henton and Phylyps Norton and demesnes and house of Henton, Longlete, Luttcumsmyll, Greneworth, and Yford'. Hungerford also complained to Cromwell that Thomas Arundel had visited Hinton in his absence and had taken away parts of the church and buildings for which he, Hungerford, had already paid.[111] Aside from its immediate properties, Hinton charterhouse had also held lands in the counties of Somerset, Wiltshire, Dorset, Gloucestershire, as well as elsewhere in England and Wales. Alan Horde's assistance in persuading his brother to surrender the house did not go unrewarded. A grant of 20 September 1540 records that Robert and Alan Horde were given Greneworth grange upon Mendyppe in the parish of Chewton, Somerset (now Chewton Mendip), with two 'sleightes for sheep' there and a sleight called Whytnell, in lieu of a sixty years' lease by Hinton priory.[112] Alan Horde had also acquired other Carthusian property, this time from Sheen: a record of 9 July 1540 notes a grant for £959 5s in fee simple, of the manor of Oune (or Onne), Staffordshire, 'belonging to the late priory of Shene, late in

---

[107] *LPFD Henry VIII*, 14.i.106 (30 Henry VIII, no. 269). Edmund's original letter survives in BL, MS Cotton Cleopatra E. IV, f. 328, viewable through *State Papers Online*.

[108] *LPFD Henry VIII*, 14.i.247 (30 Henry VIII, no. 637). Enrolled as acknowledged, same day, before John Tregonwell, King's commissioner.

[109] *LPFD Henry VIII*, 15.543 (32 Henry VIII, no. 1032: 242); *LPFD Henry VIII*, 17.127 (33 Henry VIII, no. 258), paid to William Horde.

[110] *LPFD Henry VIII*, 14.i.247 (30 Henry VIII, no. 636).

[111] *LPFD Henry VIII*, 14.i.518 (31 Henry VIII, no. 1154).

[112] *LPFD Henry VIII*, 15.557 (32 Henry VIII, no. 1032, grant 78b).

the tenure of dame Anne Hyll, widow, deceased, and now in that of Alan Hord; and all lands etc., in Plardwicke and Westwodd, Staff., which belonged to Shene, late in the tenure of John Blakmare'.[113]

Walter Hungerford's appeal to Cromwell of 24 June 1539 contained another grievance. He reported that during Arundel's survey of Hinton, the back door of the prior's cell was broken down and the contents, which included important documents and charters, disturbed; this he claimed was done by local men, without Arundel's knowledge. Hungerford was concerned at the threat to his own interests, but the vandalism he describes highlights the vulnerability of monastic property during this period. At the dissolution of the Coventry charterhouse, it was found that the prior had tried to preserve some items of movable property, partly by giving them away to different men, and partly by burying them, though his actions were swiftly discovered.[114] Edmund Horde was more successful in concealing what he took away. His brother's will of 25 January 1553 itemized 'a litle chalice of siluer and gilt which is in my studye at Ewell, and a pax of silver and gilt, and a crosse of siluer and gilt with relikes therin, and a lityll roser with relyques, and a vestment with an albe of clothe of baudkyn ...'.[115] These objects had not been transformed into domestic tableware, and were not included amongst the valuable objects bequeathed to family members (each of Alan's sons received a standing cup or ale cup, six silver spoons, and a gold ring). It seems significant that they are mentioned in conjunction with instructions regarding money which had been Edmund's, suggesting that their provenance was also connected with him, that is with Hinton, rather than Alan's own parish church at Ewell; if this was church plate that Alan had saved from confiscation during Edward's reign, he would presumably already have restored it at Mary's accession.[116] The fact that Alan was still administering Edmund's money also indicates that Edmund had not long predeceased him. Confusion has arisen over the date of Edmund Horde's death, with some historians recording that he was part of the Marian restoration at Sheen and that he died in Louvain in 1578. A possible source of this confusion is the wording of David Knowles's description of Edmund's resistance to the surrender of his house and his association with Nicholas Balland,

---

[113] *LPFD Henry VIII*, 15.470 (32 Henry VIII, no. 942, grant 42).
[114] *LPFD Henry VIII*, 14.i.65 (1539), no. 183.
[115] TNA, PROB 11/37/111.
[116] On such confiscations and restorations see Duffy, *The Stripping of the Altars*, pp. 478–503 and 548–50.

who vigorously denied the act of royal supremacy: it was Balland, not Horde, who was part of Maurice Chauncy's revival of the Charterhouse, and who died at Louvain.[117]

The clerical vestments and church plate were very likely to have been items which Edmund Horde had brought away from Hinton at the dissolution. At this time a large amount of monastic property of every kind passed into the possession of the ex-religious and their relatives, and it would not be surprising for Edmund also to have taken books with him.[118] He was clearly of a learned and academic disposition, and would have valued books for their textual contents, not their material cost. In his time at Oxford, and later as a member of the Carthusian order, Edmund must have handled many books. There is little evidence for the size of library collections in the English charterhouses, but A. I. Doyle is sure that the library at London was 'well provided' and notes that the complex pressmarks in the four surviving manuscripts from Hinton indicate 'a sizeable and well organised library by the fifteenth century …', that constituted: 'a collection of at least sixty-seven volumes, and probably several hundred'.[119] It is possible that JRL English 98 might have been one of these books.

Edmund Horde may be connected with two extant manuscripts. The first of these is BL Sloane 2515, a collection of Latin theological texts that comprises three short treatises on mortality – *Ars Moriendi*; *Breuis tractatus de arte moriendi*; and *Sciencia utilissima homini mortali q[.] e[.] scire mori* – and a series of patristic and pseudo-patristic writings including Jerome's *Meditatio*, Ambrose's *De bono mortis*, paraphrases of Gregory's sermons, Honorius Augustodunensis's *De cognitione verae vitae*, and the pseudo-Augustine *De spiritu et anima*.[120] Various blanks and two new runs of quire signatures indicate that the manuscript has been constructed from booklets, and it may be incorrect to think of it as always having comprised a single book. This small (220 mm x 140 mm) paper volume was copied by John Blacman (c. 1408–85)

---

[117] Knowles, *The Religious Orders in England*, iii.238. For a list of the former Carthusians who formed part of Mary Tudor's brief restoration of the order at Sheen, see Curtis, *The Passion and Martyrdom*, p. 143.

[118] Wright, 'The Dispersal of the Libraries', p. 150, comments on the likelihood that books were part of the traffic of movable monastic property, and see also remarks by Ker, 'The migration of manuscripts', p. 469, and Doyle, 'The library of Sir Thomas Tempest', p. 85.

[119] Doyle (ed.), *The Libraries of the Carthusians*, pp. 610–11. One volume passed into the library of Thomas Cranmer, see Selwyn, *The Library of Thomas Cranmer*, p. 183.

[120] For a brief description of its contents see http://searcharchives.bl.uk.

when he was a novice or postulant at the London charterhouse.[121] Its opening pages contain a meditation on the theme of Susanna's reproach to the Elders, *si hoc egero mors mihi est*, words that Blacman connected with his entry to religious life. Amongst these reflections Blacman also copied the texts of twenty-four Latin verses which were inscribed above the doors of the London charterhouse.[122] Blacman gave a substantial number of books to Witham charterhouse where he was a *clericus redditus*, and a record of these donations exists, but it has not proved possible to identify BL Sloane 2515 amongst its entries.[123] More promising is the record of a loan of *paruus liber de arte moriendi. cuius ijd folium incipit. quia malis* sent from London to Hull in the late fifteenth or early sixteenth century, but although the size and general description of the contents of this volume fit the first part of BL Sloane 2515 well, the citation of the *secundo folio* does not match.[124] Edmund Horde's signature, in black ink, is on f. 1^r, part of an originally separate sheet of parchment which has been folded and pasted in at the beginning of the volume. These leaves are cropped and are slightly smaller than the rest of the volume, and the writing on them runs vertically rather than horizontally across the page. Only the inner part of the bifolium, as it is now presented, is written upon, with its outer leaves (ff. 1^r and 2^v) originally left blank; another similarly folded section of two parchment leaves, this time written on all four sides, has been pasted in at the back of the book.[125] What is written on ff. 1^v–2^r is interesting, for it is a record, in Latin, of the visitation at Kingston-on-Hull Priory in 1440.[126] The reuse of these leaves in the binding or at least strengthening of the book could suggest that this volume was at Hull at some point before Edmund acquired it, or alternatively that the report of the visitation was sent to London and that Edmund came across it there.[127] Other annotations in the volume which may be Edmund's are the notes at the bottom right corner of the third

---

[121] Doyle (ed.), *The Libraries of the Carthusians*, pp. 630–31 and p. 645; Lovatt, 'John Blacman', pp. 426–28.

[122] Gray, 'A Carthusian *Carta Visitationis*', 92–93 and Lovatt, 'John Blacman', pp. 427–28.

[123] Lovatt, 'The Library of John Blacman'.

[124] Doyle (ed.), *The Libraries of the Carthusians*, p. 618.

[125] These contain a shortened form of the Mass and Office of St Anne, of the type found in a Sarum Portiforium of the period, see Gray, 'A Carthusian *Carta Visitationis*', p. 93.

[126] For a transcription and discussion see Gray, 'A Carthusian *Carta Visitationis*', pp. 91–101.

[127] This is what Gray, 'A Carthusian *Carta Visitationis*', p. 98 surmises.

blank leaf (foliated as 35ʳ), which read: *deus volens*, 'made of the kynges', *deus volens*, and 'Here ensueth a declaracioun'.

The second extant manuscript which may be connected with Edmund Horde is Dublin, Trinity College, MS 352.[128] This is another small (148 mm x 89 mm) paper manuscript with Edmund's signature again set at the top of f. 1ʳ. This is a collection of Latin and English prayers, English verses, and sets of quotations on religious topics with headings such as *Exhortacio resistendi contra diabolum* (f. 27ᵛ) and 'Praying for the dead' (f. 198ᵛ), compiled in the manner of a commonplace book.[129] Much of the volume is written in Edmund's own hand, a neat upright Tudor secretary script, and there can be no doubt that he began compiling it during the 1530s. As well as large numbers of quotations from the Bible and patristic writers including Augustine, Jerome, Chrysostom, Ambrose, and others, Edmund cites *Assertio septem sacramentorum*, the text Henry VIII wrote against Luther, and quotes from contemporary writers such as Thomas More. Quotations are selected in relation to matters such as the nature of the Catholic church, and a great many relate to issues of current concern, such as church supremacy. On this topic Edmund notes Augustine's opinion that 'not to graunt the prymacy to the Bisshopp of Rome, surely is a poynte ether of most higher wickednes, or of headlong arrogancye', and that of Ambrose: 'in matters touching Faythe, Bisshoppes are wonte to iudge ouer Christen Emperours, Emperours are not wonte to iudge ouer Bisshoppes' (f. 164ᵛ). He also records more recent thinking, attributing this to 'Sander':

> It is a wicked & a blasphemous othe to sweare any seculer prynce to be supreme Governoure in causes ecclesiasticall ... (f. 168ʳ) ... The kyng can not baptise, consecrate christes boddie, forgyue synnes, preache, excommunycat, blesse the pople, or iudge of doctryne by his kingly autoritie, Ergo, he can not be supreme Governoure in causes ecclesiasticall ... (f. 168ᵛ) ... For Christ said to Peter & to other Bisshoppes after him feede my sheepe: The kyng is one of the Sheepe, or elles he is not of the Churche, nor aboue the churche, then I saye boldly, that itt is agaynt the lawe of nature, for a sheepe to rule his shepeheard in any maner of suche sorte, wherin he is the shepeheard. (f. 169ʳ).[130]

---

[128] For a description see Colker, *Trinity College Library Dublin*, pp. 750–51.
[129] There is also much writing in shorthand which I am not able to decipher.
[130] The reference 'Sander' might relate to the religious controversialist Nicholas Sander (1530–81), see Mayer, 'Sander, Nicholas', or another member of that family.

These selections certainly leave no room for doubt about Edmund Horde's religious and political affiliations. There is much here that is critical of the Henrician regime and the newly established Church of England, with comments that openly advise non-participation in the new rites ('bee no soo much as present in the churche when the englisshe communion is mynistred') and other extracts that counsel a return to Rome.[131]

Alan Horde's will of 1553 noted that he held £30 that belonged to his brother's estate, over and above what he had already distributed in bequests and remembrances according to Edmund's instructions.[132] Alan specified that, depending on circumstance, these monies were to be used for a particular purpose:

> My mynde is yf it fortune that eny relygious house of thorder of charterhouse shortly to be sett up in England, that then the said xxx li, or a greatt parte therof, by the discretion of my executors, shal be bestowed on suche thinges as the munkes there most nede, according to my said brothers will, and the residue to poore people and in charitable dedes, accordinge to their said discrecion.

The executors were also charged with delivering the aforesaid plate and vestments 'to thuse of the said house', that is, returning this property to the order. Presumably Alan was here scrupulously recording his brother's last wishes which he himself as executor had not had the time or opportunity to achieve, in an attempt to ensure that they would still be fulfilled. Yet these were likely to also be Alan's own wishes too. At the time that Alan wrote his will, during the first few months of Mary Tudor's reign, there was every reason to expect that a proper restoration of the Catholic faith would be made in England, which would include the reopening of the religious orders and the re-endowment of their houses, and indeed, in 1557 the Carthusians were re-established at Sheen and the Bridgettines at Syon. In the event these foundations were short-lived, but in 1553 pious bequests offered a means of demonstrating adherence to the new regime, and Alan's will might therefore be regarded as little more than a prudent political strategy. His bequest of his soul not just to God but to Mary and the saints ('to almightie God my maker redemer and saveoure and to our blessed lady saynt Mary his mother and to all the holy companye of heaven')

---

[131] f. 161ʳ, and see extracts on f. 159ᵛ.
[132] I have not been able to trace Edmund Horde's own will.

scarcely sounds like the words of a reformed believer, and the fact that there were notable recusants amongst the next generations of the Horde family suggests that Alan's adherence to the Catholic faith was genuine. Alan and Dorothy's youngest son, also named Alan, and his wife Barbara were indicted for recusancy in 1586 and 1600; Anne Horde, spinster, probably Dorothy's grand-daughter by her second son Edmund, was also indicted in 1586.[133] Thomas Horde (Dorothy's grandson by her son Alan) is also named in the recusant rolls, described as of London and Weston, though he also had lands in Oxfordshire.[134] Dorothy and Alan's youngest daughter Ursula Horde participated in clandestine Catholic activities with her cousin William Horde; he was perhaps the same as the William Horde who is listed as collecting an annuity granted out of Hinton (for his uncle?) from the Office of Augmentations in 1542.[135] William was imprisoned for recusancy in 1586 and his lands in Winchester were seized.[136] He had been caught up in the apprehension of the nun Elizabeth Sander in 1580 and a few years later had helped her to escape to Rouen where the community of Syon was in exile.[137] Ursula, born in 1547, would have been too young to be admitted to Syon when the house was re-established under Mary Tudor in 1557, but she joined the Syon community abroad, and by 1587 when she signed the *Supplication of Poor Syon* at Rouen she was the order's thirteenth prioress; she died at Lisbon on 9 June 1598, and her burial is recorded in the Syon Martyrology.[138] These second and third generation members of the Horde family maintained the allegiance to Rome that their uncle and great-uncle Edmund Horde had so staunchly defended in the 1530s, and to which he had subsequently adhered even after the dissolution and the dismantling of his professional career. His commonplace book records this position in a resolute, even defiant, statement: 'I will kepe that faythe in my olde age, in whiche I was borne & brought upp in'.[139]

---

[133] *CAR* p. 292, no. 1716, and p. 498, no. 3064.

[134] Davidson, 'Roman Catholicism in Oxfordshire', pp. 178, 258–59.

[135] *LPFD Henry VIII*, 17.127 (33 Henry VIII, no. 258); Hutchison, 'Beyond the Margins', pp. 281–82.

[136] See McCann (ed.), *Recusants in the Exchequer Pipe Rolls*, pp. 87–88.

[137] Elizabeth Sander (d. 1607) was the sister of Nicholas Sander, see Lay, 'Sander, Elizabeth'.

[138] *Calendar of State Papers, Domestic Series, 1547–1580*, p. 688, and Hutchison, 'Beyond the Margins', p. 282; Jones and Walsham, *Syon Abbey and Its Books*, pp. 90–91 and p. 238; BL, MS Additional 22285 f. 42^r. I thank Virginia Bainbridge for sharing information about Ursula Horde with me.

[139] f. 290^v.

5

Books and Their Uses

A MATTER OF RECORD

An early eighteenth-century collection of transcripts of older records, BL Stowe 862, provides incidental insight into Thomas Roberts's use of books, particularly as a record keeper in his day-to-day work as a lawyer and manager of properties. This account of the prebend or manor of Neasden from the second year of the reign of Henry VIII (1510) up to 1707 contains much information about the various properties that the Roberts family owned or leased and the means by which these came into the family's hands, including the gradual development of their principal holding called 'Catewodes'.[1] Amongst much useful detail about the properties occur various references to the physical sources consulted by the eighteenth-century historian who left room to accommodate transcriptions of Latin documents but never supplied them, and who several times mentions 'the collections' of Thomas Roberts, and quotes entries made by Thomas himself:

> ... till Thomas Roberts, who was bred to ye law, & got a good estate, removed to Catewodes upon [f. 43^r] the death of his aunt, as he himself hath intimated *in his collections, vide ye white book* ...
>
> ... Another messuage mentioned *in the old rentall* as held by Thomas Roberts of the prebendary of Neasden, is Lyttels. This as appears by *the collections* of Thomas Roberts, who calls it severall times, Le Ferme place, alias Lyttels; and by *some old deeds* ...

---

[1] BL, Stowe 862, f. 38^r–59^r; note leaves left blank (ff. 38^v, 40^v, 41^v, 43^v, 44^r, 45^v, 50^v) and blank spaces left on ff. 46^v, 47^v, 48^v, and 50^r.

... *some deeds* relating to this messuage are still preserved among the *ancient evidences* of the Roberts's estate ...

[f. 44ᵛ] ... and it agrees exactly with a boundary of the same described by Thomas Roberts in *an old paper roll*, which though somewhat defaced and imperfect by age, yet enough is preserved ... Now from this it may be gathered plain enough, that this is the Ferme place alias Littels so often mentioned by Thomas Roberts *in his collections; and particularly in his rent-rolls* ...

[f. 45ʳ] ... with a large terrar of Thomas Roberts his estate in Willesdon, fairly written by himself on severall rolls of parchment, held together by a labell sealed with his own seal.

[f. 46ʳ] ... it descended to Thomas Roberts with the rest of his father's lands. He describes the bounds of it in *his terrar. And in his rent-roll* William Newland held it anno 1535 ...

[f. 47ʳ] ... from *ancient accounts, terrars and boundarys* of the aforesaid Thomas Roberts, & from *divers ancient deeds* of purchase & exchange of lands between the Roberts's & others ...

[f. 58r] And this yearly rent of 12 pence Thomas Roberts mentions in *his large terrar of 3 rolls of parchment*, as payable to him & his heirs ... (my emphases).

From these scattered comments and asides, we can imagine Thomas Roberts as 'the man who in his study sits' surrounded by a mountain of papers, diligently charting his properties and the monies due to him from his tenants through an 'old rentall', 'some old deeds', 'an old paper roll', 'his rent-rolls', and 'a large terrar' (a terrier was a register of landed property); the 'white book' was presumably a bound volume covered with alum-tawed skin.[2] This illumination of Thomas's working practices and the general state of his desk is all the more remarkable because of its lateness of date: apparently this archive of books and rolls remained intact at the start of the eighteenth century, some two hundred years after Thomas had begun writing in them.

A man such as Thomas Roberts, with his multifarious interests, properties, and occupations, could be expected to have kept some kind of personal notebook in the manner of those compiled by some of his contemporaries. Other lawyers such as John Port (1472–1540), who was a reader at the Inner Temple

---

[2] 'the man who in his study sits', from *Dr Faustus*, Chorus, line 28, see Steane, *Christopher Marlowe*, p. 265.

and promoted to serjeant in 1521, made collections of legal texts and notes that would assist them in their work. Port's notebook, now San Marino, Huntington Library, HM 46980, contains a yearbook from 9 Henry VIII; a collection of Westminster cases, alphabetically organized, from 1493 through 1498 with some later additions; reports; a collection of forest laws; and notes on moots and readings.[3] Almost all of these items are written in Port's own hand, and are a mixture of notes taken from books and personal observations. More varied in content, but still a useful resource for both family life and business matters, is the book assembled by the Cheshire gentleman Humphrey Newton (1466–1536). Newton, like Roberts, had bettered himself by marriage, extending and consolidating his landholdings until he was one of the largest landowners in the parish of Wilmslow. Newton's compilation, now BodL Lat. Misc. c.66, consists of a mixture of texts: secular lyrics (some composed by Humphrey himself), medical recipes, charms, religious items including prayers of indulgence and a list of pardons, courtesy tracts, prophecies, land deeds, estate accounts, and legal notes. The contents of this collection reveal a great deal about both Newton himself and his gentry context in north-west England.[4] Another personal miscellany that is similarly revealing of northern cultural preoccupations, this time of the Yorkshire yeoman class, is John Hanson's manuscript, now BL Additional 82370. John Hanson of Rastrick (1517–99) seems to have had no formal legal training but worked as a scrivener and legal agent. His compilation, probably assembled in the first half of the reign of Elizabeth I, preserves a variety of utilitarian and literary texts that mixes accounts of a locally notorious family feud, ballads commemorating the Armada victory, religious verses, and epitaphs, with proverbs, recipes for coloured inks, copies of local by-laws, and lists of local tenants.[5] Also from the Elizabethan period the Middle Temple lawyer, Ralph Stawell, assembled a collection of notes on moots and legal commonplaces, to which he added some of his own verses (now CUL Hh.3.8).[6] Unlike these men, Thomas Roberts did not keep a personal notebook or at least, if he did, it has not survived. Whilst this is regrettable, since the contents of such a volume would flesh out many aspects of Thomas's life and career that can only otherwise be inferred from the public record, the lack of a personal notebook does not mean

---

[3] Baker, *The Notebook of Sir John Port*.
[4] Youngs, 'The late medieval commonplace book'; Youngs, *Humphrey Newton*.
[5] May and Marotti, *Ink, Stink Bait, Revenge, and Queen Elizabeth*.
[6] Coatalen, 'Unpublished Elizabethan Sonnets in a Legal Manuscript'.

that we are entirely denied opportunities to hear Thomas's own voice, or unable to gain insights into his concerns. One of the uses of all old books during this period was as a place for new writing, and on what were originally blank leaves in Thomas's reading books we find the addition of lists and notes and various other entries of the kind that are commonly found in personal notebooks. Although scattered throughout several volumes, these inscriptions clearly demonstrate the impulse to record important facts pertaining to the family, recalling the earlier Italian genre of *libri di famiglia* or *ricordanze* in which the head of the family preserved familial, financial, and legal information for future generations.[7]

Most prominent amongst these inscriptions are the lists that preserve records of births of children in the family, evident in four of the extant manuscripts from the Roberts library. The earliest of these lists was made by Thomas himself, probably over several years. It is in his book of hours, CUL Ii.6.2, where it occupies the whole of f. 33^r, which was originally the blank reverse of the full-page miniature of the Annunciation that prefaces the beginning of Matins. At the top of the leaf is the heading, 'The tyme of Byrth of Thomas Robertes childern', and there are then six entries below, noting the births of Dorothy, Anne, Alice, Michael, Edmund, and John, before the closing statement: 'Thise childern were lyvyng *anno xxix h viij mense junij*', that is, June 1537. Different shades of ink suggest that the first four entries were made in one stint; the ink used to record Edmund's birth is a lighter shade of brown, but then that used for John is darker again, and this last entry is more roughly written. The layout of the page is also irregular, with sizeable gaps after the entries for Alice, Michael, and John. Under ultra-violet light it is possible to read most of an erased entry for another child after Alice: 'Frideseweide Robertes was born the Tuesday the xv day of may which day Robert .... day anno domini m v xiij'; for another after Michael: 'John ... was born on the fest of the concepcion of our lady anno domini m v xvij'; and for another after John: ' ... was born on friday on seint k ... day xvij day of July the ...'.[8] Indeed, close examination reveals that erased records underlie other text on this leaf: at the top, beneath the Dorothy entry, are two erased lines that I cannot read, though the words 'was born' can be made out indicating that another birth record

---

[7] Cicchetti and Mordenti, *I libri di famiglia in Italia*.
[8] These birthdates were, respectively, 15 May 1513, 8 December 1517, and St Kenelmus Day, 17 July, year unknown.

originally stood here. There are many other blank leaves in the manuscript, so there was no need to make a palimpsest of this particular one: instead, the erasure must have been made to serve another purpose. It seems that rather than record an obit when a child died, Thomas's practice was to remove the birth record altogether. If so, this must have happened many times; the second statement at the foot of the leaf declares: 'T Robertes hath in all xxiiij chyldern wherof xviij ben decessed'.[9] A very similar but not quite identical list of Thomas's children is given at the back of the family's other book of hours, CUL Ii.6.7.[10] This list is more of a summary: the entries are all by the same sixteenth-century hand and ink, and were made in one stint; they give details only of the six children who survived infancy, and there is no evidence of any erasures. In this instance the final statement always read 'had' ('Thomas Robertz had by godes will in all xxiiij childern'), and there are some mistakes in the entries which may be attributed to poor copying from the original in CUL Ii.6.2. The most glaring concerns the year of John Roberts's birth, which in CUL Ii.6.2 is given as 1531 but in CUL Ii.6.7 is said to be 1523. Comparison of the two entries shows exactly how this error arose: in CUL Ii.6.2 John's birth is described in terms of both the year of grace and the regnal year ('anno domini m l v c xxxj & anno Rex H viij xxiij'), whereas in CUL Ii.6.7 these two dates have been telescoped into one ('anno domini millesimo v c xxiij'). Collectively these mistakes and alterations and erasures make the lists in the two books of hours seem casual and rather scruffy. By contrast, a third list of Thomas's six children inscribed at the back of the family's copy of Love's *Mirror*, JRL English 98, was clearly intended for public display. This list is carefully copied in a magnificent textura script with elaborate letter-forms and decorative detail. It was not copied by Thomas himself (the final entry records his death), and although it contains some information not available elsewhere, such as the names of his wives, there are also small omitted details in the entries for Anna and Alice, suggesting that the writer did not know the exact dates on which these children were born.

The repeated copying of the names of Thomas Roberts's offspring suggests an intense interest in the documenting of family history, either on his part or stemming from his children themselves, and in both Dorothy's and Edmund's families this tradition of recording details of births was continued. Such lists of

---

[9] A later hand has altered 'hath' to 'had'.
[10] f. 132^r.

births in themselves are not uncommon features of medieval manuscripts, but as in these instances they were most usually added by late medieval or early modern handlers, rather than the commissioners or first owners of the books. Another fifteenth-century book of hours, CUL Gg.6.25, preserves details of the Pagnell family relating to the period *c.* 1485–1540, with English annotations in the margins of the Latin calendar (ff. 4^r–9^v) that record the marriage of Thomas Derham and Isabell Pagnell, and the births and deaths of their children and of other members of the Pagnell family.[11] A Wycliffite Bible owned by Sir Henry Gate carries notes of the births and baptisms of his children in the mid sixteenth century.[12] There are so many later examples of such inscriptions that this concern to preserve personal detail for posterity is often regarded as an exclusively post-Reformation phenomenon, an impression bolstered by the fact that many seventeenth-century manuscript notebooks contain familial information of this type: see, for example, the recipe books associated with the Bourne and Napier families.[13] Yet a fifteenth-century hours of the Virgin, Edinburgh University Library, MS 39, which has a note of the birth of Francis Bodley in 1532, also carries a list of the fourteen children of the London grocer Thomas Babham. The births occurred in the period 1451–74, with the first seven entries all written in one stint, indicating that the record was probably started around 1460.[14] Similarly Robert Thornton's Lincoln manuscript has a note of the birth of his grandson, also named Robert, in 1453.[15] Early modern scholarship has also tended to emphasize the role of women, and especially elite women, in the compilation of family records: one example of this is Grace Mildmay, 1552–1620, who bequeathed an archive of family records to her daughter Mary Fane.[16] Indeed, it has often been implied that the recording of family history, the transfer of family lore from one generation to the next, and the handing down of personal notebooks was an exclusively matrilineal occupation; the evidence of the Roberts family's preservation of family knowledge,

---

[11] Described by Binski and Zutshi, *Western Illuminated Manuscripts*, p. 159.

[12] Dublin, Trinity College, MS 75, with inscriptions on f. i^v and f. 281^v, discussed by Scattergood and Latré, 'Trinity College Dublin MS 75', pp. 230–34.

[13] Respectively, BodL MSS Tanner 397 and Top Oxon C 757, both discussed by Leong, 'Collecting Knowledge for the Family', 87–89.

[14] For a transcription see Borland, *A Descriptive Catalogue*, Appendix IV, iii (p. 333), and see further Connolly, 'Late Medieval Books of Hours'.

[15] Lincoln, Lincoln Cathedral Library, MS 91, f. 49^v, see Fein, 'The Contents of Robert Thornton's Manuscripts', p. 22.

[16] On Grace Mildmay see Pollock, *With Faith and Physic*.

though dispersed through several volumes, helps to demonstrate that this was a patrilineal concern too.[17]

The involvement of the male head of the household in recording family history is particularly evident from BodL Rawlinson C. 894, the fourth of the Roberts books to carry genealogical information. This manuscript has an extra quire added at the beginning (now ff. iv^v–xi^r) which is now filled with records of family births, marriages, and deaths in the period 1548–1670. Various hands contributed these records over several generations, and two of the hands are self-identified as those of Edmund Roberts and his son. The entries were begun on f. iv^v by Edmund Roberts in 1549 with a note of his marriage to Frances Welles. On f. vi^v Edmund's eldest son, Francis, notes his own marriage to Mari Barne in 1575, and starting on the facing page (f. vii^r) is a list of the births of their children, which continues to f. ix^r. Another generational shift occurs on f. viii^v when Francis noted the marriage of his eldest daughter Frances to Richard Franklin in 1598 and then the birth of their son John in 1600. Records pertaining to the offspring of Francis's sons, William and Barne, and to William's son, also named William, appear in more cursory lists on ff. ix^v–x^r; other records on ff. ix–xi give details of the marriages and children of several daughters, bringing the surnames Nelthrop, Gibbs, Cordewell, and Harrison into the family. Birth records of those who joined the family could also be entered here retrospectively, as is clearly the case with the note of the birth of Eleanor Aty in 1608, added to the bottom of f. ix^r in correct chronological sequence, but evidently only placed there following her marriage to William Roberts.

BodL MS Rawlinson C. 894 was Edmund's book rather than his father's; in this volume information about Thomas and his six children does not appear, but the lists provide very extensive information about Edmund's wives and children.[18] The records were started by Edmund, who notes his marriage to Frances Welles at Candlemas (2 February) 1548, and the births of their first four children. These entries, all made in one stint on f. iv^v, are incomplete in that they give years but not days of birth for some of the children, and no dates at all for the others, even though the names of godparents and the places of baptism

---

[17] A helpful list of studies of individual women in the context of domestic notebooks is given by LeJacq, 'The Bounds of Domestic Healing', p. 454, note 11.

[18] A more abbreviated list, with the date 1575 and just the names of Edmund's seven children who were alive at that time, is in CUL Ii.6.2, f. 109^v; this list does not contain details of place of baptism or names of godparents.

are carefully recorded. Perhaps dissatisfied with this, Edmund started again on f. v^r and this time was more careful about matters of timing; the two sets of entries between them offer a lot of information, and so of his eldest daughter, for example, we are told firstly: 'Lady Katheryne Chester & mestres Grysell Sadler & master Johan armynster master of the temple & lord of Nesdon were godmotheres & godfather and Katheryne Robertes was was [sic] crystynyd at Wylesdon anno 1552', and then secondly: 'Katheryne Robertes was borne the last daye of June betwen v and vj of the cloke in the mornyng beyng thursdaye in the vjth yere of the rayne of owre soverayne lord kyng Edward the vjth & anno domini 1552' (see Figure 14). From f. v^v with the record of the birth of 'Thomas Robertes' in 1558, the entries settle into a pattern that presents all this information more succinctly: 'Thomas Robertes was borne at Neasdon the xxxth daye of July at v of the cloke in the afternone beyng frydaye in anno domini 1558 & crystenyd the laste daye of August & Mr T Gressham and Mr John Newdegat godfatheres & Mistres Brydeman godmother I pray god make hyme hys seruant'. The death of Frances in July 1560 six weeks after the birth of her sixth child, and Edmund's second marriage to Faith Pattenson three years later, are also noted, along with the births of three more children from this second marriage.

Two of the entries in the list of Edmund's children, for Marie the younger (born 1554) and Thomas (born 1558), have been struck through, indicating their deaths in infancy, confirmed by the note of the death of Edmund's first wife which states that she 'lefte iiij chylldeyne alyue'. The entries made by Francis record the places, days, dates, and hours of his children's births, as well as the places of their baptisms and the names of their godparents. In addition Francis gives information about those children who did not survive: his third child, 'George Robertes was borne at Neasden and died within ye monethe being christened' (f. vii^r); the seventh child, Mari,'died within the moneth and was buried in mi chapyell' (f. vii^v; this entry is marked 'ded' in the left margin); the eleventh child, also named Mari, born in 1592, also perished: 'This mari died within the monethe at marke halle and there liethe buried' (f. viii^r). Mark Hall was the property of James Altham (d. 1583); Mistress Mari Altham stood as godmother to this child, and also to William Roberts born in 1595, and the names of other members of the Altham family feature elsewhere amongst the godparents of Francis's children. In the seventeenth-century birth records, death dates are also given in many instances, even when the children evidently lived to adulthood, and quite a few entries use the formula 'since dead &

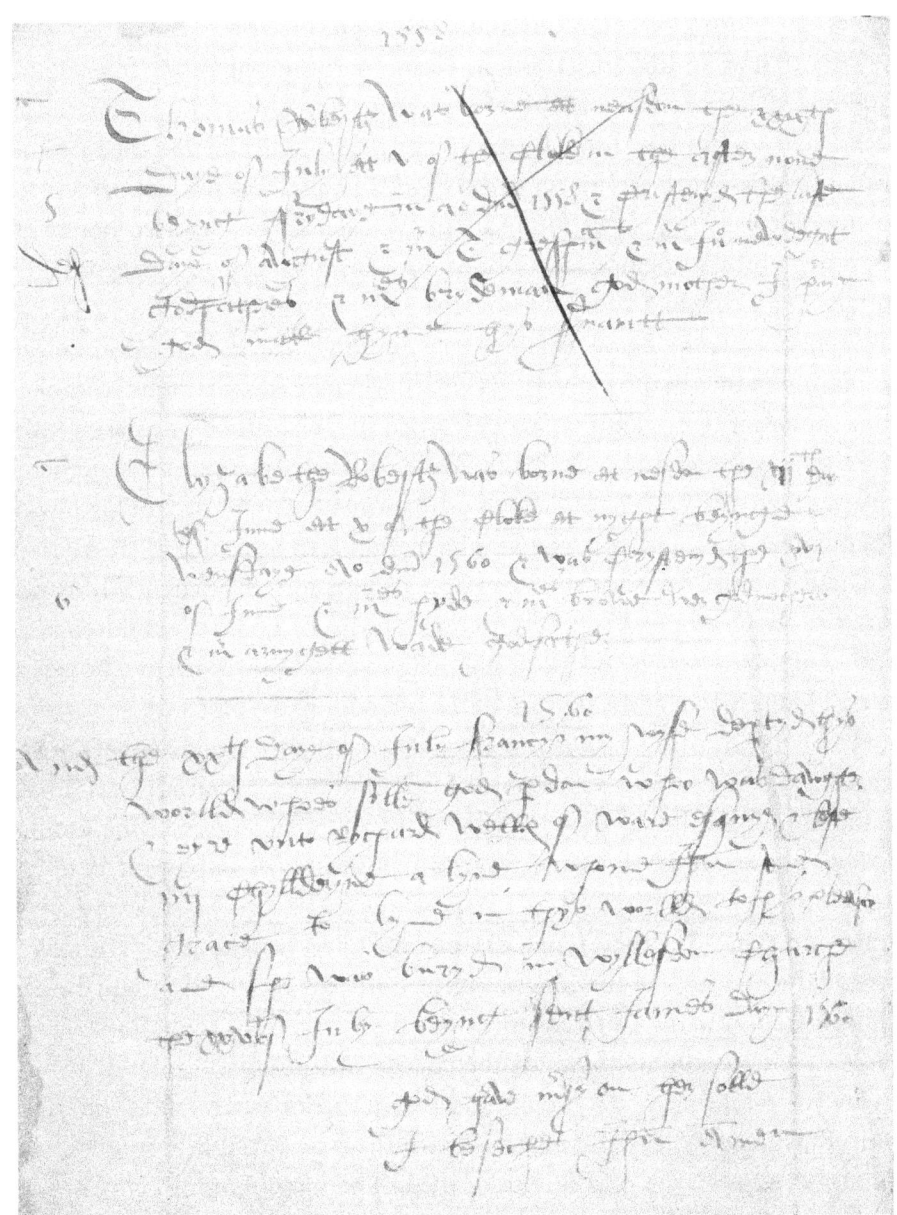

Figure 14 Oxford, Bodleian Library, MS Rawlinson C. 894, f. v^{v}. Birth records of the children of Edmund Roberts. Reproduced by permission of the Bodleian Libraries, the University of Oxford.

buryed at …', noting places of burial in Willesden, Harrow, and Clerkenwell (ff. ix^v–x^v). Thomas Roberts, though, seems to have had little interest in preserving a record of the lives of all of his twenty-four children; his preference for erasing entries from the list of births in CUL Ii.6.2 indicates that the focus of his attention was on the living, not the dead. He also was not concerned to enter any obits relating to his forebears in the calendars of his two books of hours, though on the opening leaf of BodL Rawlinson C. 299 he did record one important death that had affected him personally: his father John Roberts died on 11 September 1476. Below this Thomas inscribes the crucial information about his inheritance of the manor of Neasden when he was just eight years old. On this same leaf (f. 1^r) Thomas also recorded his own birth, calculating this from a significant historical event, the Battle of Barnet in 1471; his statement that he was then thirty weeks old allows us to estimate that his date of birth was mid-September 1470. Other personal information is to be found in BL Harley 1859, where Thomas recorded the dates of his admission to Clement's Inn and later to the Inner Temple. Whoever inscribed the list of Thomas's children and the names of their mothers in JRL English 98 preserved the record of Thomas's death on 1 January 1542 at the bottom of the list, adding the pious wish: *quarum animarum miseriatur* [sic] *omnipotens deus* '(May almighty God have mercy on whose souls)'.[19] In a similar way, a note of Edmund Roberts's death in 1585 has been added to CUL Ii.6.2, showing that successive generations of the family used these old books in the same way, as repositories of important familial information.[20]

Some additions of other types of material give insight into Thomas's professional activities. At the beginning of both BL Harley 1859 and BodL Rawlinson C. 299 is inscribed a short text, the measure of the tailor's yard, which was perhaps a mnemonic for the correct measurement of land, a skill that a lawyer would need.[21] A memorandum on thick parchment at the back of BodL Rawlinson C. 299 is connected with the type of public commissions in which he, as a lawyer, was often engaged. The memorandum consists of a list of names under the heading 'Westminster'.[22] There are thirty names in

---

[19] f. 137^v.

[20] f. 109^r.

[21] Discussed in Chapter 2, section titled 'A Lawyer's Book: British Library, MS Harley 1859'.

[22] On ff. 52^v–53^r. The leaves seem to have been pasted down at some point and are now hard to read.

total, and in each case they are bracketed into a category; the final four are under the heading 'Savoy'. None of the names are those of Thomas's known associates, and this looks very much like the type of list drawn up as preparation for visiting a district to carry out some particular commission, such as, for example, the privy searches of London properties in which Thomas was involved in the 1520s.[23] Similarly the copying of the formula for the serjeant's oath in BL Harley 1859 must relate in some way to Thomas's work as a lawyer, even though there is no evidence that he ever gained the rank of serjeant.[24] Other additions on the rear flyleaves of BL Harley 1859 are of a non-legal nature, displaying a lack of concern for generic homogeneity, or perhaps just the need to make use of space for writing wherever this was available. The copy of the indulgence granted to Ralph Roberts in 1395 which is written out at the back of this manuscript has a clear family significance, and the motivation to preserve it is readily understandable; less obvious, in terms of the reason for its inclusion, is the text about the nature of the antichrist.[25] To the modern observer these religious items seem misplaced in what is otherwise an anthology of legal texts, but our desire for homogeneity in contents is probably at odds with what earlier generations of readers encountered and desired in their books.

A BOOK OF PRACTICAL USE: BODLEIAN LIBRARY, MS RAWLINSON C. 299

Amongst the remnants of what was presumably once a larger library, BodL Rawlinson C. 299 now stands out as rather different from Thomas Roberts's other books. Whilst most of the family's other surviving manuscripts are of a religious or devotional nature, this small fifteenth-century volume of medical prescriptions bespeaks a more practical use. Very many such collections survive, indicating the range of therapeutic knowledge that was available in the late medieval gentry household, and contemporary references also demonstrate that the home was the trusted location for medical treatment: John Paston I was warned by his mother in 1464 not to put faith in London physicians, and other men such as Robert Thornton (c. 1397–1465) took the trouble to copy out

---

[23] See Chapter 2, section titled 'On Commission: Thomas Roberts and His Associates'.
[24] Discussed in Chapter 2, section titled 'Thomas Roberts at the Inns of Court'.
[25] See Chapter 2, section titled 'A Lawyer's Book: British Library, MS Harley 1859'.

collections of remedies for themselves.[26] BodL Rawlinson C. 299 was professionally prepared in the first half of the fifteenth century; it measures 210 mm x 130 mm and consists of 53 folios. The original core of the manuscript (five gatherings of eight leaves, the section now numbered ff. 4^r–41^v) contains a collection of 314 recipes that offer treatments for many ailments, broadly organized *de capite ad pedem* (from head to foot), though this arrangement is not slavishly adhered to. The recipes typically outline the medical problem in their opening words, advise what substances should be used and how they should be prepared, and then give instructions as to application. Often alternative treatments are offered for the same problem, though these are frequently very similar to each other in terms of the ingredients and uses that are recommended. There are recipes for topical applications such as washes, ointments, and plasters, and for concoctions that are to be ingested – usually drinks, or powders to be dissolved and drunk. Sometimes the recipes are purely pharmacological and not directed towards the treatment of any particular problem, suggesting that certain salves and ointments were well-known and widely desired, such as nerval, for the treatment of nerves and sinews. Another such prescription was 'the grene oyntment' that may be kept for forty years. This was used on wounds to clean them and promote the growth of new flesh; its green colour derived either from herbs or from the addition of verdigris.[27] General dietary advice or advice on a healthy lifestyle is provided as well, and occasionally there is comment on which herbs might prove most effective against a particular affliction; for example, a list of substances that provide good protection against venom is given on f. 37^v, after various recipes for animal bites and for when poison has been ingested. The recipes typically end with reassurances about their efficacy: for example, various recipes for deafness on f. 5^v claim: 'withynne ix tymes he schal ben hool'; 'and it schal done awey the werkynge wonderwel'; 'þis is a good medecyne proued'; the tag 'Proved', often rendered in Latin (*Probatus*), is very frequently written in abbreviated form at the end of a recipe. These claims and comments on efficacy are part and parcel of the original text, written in the hand of the main scribe, and form an integral part of the medical knowledge presented in the collection, though they may of course be accretions from an earlier stage in their copying history.[28]

---

[26] Voigts and Kurtz, *Scientific and Medical Writings*, note more than 1200 surviving codices; Orlemanski, 'Thornton's Remedies and the Practices of Medical Reading', p. 239.
[27] f. 24^v.
[28] On such efficacy statements see Jones, 'Formula and Formulation'.

The collection is not exclusively one of prescriptions: it also includes a few texts of a diagnostic or prognostic nature. A brief list of the zodiacal signs, 'Whan þe mone is in ony signe of þe sunne' (ff. 33ᵛ–34ʳ), explains the names of the signs in English and links them to their calendar months and the parts of the body they were believed to govern; the climatic conditions in particular months, and their effects on man's life are also noted. A short text on ff. 17ᵛ–18ʳ, 'dyuers sightes of uryne', tells how to interpret the appearance of urine, and what this reveals about disease in other parts of the body.[29] Other texts focus on the ingredients needed for medical preparations, discussing the best ways, times, and locations for gathering herbs.[30] The properties of elements used in medicines are explained in terms of their strengths and humoral definitions (hot, cold, dry, or wet).[31] Although not strictly recipes, these texts relate closely to the prescriptions: they discuss ways to identify maladies, and provide more advice about ingredients, preparation, and therapeutic application. In short, this is a coherent collection of remedies, very much the type of compendium of useful medical knowledge that members of an ordinary late medieval household might consult for advice and self-medication. By its contents it may be defined as a remedy book rather than a leechbook. The latter was the kind of book used by a professional doctor, and would contain more diagnostic tools such as astrological tables, diagrams, texts on bloodletting, and texts that specify the auspicious days for medical treatment; BodL Rawlinson C. 299 has none of these.[32]

It is not clear how this collection of medical recipes came to be in the Roberts family library. The name of its scribe is not known, but his scribal dialect has been localized to Norfolk, and *LALME* places the linguistic profile of this manuscript close to two others of a similar medical nature. Intriguingly, both of these have inscriptions that include the Roberts name:

---

[29] Tavormina, *Uroscopy in Middle English*, classifies this as simple token-list, 'Urine White and Red', with a four-parts prologue, and identifies six other manuscript witnesses, see p. 38 §4.2.1.

[30] ff. 30ᵛ–31ᵛ, 'Medecynys ben done some be lefes and some be 3erdys . . .'. Mooney, *IMEP XI*, records another copy of this text in Cambridge, Trinity College, MS R.14.32 ff. 113ʳ–114ᵛ.

[31] ff. 40ᵛ–41ᵛ, 'Symple medecynes of gresys of rotys of sedys of gommys of metallys . . .'.

[32] For a fifteenth-century leechbook that was associated with a particular individual see BL Harley 1735, compiled by John Crophill of Wix, Essex. The volume was described by Talbert, 'The Notebook of a Fifteenth-Century Practising Physician', and edited by Ayoub, 'John Crophill's Books'; see also Jones, 'Crophill, John'. For a recently published example of a remedy book see Almeida, *A Middle English Medical Remedy Book*.

Stockholm, Royal Library, MS X.90 has the inscription 'Nicholas Roberts', and Glasgow, Glasgow University Library, MS Hunter 117, which belonged to Bishop Richard Nix, has the name 'Thomas Roberts' in a list of names on one of its final flyleaves.[33] I have not been able to connect these names with the Robertses of Middlesex, but the possible Norfolk provenance is suggestive because Thomas Roberts's first and second sets of in-laws probably derived from there.[34] As yet the original owner or commissioner of BodL Rawlinson C. 299 remains unknown. It was already an old book by the time it came into Thomas Roberts's hands, and as no previous indications of ownership are present it is impossible to tell whether it had been handed down within the family, or whether Thomas had newly acquired it as a bequest or gift, or even by purchase. As was his practice with other books that he owned, Thomas made sure to inscribe his name frequently throughout the volume. Typically he wrote the abbreviated form of his surname in several of the upper margins.[35] Some of these inscriptions occur at the beginnings or ends of gatherings that may at that point have remained unbound, and their purpose may simply have been a declaration of ownership. Once, his name is placed in the right margin alongside a remedy, which might be interpreted as a sign of special interest. This occurs on f. 16^r, in a section that deals with cancer in the body: the particular remedy advises the patient to take 'mannys felthe and brenne it and mak poudur þerof and medle it with poudur of pepyr & anoynte þe canker with þat poudur aȝens þe feer til it be hool'. More frequently Thomas wrote his name into blank spaces within the text frame where the originally written text had not quite filled the line; the adjacent texts in these cases are: dietary advice for epileptics (f. 21^r); a prescription for 'water de copurose' (f. 24^r); a recipe for making a gummed cloth which was good for wounds (f. 26^r); a list of the signs of the zodiac (f. 34^r); and a recipe to make a drink to cure a swelling (f. 39^r). One recipe that was definitely marked out for special attention is the prescription 'for echyng' on f. 4^v. This remedy for nits and lice suggests mixing the juice of walwort with quicklime and

---

[33] McIntosh, Samuels, and Benskin, *LALME*, i.151, LP 4647; i.165, LP 4665; i.88, LP 4622; see further discussion in Appendix IV below. Jones, 'Vernacular Literacy in Late Medieval England', gives an account of vernacular medical manuscripts derived from East Anglia.

[34] See Chapter 1, section titled 'Father and Son: John Roberts (d. 1476) and Thomas Roberts (1470–1542)'.

[35] On ff. 12^r, 21^r, 24^r, 25^r, and 25^v.

using this as an ablution.[36] The comment in the left margin reads: 'This is þe best medicyne what place ben it be in', though this was probably not contributed by Thomas Roberts: the ink is much lighter than the black ink habitually used by him, and the formation of the letters is less practised than his legal script, bespeaking a less educated annotator. Nevertheless, this is a contemporary addition, and one that clearly shows that the recipes were put to practical use, though this is the only such comment on their value.

Many other readerly traces in the remedy collection of BodL Rawlinson C. 299 reveal a sustained interest in the volume and demonstrate its regular use in the first decades of the sixteenth century. Throughout the volume Thomas Roberts added headings to the margins to mark the location of individual recipes. These headings function as reader's aids, enabling the searcher (Roberts himself, and other members of his household) to find the desired remedy more quickly. The margins of the volume actually present layers of such annotation, showing repeated consultation by different users, probably from successive generations of the family.[37] For example, in the first set of recipes for the head, on f. 4ᵛ, Thomas adds four headings: 'for lyse & nyttes'; 'to purge þe hede'; 'for hede ake'; 'for þe mygrene'. The last has another heading, 'for de demigren', supplied by another much smaller hand. The less practised hand that contributed the comment about the nit cure also wrote 'fenil' to clarify an unclearly written ingredient in the third recipe on this leaf. The headings added by Thomas Roberts have a dual purpose. Not only do they make the information on each individual leaf easier to navigate, they also relate to a list of the volume's contents that he prepared and placed at the back of the original book. The list is arranged as a single column of entries, within which recipes are grouped together with brackets and keyed to Roman numerals; these numerals relate to the numbers that Roberts added at the top right corner of each recto leaf in the volume. This apparatus makes it possible for a reader to gain a rapid overview of the recipes in the collection, and also to see where remedies for particular ailments are located; when turning to the numbered leaf in question the reader is further helped by the marginal headings. The list of contents

---

[36] *MED* glosses walwort as a plant, usually Danewort or dwarf elder (*sambucus ebulus*), but notes that the name might signify other plants such as chicory and hellebore.

[37] Parkes, 'The Influence of the Concepts of *Ordinatio* and *Compilatio*', p. 135 notes the provision of such marginal apparatus in medieval manuscripts, and, from the fourteenth century onwards, the increasing tendency of readers to provide their own. On finding aids in medical manuscripts in particular see Almeida, 'Finding-information Aids'.

consists of a list of ailments rather than a complete list of remedies, and consequently is rather condensed, containing 287 entries even though there are 314 recipes in the volume. The list does not itemize all of the different remedies for the same problem; rather, the word 'dyuerse' is used to indicate that alternative recipes for the same complaint will be found.

Thomas Roberts's investment of his time and labour in preparing this list bespeaks a high regard for the recipe collection and the knowledge it contains; the considerable effort involved in this exercise would only have been worthwhile if the volume were consulted on a regular basis. Despite the fact that by the sixteenth century the contents of the remedy book were very old, this was clearly still a valued household manual to which regular recourse was made. There are few signs to show which particular medieval recipes were the most frequently consulted, and it is not possible to extrapolate what particular illnesses beset the family. Signs of wear and tear on the manuscript are largely lacking, except that two leaves are now missing from the second gathering. These would have been numbered xij and xiij in Thomas Roberts's scheme, and were located between what are now ff. 14^v–15^r. These leaves were still present in the manuscript when Thomas Roberts handled it and from his list of contents we can reconstruct their contents, which were recipes for: gout, pains, sleep problems, speech problems, warts, stinking nostrils, and constipation; and prescriptions to make the face fair, the hands white, and to remove freckles from the face, for sickness, swelling, and contractions in the stomach, and for discharge from the anus.[38] Was there a remedy here that was often needed? Perhaps the stitching of this particular bifolium was worn out by frequent consultation, though as the central unit of the gathering it was always the most vulnerable.

The remedy book was not only much used in this period, it was also extended. In order to accommodate his list of contents, Thomas added two units of parchment of rather finer quality than that used in the original volume, one gathering of four (ff. 42^r–45^v), and one of only three leaves (46^r–48^v). These are followed by a strip of parchment, half the size of a normal leaf (f. 49), a unit of stiffer parchment (ff. 50^r–51^v), and then a final unit of stiff parchment (ff. 52^r–53^v), slightly different in size, of which the inner leaves seem to have been pasted down at some point. One of these added leaves, f. 51^v, remains blank, except for a small applied circular seal in red wax, impressed by a signet ring; the seal impression, which is very small, shows a prancing horse, its head facing towards the right, and

---

[38] Listed on f. 43^v.

the tiny letters 'W R', almost certainly for William Roberts. The other leaves have been written on by a variety of sixteenth-century hands. Three other parchment leaves at the beginning of the volume were originally blank, except for the second which has a partial copy of a uroscopy text written by a fifteenth-century hand that differs from that of the main scribe; jordans, or urine flasks, are drawn roughly at the start of each entry.[39] The reverse of this second leaf is still blank, but the other leaves at the front of the manuscript have been filled with later additions.

With the exception of the personal records written on f. 1^r, for which see the discussion above, these additions are almost all of a medical nature, and serve to extend the original collection of 314 recipes by a further 43 prescriptions.[40] Variations in ink colour and script show that these were added at a variety of times, and by a variety of hands, including that of Thomas Roberts and, presumably, those of other members of his family and household. Nine recipes have been added at the front of the volume and thirty-four at the back, with a few copied out more than once. Three recipes lack any indication as to their use, and two are for treating horses; the rest were for: phlegm, affecting mainly the chest but also the head and stomach; toothache; aches in other parts of the body; constipation; plague and the sweating sickness; ague; colic; stone; flux; watering of the eyes; a broken limb; a persistent sore; drunkenness. Arguably these added recipes offer the greatest insight into Tudor use of the collection. Although Thomas Roberts and his family clearly made use of the whole volume, the remedies that they themselves inscribed must have been the ones which they had cause to use and regarded as effective prescriptions that were worth preserving. To a certain extent, these additions make good deficiencies in the coverage of the original remedy book which offered no prescriptions to help with ague, colic, aches in the body (except in the legs and feet), broken limbs, or phlegm in the stomach. The original collection has prescriptions which promise to open or purge the breast, but none specifically to treat phlegm which seems to have been a complaint that troubled Thomas Roberts considerably: at the beginning of the book he added three recipes for phlegm on f. 1^v, one of which he copied again at the back of the book (f. 41^v), and three more on f. 3^v (see Figure 15). He also added two very similar prescriptions for constipation,

---

[39] Tavormina, 'The Twenty-Jordan Series', p. 62, has identified this as an incomplete copy of a Twenty-Jordan text, noting that it belongs to a recognized subgroup of this most common type of Middle English uroscopies.

[40] The additions are discussed more fully in Connolly, 'Evidence for the Continued Use'.

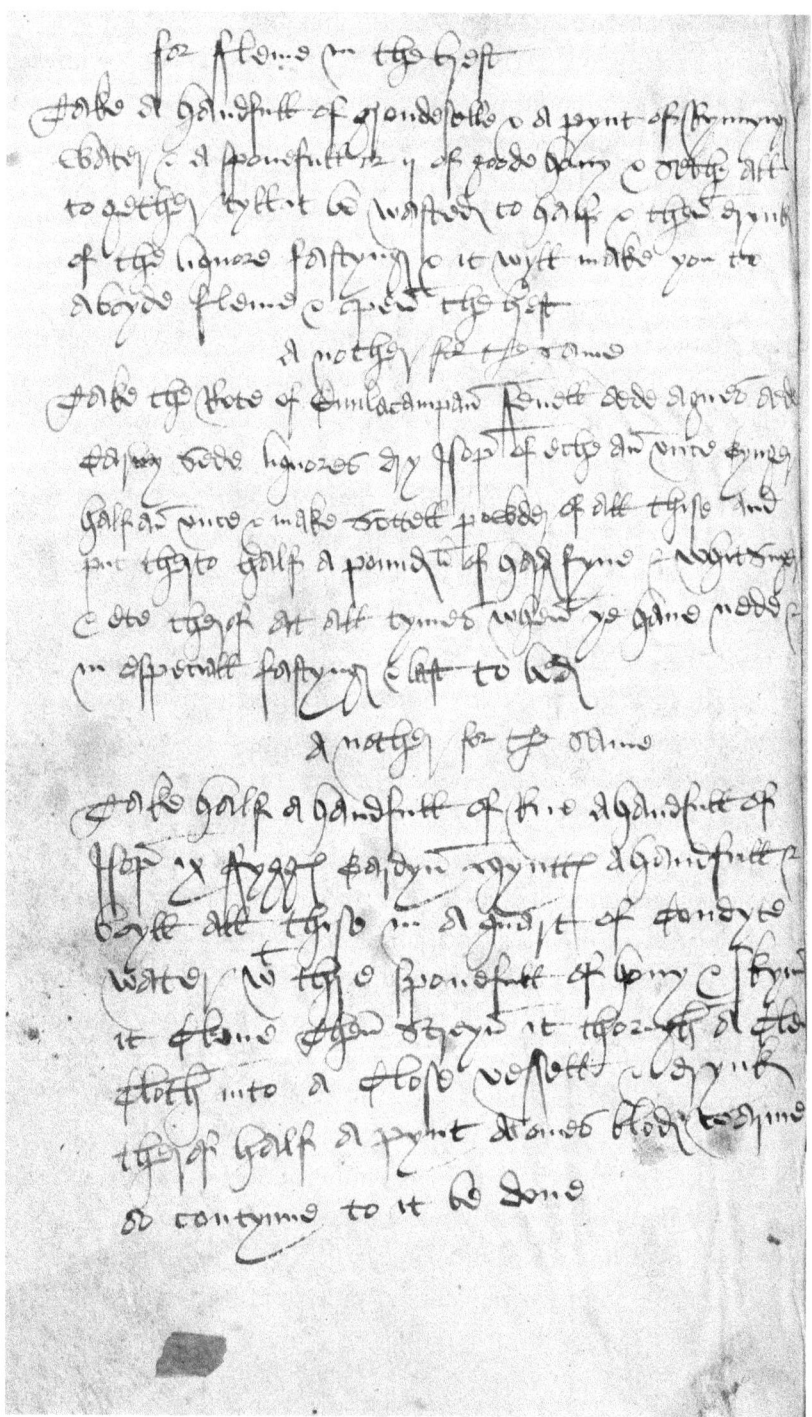

Figure 15 Oxford, Bodleian Library, MS Rawlinson C. 299, f. 3ᵛ. Medical recipes added by Thomas Roberts. Reproduced by permission of the Bodleian Libraries, the University of Oxford.

on ff. 41^v and 47^v; a third added recipe for 'a goode lax' occurs on the very last leaf, f. 53^v. The original collection seems to have included only one laxative, so the provision of these additional recipes was a useful augmentation of the existing volume, and would seem to indicate that constipation was a common problem for which relief was regularly sought. Similarly the original remedy book offered only one recipe to help against pestilence (f. 26^r); given the regular outbreaks of plague and the 'sweat' in London in Thomas's lifetime, it is not surprising to find several remedies for these problems amongst the sixteenth-century additions. In other cases, however, the recipes that were added to the volume by its sixteenth-century users serve only to duplicate aspects of the original collection where, for example, prescriptions for the stone, flux, and watering of the eyes might already be found. Indeed, the original collection has no fewer than nine remedies for drunkenness (f. 22^r), so another, as offered on f. 47^v, can scarcely have been needed. In several cases the added recipe not only duplicated a remedy already contained in the book, but used the same key ingredients: such recipes cannot have been very different in either practice or outcome. Another inscription that offers a means of practical help occurs at the top of f. 1^v where Thomas Roberts wrote informatively: 'Thomas Warde surgeon at seynt Andrewes Vndershaft can hele & help all diseases & sores with one medycine or salue'.

There were various medical practitioners of this name in late medieval London; the closest in date and description seems to be the Thomas Ward, surgeon of London, who died in October 1521 leaving his estate to his son Christopher, although this Thomas Ward wished to be buried in the church of St Bride in Fleet Street.[41]

One other aspect of BodL Rawlinson C. 299 deserves attention. Most of this discussion has focussed on the annotations and additions made to the original fifteenth-century collection of recipes by its sixteenth-century users, and my examination of the volume has been alert to signs of readerly use such as underlining, accumulated dirt, and general wear and tear. Yet also worth noting is a particular instance where there has been no disturbance to the original text, since occasionally there is something that may be learned from an *absence* of readerly activity. In common with other similar collections of medieval recipes, BodL Rawlinson C. 299 contains a few charms, all of which are examples that

---

[41] Talbert and Hammond, *The Medical Practitioners in Medieval England*, list five individuals named Thomas Ward(e). The comments on Warde and on BodL Rawlinson C. 299 in Gottfried, *Doctors and Medicine*, p. 62 are unreliable.

were widely known in medieval Europe. Two are for toothache: the first, in Latin, is an invocation to St Apollonia; the second, in English, is a brief version of the 'God was Born in Bethlehem' charm.[42] These both occur on f. 33^v, where there is also a Latin charm to staunch blood, a version of the 'Flum Jordan' charm.[43] The fourth and most extensive charm, on f. 13^v, is mostly in English, and was a text known as the 'Three Good Brothers' charm which incorporated material from another similar charm, known as the 'Uncorrupted Wounds of Christ' charm.[44] The scribe drew attention to this last item with the marginal marker 'Charme', and it is visually distinguished from the ordinary recipes that surround it by the frequent occurrence of crosses throughout the text, including one particularly elaborate marker that divides Christ's name; these are prompts to show the reader that he must make the sign of the cross on his own body at these points. Thomas Roberts's response to these texts was to treat them just like the other remedies. In the margin of f. 33^r he has added the heading 'Charmes for the Tothe ache', showing that he recognized the true nature of these texts. He indexed these charms along with the recipes in his list of contents, making no distinction between the two categories of material, except in his entry for the various prescriptions to staunch blood which reads: 'for to staunche blode diuerse & a prayer'. The description 'prayer' for the charm reveals his positive regard for the text: to him this was an ordinary devotion, not superstitious or magical in any bad sense. Frequently later Protestant readers crossed out such texts, believing them to be devilish. The fact that the charm texts in BodL Rawlinson C. 299 are not defaced in any way shows that for as long as the book was in use by members of the Roberts family, these texts were believed to be equally as effective as the other remedies, or at least were held in sufficient respect not to be cancelled.[45]

It is apparent is that Thomas Roberts had a high regard for all of the contents of this medieval remedy book, and that he and his family made use of it in the way that it was intended to function, namely, as a practical guide to maintaining good health. Collectively the additions and annotations within this small collection of medieval recipes reveal a sustained level of engagement

---

[42] Keiser, 'Works of Science and Information', p. 3671, no. 333, and p. 3673, no. 351.
[43] Keiser, 'Works of Science and Information', pp. 3670–71, no. 328.
[44] Keiser, 'Works of Science and Information', p. 3672, nos. 343 and 341.
[45] Note also the presence of other charm texts in their other books: in BL Harley 1859, discussed above, and amongst the items added to CUL Ii.6.2, discussed in Chapter 6, section titled 'I Youse Thys Prayer Well Every Daye: How Edmund Roberts Said His Prayers'.

with its written text by readers of a much more modern vintage than could have been expected by the volume's original fifteenth-century compiler. The most significant additions to the manuscript were those contributed by Thomas Roberts, and even though not all of the non-original recipes can be attributed to him, it is clear that in his eyes this old manuscript represented a store of currently relevant advice and practical application. Thomas Roberts and his family found that the *old* science of old books was still relevant and applicable; despite their age, these medieval remedies were still needed, used, and valued in the early modern period. As modern scholars it is easy to overlook the value of old books, especially if we regard the sixteenth century as a period when printing had rendered manuscripts redundant (a change that was not effected as rapidly as has been assumed).[46] For these Tudor readers 'old' in this context was synonymous with reliable, tried and tested, and the old book was a source of authoritative wisdom, not outmoded knowledge. Not all of the family's remedies were enshrined in this book, however; some appear in other contexts, perhaps just noted down on whatever was most immediately to hand. Thus, for example, in addition to the three recipes offered in this volume for drinks that might cure colic, another quite different remedy for the same complaint may be found tucked away at the back of one of the family's books of hours.[47]

THE USE OF SARUM: CAMBRIDGE UNIVERSITY LIBRARY, MS Ii.6.7 AND CAMBRIDGE UNIVERSITY LIBRARY, MS Ii.6.2

In the later Middle Ages the form of the liturgy varied across different English dioceses according to the uses of Sarum, York, or Hereford, but by the mid fifteenth century Sarum (originally the form of the Roman rite used at Salisbury) had become the dominant form that was widely used throughout the English province. Books of hours, configured to the correct use, allowed individual Christians of all ranks to follow their daily devotions at home or in church. Two such books of Sarum hours may be connected with the Roberts family; both were manuscript hours, even though by the sixteenth century

---

[46] For a recent assessment of the early years of print production in Britain see Gillespie and Powell (eds.), *A Companion to the Early Printed Book*.

[47] CUL Ii.6.2, f. 110ʳ: 'For the collyk: take wurminholde comyn sauge bred and veneger and make a playstre, & ley it to your laske, and ye xal be holl, by þe grace of God.'

printed *horae* were being produced in significant numbers.[48] Since the book of hours was, above all, a book of private devotion it might seem odd that Thomas Roberts possessed two, but in fact it was not at all uncommon for individuals to own more than one copy; this type of book was frequently handed down through generations or bequeathed to friends or associates outwith the family, as is apparent from the evidence of medieval wills and book inscriptions.[49] Amongst educated lay readers, the book of hours had been a popular aid to personal devotion since at least the beginning of the fourteenth century. Using a book of hours allowed the lay reader a virtual participation in the institutionalized worship offered by enclosed monks and nuns because its contents, principally the 'Little Office' of the Virgin (*Officium Parvum Beatae Virginis Mariae*), laid out the prayers, lessons, and psalms that were to be read at the regular intervals prescribed in the monastic office. These were Matins and Lauds, which together formed one long office said during the night and early morning; the first, third, sixth, and ninth hours of the day (Prime, Terce, Sext, and None); and Vespers (at sunset) and Compline. Sometimes the Office of the Virgin was followed by other offices, such as the Hours of the Cross and the Hours of the Holy Ghost; the other usual elements of the book were the Seven Penitential Psalms, the Fifteen Gradual Psalms, the Litany of Saints, and the Office of the Dead.[50] The beginning of each major section was usually distinguished by some element of decoration; depending on where the book was made and how much money was spent on its production, this might be through the inclusion of highly decorative historiated initial capitals or full-page miniatures, or through elaborate full or partial borders, or some lesser level of illustration. Over time various other prayers accumulated around the core elements; amongst devotions to Mary that regularly appear are the prayers *O intemerata et in eternum benedicta* and *Obsecro te domina sancta maria*; another item that frequently features in books of hours in England is the 'Fifteen Oes', a set of fifteen invocations to Jesus traditionally ascribed to St Bridget.

---

[48] Another 'Roberts' hours, BL Additional 73518, belonged to a different family, see Appendix V.

[49] Many examples of such bequests in northern wills are cited by Wordsworth, *Horae Eboracenses*, pp. xxxviii–xxxix.

[50] The classic study of books of hours is Wieck, *Time Sanctified*; for a briefer introduction see Sutton and Visser-Fuchs, *The Hours of Richard III*, pp. 2–3. Erler, 'Devotional Literature', provides a description of a typical hours.

One of the Roberts family's books of hours, CUL Ii.6.7, fits the general pattern described above quite closely. This small (180 mm x 130 mm) parchment manuscript of 132 folios was produced in England, probably in London, *circa* 1440.[51] It contains the Hours of the Virgin followed by the Hours of the Cross, the Penitential Psalms, the Fifteen Gradual Psalms, the Litany, the Psalms of the Passion, and the Office of the Dead with the Commendation of Souls. It also includes the Fifteen Oes; the *O intemerata* and *Obsecro te* prayers and other short prayers to Mary; the prayer on the 'Seven Words' spoken by Christ on the cross (*Domine ihesu christe qui septem verba die ultimo vite tue in cruce pendens dixisti*); and the 'Verses of St Bernard', an instruction to say eight particular verses from the psalms every day in order to be saved.[52] The major divisions of the manuscript are marked with four full-page miniatures, each surrounded by blue and purple bars, gold frames, and green-leaved sprays tipped with gold disks and leaves. As is usual the image that prefaces Matins (f. 7^v) is of the Annunciation, but two of the other miniatures depart from standard iconography to show St Christopher prefacing the Penitential Psalms (f. 44^v, not Christ in Judgment), and St Margaret prefacing the Office of the Dead (f. 84^v, not the usual depiction of monks chanting the funeral service); the Psalms of the Passion is prefaced by an image of the Mass of St Gregory (f. 62^v). Full border decoration surrounds the beginning of the text at each of these points, and also at the start of the *Commendatio animarum* (f. 114^r). There is a clear hierarchy in the system of decorated initials, with the largest (three to five lines high) in blue or purple patterned in white and filled with blue, rose, purple, orange, and green leaves on burnished gold ground, and also burnished gold initials mainly on blue and rose ground patterned in white; lesser divisions are marked with two-line burnished gold or blue initials with brown or red penwork flourishing, and one-line initials, alternating blue and red, are also used.[53] Though nicely decorated this was by no means a lavish

---

[51] Binski and Zutshi, *Western Illuminated Manuscripts*, p. 217 date it to the second quarter of the fifteenth century and Rogers, 'Books of Hours produced in the Low Countries', p. 223, note 55, describes it as 'of 1440s'.

[52] f. 74^v, *inc. inuenitur in libro bernardi quando diabolus dixit ei quis sciebat octo uersus psalterij quos qui dixerat omni die saluaretur et sunt isti uersus*. Each of the verses is marked with a coloured initial, alternately blue and red. On this text see Sutton and Visser-Fuchs, *The Hours of Richard III*, p. 50; versions in English are also known, see Revell, *Fifteenth Century English Prayers*, no. 206.

[53] For a full description see Binski and Zutshi, *Western Illuminated Manuscripts*, pp. 217–18; see also Scott, *Later Gothic Manuscripts*, i.41, note 20; ii.278.

production. The parchment is thick and feels rough to the touch; the layout is professionally done with pricking and ruling, and the script is a gothic textualis bookhand, but there are many mistakes in the text which have been visibly corrected in the margins. The decoration remains uncompleted in the text of the Fifteen Oes (ff. 76^r–81^v), where spaces three and two lines high have been left for initial capitals that have never been supplied except for crudely drawn small 'o's encircled in black ink.

The manuscript as a whole is comparatively free from annotations and additions. One layer of marginal additions may be distinguished as a programme of textual correction, with amendments to the main text written by a large, unpractised hand in a variety of ink shades. These usually supply omitted words or phrases, as for example in the short lection used during Compline, *Sicut cynamomum et balsamum aromatiratis odorem dedi quasi mirra electa dedi suauitatem odoris* on f. 42^r, where the words *quasi mirra electa dedi*, mistakenly omitted by eyeskip, have been supplied in the right margin.[54] The same type of corrections rectifying minor omissions occur throughout the Penitential Psalms and Office of the Dead.[55] Occasionally the correction is an erasure, as on f. 64^v, towards the bottom, where the corrector was removing an inadvertent repetition.[56] In one instance a word has been both supplied and erased, as on f. 46^v where the correct reading of Psalm 38 verse 2, *confirmasti super me manum tuam*, has been achieved first through the addition of *meum* in the left margin in light brown ink, and then the partial erasure of the word to give *me*. The hand that supplied these corrections knew the psalms well, but such knowledge could be accrued just as easily by a devout reader as by a text writer, and the script is not a professional one. Another improvement to the volume's usability is the provision of numbers for the Penitential Psalms, added neatly in the margins in a dark grey ink.[57] The numbers are Arabic, though still not easy to date, but fortunately the same ink is used on f. 38^r to mark out the start of Vespers by the addition of *Vesperas* in the right margin alongside the

---

[54] The lection is from Ecclesiasticus 24.20; see Wordsworth, *Horae Eboracenses*, p. 60.

[55] To cite just a few of many examples: f. 45^v, *meos*, marked with a caret for insertion after *omnes inimicos* (Psalm 6 v.7); f. 47^v *meus*, marked with a caret for insertion after *tu exaudias me domine deus* (Psalm 38 v.15); f. 50^v *filios*, marked with a caret for insertion after *ut solueret* (Psalm 102 v.20).

[56] The erased portion began *in conspectu eius cadent . . .*, which are exactly the words that were copied next (Psalm 22 v.29).

[57] The supplier uses the numbers according to the Vulgate sequence, marking 6 (f. 45^r), 32 (f. 45^v), 38 (f. 46^v), 51 (f. 48^r), 102 (f. 49^v), 130 and 143 (f. 51^r).

opening *Deus in adiutorium meum intende*, and here the script is clearly of the sixteenth century. Sometimes little marginal crosses have been used to mark particular lines, as on f. 43ᵛ by the phrase *fructum ventris tui*; on f. 44ʳ by *memoriam agimus*; and on f. 54ʳ a phrase from Psalm 132: *illuc producam cornu dauid*.⁵⁸ Collectively these small markings show that the book was used diligently and with care, with improvements made to its text and passages labelled for special attention.

Another part of the book that has clearly been much used is its calendar. Books of hours were usually prefaced by perpetual calendars, with a page allocated to each month, which in more deluxe products than Ii.6.7 might by illustrated by the signs of the zodiac or seasonal labours. The calendar listed the saints' days and fixed feasts of universal and local importance, and provided the means by which the date of Easter might be calculated, thus allowing the reader to grasp a sense of the liturgical year. In Ii.6.7 major feasts and saints are noted in red ink and minor saints in black, with contrasting initials in blue and red. To the left of the feast-day entries are four columns of numbers and letters. The first, a series of Roman numerals in red, gives the so-called golden number of the year and indicates the day of the new moon; the second, a series of letters a–g in black ('a' is in red), gives the dominical or Sunday letters; together these two columns provide the materials to calculate the date of Easter (the first Sunday following the first full moon on or after 21 March). The third column offers another series of Roman numerals in red; and the fourth gives the abbreviations for Nones (N), Ides (Id), and Kalends (Kl) alternately in black and red; together these two columns contain the information to allow calculation of the date according to the Roman practice of counting backwards from the named days of Kalends, Nones, and Ides.⁵⁹ At the bottom of each page is a statement in red of the relative length of day and night in each month: in July, for example, *Nox habet horas viii dies uero xvi*.⁶⁰ The July page also has a note of *Dies caniculares* at 14 July, and there is another similar entry on the September page.⁶¹ The 'dog days', as they are colloquially called, are the days about the time of the heliacal rising of the dog-star, and were traditionally regarded as the hottest and therefore

---

⁵⁸ Psalm 132 v.17.

⁵⁹ For a succinct and clear explanation of both methods of calculation see Sutton and Visser-Fuchs, *The Hours of Richard III*, pp. 94–95.

⁶⁰ f. 4ʳ: 'Night has eight hours, day truly sixteen'.

⁶¹ f. 5ʳ, at 6 September.

unhealthiest time of the year, and a period in which malignant influences might prevail. This was therefore a point when some activities – surgery, for example – ought to be avoided. In this respect some other calendars also note the year's twenty-four unlucky days (so-called 'Egyptian' days or *dies mali*, hence 'dismal'), but this information is not included here. There is, however, a note of the sun's entry into each different house of the zodiac: at 18 January *sol in aquario*, at 17 September *sol in libra*, and so on.

The standard format of the calendar thus provided a great deal of information whose use extended beyond the strictly liturgical. It offered the means to calculate the passage of time for secular purposes, facilitating forward planning and the avoidance of inauspicious dates. There was space too to add information of particular interest; the names of local saints, too obscure to have been included in the official template, or simply saints who were the objects of special veneration by the book's owners, could be written in, either by the owners themselves or by a professional text-writer. Four saints have been added to the calendar of Ii.6.7. One, St Alphege (19 April), is a very subtle addition that blends in well with the original entries, and only the darker shade of red used for the initial 'S' and the brown ink used for the rest of the entry betray its different status; it might have been made at a very early stage, perhaps even as a correction by the original scribe, since commemoration of St Alphege, an eleventh-century archbishop of Canterbury, was usually included in English calendars. The other three additions are much easier to spot since they were all made by the same rough hand. The first is at 3 March: 'Sancti Wenswali' or possibly 'Wenlwali', signifying St Winwaloe or Winwalocus who was a Breton abbot. In England Winwaloe was best known in Cornwall where two churches and a chapel were dedicated to him, but he was also known in Wales and in East Anglia: his feast was celebrated at Norwich where a church was dedicated to him.[62] The other two additions appear on the October page, where the translation of St Etheldreda and the feast of St Frideswide have been added inexpertly; the writer knows how to imitate the abbreviated form 'St', but the writing is unpractised and too large for

---

[62] Arnold-Forster, *Studies in Church Dedications*, ii.285–86; Linnell, *Norfolk Church Dedications*, pp. 18–19; Farmer, *The Oxford Dictionary of Saints*, pp. 409–10. There was also a very small alien cell at Wereham, due south of Fincham in Norfolk, that was dependent on Monsterel, Amiens (dedicated to St Guénolé), see Knowles and Hadcock, *Medieval Religious Houses*, p. 91.

the line space.⁶³ St Etheldreda was an East Anglian saint associated with Ely.⁶⁴ St Frideswide, virgin and abbess, was the patron of Oxford and her cult was strengthened after her formal adoption as patron of the university (by 1434); her relics were housed in the church dedicated to her and her tomb was honoured as a principal shrine until its suppression in 1538. Special interest in these saints cannot be associated with either Thomas or Edmund Roberts, but to some extent this is irrelevant since it is clear that they were not responsible for adding them. The same rough hand that wrote the three saints' entries has also contributed other additions of a different nature, inscribing obits in four places: two in July, one in September, and one in November. Remembrance was an important function of calendars, and this included not just the remembering of days of religious obligation but also the memorializing of the dead. Christians had a duty to pray for the souls of the departed, and a useful way of ensuring that this would happen perpetually was to record the obits of immediate family members in calendars that would be used by future generations. Quite often subsequent and unrelated owners of books of hours attempted to erase such obits, as has happened here, but enough remains visible to demonstrate that the Roberts book was pre-owned, seemingly by an entirely different family. The first entry on the July page, f. 4ʳ, is the least damaged and reads: *Obitus Constancie Coldhill anno domini millesimo CCCC lxxvi*, that is, 1476 (see Figure 16).⁶⁵ The obit has been crudely set into the available space at the end of the line for 17 July and along the whole blank line for 19 July, with just the final numbers extending out into the margin and so vulnerable to erasure. Immediately beneath this, squashed into the ends of the lines for 20–21 July, is a second obit which extends to the full width of the right margin and so has been more heavily erased. This can be read with the aid of ultra-violet light as: *Obitus Rogeri Coldhill anno domini millesimo ccccliij*, that is 1453.⁶⁶ The obit on the September page, f. 5ʳ, is set in the right

---

⁶³ At 17 and 19 October, respectively; the entry for the feast of St Etheldreda (23 June) was copied by the original scribe, see f. 3ᵛ.

⁶⁴ On the medieval cult of St Etheldreda see Blanton, *Signs of Devotion*.

⁶⁵ Hardwick and Luard, *A Catalogue of Manuscripts*, iii.503 read 'lx' wrongly as 'ix' and ignored the erasure, thus giving the date as 1409. Binski and Zutshi, *Western Illuminated Manuscripts* tentatively suggest that the date reads 'cccc°lxxxii (? last four letters erased)'; this would be 1482.

⁶⁶ Binski and Zutshi, *Western Illuminated Manuscripts*, do not mention this entry, nor the others on ff. 5ʳ and 6ʳ.

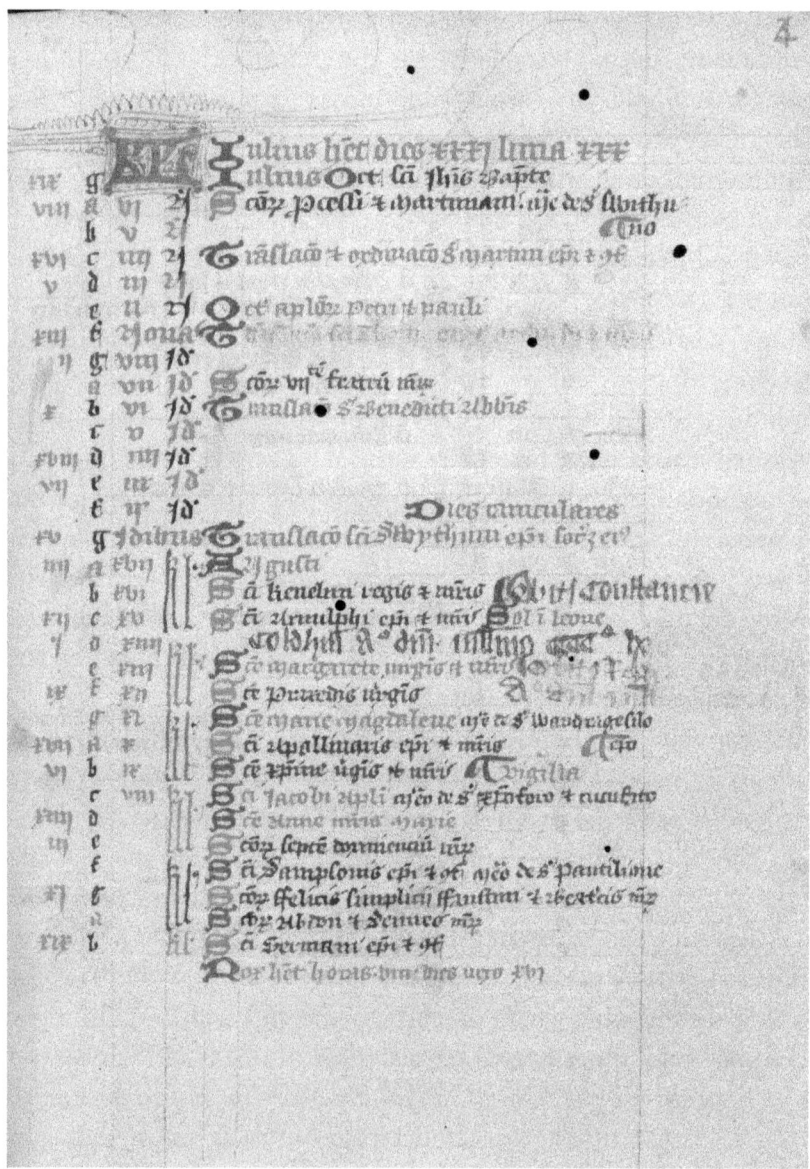

Figure 16 Cambridge University Library, MS Ii.6.7, f. 4ʳ. Book of Hours: July section from the calendar with added obits. Reproduced by kind permission of the Syndics of Cambridge University Library.

margin alongside the entries for 26–29 September; it can be deciphered under ultra-violet light as *Obitus Robert Page anno domini cccc lxviii*, that is 1468. The final obit, on f. 6ʳ, is set alongside the entries for 17–19

November. The opening word is *Obit* and the date seems to be *anno dominus millesimo cccc lxx*, that is, 1470, but the rest of the inscription is very unclear. I know of no associations between the Robertses and individuals named Coldhill or Page (with the exception of Thomas Roberts's legal involvement with the Pages of Harlesden),[67] but there need not necessarily be a direct connection: books might be purchased second-hand as well as bequeathed, and if bequeathed there might be several links in the chain between new and original owners.

In CUL Ii.6.7 there are few sustained additions to the volume's original contents from which to gain a better sense of who used the book during which period. Most of the volume's originally blank leaves remain entirely blank; the exception is the list of the births of Thomas Roberts's children f. 132^r, copied in a single stint probably from CUL Ii.6.2 as discussed above, and so probably added by Edmund Roberts. No other additions by Edmund occur in this hours however, in contrast to his treatment of CUL Ii.6.2, and it has neither his characteristic signatures nor the 'Robtz' monogrammatic form preferred by his father. Other marks and traces amongst the leaves of CUL Ii.6.7 are not especially attributable to any particular reader. Overall the volume is in good condition; it is not especially dirty, suggesting either that it was treated with care or that it was not much used. Certainly there is more evidence that the family's 'main' book of hours, used first by Thomas, and later by Edmund and then his son Francis, was CUL Ii.6.2. The inclusion of the list of birth records of Thomas's children in CUL Ii.6.7 might indicate that this volume belonged to another sibling of Edmund's (in the same way that his half-sister Dorothy had JRL English 98 with another list of those same records at the back); if so, this sibling was not such a habitual annotator as Edmund. Regardless of which family member used it, this book evidently did not stray far: circumstances kept it together with CUL Ii.6.2, which was demonstrably in the hands of the Robertses until the late sixteenth century at least before entering the collection of John Moore.[68]

CUL Ii.6.2, the family's other book of hours, is both older and more copiously annotated than Ii.6.7, making it a richer resource for tracing readerly activity, and Edmund Roberts's diligent use of its contents will be explored in detail in the next chapter. This small (190 mm x 130 mm) parchment volume of

---

[67] See Chapter 1, section titled 'The Family Seat and Some Family History.'
[68] See further discussion of this manuscript in the Postscript below.

100 folios was produced in Flanders in the last decade of the fourteenth century. Its script is a gothic textualis bookhand, and its full-page miniatures have distinctive architectural frames which allow an identification with the so-called 'Pink Canopies Group' of artists who were active in Bruges in that period.[69] From the outset this was a volume intended for the English market: its text follows the use of Sarum, and its calendar contains the names of some English saints who were not much known on the other side of the North Sea.[70] Geographical proximity and long-established trade routes between the Low Countries and East Anglia meant that Flemish books of hours were popular in that region, and it is not surprising to find various indications that the earliest owners of CUL Ii.6.2 had connections there. Most clearly indicative of this is the earliest addition to its original textual contents. At the end of the Commendations on f. 102ᵛ is the addition of a prayer to St Etheldreda, patron saint of Ely:

> [A]ve gemma preciosa, virgo decens et formosa, ethedreda deo digna, pia mater & benigna, fac hec digna familia tua cauat preconia. Beata ethedreda uirgo deo dilecta. Intercede pro nobis ad deum qui te elegit. Oremus.
>
> [D]eus qui eximie castitatis preui legio sanctissimam uirginem tuam etheldredam multipliciter decorasti da nobis famulis tuis ut sicut eius commemoracio nobiscum agitur in terris ita per eius interuentum nostri memoria apud te semper habeatur in celis. Per christum dominum nostrum.

The hand of the added prayer is not that of the main scribe, but it is a good scribal hand and clearly the work of a professional. Room has been carefully left for the initial capitals in the added text to be decorated in line with those in the rest of the volume: a space one line deep is allowed for the 'A' of 'aue' to be coloured, and the 'D' of 'deus' was allocated a space of three lines, presumably in the expectation that this would be finished like the burnished gold initials used elsewhere in other prayers and verses. There is generous spacing before the words *Beata* and *Oremus* which would have accommodated some colour too. None of this decoration has been supplied; if it had been it would be harder to

---

[69] Smeyers, *Flemish Miniatures*, pp. 203–5.
[70] For example, SS Alphege (19 April 'Alphegi') and Frideswide (17 October: 'Fredeswithe'), both in the hand of the original scribe. On Flemish books produced for the English market see Arnould and Massing, *Splendours of Flanders*, pp. 113–15.

discern that these lines were an addition to the originally planned contents of the volume.

Another feature that points towards the volume's early ownership in East Anglia is the addition of two obits to its calendar. The first of these, written by a small neat hand on f. 5^r alongside the dates 4–6 March, reads: *Obitus domine Margerie Carbonell uxor d. J.C. m anno domini millesimo cccc^{mo} vicesimo vj^{to} littera dominical e*, that is, 1426.[71] Margery (née Fitzrauf) was the wife of Sir John Carbonell of Badingham in Hoxne Hundred, Suffolk.[72] Her husband predeceased her, and in a grant of 1426 she adjusted her will so that her manor in Watton, Norfolk would pass to Richard Carbonell and his wife Elizabeth on condition that they gave 100 marks to Margery's daughter Elizabeth when she turned fifteen, either as a marriage portion or as payment for her profession as a nun at Marham Abbey.[73] The second obit has been added by a large rough hand on f. 8^r, alongside the dates for 1–4 September, and reads: *Obitus margarete heueyngham anno domini millesimo cccc xxxij littera dominical g*. The surname probably indicates a connection with Heveningham, a settlement only a few miles from Badingham, and it has been suggested that this lady was Margaret Heveningham (née Redisham), the wife of Sir John Heveningham, Suffolk (d. 1453).[74] In a letter to his son John Paston reported the death of his neighbour: 'And on Tuysday Sere Jon Henyngham 3ede to hys chyrche and herd iij massys, and cam hom agayn nevyr meryer, and seyd to hese wyf that he wuld go sey a lytyll deuocion in hese gardeyn and than he wuld dyne; and forthwyth he felt a feyntyng in hese legge and syyd doun. Thys was at ix of þe clok, and he was ded or none'.[75] Between them these obits clearly show that during its early history the book was owned in East Anglia. Badingham lies north of

---

[71] The hand responsible for this obit is not the same as that which added the note of St Ethedreda's translation on 17 October (f. 8^v).

[72] Binski and Zutshi, *Western Illuminated Manuscripts*, p. 343; Rogers, 'Books of Hours produced in the Low Countries', p. 71. John Carbonell's will is Norwich Consistory Court, Will Register 3 (Hirning), 134. On this and other books connected with the deanery of Dunwich, Suffolk, see Middleton-Stewart, *Inward Purity and Outward Splendour*, pp. 285–88.

[73] Oliva, *The Convent and the Community*, p. 46, referring to Norfolk Records Office Microfilm Reel 124/7, notes that there is no further evidence to show whether Margery's daughter became a nun.

[74] Binski and Zutshi, *Western Illuminated Manuscripts*, p. 343 and Rogers, 'Books of Hours produced in the Low Countries', p. 71; the surname occurs in various forms.

[75] Davis, *Paston Letters and Papers*, i.39. Duffy, *Marking the Hours*, repeats this, painting a vivid picture of the man 'saying a little devotion in his orchard; perhaps he was using this very book' (p. 83).

Framlingham in Suffolk, and Heveningham is a little further north and east. Watton and Marham are in Norfolk, but John Carbonell was lord of various places in both counties. Further East Anglian connections are indicated by the large shield which has been added to f. 2^v.[76] This shows two sets of quartered arms: those to the heraldic left (dexter), variously claimed as the arms of the Sutton or Thorpe families,[77] and those to the heraldic right (sinister) identified as the arms of Tilney of Ashwellthorpe.[78]

The obits and heraldry are not connected in any obvious way with the Roberts family, and it is not clear how the manuscript came into their hands. From the various lists of family records it is apparent that the book was owned by Thomas Roberts before it came to his son Edmund. Not only are there separate lists of the children of both men (Thomas's children are listed on f. 33^r, Edmund's on f. 109^v), more tellingly at the bottom of the list of Thomas's children is a note that records: 'Thise childern were lyvyng anno xxix h viij mense junij', that is June in the twenty-ninth year of Henry VIII's reign (1537). The implication is that the note was written in that same year, and this is borne out by the present tense used in the following statement: 'T Robertes hath in all xxiiij chyldern wherof xviij ben decessed'. A later hand has clumsily altered 'hath' to 'had' by erasing the 'h' and converting the 't' to a 'd'. This alteration might have been made at any point after Thomas's death, but the present tense of 'hath' suggests that the original inscription was made prior to 1542, and probably by Thomas himself. Another indication of Thomas's possession of the book is the inscription of his monogrammatic signature 'Robertz'; this occurs in a total of eleven places throughout the volume, usually though not invariably at the top corners of folios that face full-page miniatures.[79] Half of these signatures have been adapted by Edmund so that they stand in place of his own; this is cleverly done, and only careful attention to the different shades of

---

[76] Illustrated in Duffy, *Marking the Hours*, p. 85. Rogers, 'Books of Hours produced in the Low Countries', p. 71 notes that the coat-of-arms is of a sixteenth-century form.

[77] Duffy, *Marking the Hours*, p. 85 says Sutton; Binski and Zutshi, *Western Illuminated Manuscripts*, p. 343, following Rogers, 'Books of Hours produced in the Low Countries', p. 71, say Thorpe.

[78] cf. the heraldry in the Tilney scroll (NRO; a copy is kept at Tilney All Saints Church, and some images are viewable online via the website of the local newspaper, the Ely Standard: www.elystandard.co.uk).

[79] At the top right corners of ff. 4^r, 34^r, 38^r, 45^r, 54^r, 56^r, 76^r, 85^r; at the top left corner of f. 68^v; and in the left margins of f. 65^v alongside the start of the Latin prayer *Virgo templum*, and f. 95^v close to the start of *Beati imaculati*.

ink betrays the deception. The inscriptions across the double opening of ff. 33ᵛ–34ʳ, at the beginning of the Matins of the Virgin, are typical: 'Robertz' was written first in black ink at the top right corner of f. 34ʳ, and 'Edmond' was added subsequently in grey ink at the top left corner of f. 33ᵛ. As well as his forename Edmund also added the date, '1553', to the centre of the top margin of f. 33ᵛ above the full-page miniature of the Annunciation, so that the inscription across the double opening reads: 'Edmond 1553 Robertz'.[80] There is one instance that could not be so easily customized: at the start of the Meditations on the Cross the 'Robertz' monogram is placed at the top left of f. 68ᵛ, causing Edmund to add the more awkward inscription *Edmond est istas liber* at the top right corner of the same folio (see Figure 17).

Edmund's addition of the date '1553' along with his name suggests that this was the point at which he acquired the manuscript. When Thomas died in 1542 the book probably became the property of his heir, Michael, Edmund's elder brother, and there is one tiny piece of evidence that could support this theory. Above the large coloured shield on f. 2ᵛ are two other small sketches of shields. The one to the left is the Roberts family shield and it has the initials 'M R' set around it, perhaps indicating Michael Roberts.[81] This passage of the book, from Thomas to Edmund via Michael, is more than likely, and the delay in Edmund receiving it (Michael died in 1544 but Edmund's possession of the volume is only apparent from 1553) may be attributed to Michael's widow's continued occupation of the family home. This was Ursula's right under the terms of Michael's will, but following her remarriage to Benjamin Gonson her possession of this and other properties was disputed by Edmund. A complaint against him brought by Ursula and her husband in about 1550 accuses him of making various disturbances at the capital mansion where he 'hath broken vp the dores & windowes of the sayed mansyon howse & the chestes theare & hath taken awaye diuers parcelles of goods'.[82] Amongst these goods were 'evydences' and 'writinges', that is, deeds and charters proving entitlement to property; it is possible that Edmund might have seized other books at this point since he

---

[80] See similarly ff. 37ᵛ–38ʳ, 44ᵛ–45ʳ, 55ᵛ–56ʳ, 75ᵛ–76ʳ, 84ᵛ–85ʳ; one instance where Edmund missed the opportunity of adding his name is on ff. 53ᵛ–54ʳ at the start of Vespers.

[81] The other shows a design of three shields set 2 and 1, somewhat coloured, and might possibly represent the Barnes arms. It is not the arms of Michael's wife, Ursula Huse: her father Anthony Hussey's arms shown on www.ancestry.co.uk are barry, Ermine and Gules, over all a canton Gules a cross Or.

[82] TNA, C 1/1223/29.

Figure 17 Cambridge University Library, MS Ii.6.2, f. 68ᵛ. Ownership inscriptions added by Thomas and Edmund Roberts. Reproduced by kind permission of the Syndics of Cambridge University Library.

certainly became the owner of this book of hours a short time later. It is less clear how the book had come into the Roberts family, and whether its earliest traceable owners, Margery Carbonell and Margaret Heveningham, were Edmund's ancestors or not. If these women were long-dead family members, then in using the book Edmund might have felt a deep sense of personal connection with both the past and the afterlife. Yet even if they were not, a sense of connection would still have obtained, because these were individuals who were part of the community of souls, to be remembered and prayed for after death, as part of the Christian duty of the living.

Owning a book of hours indicates participation in a common religious culture rather than any special level of individual devotion. Use, rather than mere possession, is a more reliable indicator of piety and, as in the case of other books, annotations can reveal just how much these books of hours were used, and for what purpose. One significant use of these books, as secure repositories for records of births and deaths in the Roberts family, has been discussed in the present chapter, but this type of engagement reveals little about contemporary reading practices. In the next chapter attention will be focussed on just one of these books of hours, CUL Ii.6.2, and particularly on the texts and annotations that were added to it after its initial period of production. Some of these additions may be attributed to Thomas Roberts and others to Edmund. Unpicking which man added which materials to the volume reveals their different individual responses and concerns, and also demonstrates that although they both in turn owned the same physical book, each of them nevertheless possessed a slightly different book of hours and one which, by the time it was handed down to Edmund's son Francis, was quite transformed from the book that had belonged to the Carbonell family in the early fifteenth century.

6

Devotional Reading in the Reigns of Mary Tudor and Elizabeth I

Thomas Roberts is the earliest member of the Roberts family who can be identified as the owner of the manuscripts now associated with them. After Thomas's lifetime his books passed to his children, and remained in the family for several generations. His son Edmund was a keen reader and annotator, using the family's old books but also acquiring books of his own. This chapter will explore Edmund's engagement with two kinds of religious books, the book of hours and the devotional anthology.

I YOUSE THYS PRAYER WELL EVERY DAYE: HOW EDMUND ROBERTS SAID HIS PRAYERS

As his father had done before him, Edmund Roberts used a book of hours in his personal devotions. Of itself this was not particularly remarkable, nor can it be taken as evidence of any special degree of piety: books of hours were widely owned by members of all classes in the later Middle Ages, with income and aspiration dictating whether their format was that of the richly illuminated *objet d'art* or the more humble continental volumes which were mass-produced for the English market. These were books designed for lay people to use daily at home and to carry to church services on Sundays and other holy days; they were also books which were typically handed down through generations of the same family, or bequeathed to particular relatives or close friends. This type of book reached the peak of its popularity in the mid to late fifteenth century, and copies (in both manuscript and print) continued to be produced in large numbers well into the sixteenth century.[1]

---

[1] The following discussion depends on the overview given by Erler, 'Devotional Literature', pp. 495–515.

Even in the 1530s, when religious change was well-advanced in England, the book of hours remained central to the practice of individual spirituality; instead of trying to forbid the possession and use of this type of book, the secular authorities wisely sought to adapt it so that it would conform more closely to reformed religious thinking. After the publication in 1534 of *A Prymer in Englyshe*, a book of hours which used the English language rather than Latin, various reformist versions followed with new additions that replaced the original indulgenced devotions.[2] Royal approval was given to *The primer set foorth by the kynges maiestie* which appeared in 1545; a decade later, under a very different regime, the prescribed Marian imprint was *An vniforme and catholyke prymer in latin and Englishe*.[3] Sixteenth-century printed hours were issued in different formats, on parchment or paper, with richly coloured or plain cuts, and in considerable numbers; they would have been widely available and also very affordable, retailing in the shop of one Cambridge bookseller at prices between two pence and fourteen pence.[4] These were products designed to meet the demands of a mass market and to suit every pocket, yet when Edmund Roberts took up his hours it was not one of these modern books but an old manuscript; if he possessed a printed hours it has not survived.[5]

The physical artefact that Edmund held in his hand as he knelt to pray was old, but its contents were even older. The format of the book of hours had originated in the mid thirteenth century with the intention of helping lay readers to follow the patterns of daily prayer prescribed in the Divine Office used by the clergy. Those services or hours were found together in the book's central text, the Little Office of the Virgin, which was followed by particular groups of psalms, the Litany, and the Office of the Dead, and usually preceded by set passages from the gospels and a calendar; these were the standard contents but were subject to local variations and the accretion of other elements over time.[6] These are broadly

---

[2] *STC* 15986. For an earlier group of manuscripts that translated the book of hours into English see Kennedy, 'Reintroducing the English Books of Hours'.

[3] *STC* 16034 and *STC* 16060.

[4] Erler, 'The Laity', p. 140.

[5] Survival rates for printed hours are low: Erler, 'Devotional Literature', p. 506, estimates a total of about 375 surviving copies. A printed hours that might be connected with a different branch of the Roberts family is *STC* 16042, sold at Sotheby's 2 July 1963, lot 338: it has the name 'Henri Roberte' and the date 1546; I am grateful to A. I. Doyle for bringing this volume to my notice.

[6] See the fuller description given in Chapter 5, section titled 'The Use of Sarum: Cambridge University Library, MS Ii.6.7 and Cambridge University Library, MS Ii.6.2'.

the contents of CUL Ii.6.2, but the ordering of the individual elements after the calendar is different: here the *memoriae* (prayers to the saints) come first, followed by the Hours of the Virgin, the Penitential Psalms, and the Office of the Dead with the Commendations.[7] This variation in ordering was a usual feature of Sarum Hours that were produced in the Low Countries; in these volumes the *memoriae* were placed first, and typically included suffrages (intercessory prayers) to the Trinity, and SS Michael, John the Baptist, John the Evangelist, George, Thomas of Canterbury, Christopher, Mary Magdalene, Katherine, Margaret, Barbara, and Anne. These seem indeed to have been the original contents of CUL Ii.6.2, though there are now some omissions, and one additional item is the miniature of the Vernicle on f. 12^v with prayers from the Office of the Vernicle or Holy Face following on f. 13^{r-v}. The omissions are Thomas of Canterbury, Mary Magdalene, and Barbara, but all three may well have been present originally. Two leaves are now missing between the full-page miniature of St Anne with the Virgin and Child on f. 28^v and f. 31^r where the text refers to Mary Magdalene (*Gaude pia magdalena spes salutis uite uena lapsorum fiducia . . .; Deus qui beatam mariam magdalena penitentiam . . .*), making it clear that the missing leaves must have carried the memoria to Anne and the image of Mary Magdalene. Another missing leaf, f. 32, might have contained the miniature of Barbara and related prayers, though none survive to substantiate this. A longer omission (ff. 20^v–21^r) occurs exactly where we might anticipate the miniature and texts associated with Thomas of Canterbury. Omissions, unlike additions, are almost impossible to date, and their causes may have been as much accidental as deliberate. Possibly these losses might have arisen from greater wear and tear at these points in the codex, which might signal that members of the Roberts household had a personal devotion to these particular saints. There is no reason to suppose that all three losses must have occurred at the same point, and no way to be sure whether they happened before or after Edmund's possession of the book. However, the 1538 decree that Thomas of Canterbury's feast should be suppressed suggests that the removal of ff. 20^v–21^r might have already taken place before the book came into Edmund's hands. It might be noted that in the calendar the entries for Thomas's martyrdom on 29 December (f. 9^v) and the octave of this feast on 5 January (f. 4^r) have been obediently erased, and those saints who were popes have been restyled as bishops (*episcopi*); the dark ink and

---

[7] Rogers, 'Patrons and Purchasers', p. 1167.

approximation of textura script used in these alterations is characteristic of Thomas Roberts's writing.⁸

When Edmund used this book for his devotions he inevitably followed in the footsteps of his father who had owned it before him. Quite aside from Thomas's inscription of their family records on f. 33ʳ, which Edmund would have encountered every time he looked for the place where the Little Office began, Thomas also marked some of the original prayers and devotions for special attention. One such is the metrical devotion on the Seven Joys of Mary, *Virgo templum trinitatis ...*, copied on ff. 65ᵛ–67ʳ as part of a sequence of prayers to the Virgin introduced by the full-page miniature of Our Lady of Humility.⁹ The devotion is signalled to the reader by a substantial five-line rubric, but has been further marked out by the addition alongside in the left margin of Thomas Roberts's monogram. The beginning of the *Commendatio animarum* on f. 95ᵛ, already distinguished by a five-lines high illuminated initial 'B', is emphasized in the same way. When these monograms occur at the top corners of leaves, as noted in the previous chapter, they seem to function primarily as stamps of ownership; but when they are set in other places the aim seems to be to draw attention to particular texts. Regardless of the intention, the effect would have been to remind Edmund of his father and his father's previous use of the book whilst he performed his own devotions. Another instance where Thomas annotated the original contents of the volume is the prayer for protection against enemies on f. 11ʳ: *Domine deus omnipotens pater & filius et spiritus sanctus da michi famulis tuo uictoriam contra omnes inimicos meos ...*; this prayer invokes the power of the Trinity, and so is often, as here, paired with a depiction of the Throne of Mercy (f. 10ᵛ). Towards the bottom of f. 11ʳ the opening words of two psalms are cited in the text of the prayer, *Deus in nomine tuo*, Psalm 53 (54), and *Deus misereatur*, Psalm 66 (67), each signalled by the rubricated abbreviation 'Ps' (for *Psalmus*). Alongside in the left margin Thomas has added the instruction: *Oremus*. Another addition in the right margin gives the opening words of Psalm 129 (130), *De profundis etc*, with a caret marking the point of insertion in the text, followed by *Kyrie christi*

---

⁸ For the substitution of *epi* (*episcopi*) for *pape*, see for example the entries for St Marcellus on 16 January (f. 4ʳ) and St Gregory on 12 March (f. 5ʳ). Sutton and Visser-Fuchs, *The Hours of Richard III*, suggest this reason for the erasure of St Edward's feast from the Hours of Richard III, see p. 46 and p. 95 note 118; for the 1538 decree see Hughes and Larkin, *Tudor Royal Proclamations*, i.270–76 (no. 186).

⁹ f. 59ᵛ; the opening devotion is *Salve virgo virginum*.

kyrie. The addition to the right margin has a less careful aspect, and was either made on a different occasion when Thomas was writing more hastily, or possibly added by Edmund rather than his father; both men used dark ink, and it is not always easy to distinguish between their hands in this volume. Whichever man was responsible, the citation of the *incipit* to Psalm 129 (130) shows that he knew this prayer well enough to supply the omission; other copies of the prayer, as in Robert Thornton's book, usually cite this and other psalms at this point.[10]

Thomas Roberts had also augmented the original contents of CUL Ii.6.2 by including many other prayers. The addition of extra devotional materials was a common practice in books of hours, where individual owners tended to add their own favourite prayers, often on blank leaves at the ends of the books. At the front of the manuscript, on the blank leaves before the calendar begins, there are various additions, not all attributable to Thomas, but amongst those that are in his hand are a rhyme on the life of the Virgin and a couplet on the Passion of Christ (both in Latin, f. 1^v), and a form of confession in English (f. 3^r). At the back of the book, on f. 110^r Thomas added a Latin prayer to St Erasmus, signing the ten lines of text with his 'Robertz' monogram and separating the prayer from the preceding item, a recipe for colic, by drawing a line across the page. There are other contributions by other hands in both these locations, but these are not the only places in the volume where extra materials have been added. The physical composition of CUL Ii.6.2 provided its owners with a great many opportunities to add other items to the original textual contents, because in this case the text and the illustrations had been produced independently.[11] The fifteenth-century Flemish artist painted the full-page miniatures on the versos of singletons, following a standard iconographic programme. This method of production meant that a stationer could buy a job lot of illustrations and allow individual clients to select whatever pictures they desired. The pictures might then be inserted into otherwise undecorated books of hours, and placed according to taste.[12] Such flexibility must have suited all concerned, but one consequence was

---

[10] For the copy in Thornton's miscellany, Lincoln, Lincoln Cathedral Library MS 91, f. 177^r, see Brewer and Owen, *The Thornton Manuscript*; the prayer is transcribed by Horstman, *Yorkshire Writers*, i.377.

[11] Arnould and Massing, *Splendours of Flanders*, p. 114 discuss this practice in relation to this manuscript. Another manuscript which has miniatures from the same Flanders workshop is BL, MS Sloane 2683, illustrated in Duffy, *Marking the Hours*, p. 82.

[12] Rudy, *Piety in Pieces*, discusses ways in which medieval manuscripts could be customized.

that the finished volumes would contain numerous blank leaves which were the rectos of the full-page miniatures. Moreover, since the original text that accompanied the images did not always take up the whole of the room allowed, there would be other blank spaces as well, and collectively these offered ample scope for the addition of extra prayers or other texts.[13] In CUL Ii.6.2 Thomas Roberts used the blank reverses of nine of the miniatures to inscribe further materials.[14] He chose to use more of the blank leaves that occur towards the beginning of the volume where, in the *Memoriae*, he wrote on six out of nine originally blank reverses; conversely, in the Hours of the Virgin, he wrote on only three, and the rest remain blank.[15] At first sight this might seem no more than an orderly method of using up any available writing spaces in the volume in the order in which they presented themselves, but in fact Thomas seems to have been concerned to place his additions in the most appropriate locations.[16] On the originally blank reverse of the full-page miniature of SS John the Baptist and John the Evangelist, Thomas inscribed two Latin prayers to John the Baptist: *Sancte Johannes Baptista electe dei tu es angelus dei qui venisti ante faciem domini* ... and *Sancte Johannes Baptista qui meruisti saluatorem mundi tuis manibus* ....[17] On the reverse of the image of St George Thomas added a prayer addressed to him: *George deo care saluatorem deprecare ut gubernat angliam* ....[18] In other cases the prayers that he added introduce saints not otherwise represented in the original text. For example, on the reverse of the miniature which portrays St Margaret he added two prayers to St Frideswide, *De regali stupe nata Frideswida nobilis* ... and *Deus qui beate Frideswide virgini tue*

---

[13] CUL Ii.6.2 has twenty-one full-page miniatures and two instances where the written text did not fully fill the page, ff. 19^v and 43^v; there are two other blank leaves as well, ff. 46^v and 83^v. Another Flemish book of hours that was assembled in this way is Cambridge, Fitzwilliam Museum, MS 49, see Rogers, 'Some *Curiosa Hagiographia*', pp. 199–202 and Rogers, 'Patrons and Purchasers', p. 1169.

[14] The reverses of miniatures which remain unfilled are: f. 12^r Vernicle; f. 28^r St Anne with the Virgin and Child; f. 44^r Nativity; f. 47^r Annunciation to the Shepherds; f. 49^r Adoration of the Magi; f. 51^r Massacre of the Innocents; f. 53^r Flight into Egypt; f. 59^r Our Lady of Humility; f. 68^r Crucifixion; f. 84^r Funeral Service.

[15] The reverse of one miniature, the Visitation (f. 37^v) has written text that seems to be the work of the original scribe rather than an addition, which may be an indication that the pictures were purchased first.

[16] Note that ff. 12^v and 28^r remain blank.

[17] f. 18^r.

[18] f. 22^r, twelve lines in rhyming couplets, laid out as verse.

felicitatem . . ..[19] In the Hours of the Virgin where Thomas made fewer additions there are also indications that material was directed to the most appropriate place. A Latin metrical prayer in praise of Mary, *Aue virgo graciosa stella sole clarior* . . . is written on the reverse of the miniature that depicts the Presentation in the Temple, laid out over five lines though actually constituting ten lines of verse.[20] Similarly a range of other texts added to the back of the miniature depicting the Man of Sorrows are all of a Marian or Christological nature.[21]

The effect of all Thomas's additions was to extend the volume's original contents by some considerable measure, and as a result Edmund found within the book of hours that he inherited not just the usual devotions to the Virgin and major saints, but also a range of extra prayers and hymns addressed to these figures, as well as prayers that invoked other saints who were less central to the liturgy, such as SS Clement, Cornelius, and Frideswide.[22] Still other prayers had been inserted in the volume even before Thomas's time, including the suffrages to St Etheldreda which have already been discussed in Chapter 5 above.[23] Another such early addition is the inscription of two Latin prayers to St Botolph on f. 58^v: *O lilium odiferum spergens ubique vivificum suavitatis odorem sancte pater Botulphe* . . . ; and *[D]eus qui es uera felicitas et requies beatorum beati Botulphi confessoris* . . .. These are written in a dark brown ink by a hand that tries to conform to the appearance of the original textura script. At the beginning of the second prayer a space two lines high has been left for a decorated initial capital 'D' to be supplied. The absence of the capital calls attention to the text and betrays its addition. Notably a little letter 'd' has been written into the space to complete the word, and the same black ink that supplied this letter has also written 'Botulphe' in the left margin. Written casually by Thomas Roberts's hand, this note reveals that St Botolph carried some significance for a new generation of readers. Whilst the actual inscription of the two additional prayers to St Botolph was probably done at the request of an earlier owner, and was most likely connected with the volume's East Anglian origins where church dedications to the saint are most numerous, the sixteenth-century note attests to a later interest in the saint, and one that is more likely to have been related to

---

[19] f. 26^r.
[20] f. 55^r; the rhyme scheme is abababcccb. See further below.
[21] f. 75^r.
[22] Material relating to these less well-known saints occurs, respectively, on ff. 10^r, 15^v, and 26^r.
[23] See Chapter 5, section titled 'The Use of Sarum: Cambridge University Library, MS Ii.6.7 and Cambridge University Library, MS Ii.6.2'.

the Robertses' London milieu where four churches were dedicated to him.[24] Similarly, Thomas's addition on f. 10[r] of two prayers related to St Clement (*Dedisti domine habitaculum martiri tuo Clementi in mari . . .* and *Deus qui nos anima beati Clementes martiris tui atque pontificis . . .*) seems almost certainly connected with the dedication of Thomas's London parish church, St Clement Danes.[25]

Some of Thomas's additions were prayers for particular purposes or circumstances. On f. 25[v], after writing two prayers addressed to St Dorothy: *Inuictissima cristi martiri & virgo sancta Dorothea martiris scoleribus . . .* and *Omnipotens sempiterne deus cuius nomine gloriosa virgo & martir Dorothea . . .*, Thomas wrote another short Latin prayer (*Te veneranda caro cristi venerantur adoro corpus . . .*) with an English heading that explains when the prayer is to be used: 'Sey this prayer at the leuacion'.[26] Beneath the two prayers to St Clement on f. 10[r] he inscribed a Latin prayer addressed to Christ which recalls various Biblical couples whose wives conceived in old age. Abraham, Sarah and Isaac, Zachariah, Elizabeth and John are all named, and the second part of the prayer allows for the insertion of the supplicant's name (*est michi famule sue N ad honorem & gloriam nominis sui . . .*). The English heading makes clear that this is a 'Prayer for women to Conceyue Childe', but the invocation of holy names recalls a strategy familiar from charms, blurring the border between devotion and superstition a little. Another short text added by Thomas at the start of the volume crosses that border entirely, purporting to offer physical help in a particular circumstance by detailing the form of injunction to be used 'to staunche fyre yf a house be bryni–': *mentem cauetam spontaneam honorem deo et patre liberacionem.*[27] The English headings clarify the proper application or context of these Latin texts, perhaps to help female members of the family since

---

[24] On Botolph see Arnold-Forster, *Studies in Church Dedications*, ii.52–56; the four London dedications were in Aldgate, Billingsgate, Bishopsgate, and Aldersgate. Yet Botolph has not been added to the calendar (June 17, see f. 6[v]); his feast does not usually occur in the Sarum hours.

[25] On St Clement see Rogers, 'Patrons and Purchasers', pp. 1167–71, and Arnold-Forster, *Studies in Church Dedications*, i.275–88 who notes that 'a fair fountain called Clement's Well' located close to Clement's Inn survived as late as the sixteenth century. St Clement does not occur frequently in books of hours, though Robert Bartlett, *Why Can the Dead Do Such Great Things?*, p. 114 notes that his name is mentioned in the *Communicantes* and so would be familiar to anyone who attended Mass regularly.

[26] Other prayers to St Dorothy on f. 3[v] are not in Thomas's hand.

[27] f. 2[r]; the final letters of the English are lost due to a hole in the leaf.

Thomas and his sons were evidently proficient in Latin. Only a few of Thomas's additions are furnished with English prompts. More typical is the prayer for daily use that he added to f. 27^v, *Omnipotens sempiterne deus te adore to [sic] glorifico tibi gracias ago ...*, which is all in Latin with a Latin heading: *Oracio cotidiana pro beneficijs dei & vocetur deo gracias ....* Yet elsewhere Thomas included prayers that were composed entirely in English, such as the form of confession that he copied on f. 3^r, 'Oure most mercyfull fader, Lord God, knowyng oure frelite and redynes to all synners ...'.

Not all of the extra devotional items that Edmund found within his augmented book of hours had been contributed by his father's hand. Some had clearly been inscribed before Thomas's time, such as the prayers to St Botolph mentioned above. Other fifteenth-century additions include the single rhyme royal stanza beginning 'The merites of mas who can expresse' which is set centrally in the upper half of f. 2^r, and two Latin texts on f. 3^v that relate to St Dorothy.[28] Two other added items from this period are the Latin prayers to St Peter and Mary that are set at the top of f. 23^v, both by the same small, neat hand and light brown ink.[29] Other added texts seem of a more contemporary appearance. The second of the two added prayers to St George on f. 22^r is written in a sixteenth-century secretary script that seems more casual, and with letters more thickly formed, than is usual in Thomas Roberts's hand, and so perhaps might have been added by Edmund or his older brother Michael.[30] The hand that added two Latin prayers on f. 24^r is more casual again, and might also be responsible for two other Latin items on f. 103^r, but it is often hard to be sure whether contributions were made by different individuals, or by just one person writing on different occasions and under different, perhaps more rushed, circumstances.[31] In a volume such as this it can be difficult to disentangle the many layers of textual production. Thomas Roberts was responsible for adding many of the extra prayers and devotions, but some clearly pre-date

---

[28] *NIMEV* 3427, the only recorded instance of this poem. The first text on f. 3^v (*In quacumque domo nomen fuint vel imago ...*) expresses the benefits of keeping an image of St Dorothy in the home as a protection against miscarriage; the second is a prayer to the saint, *Virgo pia Dorothea polleus miraculis ...*.

[29] *Janitor celi qui accepisti claues regni celorum ...* and *Aue & gaude mater domini nostri ihesu christi regina celi domina mundi imperatrix inferni ...*.

[30] *Deus qui nos beati Georgii martiris tui meritis ...*.

[31] On f. 23^v *Per crucis hoc signum fugiat ...* and the prayer to St Erasmus, *Pra quis omnipotens deus vt qui beati herasimi ...*'; on f. 103^r *Adesto domine supplicacionibus nostris ...* and *Angele qui meus es custos pietate superna ...*.

his possession of the book, and others were contributed by his son. Some of the more securely identifiable instances added by Edmund will be discussed further below. In other cases it is impossible to be sure whether prayers or notes were added by Edmund or his father, or even by his brother Michael or another of his siblings. Rarely, it is possible to say with some confidence that both father and son have left traces on the same page: one such instance occurs on f. 15^v where Thomas copied a prayer to St Cornelius. In both the heading and the opening line the epithet *papa* has been struck through and 'epo' (*episcopo*) and 'epi' (*episcopi*) written above, probably by Edmund, perhaps by Michael (four letters do not provide much of a sample for comparison, but the addition is clearly later). Yet ultimately the difficulty of identifying exactly which member of the family may have been responsible for which additionally inscribed item does not undermine the main preoccupation of this discussion, which is to examine Edmund's *reading* of the book and his use of it in his personal devotions.

A consequence of the layering of additional texts in CUL Ii.6.2 was that when Edmund used this book in the second half of the sixteenth century he had at his fingertips a store of prayers to use for different occasions and to suit a wide selection of devotional needs; moreover, he could choose between texts written in either Latin or English. Prayers concerning the sacrament include the text *Anima Ihesu christi sanctifica me* (f. 103^r), a devotion to be said at or after communion, and also the English poem on the merits of the Mass (f. 2^r). An instruction as to what to say at the elevation of the host, the holiest moment in the Mass, details the recitation of the hymn *Stella celi extirpavit* (f. 103^r), but it is clear that Edmund actually used a different levation prayer *Te veneranda caro cristi* . . . (f. 25^v) because he replicates part of its English heading ('At þe lauacion') in the left margin where it is more visible. An English verse levation prayer was copied twice by different hands on ff. 102^v and 103^v, once set out roughly as verse though not always keeping to the proper lineation, and once as prose:

> O Ihesus lorde wellcum thu be
> in forme of brede as Y the se.
> O Ihesus for thy holy name
> schelde me thys day fro sorro & schame,
> And lete me lyfe in trewthe and ryght
> before my dethe hafe hosyll and schryfte.
> O Ihesus as thus were of a mayden borne

> Let me neuer be forlone,
> And let me neuer for no syne
> Lese the blysse that thu art jn.³²

Reminders of the importance and benefits of Christ's passion occur throughout. A formula for meditation, whose opening words 'Meditacio est' are bracketed to three phrases, concludes with the advice that thoughts should be constantly focussed on Christ's passion (*In passione cristi constante infixa*).³³ A Latin prayer to Christ, *Adoramus te cristi ihesu & benedicimus tibi* . . ., said to be uttered by Joseph of Arimathea at the crucifixion, seems to show indications of Edmund's use. The prayer was copied by Thomas Roberts on the originally blank reverse of the image that shows St Michael and the dragon, and consists of a series of statements beginning *adoremus te*, each followed by the Pater Noster and Ave, the sign of the cross, and at the end *Credo in deum*. The prayer occupies the top half of f. 14ʳ and beneath it a line has been drawn in lighter ink, with the initial 'R' added at the far right hand side; this 'R' is not the heavy monogrammatic form favoured by Thomas Roberts, but might be a similar signature used by Edmund. Another prayer addressed to Christ, this time in English, that asks for the forgiveness of sins, has no annotations but was evidently used a great deal:

> O my seuereyn lord Iesu, þe very sone off allmyty God, and of þe most clene and gloryous virgine Seynt Mary, þat suffryd deth for my sake and for all mankende upon good fryday, and arose ageyn be þi godhed on þe thred day. I beseche þe lord to haue mercy upon me þat arn all a vrechyd synner. But ȝet lord I am þi creature, and for þi presyeus passyon, saue me and kepe me from all perell bodely and gostely, and specyally from all thynges þat may turne þe to displesans. And wyth all my hert I thanke þe most mercyfull lord for þe grete mercyee þu hast schewyd me in my grete dawngeres that I haue ben in [. . .] vele in my

---

³² This is the copy written on f. 103ᵛ: there are only minor variations between the two copies. The prayer closely resembles that printed from the Gurney manuscript (now British Library, MS Egerton 3245) by Robbins, 'The Gurney Series' p. 378, 'Iesu, Lord, welcom þow be', but with several lines transposed. *NIMEV* records several versions of this prayer (3882; 3883; 3884); the version here is closest to 3882, but is not listed there, nor in the equivalent entry in *DIMEV* 6195. On levation prayers in English verse more generally see Robbins, 'Levation Prayers'.

³³ ff. 1ᵛ and 75ʳ.

sowle as in my body and þi [...] grete and enlest [*sic*] mercy hath euer kepyd me sparyd me and savyd me from þe owr of my by[rth] [f. 24ʳ] in to þis tyme. I thanke þe lord wyth my myghte and where I kan nott ne doo natt lyffe as þi seruaunt, lord allmyghty God, Iesu, I synfull creature aske þe mercy, Amen.

Copied across ff. 23ᵛ–24ʳ, its text becomes progressively less clear towards the foot of f. 23ᵛ where some of the words that lie closest to the central gutter are so rubbed as to be almost illegible. The damage arises from the position of the hand holding the open book, and bespeaks much use in devotion, despite the fact that this addition was written by an unpractised hand that is neither Thomas's nor Edmund's. The prayer is known from other similar contexts including the book of hours made for John Talbot, first Earl of Shrewsbury.[34]

The standard format of the book of hours contained no shortage of suitable devotions to Mary, but nevertheless several other Marian texts have been added to CUL Ii.6.2. The most extensive is the prayer that Thomas Roberts copied on f. 31ᵛ: *Euge dicta sanctis oraculis antequam nata visu ...,* with a heading that ascribes its composition to the theologically conservative bishop of London, Richard Fitzjames (d. 1522), a staunch defender of orthodoxy.[35] A short rhyme on the life of the Virgin was important enough to be inscribed twice, on f. 1ᵛ and f. 75ʳ:

> Anno quartodecimo virgo concepisti
> Annis triginta tribus cum nato vixisti
> Et post mortem filij quem tu peperisti
> Anno duodecimo assumpta fuisti.[36]

Further down on f. 75ʳ Thomas made a note about the date of the foundation of Mary's shrine at Walsingham. There is also the metrical devotion *Aue virgo graciosa* mentioned above, that he copied on f. 55ʳ:

---

[34] Cambridge, Fitzwilliam Museum, MS 40–1950, where it has been added to f. 133ʳ, see Wormald and Giles, *Descriptive Catalogue*, ii.446. In another fifteenth-century book of hours, CUL Ff.6.8, this prayer is the first of two English prayers added to the first leaf, see Connolly, *IMEP XIX*, p. 151.

[35] Fitzjames became bishop of London in August 1506, see Thompson, 'Fitzjames, Richard'.

[36] On f. 75ʳ (the version quoted here) and in a more abbreviated version on f. 1ᵛ, both copies by the same hand.

> Aue virgo graciosa, stella sole clarior,
> Mater dei gloriosa, fauo mellis dulcior,
> Rubicunda plusquam rosa, lilio candidior,
> Omnis sanctus te honorat, omnis virtus te decorat,
> Ihesus Cristus te coronat, in celis sublimior.[37]

A final line: *Pater noster aue maria ab alexanda papa vj concedare plena*, apparently written at the same time, seems to attribute the poem to Pope Alexander VI whose pontificate was 1492–1503, and implies an indulgence of some kind. Thomas noted another indulgence connected with devotion to Mary at the start of the book:

> Virginis egregie faciem cum veneris ante
> Tunc aue deuote non cesses fundere pro te
> Illud dicenti conceditur sapienti
> Anni milleni trescenti septuageni
> per quintum urbanum Episcopum tibi dico romanum
> Adde Jesus fine quotiens tu dixeris aue
> bis triginta dies venie tibi merces.[38]

The first five lines are bracketed to the words *urbanus v^{tus}*, and the last two lines to the words *urbanus $iiij^{tus}$* and *Johannes 22*. The text therefore indicates various concessions: the indulgence granted by Urban V for reciting the 'Ave Maria', and the indulgence granted by Urban IV and John XXII for saying the name of Christ at the end of the prayer. At the back of the book is a note of another indulgence: *Pardon vj m^l dayes & $iiij^{xx}$* (6080 days), added at the foot of f. 102^r below another carefully written addition addressed to Mary but concerning St Anne: *Et benedicta sit sannctissima mater tua anna ex qua sine macula tua caro processit virginea Amen.*[39] Attention is further drawn to the text by a symbol like a hooked 'g' in the right margin – not a form of the Roberts monogram, but some type of *signe de renvoi* whose significance is now unclear. There have been no attempts to hide or delete any of these indulgence texts despite the fluctuating fashions of religious devotion that characterized the mid to late sixteenth century. However, close examination of the text that Thomas inscribed on f. 2^r reveals that

---

[37] The word *Alleluia* has been added in a lighter ink to the end of the final line of the text.
[38] f. 2^r.
[39] The Latin text is written in a style that imitates the textura of the original script on this page; the note of pardon is less formally written.

the word *Episcopum* in line 5 has been carefully worked into a space that is really too small for it, replacing an erased *pape* of which the faint outline of the descender of the initial 'p' is just still visible. Thomas here made an effort to stay within the letter of the law, converting *pape* to *episcopum* in a similar way to the substitutions he made throughout the calendar. Allowing the rest of the text and others like it to stand is a clear indication that Thomas and Edmund and other members of the Roberts family continued to cherish the promise of remission that indulgences offered, resisting reformist advice that such promises were worthless.

Another form of devotion that focusses on the saying of the 'Ave Maria' occurs close to the back of CUL Ii.6.2 on ff. 108ᵛ–109ʳ. Written by Thomas's hand, this text mixes Latin and English, beginning with some instructions in English which direct the reader to say the 'Ave Maria' one hundred times a day for ten days running:

> Ye shall say a ml tymes Aue Maria, and ye shall sey theym in x dayes, that is euery day a hunderith; and ye shall sey them standyng, goyng, knelyng, or syttyng. And ye shall haue a certen almes in your hand while ye make your prayers. And after say this orisoun or prayer that folowith.

Some lines in Latin follow, invoking Christ's incarnation through Mary and making a plea for protection against enemies:

> Adonay domine deus magne & mirabilis qui dedisti salutem humano generi in manus Gloriosissime virginis & matris tue Marie per uterum & merita ipius & per illud sacratissimum corpus quod de illa sumpsisti exaudi preces meas & imple desiderium meum in bonum ad laudem & gloriam nominis tui & libera me de omni tribulacione impugnatione et ab omnibus insidijs jnimicorum meorum michi nocere cupientum & a labijs jniquis & linguis dolosis & conuerte tribulacionem meam modo in gaudium & leticiam Amen.[40]

---

[40] Duffy, *Marking the Hours*, p. 92 offers a translation of the Latin: 'O Adonai, Lord, great and wonderful God, who gave the salvation of human kind into the hands of the most glorious Virgin, your Mother Mary: through her womb and merits, and through that most holy body which you took from her, in your goodness hear my prayers and fulfil my desires for [my] good, to the praise and glory of your name. Liberate me from every tribulation and assailant, and from all the snares of my enemies who seek to harm me, and from lying lips and sharpened tongues, and change all my tribulation into rejoicing and gladness. Amen.'

At the conclusion of the Latin is the further instruction:

> And when ye haue seid this orisoun kysse youre almes and after geve it to a pore mann or womann, in honoure of that blyssed joy that Seynt Gabriel gret Our Lady. And for what thyng ye do this x dayes togeder, without dought ye shall sure haue that thyng ye pray for laufully, with Goddes grace.

Though cast in the form of a prayer, this text is closer in nature to a charm.[41] The repetition of the same words in the short prayer of the 'Ave' and the mathematical formula prescribed for its iteration are characteristic of the semi-magical instructions given in charms. Similarly the holding and kissing of the money during and after praying bespeaks a superstitious belief that some kind of transformation or investing of special power will result from the power of the spoken words. Other additions to the book demonstrate a belief in this type of power, most notably the instructions for emergency action in the case of a house fire (f. 2^r); and the Latin charm/prayer 'for women to conceyue childe' (f. 10^r), another context where the magical power of words was habitually relied upon for assistance.[42] Various other additions demonstrate a firm belief in the power of signing: a short Latin prayer on f. 24^r invokes the power of the sign of the cross to repel evil; and a longer charm against fevers on f. 108^r uses the sign of the cross and various names for God, along with an anecdote about St Peter.[43] Yet not all of this volume's prayers for protection rely on such strategies; some are more straightforwardly devotional, such as the Latin collect *Adesto domine supplicacionibus nostris* and the prayer to one's guardian angel, *Angele qui meus es custos pietate superna*, both copied by the same hand on f. 103^r.

The concluding instructions to the prayer-charm on ff. 108^v–109^r promise certain benefits for the user: 'without dought ye shall sure haue that thyng ye pray for laufully, with Goddes grace'. Edmund Roberts certainly seems to have been convinced of its merits. He marked the beginning of the text on

---

[41] Duffy, *Marking the Hours*, p. 186, note 10 notes two other instances of the devotion of the One Thousand Aves, in Durham, Ushaw College, MS 10, f. 11^r, and in BL, MS Harley 494, f. 89^v. A summary list of contents of the latter is given by Barratt, 'Singing from the Same Hymn-Sheet', pp. 158–60, and see further Barratt, *Anne Bulkeley and her Book*.

[42] For English or macaronic charms to aid successful childbirth see Keiser, 'Works of Science and Information', p. 3673 and pp. 3873–74.

[43] The prayer on f. 24^r is added by an unidentified sixteenth-century hand; that on f. 108^r was written by Thomas Roberts. Another short prayer against plague is given on f. 102^v.

f. 108ᵛ with a marginal 'nota', and at the end on f. 109ʳ he added the affirmation 'I youse thys prayer well every daye', filling up the remainder of the last line with these words, and then adding his signature 'Edmond Robertes' on the line beneath. He also gives an indication of when he used the prayer. In the top margin of f. 109ʳ he wrote *Anno 1553*, and he set the same date, in a more expansive formula, *Anno domini 1553 anno primo maria regina nostra*, across the top of f. 108ᵛ, in the manner of a running header. The same date is written, along with his signature, in the top margin of several of the volume's miniatures. Its presence allows us to locate Edmund's use of the 'Thousand Aves' prayer-charm very exactly, to the part of 1553 which was also the first year of Mary Tudor's reign, that is the period between 19 July and 24 March.[44]

Edmund made other additions to his hours as well, following his father's example of filling up blank spaces in the earlier part of the book. Sometimes his additions show a reworking or reframing of the religious material that Thomas had added, as for example on f. 14ʳ. Here Edmund repeated the opening lines of five well-known psalms that occur within the *Adoramus te* prayer that Thomas had written out on the top half of the leaf: *Ad te levaui occulos meos* (Psalm 123); *Deus in nomine tuo saluum me fac* (Psalm 54); *Deus miseriatur nostri* (Psalm 67); *Laudate dominum in sanctis eius* (Psalm 150); and *Leuaui occulos meos in montes unde venyt* (Psalm 121).[45] Edmund marks the end of each incipit with the sign of the cross, again mimicking Thomas's use of the same practice in the text above, and then concludes by reiterating another formula that occurs several times in the *Adoramus te* prayer: *Qui crucis in patibulo / adoramus te Christi Ihesu pater aue & credo*. These repetitions are in one sense needless, since all this information is included on the page already, but the reiteration reveals Edmund's engagement with the text, and perhaps implies his frequent recourse to it; his reproduction makes more apparent which psalm texts are cited, and its open layout might have made consultation easier. Such openness and generosity of spacing is a characteristic trait of Edmund's other contributions to the volume; he also has the tendency to draw brackets and lines that end in diamond shapes. These features are all evident in the meditative scheme that he added to another

---

[44] In modern style between 19 July 1553 and 24 March 1554. The first regnal year of Mary Tudor ran from 19 July 1553 to 5 July 1554.

[45] The last entry originally read *Leuaui occulos meos qui habitas in celis*, showing confusion with the already cited Psalm 123; Edmund has struck through the last four words and substituted *in montes unde venyt* above.

	Saperent	preterita:	malum comissum
			bonum omissum
vtinam			tempus amissum
homines	inte lige ent	presentia:	vite breuitatum
	tia		saluandi difficultatem
			saluando in partitalem
	providerent	futura:	Mortem qua nihil miserabilius
			Iudicium quo nihil teribilius
			Penam inferni quo nihil ^in^tolerabilius

originally blank leaf, f. 73^v, laying this out as a diagram that runs from left to right. At the leaf's top corners Edmund drew his initials 'E' and 'R', on this occasion rather crudely formed, and also added the date, '1581', which makes clear that Edmund was still using this book in the final decade of his life, indicating that he had been interacting with its contents over a period of some thirty years.

The material that Edmund inscribed within the book of hours is more varied than that added by his father: whilst Thomas's contributions were largely religious and devotional, Edmund's have a more moralizing nature. This aspect is apparent in some verses, seemingly authored by Edmund himself, which he wrote on f. 109^v. These consist of eight lines of verse rhyming ababcdcd, laid out as two quatrains:

> Joye in god whoes whoes [sic] grace is beste
> Obeye thy prince & lyue in awe
> Hellpe the poore to lyue in reste
> and nevar spurne againte the lawe
> Hepe nott syne in hope of grace
> Estueve[46] all vyce & learne to dye
> Refrayne to syne in tyme & space
> more nere ys deathe then thowe censt espye

---

[46] i.e 'eschew'.

Beneath the final line is written 'inqut E Robertz', evidently both a signature and a statement of authorship, since there are no other known attestations of this poem.[47] The verses are set in the upper half of the page; in the lower half Edmund has written a list of the births of his seven children, drawing a line between the poem and the records to create a separate space. The records relate to both his marriages and were copied all in one stint in 1575.[48] Edmund's list matches the earlier account of Thomas's children on f. 33^r, and its inscription is another way in which Edmund imitated his father's habits and use of the book. Like Thomas he made more than one copy of these records, keeping a more informative list of his children's births and baptisms in another volume; perhaps the true purpose of the addition of this briefer list here was connected with an intention to pass on the book to one of his children.[49] Other family members certainly used the book after him, if only to continue the practice of adding family records. A memorandum noting the birth of Anne Barnesdale on 16 September 1588 has been added in a large italic script at the top of f. 103^v, though what her connection with the family may have been is not clear. More straightforward is the notice of Edmund's death on 1 June 1585 and a note of his burial at Willesden; this is written by a forward-sloping and confident secretary hand that might be that of Francis Roberts or another of his children, and is appropriately set on f. 109^r beneath the prayer that Edmund claimed he used every day (see Figure 18).

þOU SHALT MOCH PROFETT IN REDYNG: WHAT EDMUND READ

The layers of annotation in CUL Ii.6.2 provide much insight into the devotional habits of Thomas and Edmund Roberts, but books of hours were designed primarily as prompts for the articulation of personal devotions, and evidence of more assiduous religious reading must be sought in other kinds of books. Of the four fifteenth-century volumes of vernacular devotional texts which may be

---

[47] Ringler, *Bibliography*, p. 142 lists this as TM 863, there described as 'Exhortations copied by E. Robert' and given the date 1536, but this is too early. The verses were originally listed by Brown and Robbins as *IMEV* 1806 but this entry was deleted by Robbins and Cutler, *Supplement*; listed as *DIMEV* 0.1806.

[48] This date is written in the bottom right corner of f. 109^v.

[49] See the discussion of BodL Rawlinson C. 894 in Chapter 5, section titled 'A Matter of Record'.

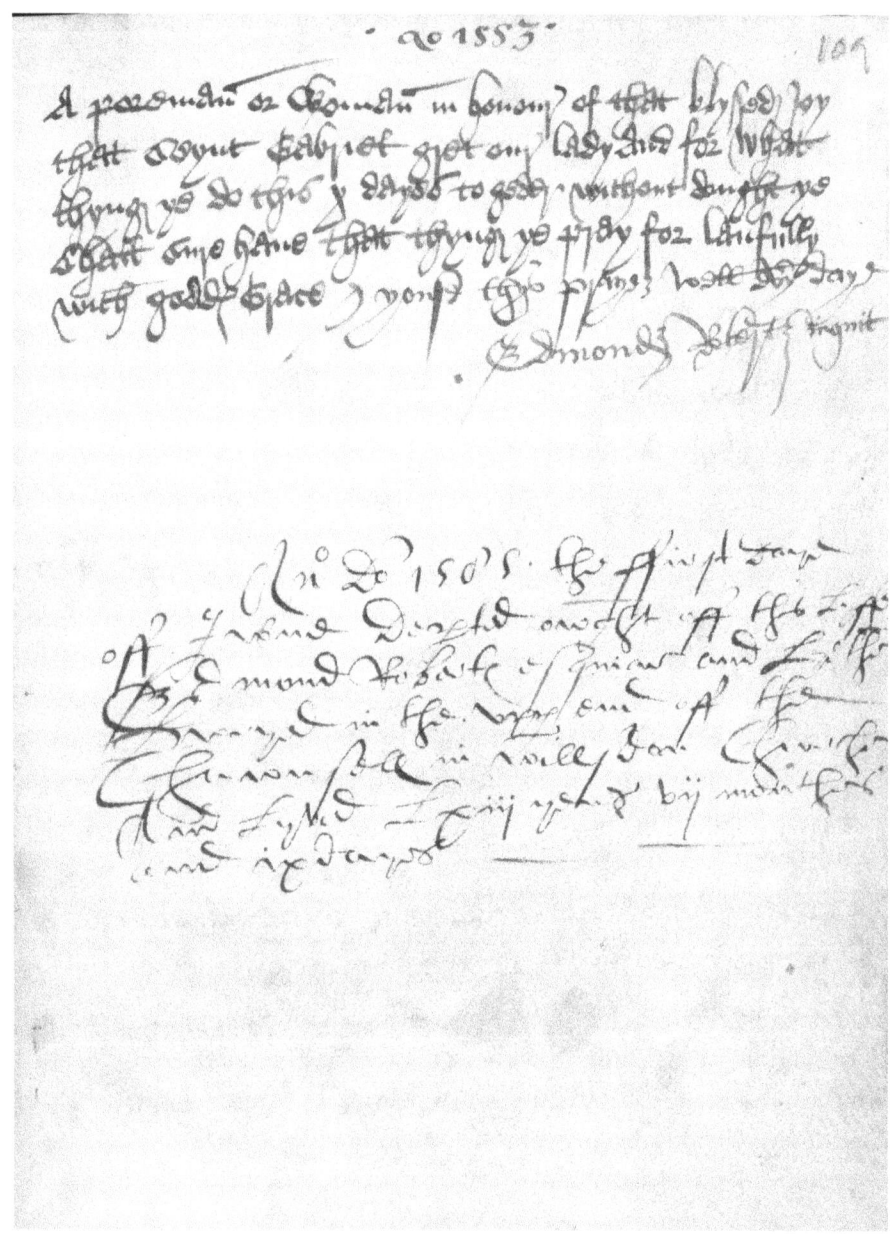

Figure 18 Cambridge University Library, MS Ii.6.2, f. 109[r]. Inscriptions by Thomas, Edmund, and Francis Roberts. Reproduced by kind permission of the Syndics of Cambridge University Library.

associated with the Roberts family, Edmund's presence may be detected in only one. There are no traces of additions by his hand in their manuscript copies of

Nicholas Love's *Mirror of the Blessed Life of Jesus Christ*, the pseudo-Augustinian *Soliloquies*, and the *Pore Caitif*, though he may of course have read these texts and left behind no signs of his handling. The manuscripts of the first two of these are comparatively fine, which may have been a deterrent to readerly annotation, and in these cases even Thomas Roberts, who was clearly in the habit of indexing and annotating his books, only added his name or monogram. By contrast, in the family's fourth volume, an anthology of short devotional works, there are copious additions – not by Thomas, who does not seem to have had this book, but by Edmund. This manuscript, BodL Rawlinson C. 894, is a small, relatively shabby, parchment codex. Its original contents consist of a series of short texts or extracts, all but one in English, and all in prose. In brief, and in order, these are: *Six Masters on Tribulation* (ff. 1^{r-v}), followed on ff. 1^v–2^v by the Latin *Nota de paciencia infirmitatis* which often accompanies this text; *The Twelve Profits of Tribulation* (ff. 2^v–18^r); *The Boke of Crafte of Dying* (ff. 18^v–33^r); *A Tretyse of Gostly Batayle* (ff. 33^r–48^r); an extract from Hilton's *On the Mixed Life* (ff. 48^r–54^v); extracts from the *Abbey of the Holy Ghost* (ff. 55^{r-v}); extracts from Hilton's *Scale of Perfection* (ff. 55^v–65^r), with interpolations of a chapter from *Contemplations of the Dread and Love of God* (ff. 56^r–58^r), and the text 'A good contemplacion for a prest or he go to masse' (ff. 58^r–59^v); *Twelve Degrees of Humility* (ff. 65^r–67^v); Hilton's *Eight Chapters on Perfection* (ff. 68^r–74^r); the Pseudo-Bernard *Meditationes Piissime* (ff. 74^r–86^v); *The Counsels of Saint Isidore* (ff. 86^v–91^r); part of the *Epistle of Pelagius / Jerome to Demetrias* (ff. 91^v–97^v); and an anonymous treatise against fleshly affections which was sometimes incorporated into *Disce Mori* (ff. 97^v–106^r). Before considering how Edmund responded to this compilation of devotional material it will be helpful to have some sense of its overall scope, and of the particular contents and nature of each item.

The opening short text, *Six Masters on Tribulation*, is essentially a summary of the benefits of tribulation or suffering. Voiced by 'vj maistris asemblyd togidyr', the text proclaims that remembering and sharing in the suffering that Christ endured for man's sins is more worthwhile than enjoying earthly rewards, and of greater benefit to the soul than the intercession of the saints.[50] The multiple benefits of tribulation are outlined, and reasons suggested to explain why the imposition of this suffering is resented. The brief Latin text *Nota de paciencia infirmitatis* which follows serves to

---

[50] f. 1^r; Jolliffe, *A Check-List*, J.2; Lagorio and Sargent, 'English Mystical Writings', p. 3128; printed by Horstman, *Yorkshire Writers*, ii.390.

connect this short summary to the much longer work on the same topic from which it derives, *The Twelve Profits of Tribulation*.⁵¹ This was a text with a long history. Its ultimate source was a Latin treatise, *Tractatus de tribulacione*, which dates from the third quarter of the thirteenth century, and which exists in two versions. The shorter of these, *De duodecim utilitatibus tribulationis* (falsely attributed to Peter of Blois), gave rise to two Middle English translations, of which the one copied here seems to have been the more popular. It consists of twelve points, each illustrated with scriptural and patristic quotations and with extensive analogies, and preceded by a brief prologue which explains that God sends tribulation for the good of the soul. The third English item in this collection of texts is *The Boke of Crafte of Dying*, another work translated from Latin, this time derived from a treatise with various titles but known generally as *Ars Moriendi*.⁵² The Middle English text is based on the third part of Jean Gerson's *Opusculum tripartitum* but draws on other sources too and so comprises a compilation within itself. Through its six chapters it aims to instruct its readers in the spiritual issues that arise at the time of death, acknowledging that death 'semith wonderfull harde & ryȝt perlouse & also ryȝt ferefull & horrible' not just to lay people but to religious and 'deuoute personys' as well.⁵³ Accordingly the first chapter aims to demonstrate how to die well and the second to identify the five principal temptations that the devil brings to those who are dying. The third chapter outlines seven questions that ought to be addressed to the dying person, whilst the fourth and fifth chapters offer instruction in the proper behaviour of the dying and in preparation for the moment of death. The last chapter details the prayers that should be said by those present when a person dies. The next text, *A Tretyse of Gostly Batayle*, focusses on living rather than dying, and details how Christians may best resist the spiritual enemies of the world, the flesh, and the devil.⁵⁴ Beginning with the conceit that the body's relation to the soul may be likened to a horse that

---

⁵¹ The *Nota de paciencia infirmitatis* is printed by Horstman, *Yorkshire Writers*, ii.390–91. For *The Twelve Profits of Tribulation* see Jolliffe, *A Check-List*, J.3(b); Lagorio and Sargent, 'English Mystical Writings', pp. 3127–28; Horstman, *Yorkshire Writers*, ii.391–406.

⁵² Jolliffe, *A Check-List*, L.2, L.4; Raymo, 'Works of Religious and Philosophical Instruction', pp. 2361–64; printed by Horstman, *Yorkshire Writers*, ii.406–20.

⁵³ f. 18ᵛ.

⁵⁴ Jolliffe, *A Check-List*, H.3; Raymo, 'Works of Religious and Philosophical Instruction', pp. 2331–32; printed by Horstman, *Yorkshire Writers*, ii.420–36, and edited by Murray, 'An Edition of a Tretyse of Gostly Batayle'.

carries its rider safely, the text allegorically details the elements of the horse's tackle before moving on to describe the rider's attributes (the shield of faith and so on), using familiar terms borrowed from Ephesians 6.

After these texts comes a series of extracts from longer works, none of which is identified or acknowledged. In this miniature compilation the first item is an extract from Walter Hilton's *On the Mixed Life*, comprising the first four hundred and fifty lines of Part I.[55] This section discusses bodily and spiritual matters and provides definitions of the active, contemplative, and mixed lives, using the Biblical models of Rachel and Leah, and imagery associated with fire, to demonstrate the complementary nature of action and contemplation. This extract from *On the Mixed Life* is joined seamlessly to the conclusion of the twenty-third chapter from Book I of the *Scale of Perfection*, and to definitions of prayer and meditation taken from the *Abbey of the Holy Ghost* with further selections from the *Scale* (Book I, chapters 24–36) following.[56] The combining of materials from Hilton's two texts is unsurprising: selections from both circulated together in a number of manuscripts, and the full-length works were associated in transmission in both manuscript and print.[57] Here however, between chapter 25, on how to pray, and chapter 26, on the fire of love, two other items, not attributable to Hilton, have been slotted in. The first of these comprises the final chapter from a devotional text known from its printing by Wynkyn de Worde as *Contemplations of the Dread and Love of God*.[58] The chapter extracted here offers advice on how to pray, a meditation on Christ's passion, and some forms of prayer to use, and as such it is an appropriate insertion to this mini-compilation on prayer and meditation. The second text that is sandwiched in at this point, 'A good contemplacion for a prest or he go to masse', offers advice on prayer in the more specific context of receiving the sacrament, first outlining through six points the proper

---

[55] Equivalent to pp. 1–39 in the edition by Ogilvie-Thomson, *Walter Hilton's Mixed Life*; see also Lagorio and Sargent, 'English Mystical Writings', pp. 3076–77.

[56] As noted and discussed in detail by Jones, 'The Compilations of Two Late-Medieval Devotional Manuscripts', p. 83, pp. 88–92. Jolliffe, *A Check-List*, lists the extracts from the *Abbey of the Holy Ghost* separately as M.12; for an edition of the text see Blake, *Middle English Religious Prose*, pp. 88–102. For the *Scale of Perfection* see Lagorio and Sargent, 'English Mystical Writings', pp. 3075–76 and the edition by Bestul, *Walter Hilton*.

[57] Lagorio and Sargent, 'English Mystical Writings', pp. 3076–77 and 3433–34 note that *On the Mixed Life* was added as a 'third book' to five of the thirteen known copies of the *Scale of Perfection* printed by Wynkyn de Worde in 1494 (*STC* 14042).

[58] See Connolly (ed.), *Contemplations*.

state of mind for the communicant, and then providing sample affective meditations for use before and after communion.[59]

This compilation on prayer and meditation is followed by a work that stresses the necessity of meekness. Like *The Twelve Points of Tribulation*, *The Twelve Degrees of Humility* is another didactic text with a numerical structure.[60] Its practical advice about humble behaviour is drawn from St Bernard's *De duodecim gradibus humilitatis*, even though it begins by citing St Gregory, and these points are framed by an insistence on the overarching importance of humility. Another work of Hilton's follows, the *Eight Chapters on Perfection*, which focusses on love and the need for prayer and confession to combat temptation.[61] The perfect love of Christ and his role as man's spiritual exemplar are upheld as the antidotes to those dangers that are inherent in the spiritual life and that beset holy love in particular. As with the other texts grouped together here there is a tendency to structure advice numerically, with the fourth chapter listing five degrees of contemplation. Various texts that rely on borrowed patristic authority lead up to the volume's conclusion. First is a set of meditations ascribed to St Bernard beginning 'Many knoweth many thynges & knoweth not hem selfe ...', a translation of the Latin Pseudo-Bernard *Meditationes Piissime*.[62] This is followed by *The Counsels of Saint Isidore*, a collection of moral admonitions to good conduct arranged in brief paragraphs, with topics ranging from practical instruction on prayer and fasting, drink, women, good speech, and swearing, to advice on less tangible concepts such as conscience, curiosity, and sovereignty.[63] Then comes the Middle English translation of Pelagius's *Epistula ad sacram Christi virginem Demetriadem*, a widely circulated Latin work in thirty chapters which in the Middle Ages was falsely attributed to St Jerome. The Middle English translation carefully avoids the text's heretical content by excising its first eight chapters, and the particular version included here truncates the original still further by beginning with material found in the twenty-first chapter of the

---

[59] Jolliffe, *A Check-List*, N.17.
[60] Jolliffe, *A Check-List*, G.19; Raymo, 'Works of Religious and Philosophical Instruction', pp. 2296–97.
[61] Lagorio and Sargent, 'English Mystical Writings', pp. 3078–79; edited by Kuriyagawa and Takamiya, *Two Minor Works*.
[62] f. 74^r; Jolliffe, *A Check-List*, H.19; Revell, *Fifteenth Century English Prayers*, no. 111.
[63] Jolliffe, *A Check-List*, I.22(c); Raymo, 'Works of Religious and Philosophical Instruction', p. 2323; ed. by Horstman, *Yorkshire Writers*, ii.367–74.

Latin, and concentrating on the spiritual temptations that accompany the life of perfection.⁶⁴ Finally the collection concludes with an anonymous treatise against fleshly affections that is here introduced as 'A litill tretise ayence flesshly affeccions and all unþrifty loves'. This text offers an account of the differences between bodily and spiritual loves, making a distinction between the two types by referring to seven tokens of carnal love that derive from David of Augsburg's *De exterioris et interioris hominis compositione*.⁶⁵

Collectively these texts offered Edmund much advice for good living, of both a generally moral and more specifically Christian nature. Some of the texts model the proper behaviour expected from the diligent Christian, covering a range of contexts, whereas others concentrate on conveying a deeper understanding of difficult issues such as suffering and death. In several instances challenging material is made more accessible by the use of numerical structures which marshall complex content into manageable chunks; such enumeration was a frequently used technique in later medieval devotional compilations and instructional manuals, as well as in practical anthologies, favoured because it facilitated both assimilation and recall.⁶⁶ As well as this instruction, Edmund could find within this volume various exhortations to prayer; and if he tired of the diet of devotions offered by his book of hours he could find other sample prayers and meditations in this devotional compilation.

There is no doubt that Edmund read these texts with a degree of diligence. Amongst five different annotating hands which may be distinguished in the manuscript, his is by far the most prolific, the others are not significant in that two contribute only one annotation each, one adds only doodles and pen trials, and one is in modern pencil.⁶⁷ Some of Edmund's annotations serve to elucidate terms or spellings which were clearly becoming unfamiliar to the mid sixteenth-century reader. On f. 1ʳ he wrote 'mighte' in the right margin by the rubric apparently to explain the unfamiliar spelling 'myȝt' in line 3. Similar glosses occur later on in the *Twelve Degrees of Humility* where on f. 67ʳ 'reft' is underlined in the text and the word 'bereft' added to the right margin; on f. 67ᵛ 'buxomness' has been underlined in the text but ironically the explanatory term in the left margin ' . . . renes' is now hard to read.

---

⁶⁴ Jolliffe, *A Check-List*, H.5, O.11; see the discussion by Jones, 'The Heresiarch'.
⁶⁵ Jolliffe, *A Check-List*, K.1; see the discussion by Patterson, *Negotiating the Past*, pp. 115–53.
⁶⁶ On this see Connolly, 'Practical Reading for Body and Soul', 156–57.
⁶⁷ For fuller details of the less significant annotations see Connolly, 'Sixteenth-Century Readers', p. 251.

Two of the texts in particular attracted Edmund's close attention: *The Twelve Profits of Tribulation* and *A Tretyse of Gostly Batayle*. In the case of the former, Edmund rewrote the rubric heading in the left margin: 'Here sewith xij profytis & vauntages of tribulacion', presumably as an aid to quick location, so perhaps this text was a particular favourite. On f. 3ᵛ what initially looks like a finding reference: 'ix^m' (i.e. chapter 9) has been supplied alongside a citation in the first chapter of the text, 'as we rede in the boke of holy faders Seint Anton . . .', introducing an episode from the life of St Antony. This relates how, apparently fatally wounded by the temptations of devils, the saint's body is carried away by a servant; however, when Antony revives he insists on being carried back to the place of temptation where he faces his tormentors again, but is also visited by Christ and comforted by him. Christ explains that he has been with Antony throughout, ready to reward him as he rewards his 'chosin childerne'.[68] This episode occurs towards the beginning of the life of St Antony in the *Gilte Legende* and its sources, and in those collections the saint's life forms either the twentieth or the twenty-first chapter.[69] Rather than identifying a source, Edmund's marginal note of a ninth chapter here seems to refer the reader forward to the ninth section of the present text, where the description of the ninth profit of tribulation claims that suffering draws down greater attention from God: 'for hym þat he sendyth tribulacion he hath in mynd, ȝeuyng goostly comforte & incresyng of grace'.[70] The concluding parts of this ninth chapter repeat the notion that 'Crist is present with hem þat be in tribulacion, & yeueth hem refresshyng in desese . . . for in tribulacion God is with þe, & fro tribulacion he schall delyuer the . . .', which seems to be the point that Edmund was recalling and noting in the earlier chapter.[71] Near to the beginning of the description of the sixth profit, on f. 13ʳ, the words 'in christe' have been added in the right margin alongside the explanation of how everlasting penance is commuted to temporal penance by contrition and confession, '& fterthermore it is foryeuen by satisfaccion, & somtyme it is all relesed namely by tribulacion', with the word 'satisfaccion' also underlined. Other additions of words and phrases in this text seem to be merely for

---

[68] f. 4ʳ.

[69] The Life of St Antony is the twentieth chapter of the *Gilte Legende*, and the twenty-first in the *Legenda Aurea* and *La Légende Dorée*, see Hamer and Russell (eds.), *Gilte Legende*, i. 97–102 and iii.107–8.

[70] f. 15ʳ.

[71] f. 15ᵛ.

clarification or emphasis: for example, on f. 3ʳ the words 'which enemyes' have been added to the right margin and marked for insertion in the text so that the relevant line will now read 'his enemyes *which enemye* ben þese preuy suggestions ...'. Lower down on the same page 'þan' has been added in a similar manner, to make the text read 'for als much *þan* as god is with vs ...'; another addition in the margin at this point is placed to run on from the end of the line, giving the reading 'and so with his swerd *in þat oder hond* ...'.

The beginning of *A Tretyse of Gostly Batayle* has also been picked out for attention with the addition of 'nota' in the right margin of f. 33ʳ. In this text many words and phrases have been underlined: on f. 34ʳ the terms 'abstinence' and 'temperaunce' are both underlined and also rewritten in the right margin, and the phrase 'the two reynes of þis bridill' has been underlined as well; on the next leaves more terms from the text's allegorical framework of the horse's armour have been underlined ('that on rayne', 'that oþer rayne' on f. 34ᵛ, 'the saddell of patience', 'the stirripes' on f. 35ʳ), and on f. 35ʳ other phrases such as 'þin horse behoueþe to haue a saddell' and 'the sterruppes of his sadel shuld be lowness' are also picked out; on f. 36ᵛ some more abstract concepts such as 'in trouþe', 'chastite', 'ryȝtwisnes', 'gospell of pes', along with the allegorical constructs 'scheld of feyth', and 'basnet of helth & þe swerd of þe holy gost þat is goddis word' have caught Edmund's attention (see Figure 19).

Underlining is perhaps the simplest level of readerly interaction with a text, but its purposes are manifold and not always recoverable by a subsequent observer. Edmund uses underlining frequently, sometimes it would seem because a particular thought has caught his attention and been judged especially worthy, as perhaps in the following instance from the *Six Masters on Tribulation* where he has singled out the following sentence on f. 1ʳ: 'But I sei we schuld rather and by more ryȝt and reson haue in mynde of þat tribulacion þat he suffred þere upon for oure giltis and oure trespassis'. He also used a marginal 'nota' for the same purpose, as may be seen on f. 21ᵛ, in *The Boke of Crafte of Dying*, where he wished to note the comforting line: 'In what oure þat euer it be þat the synful man is sory inward & conuerted fro his syn he schal be saued ...'. Underlining is not used in this instance, but on another occasion Edmund used both underlining and a comment to distinguish a favourite passage: on f. 57ʳ, in the extract from *Contemplations of the Dread and Love of God*, he underlined the opening words of the prayer 'a lord god allmyȝty blessid mot þou be', and wrote alongside in the margin 'here begennethe a vere good

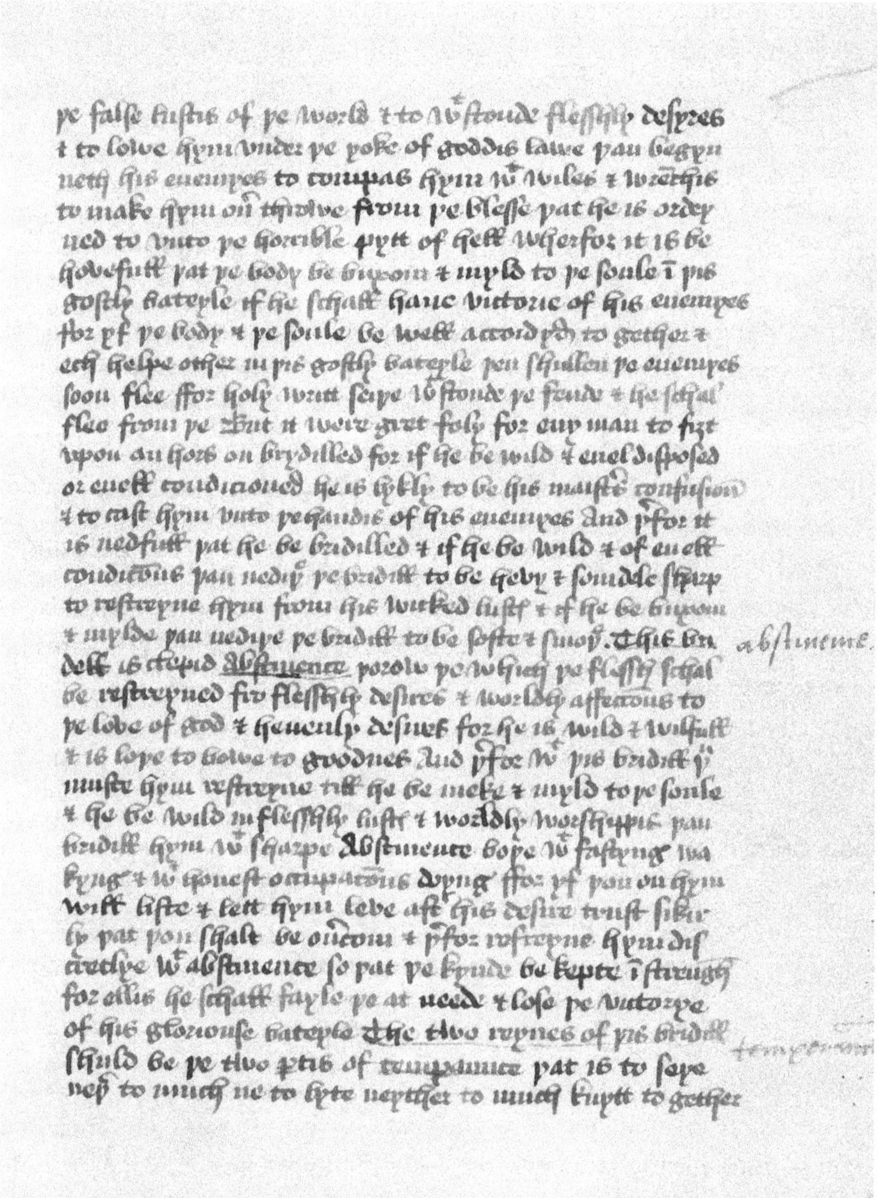

Figure 19 Oxford, Bodleian Library, MS Rawlinson C. 894, f. 34ʳ. Annotations and underlining by Edmund Roberts in 'A Tretyse of Gostly Batayle'. Reproduced by permission of the Bodleian Libraries, the University of Oxford.

praer'. This is a helpful annotation since there is no other indication in the text that anything new begins at this point; by contrast, four lines further on, a red paraph prominently marks the beginning of the following sentence, 'Now lord with sorowfull herte ...'. The other way in which Edmund and members of his family habitually marked their books was with the Roberts name, most often set at the uppermost and outermost corners of a single leaf or of a double-page opening, and usually placed on a leaf which contains some form of decoration.[72] In BodL Rawlinson C. 894 there are no illustrations, but there are two points where this style of inscription occurs. One occasion is at the top left corner of f. 87^v where the name 'Robertz' has been written in the light grey ink that Edmund used when inscribing his name in CUL Ii.6.2. The addition here is made to *The Counsels of Saint Isidore*, where comments in the text concern lechery and idleness, generally linked by advice to avoid the causes of sin, but there is no annotation or underlining on this leaf to indicate what specifically attracted Edmund's attention. An earlier such instance is on ff. 26^v–27^r, where 'Robertȝ' has been written in an elaborate script at the outer top corner of each of the leaves. Again, just why this opening should have been selected for special treatment is not immediately apparent: there are no other marks on these leaves to reveal what might have attracted Edmund's special interest. The text at this point is *The Boke of Crafte of Dying*, and the rubric and chapter number towards the top of f. 26^v indicate that this is the beginning of its fourth chapter: 'the iiijth chapiter conteyneth an instruccion with certeyne obsecracions to hem þat schullen dye'. This chapter advises that the man facing death should do the five things that Christ did on the cross, that is, pray, desire forgiveness, weep for his sins, commend his soul to God, and 'yafe up wilfully his spirit' (f. 26^v). The 'certeyne obsecracions' that it offers consist of a series of English prayers addressed to the Trinity, God the Father, Christ, the Virgin, and the angels in heaven, with instructions for other prayers and an emphasis on the proper order of these intercessions ('Let hym sey also ... Þan lat hym pray ... Þan afterward lett hyme sey ...'). This series concludes with two particular prayers, 'The pese of oure lord Ihesu Criste ...' and 'Graunt me lord a clere ende ...', both of which are to be said three times by the dying man:

> And if he þat is sike can not all þis prayers, or may not sey hem for greuouse of his siknesse, lett som man þat is about hym sey hem before

---

[72] As discussed in Chapter 5, section titled 'The Use of Sarum: Cambridge University Library, MS Ii.6.7 and Cambridge University Library, MS Ii.6.2.'

hym as he may clerely here hym sey hem, chaungyng þe wordis þat ought to be chaunged in his seyng . . .'.[73]

This part of *The Boke of Crafte of Dying* has a very pragmatic function, offering detailed information about the procedures to be followed when approaching the point of death, and also indicating what can be done to assist a dying person in the absence of a priest. The chapter ends with reassurances that, if these guidelines are followed, all shall be well: provided that the dying man prays devoutly 'and as he cann & may and so yeld þe gost up to God and he shal be saued'. The final clause 'he shal be saued' is reminiscent of the efficacy formulae that occur at the close of medical recipes (*probatum est*), used there, as here, to encourage faith in the power of their contents to effect a positive outcome. Like the medical prescriptions preserved in the Roberts remedy book, BodL MS Rawlinson C. 299, the devotional prescription offered here is one that Edmund and other family members may have needed recourse to on various occasions; it would have been important in the circumstances to be able to locate this section of the text with relative ease, hence the particular marking out of these leaves. A further indication that Edmund held this part of *The Boke of Crafte of Dying* in high esteem is to be found in the instruction that he set at the very front of the manuscript: 'Rede well the iiijth chapter'.[74]

The remainder of this instruction reads '& Disse mori', followed by the date '1575'. The date is a helpful indication of Edmund's period of reading, but the reference to *Disce mori* is rather more opaque, since there is no copy of this text in the manuscript. *Disce mori* was a mid fifteenth-century manual of religious instruction in the Pechamite tradition with particular sections focussed on sins, temptations, penance, and virtues; its concluding part focusses on the love of God, contemplation, and the need for perseverance.[75] Although no part of *Disce Mori* is included in BodL Rawlinson C. 894, the manuscript compilation manifestly contains much

---

[73] BodL Rawlinson C. 894, ff. 27^{v}–28^{r}.

[74] In the top margin of f. xi^{v}. Previously I had not been able to make proper sense of this instruction, see Connolly, 'Sixteenth-Century Readers', p. 253.

[75] Raymo, 'Works of Religious and Philosophical Instruction', pp. 2263–64 and Lagorio and Sargent, 'English Mystical Writings', p. 3098; Jones (ed.), *The 'Exhortacion' from Disce Mori*, gives the text's final section the non-authorial title 'Exhortacion'.

material of a similar nature, and furthermore its final text, 'A littil tretise ayenes fleshly affeccions and all vnþrifty loves', does have some relationship with *Disce Mori*, as either a source or a congener of one of its later chapters. The relationship of the two texts is not yet fully understood, but if Edmund's note is not a reference to another separate book that he possessed, it might be taken as evidence that he regarded the 'littil tretise' as either synonymous with it or at least as part of the longer work.[76] Though if Edmund's reference to 'Disse Mori' does relate to the 'littil tretise' then we might have expected to find at least some measure of annotation within that text, whereas in fact it contains none at all – but readers are not obliged to always mark the material that catches their interest.

Edmund's annotations in BodL Rawlinson C. 894 demonstrate that he made regular use of this anthology and read its contents closely. He marked and identified key points, either as part of an immediate process of assimilation, or perhaps as notes for commonplacing at a later date. In the process Edmund may be seen conforming to the advice of one of the anthology's texts; the prologue to *The Twelve Profits of Tribulation* concludes with this exhortation to the reader:

> the which whoso will with good diligens reed or here, he schal lyghtly with Goddis grace fynde gostly sauoure. For ryght as mete euel chewed is euel to defye, ryght so techyng of hooly writt neccligently redd or herd profiteth lytell or ellis nouȝt.[77]

Edmund's underlinings and marginal additions in both this text and more widely throughout the manuscript reveal that he was indeed an attentive reader, concerned above all with spiritual and moral edification. He was an active reader who devoutly attempted to follow the advice on reading given in *The Counsels of Saint Isidore*:

> Yeve þe much to redyng. Take hede in mediacion of sett scripture; besy þe in þe lawe of God; haue acustomable use in devyne bokes, redyng truly what þou shalt shoun. Redyng sheweth what þou oweth to drede;

---

[76] For the relationship between the two texts see Hudson, 'A Chapter from Walter Hilton', 416–21, Patterson, *Negotiating the Past*, pp. 115–53, and Jones (ed.), *The 'Exhortacion' from Disce Mori*, p. xxxiv.

[77] f. 3ʳ.

redyng tellith where þou goste; in redyng witt & understondyng encrosyth. Þou shalt moch profett in redyng if þou do as thow rediste.[78]

Even though over time it is clear that this manuscript was transformed into a notebook that offered a safe repository for family records, in Edmund's lifetime it retained its primary function as a reading book, offering guidance to be followed and knowledge to be consumed. In the late sixteenth century it is evident that this compilation of devotional texts was still being used according to the intentions of its fifteenth-century compiler, despite the very extensive changes of a linguistic, social, and above all religious nature that had complicated its reading context.

[78] f. 87ᵛ.

Conclusion

Newly Reformed Readers?

Amongst other devotional texts that Thomas Roberts added to his book of hours, CUL Ii.6.2, is a long prayer in English that fills the entirety of f. 3^r:

> Oure most mercyfull fader, Lord God, knowyng oure frelite and redynes to all synners is euer redy duryng this wrecched and mortall lyfe, by many and dyuerse weyes, to foryeue us oure trespas and to graunt us his grace, yf so be that truly we ordeyne unto hym thise thre treuthis folowyng, seid and doun with all our hart.
>
> The first thou shalt sey: 'Blessed Lorde, I knowlegge that I haue synned ayenst thy goodnes thus & thus, rehersyng thy synnes, & I am displeased therwith be reason of the which I shall doo penaunce and will doo, for I knowe well that I haue greued the & broken thy commaundementes in which thou only ought to be worshipped.'
>
> The secunde sey this truthe: 'Goode Lorde, I haue goode purpose & desire with thy help to be right ware herafter that I fall nat in synne, & I intende to fle the occasions after the possibilitis of my powers.'
>
> The third is this: 'Mercyfull Lorde, I haue a goode will to make a hole confession of all my synnes whan place & tyme conuenyent may be had, acordyng to thy commaundementes & all holy church.'
>
> These thre truthes whosoeuer saith with his hart onfeynyngly, in what place so euer it be, he may be sure that he is in the state of helthe & grace, & he shall haue euerlastyng lyfe though he has don all the synnes in the worlde. And yf he decesse without any other confession, for lak of a prist, as slepyng or soden deth, he sal be saafe soferyng afore hard payn of purgatorye. Wherfore it is a goode counsell that euery cristen man ones or twis in the day, erly or late, or elles at lest on holy dayes, examyn

his conscience & remembre yf he may with all his hart, onfeynyngly sey thise thre truthes. And yf he doo, he may be sure that he is in the state of grace. And yf he may nat, but is in will to synne ayen & to have his dilectacion with the dede, & will nat fle thoccacions of mortall synnes and so drownes, [he] will nat arise, as userers, fals marchauntes, or that desiren vengaunce with suche other; suche may be certen that the pope may nat assoyle theym. Therfor my holsom counsell is that such pray & yeue almes & do other goode dedes after their power, that God the rather may lighten their hartes and the soner turn theym to goodenes and grace. Amen.

This prayer, which may be classified as a form of confession, is one of many that survive in later medieval manuscripts.[1] Its combined emphasis on contrition, confession, and repentance, together with associated prayer, almsgiving, and good deeds, make it a typical expression of late medieval piety. Thomas's choice of this prayer demonstrates how comfortable he felt with styles of personal devotion that were very established and already quite old by his lifetime; his inscription of it also preserved access to such formulas, now even older, for his son Edmund.

The prayer's references to purgatory and the pope locate its composition to a pre-reformed period when such concepts were unproblematic. Other aspects, such as confessing without the assistance of a priest, indicate a measure of independence and self-help which might seem to prefigure a devotional self-reliance that is more in tune with reformed sympathies. Thomas Roberts might not have found any of this very troubling. When he died in 1542 his will demonstrated a typically unreformed devotion to Mary and the saints: his first instruction concerned the disposition of his soul which he bequeathed to God 'and to the blissed virgine marye his mother and to all the holly companye'.[2] The will of his eldest son Michael, made only two years later, repeats the same bequest of his soul to God, Mary, and 'all the holy company of heaven' whilst also being careful to style Henry VIII as 'defendour of the faithe and in earthe the supreme hedde of the churche of

---

[1] Raymo, 'Works of Religious and Philosophical Instruction', pp. 2562–64 identifies fifty-three different forms of confession in prose, along with four versions in verse, and this is probably not an exhaustive list. Most of these exist in single copies, suggesting that they were highly individual texts whose origins lay in personal or perhaps family devotional contexts, and that their circulation was very limited.

[2] LMA, DL/C/356.

Conclusion: Newly Reformed Readers?

Englonde and Irelande'.³ Such bequests were typical of mid sixteenth-century wills, in which Susan Brigden notes that despite various reforms the large majority of testators still remembered the Virgin and the saints in Heaven.⁴ Similarly both men left bequests that would cover prayers for their souls, demonstrating a continuing belief in purgatory. Thomas allocated six shillings and eight pence (half a mark) to the vicar of Willesden, Mr William Garrard 'to pray for me'; Michael Roberts was both more generous and expansive, stipulating: 'I gyue and bequethe to sir John Busshopp preste all my landes and tenementes lieng and beyng in Totehill strete in the citty of Westminster, to haue and to houlde to hym and his assignes for terme of his lief to praye for my father and mother soules and myne'.⁵ Despite the efforts made by the reformers to dismantle the doctrine of purgatory, chantries continued to exist in the final years of Henry VIII's reign, meaning that it was still possible to leave such instructions. This situation changed with the introduction of the Chantries Act in Edward VI's reign, and other injunctions issued in this period were designed to denigrate many late medieval devotional practices, outlawing as idolatrous the use of images, candles, beads, and going on pilgrimage.⁶

Unlike his father and elder brother, Edmund lived through this period of reform and faced much greater challenges in terms of complying with religious and political change, partly because of the rapid pace at which those developments occurred, and partly because there were just so many changes during his adult life. Edmund was born in 1520. He was in his teenage years when Henry VIII's attacks on the monasteries began, and within a short period would have seen a complete transformation in the fabric of religious life and society. These dramatic changes were documented by the author of *A London Chronicle* who records how in 1535: 'Then was dyverce halidays put doune, and then began the abbes to go down'.⁷ Subsequent entries, for the period 1537–40, record the destruction of various holy images: 'Then was the pictour of our lady of

---

³ TNA, PROB 11/30/205.

⁴ Brigden, *London and the Reformation*, p. 383.

⁵ William Garrard died in 1543; his will is TNA, PROB 11/29/332. John Busshope was vicar of Willesden 1546–52, and later parish clerk of St Nicholas Acon, as described in the will of Thomas Salter in 1558, TNA, PROB 11/42A/143; see Barron, 'The Will as Autobiography', p. 179.

⁶ 31 July 1547, see Bridgen, *London and the Reformation*, pp. 427–28, and Duffy, *The Stripping of the Altars*, pp. 448–77.

⁷ Hopper, 'London Chronicle', p. 10 (entry for 1535).

Worcetter brought to London. Then was the Roode that stode in Saynt Margit Pattens churche yarde takyn a waye', and the dismantling of St Thomas's shrine at Canterbury, St Edward's shrine at Westminster, and the lofts and shrines in St Paul's.[8] Other chroniclers record the bonfire at Chelsea in which images, including those of Our Lady of Walsingham and Ipswich, 'and divers other images, both in England and Wales, that were used for common pilgrimages', were destroyed; clearly this was the fate met by the image of the Virgin at Willesden too.[9] These events took place in Thomas Roberts's lifetime, but his death soon after meant that he did not have to address the issue of responding to them by altering his devotional practices, except in the most superficial ways such as deleting references to the pope and removing the feast of Thomas Becket from the calendar of his book of hours.

Edmund, on the other hand, experienced the more radical Protestant reforms of Edward VI's reign and would have seen the impact in his local church as altars were taken down, walls and windows whitewashed, and vestments and plate surrendered to the royal commissioners.[10] Nevertheless, he may have been quietly resistant to making changes to his beliefs and observances. As noted in Chapter 2 above, Edmund does not seem to have enjoyed any public advancement under Edward VI, which is probably an indication that his religious preferences did not sit well with those of the ruling regime. Certainly the accession of Mary Tudor in 1553 and the re-establishment of a Catholic regime seems to have presented him with opportunities rather than difficulties, and from this point onwards Edmund Roberts's name begins to appear in the public record in very much the same capacities as had his elder brother's and his father's. He is recorded as a justice of the peace for Middlesex in 1555 when he would have been about thirty-five years old, and later that year was made a keeper of Waltham forest. He served on other commissions in Middlesex and London in the late 1550s too, but these appointments peter out in the early years of Elizabeth's reign. On the whole Edmund seems to have prospered less in public life than his father, which may of course be connected with the personal attributes or inclinations of both men. It is still notable however that the most richly documented period of Edmund's life coincides with the reign of Mary Tudor and the short Catholic restoration, and it may be

---

[8] Hopper, 'London Chronicle', pp. 13–16.
[9] Hamilton, *A Chronicle of England*, (1875–77), i.83.
[10] See Duffy, *The Stripping of the Altars*, pp. 478–503.

that his absence from public life in the reigns of Edward VI and Elizabeth was connected with a distinct preference for the ways of the old religion. Documented evidence of such preferences is naturally hard to find. Problems arising from the survival of material sources and their correct interpretation are in this instance compounded by what may have been a deliberate obfuscation; it must often have been more politic in the middle years of the sixteenth century to disguise one's true spiritual predilections. Nevertheless, close observation of Edmund's known personal associations yields some indications that he was part of a network of Catholic adherents, and although some of his connections might have been no more than serendipitous, others were deliberate choices, and collectively add up to a meaningful participation.

Evidence of friendships and associations made through work or public service is less substantial in Edmund's case, compared with his father, since Edmund just seems to have been less active in this respect. The service Edmund performed on commissions in 1553 and 1554 shows him working with many lawyers, some of whom, such as John Tawe and John Baker of the Inner Temple, and Humfrey Browne (d. 1562) of the Middle Temple, had also served in latter years with his father.[11] John Baker (d. 1558) had been under-sheriff and recorder of London in Thomas Roberts's time, and latterly (from 1540) chancellor of the exchequer, a post that he held until his death. John Tawe's career as JP for Middlesex 1537–47 similarly intersected with both Thomas's and Edmund's time in public office, as did periods of service by Edmund Peckham. In 1554 Edmund found himself serving on the Commission of the Peace with Jasper Fesaunt, a link not so much with his father as with his elder brother Michael. Another man with whom Edmund later served in 1559 was John Hales; he may have been related to several men of this surname, all of whom were lawyers, who had served on commissions with Thomas.[12] Some of these perceived overlaps and connections may only have been coincidental, showing little more than that these were the men of the moment in terms of local government; some may also have been younger men coming into these

---

[11] On these men see Baker, *Readers and Readings*, pp. 81, 77, and 151, respectively. For fuller details of the commissions on which Edmund served see Chapter 2, section titled 'On Commission: Thomas Roberts and His Associates'. Jones, *The English Reformation*, describes the conservative and essentially tolerant atmosphere that prevailed at the Inns of Court during the 1550s, see pp. 124–30.

[12] See Baker, *Readers and Readings*, for details of Edward Hales (p. 72), Christopher Hales (p. 33), and John Hales; the latter died in 1540, so was not the John mentioned here (pp. 30–31).

roles just as Thomas Roberts was retiring from public life, and so not necessarily well known to him. Certain individuals, however, came from Middlesex families that had long enjoyed such local representation, and it is clear that in these cases there were meaningful connections on which Edmund could rely. The Thomas Elrington with whom he served on four commissions in the 1550s was the younger brother of Robert Elryngton with whom Thomas had served in the 1520s and early 1530s; and the John Newdigate with whom Edmund served on five commissions in the 1550s was the grandson of the John Newdigate who had been his father's close associate. Both John Newdigate and a relative of Thomas Elrington, Edward Ellryngton, stood as godparents to Edmund's children in 1558 and 1574, respectively, demonstrating a very long period of acquaintance and trust between these families.

In Thomas Roberts's time these Middlesex men had naturally shared links with the county's religious houses through paid employment as stewards: Thomas's associations were with Kilburn Priory, his friend John Newdigate's with Halliwell. The dissolution of the monasteries brought to an end this type of employment, and ostensibly ended the possibility of religious profession as well, pensioning off the monks and nuns in a process that was completed by 1540. In the case of Syon Abbey, and perhaps in other less well-documented instances as well, there were attempts to continue these communities quietly, with small groups of religious choosing to live together in different locations in England and abroad.[13] During Mary's reign the Syon community was briefly re-established at Sheen, at which point a small group of exiles which included the eighth abbess Katherine Palmer, Anne Daunsey, and Mary Nevell, returned from the Continent. Men with these family surnames had served with Thomas Roberts (John Palmer, *fl.* 1523–40; Sir John Daunce *fl.* 1512–40; and Sir Thomas Nevill *fl.* 1516–40), suggesting potential connections between the Roberts family and those families that were instrumental in maintaining the Syon community after the dissolution. Firmer evidence of such a connection is to be found in the person of Lady Joanna Dormer (d. 1571), the wife of Robert Dormer of Ascott, but by birth one of the daughters of John Newdigate (d. 1528) and the sister of the Carthusian martyr, Sebastian Newdigate.[14] Joanna Dormer was a notable benefactor of Syon: she supported

---

[13] *VCH* Middlesex vol. 1.189; see also Erler, *Reading and Writing During the Dissolution*, pp. 121–23.

[14] See Chapter 4, section titled 'Augmentations'.

leading Catholic intellectuals during the reign of Edward VI, and these were figures who were later promoted to positions in the Church and the universities during Mary's reign.[15] Other friends of Syon with whom Edmund had at least some acquaintance included Thomas More's son-in-law William Roper, with whom Edmund served on the Peace in 1554 and as justice of the peace for Middlesex the following year. Another Middlesex justice of the peace was Sir William Cordell, solicitor-general under Mary.[16] The accession of Elizabeth in 1559 and the Syon community's final exile removes from easy view any connections between it and Edmund Roberts; those networks, though hidden, were still very much present in terms of his own extended family, as is demonstrated by the fact that some years later his niece, Ursula Horde, became Syon's thirteenth prioress.[17]

Ursula was the youngest daughter of Edmund's half-sister Dorothy Roberts. Dorothy's marital family, the Hordes, was one of firm Catholic conviction, as has been documented in Chapter 4 above. Dorothy was much older than Edmund, and the product of an earlier marriage of their father's, which are factors that might suggest limited personal contact. Certainly her name does not appear amongst the godparents that Edmund chose for his children, though that of another female family member, Mrs Grysell Sadler, does occur.[18] Yet when Dorothy's husband Alan Horde died Edmund Roberts, though not a named beneficiary or executor of Alan's will, was named as *procuratoris* in the granting of probate in 1554, indicating that Dorothy was relying upon his help in protecting her interests. There is certainly no mistaking the Catholic nature of Alan Horde's last will and testament.[19] He too bequeathed his soul to God, Mary, and the saints in heaven, and although he makes no stipulations about his own remembrance he is scrupulous in mentioning payments for the care of other souls. In what seems to have been an incomplete legal case for his cousin Maurice Glynn for whom Alan was the executor, he records:

> I know not þe certey some therof over and aboue moche money where
> I haue disposed for hes sowle as apperath by a lytill boke in my study.

---

[15] See Bainbridge, 'Syon Abbey', p. 99.

[16] Both men were commemorated in the Syon Martyrology, see Bainbridge, 'Syon Abbey', p. 98. On Cordell see Baker, 'Cordell, Sir William'.

[17] See Chapter 4, section titled 'Augmentations'.

[18] Grysell Sadler was the wife of John Sadler, Edmund's mother's brother, and the person given custody of Edmund's younger brother John during his minority.

[19] TNA, PROB 11/37/111.

> I will and desyre my executoures to besteye in due of charite by their discrecioun fourtee poundes in money for the soule of the said doctour Glyn.[20]

Similarly Alan's will also notes that he was administering the estate of his brother Edmund, for whom he has bestowed money as directed, and specifically that he has distributed money for his soul.[21] It might be noted that Dorothy's second husband, Laurence Taylard, had a significant range of Catholic connections from his first marriage to Margaret Mordaunt: the Mordaunts were a staunchly Catholic family. Another of Edmund's relatives through marriage was Anthony Hussey, father of Edmund's widowed sister-in-law Ursula Hussey. Hussey (1496/97–1560) was a significant man in affairs of civil law and ecclesiastical administration who was already a judge in the Admiralty court and proctor of the Court of Arches by the time of Thomas Roberts's death in 1542. After experiencing various difficulties during Edward's reign, Hussey generally prospered during Mary's when he was granted the governorships of various trading companies and the royal agency at Antwerp, and when he also sat in the Commons for Horsham and New Shoreham.[22]

This range of extended family connections does nothing to suggest that Edmund associated with those keen for religious reform, pointing instead towards a natural conservatism and a continued adherence to old beliefs.[23] Edmund's choice of godparents for his children reveals a little more in this regard. The detailed lists in BodL Rawlinson C. 894 that record the children's births also note the names of their godparents, amongst whom are many figures of public prominence. The majority of those listed are connected with the legal profession: John Armyster, Master of the Temple, and lord of Neasden; Jesper Umpton, a lawyer at the Middle Temple; Mr Armygell Wade, JP for Middlesex and clerk of the counsell to Henry VIII

---

[20] Maurice Glynn, clerk and doctor of the law, left £20 in his will of 1525 towards the building of the cathedral church of Bangor, Carnarvonshire, see TNA, PROB 11/21/564, and Thomas, 'Extracts from Old Wills', p. 151.

[21] And see further, Chapter 4, section titled 'After the Dissolution: the Hordes of Ewell'.

[22] On Hussey see Bindoff, *The History of Parliament*, ii.420–21.

[23] Jones, *The English Reformation*, pp. 33–57 gives an account of how families were affected by religious change, and how different generations might well subscribe to different religious values.

and Edward VI; Mr Losse, probably Hugh Losse, MP for Middlesex.[24] Full names are not always given, but it seems likely that Lady Broke was the wife of Sir Robert Broke, JP for Middlesex, and that Mrs Hyde and Mrs Browne were probably both the wives of Middle Temple lawyers with those names. Sir Robert Chester and Lady Kateryne Chester are both named as godparents to different children in 1550 and 1552, respectively. Sir Robert was the Receiver of the Court of Augmentations and a man of substance; the death and burial on 26 March 1563 of 'the good lade Chastur [at] Rayston, the wyff of ser Robartt Chastur knyght' was recorded by Henry Machyn, who notes what a big event this was, and what a great dinner followed.[25] Clearly Edmund hoped to forge useful connections for his children by making these relationships for them at their births. One sponsor that he chose for his first-born son, Francis, in 1550 was Sir Robert Tyrwytt. There are two individuals of this name in this period, but the man more likely to be Francis's godfather is Sir Robert Thyrwhitt I (1504–72) of Mortlake Surrey and Leighton Bromswold, Hunts. He was a member of the Commons in 1545 and again during Mary's reign, and with his wife had been an overseer of princess Elizabeth at Hatfield. After his death his widow is described as Dame Elizabeth of Clerkenwell, suggesting a local connection with the Robertses.[26] A few years later in 1554, Edmund selected Mrs 'Clarensyous' to stand as godmother to his daughter Mary. Mrs Clarencieux was the widow of Thomas Tonge, Clarencieux King of Arms, who had died in 1536. She was born Susan White (before 1510–66), daughter of Richard White of Hutton Hall, Essex, and Maud Tyrrell. Before her marriage Susan had been in the service of Mary Tudor (1525–33), and she rejoined Mary's household after its reorganization (and her own widowhood) in 1536 at Mary's specific request. After Mary's accession Susan Clarence, as she was known, became Mistress of Robes. She was with Mary when she died, and

---

[24] There is a family tree for the Wades of Belsize in Hampstead in Park, *The Topography and Natural History of Hampstead*, p. 137.

[25] Nichols, *The Diary of Henry Machyn*, p. 303.

[26] For their wills see TNA, PROB 11/54/285 and PROB 11/60/222. The alternative, Sir Robert Tyrwitt II (*c.* 1510–81) of Kettleby, Lincolnshire, was the nephew of Robert Tyrwitt I. He was a lifelong Catholic and a member of parliament under Mary; he did not sit in Elizabeth's parliaments, and towards the end of his life he and his children were harried for recusancy. For his will see TNA, PROB 11/64/82. See also Bindoff, *The History of Parliament*, iii.501–503.

in 1559 she went abroad in the household of Jane Dormer.[27] A more Catholic sponsor for Edmund's fourth child, named Mary as the short-lived third child had also been, can scarcely be imagined. And although most of these children were baptized in the church at Willesden, three of Edmund's grandchildren: Francis (born 1581), another Francis (born 1597), and Mari (born 1600), were christened 'in the parler' at Neasden, and an earlier Mari who lived less than a month was buried 'in mi chapyell', according to a note added to the record of her birth in 1587.[28] These references hint at a private family chapel where separate (and more Catholic) rites might be discreetly observed, but they are no more than hints, and the family's association with St Mary's remained significant.

In July 1553, a point at which it is clear that he was using the book of hours that had previously belonged to his father, Edmund would have been aged thirty-two. He had married his first wife, Fraunces Welles, in 1548, and by this date they had two young children and were expecting a third.[29] Edmund had been the head of the main branch of the Roberts family for almost a decade. In terms of important personal events such as marriage, birth of an heir, death, and inheritance, 1553 was not an especially significant year for Edmund, but for some reason this was the year when he seems to have become an assiduous annotator of his books: the date 1553 is written alongside his signature in both CUL Ii.6.2 and BodL Rawlinson C. 894.[30] The simplest explanation for this is to assume that this was the point at which Edmund acquired these two books. This may well have been the case with BodL Rawlinson C. 894, which he seems to have been the first member of the Roberts family to own. On the other hand CUL Ii.6.2 had been family property for much longer and ought to have passed into Edmund's hands almost a decade earlier after the deaths of his father and brother. One reason for a delay in Edmund receiving the book has been suggested in Chapter 5 above.[31] Another possible reason is that Edmund did not choose to take up residence in the family's main property at Willesden until the early 1550s. He was married in 1548 at Rysene (Royston) and his first child

---

[27] Loades, 'Tonge [née White], Susan [*known as* Susan Clarencius]'; on Jane (Joanna) Dormer see Chapter 4, section titled 'Augmentations'.

[28] BodL, MS Rawlinson C. 894, f. vii^{r-v}, viii^v, and ix^r.

[29] According to records entered by his hand in BodL Rawlinson C. 894, f. iv^v and f. v^r.

[30] f. 33^v and f. iv^r respectively.

[31] See Chapter 5, section titled 'The Use of Sarum: Cambridge University Library, MS Ii.6.7 and Cambridge University LIbrary, MS Ii.6.2'.

Conclusion: Newly Reformed Readers?

Francis was christened there. Not until 1552 and the birth of his daughter Katherine is there any mention of Willesden in the baptism records preserved in BodL Rawlinson C. 894.

There may have been other factors beyond the strictly devotional which encouraged Edmund in the habit of marking his religious books. In political terms this was a turbulent period: July 1553 was a month of three monarchs, with the death of Edward VI on 6 July, followed by the nine-day reign of Lady Jane Grey which culminated in her execution, and the accession of Mary Tudor on 19 July. These changes in the ruling monarch also entailed official changes of religion, from the Protestant regime of Edward following Henry VIII's break with Rome, to the restoration of Catholicism under Mary. Mary's reign proved to be repressive, but this would not have been apparent in 1553, and there may have been general relief and even rejoicing at a return to the ways of the old religion, since Edward's reign had introduced more extreme reformist ideas than Henry's, and these were not widely liked. Certainly Mary's accession seems to have met with popular approval, and the likelihood is that Edmund and his family shared this reaction. The Robertses' longstanding association with the church of St Mary in Willesden, where generations of family members were buried, must have given them a close sense of affinity with the Marian shrine there.[32] The shrine of Our Lady of Willesden had become a popular pilgrimage destination by the end of the fifteenth century, but it had been dismantled under Henry VIII along with other similar shrines at Walsingham, Ipswich, and Worcester.[33] Although she never did so, Mary was expected to reverse such actions; in the light of this expectation, Edmund's annotations in CUL Ii.6.2 might be viewed as an overt attempt to demonstrate that his religious practices were aligned with the devotional habits of the old religion rather than with the reforms of recent years. It is likely that he felt quite comfortable with this, and his freely added annotations that demonstrate his devotion to the Virgin and his belief in her powers of intercession may simply form part of a new-found expression of devotional freedom, in contrast to the situation which had obtained only a few years earlier. Edwardian legislation in 1550 against 'Superstitious Books and Images' had condemned the use of religious books that were not specifically approved and authorized by the

---

[32] For details of the various Roberts family memorials, including Edmund's, that survive in the church of St Mary, see www.stmarywillesden.org.uk.

[33] The general suppression of shrines and images took place in 1541, see *LPFD, Henry VIII*, 16 (32 Henry VIII, nos 1192, 1233, 1258, 1262, 1297 (p. 599), 1377).

king, ordering that they be 'abolished, extinguished, and forbidden ever to be used or kept in this realm'; instead they were to be handed over and 'openly burnt or otherways defaced and destroyed'.[34] The list of types of forbidden books is comprehensive, and includes manuals, and primers in Latin or English, as well as a full range of more liturgical works. In the light of this interdict against the possession of unreformed reading matter, it would have been sensible for Edmund to conceal his book of hours and miscellany of devotional texts.

There may also have been a more political motivation behind Edmund's devout annotations too. No doubt various anxieties about religious conformity were felt throughout the nobility and gentry at this time; the preceding two decades had been a period of unprecedented religious change, and the accession of Mary promised more such disruption even if, in 1553, there was no reason to expect her reign to be as intolerant as it turned out to be. One reasonable expectation, though, was that a Catholic monarch might wish to restore the fabric of religious communities, reopening religious orders and re-establishing their houses. This certainly seems to have been the expectation of Alan Horde, writing his will mid-way through the first year of Mary's reign.[35] For families that had benefitted in financial terms from Henry VIII's dismantling of the monasteries and redistribution of church lands, there must have been a very real anxiety in 1553 that this property and land would be requisitioned.[36] Further, it might be noted that the Roberts family had leases of lands from Westminster Abbey, which *was* restored by Mary, and so they might have feared this particularly keenly; in fact, amongst the lands granted back to the abbey in 1556 were some at Willesden in the tenure of John Roberts.[37] For materialistic reasons then, rather than through fear of religious persecution, Edmund may have wished to demonstrate his proper devotion and loyalty to the crown through religious conformity. In this light some of the additions to his personal book of hours could be seen as akin to the deletions and alterations that had been made earlier to its calendar by his father, to display outward conformity to the religious changes wrought by Henry VIII.

---

[34] On this legislation see Wright, 'The Dispersal of the Libraries', pp. 165–67.
[35] Alan Horde made his will on 24 January 1553 (i.e. 1554) in the first year of Mary Tudor's reign.
[36] *VCH: Middlesex*, i.216.
[37] *CPR Philip and Mary*, 3 (1555–57), p. 352.

Conclusion: Newly Reformed Readers?

The layers of accretions in CUL Ii.6.2 point to the volume's diligent use as an aid to devotion in the later fifteenth century and all the way through the religious upheavals of the sixteenth century. As Edmund Roberts continued to use this fifteenth-century book of hours through the middle period of the sixteenth century, the world of religious devotion must have looked rather different, and not only because of the passage of time. The forms of prayer that Edmund found there were not just older than him: they also predated the many religious reforms of his lifetime. Similarly Edmund's collection of Middle English devotional texts in BodL Rawlinson C. 894 offered instruction in the Christian faith and guidance for proper living that had been designed for a different age of religious belief and observance. The sixteenth-century readers of this book had a much more complicated religious worldview than could ever have been anticipated by the manuscript's compilers. Nevertheless, these new readers could still recognize the value of 'a vere good praer', and were clearly willing to continue using old-fashioned devotions in their post-Reformation worship. Though far distant in time from the audience originally imagined for works such as the *Pore Caitif*, Thomas and Edmund Roberts were not, it seems, particularly distant from the *type* of readers articulated by the author of that text who aimed to 'teche symple men & wymmen of good will þe riȝt weie to heuene, If þei wolen bisie hem to haue it in mynde & worche þeraftir, without multiplicacioun of manye bookis.'[38] We cannot be sure how many of the family's books passed through Edmund Roberts's hands, nor how many books in total he possessed, and we know of only a handful of manuscripts which formed part of the Roberts family library. Yet the spectrum of religious reading available in even these few books, which includes both an ultra-orthodox work such as Love's *Mirror* and the Lollard defence of vernacular scripture, 'Answeris to hem that seien that we schulde not speke of holy writt', shows the eagerness of newly reformed readers such as Edmund Roberts, who had lived through the upheavals of the English Reformation and experienced several changes in official religion, to engage with different aspects of religious issues.

The question of how reformed a reader Edmund Roberts really was is ultimately unanswerable, but in the annotations that he made to both his

---

[38] Prologue to *Pore Caitif*, quoted from Brady, 'The Pore Caitif', p. 1, lines 3–6; these lines do not actually occur in the version in BL, MS Harley 2322 which omits the prologue and begins instead with the *Pater Noster* tract.

book of hours and his anthology of devotional treatises there is little of reformist substance to be found. All the sentiments expressed by Edmund seem firmly in tune with a continuing Catholic worldview, but the details of his personal life demonstrate a mode of quiet adherence rather than a stubborn recusancy. Certainly the fortunes of the Roberts family continued to prosper. The inscription on Edmund's commemorative brass states that he 'left good land unto his sonne', and further augmentations of property during Francis Roberts's lifetime – and that of his grandson and heir – brought the estate to a position of significance by the mid seventeenth century. William Roberts, Edmund's great grandson, managed not just to buy up ecclesiastical properties during the Civil War but also to retain them at the Restoration, demonstrating that he had inherited the ability to negotiate political changes of an extreme nature. Such adaptability had been a family characteristic for many generations.

Postscript

After the Family: The Manuscripts' Later Histories

The eight manuscripts that have been discussed in this book in connection with the Roberts family of Willesden must constitute merely a small remnant of that family's library. These books were preserved and handed down through several generations, but at the same time there would have been an ongoing process of book acquisition in each period as well. Even if we restrict consideration to Thomas Roberts alone it is clear that he must have possessed more books than the handful of manuscripts that can now be associated with him. A contemporary, James Morice, clerk of works to Lady Margaret Beaufort, had twenty-three books in 1508.[1] And a comparison with some other lawyers whose lives overlapped with Thomas's shows that it was not unusual for members of this professional group to accumulate significant book collections. Thomas Kebell, serjeant-at-law, had at least thirty-three books when he died in 1500, and Roger Townshend (d. 1493), another serjeant-at-law and a practising lawyer in Norfolk, had more than forty.[2] The environment of the Inns of Court was saturated with literary culture, and by the 1560s they were home to flourishing traditions of poetic composition, dramatic performance, and classical translation.[3] Men who attended university, as several of the Roberts family did in the second half of the sixteenth century, also had a need for books, yet no copies of the texts that were prescribed by university statutes can now be associated with the family. And beyond the question of sheer need are other considerations such as edification and entertainment. Margaret Lane Ford warns against the danger of making 'fixed assumptions regarding what types of book people *ought* to have owned', and reminds us that in the late fifteenth and early sixteenth centuries members of

---

[1] Oates, 'English Bokes', recently discussed in detail by Erler, 'The Laity'.
[2] See Chapter 2, section titled 'A Lawyer's Book: British Library, MS Harley 1859.'
[3] As demonstrated by Winston, *Lawyers at Play*.

the gentry and mercantile classes read books for a wide variety of reasons including improvement and pleasure.[4] A narrow focus on only the surviving identifiable volumes from the Roberts library gives an impression that readers in this family were overwhelmingly interested in matters of religious devotion, since amongst these manuscripts there is no entertainment literature, no drama, little poetry (except for devotional pieces), no chronicles, no works of science and information, and no texts of practical application (except for medical remedies). Yet clearly their tastes must have been more wide-ranging and their book collection must have been of a more diverse nature. Furthermore, as well as manuscripts, it must have included printed books (easily obtainable in London), even though none can now be securely connected with members of the family.[5]

A study such as this necessarily introduces distortions, since it must inevitably draw its conclusions from the surviving material artefacts. To counteract this, some attempt has been made in earlier chapters to discuss various losses and absences from the extant manuscripts, and the total loss of other manuscripts and printed books is explicitly acknowledged here, but it is still worth emphasizing the chance survival of the existing evidence. Parchment is essentially a more durable material than paper, leading to the greater survival of manuscripts written on skin, and to the greater likelihood that manuscript, rather than printed, material will survive at all. Some types of manuscripts, principally those with attractive decoration, have survived in greater numbers because they have been more valued by collectors. Volumes that contain records of births and deaths had a greater chance of being retained through successive generations of the same family than did other books, and these same records provide the means by which books may be linked back to the possession of a particular family once that chain of ownership has been severed. Uncertainties of identification introduce other potential distortions. There are a number of other manuscripts that bear the name 'Roberts' that cannot be securely connected with the Roberts family of Middlesex. Sometimes this is because the names and dates of inscriptions do not fit easily with the historical and genealogical information that I have been able to recover about the

---

[4] See Ford, 'Private Ownership of Printed Books', p. 211 and pp. 217–18.

[5] A possible exception is BodL Antiq.d.F.9 (1), a copy of Ovidian commentaries printed in Lyons in 1500, which has the sixteenth-century inscription: *Possidet hunc Roberts*, not attributable to the hands of either Thomas or Edmund; see Coates, Jensen et al., *A Catalogue of Books*, iv.1920–21. See also the printed hours mentioned in Chapter 6, section titled 'I youse thys prayer well every daye: How Edmund Roberts Said His Prayers.'

Postscript: After the Family: The Manuscripts' Later Histories

Willesden family; sometimes the inscribed names may relate to later descendants about whom I do not know enough to be sure of a connection with the earlier generation, and sometimes when a genealogical connection seems probable there is simply no evidence of earlier book ownership. Occasionally the manuscripts themselves are hidden from view in private collections, preventing a full assessment of their witness.[6] I have listed these manuscripts of uncertain association in Appendix V, along with some whose connection with the family I reject. It may be that if some of these manuscripts could be attributed to the libraries of Thomas or Edmund Roberts this would subtly change the overall impression of their book collections and literary taste.

By the end of the seventeenth century the Roberts books had been dispersed, and some might have passed out of family hands before this point. This was a period in which the fortunes of the family were declining. After Sir William Roberts died in 1662, heavy debts forced first his son and then his grandson to sell off properties in what may have been a period of general asset-stripping; the estate then passed into the hands of a different branch of the family in the early eighteenth century. The fortunes of the manuscripts varied. By the middle of the eighteenth century several had already entered institutional collections, whilst others passed through the hands of a series of private owners. This short postscript to the main discussion notes the material evidence for the ongoing life of these eight manuscripts. It charts the post-Enlightenment history of the manuscripts largely in terms of their passage through salerooms and the hands of various owners and, sooner or later, into public repositories. In the process these ceased to be private family books, and consequently there is no attempt to discuss evidence of annotation and readership in this later phase of their existence, though occasionally significant interactions of modern users will be noted.

CAMBRIDGE, UNIVERSITY LIBRARY, MSS Ii.6.2 AND Ii.6.7

Since the two books of hours, CUL Ii.6.2 and Ii.6.7, both ended up in the same repository it seems safe to assume that they shared the same fortunes after they left the family's hands. Francis Roberts had Ii.6.2 after his father died in 1585,

---

[6] As is the case with the Sarum hours sold at Sotheby's on 7 December 1992 (lot 59), which bears the tantalizing inscription: 'This is Thomas Robards Booke, Witnes by me John Benfylld and Jone Russell and Walter Crayes and John Hayward the baylay'; none of these are names that I can link to Thomas Roberts of Willesden.

and probably the other volume as well, but it is not clear what happened to them immediately after this. At some point during the second half of the seventeenth century the two volumes entered the collection of John Moore (1646–1714), bishop of Ely.[7] Moore had been a book collector since his undergraduate years at Cambridge, and his career afforded him many opportunities to build up a personal library though there is not much documentation to show how and when he did so. At some point he acquired the books and manuscripts of Sir Thomas Knyvett (1539–1618) of Ashwellthorpe in Norfolk.[8] Moore also added greatly to his collection during his time as bishop of Norwich (1691–1707). His chaplain, Thomas Tanner, prepared an account of his library that was published in Edward Bernard's *Catalogi librorum manuscriptorum Angliae et Hiberniae* in 1697, and the reference numbers used in this list relate to numbers that appear on early leaves of Ii.6.2 and Ii.6.7.[9] After Moore died his library was purchased by George I, who then donated it to the University of Cambridge in 1715.

LONDON, BRITISH LIBRARY, MSS HARLEY 1859 AND HARLEY 2322

Two of the Roberts manuscripts, containing *Registrum Brevium* and the *Pore Caitif*, are now part of the Harley collection at the British Library. This collection was acquired when the British Museum was established in 1753, and had been built up over two generations by Robert Harley, first earl of Oxford (1661–1724) and his son, Edward Harley, second earl of Oxford and Mortimer (1689–1741).[10] The two manuscripts entered the collection by different routes. A pencilled note at the front of Harley 1859, written by the hand of the Harleys' librarian, Humfrey Wanley (1672–1726), reads 'Bought of Mr Noble', indicating the manner of its acquisition; however, the precise identity of Mr Noble remains unclear.[11] Plomer's directory of the printers and

---

[7] See Meadows, 'Moore, John', and Ringrose, 'The Royal Library'.

[8] On Sir Thomas Knyvett see McKitterick, *The Library of Sir Thomas Knyvett*.

[9] CUL Ii.6.2, f. 2ʳ has the number '151', and CUL Ii.6.7 has the number '122'. In Bernard's list the equivalent entries are: '9308. 122 Missale. 8vo' and '9337. 151. Alter 8vo. eadem pulchritudine & figuris', see Bernard, *Catalogi*, p. 364.

[10] See Speck, 'Harley, Robert', and Stoker, 'Harley, Edward'.

[11] On Wanley see Heyworth, 'Wanley, Humfrey', and Jackson, 'Humfrey Wanley'. Wright, *Fontes Harleiani*, p. 253 notes a total of seventeen manuscripts in the collection that were acquired from 'Mr Noble'.

booksellers active between 1668–1725 lists only one man with this surname, a Thomas Noble who was a printer in Edinburgh, which seems an unlikely provenance.[12] The inscription is too early to refer to the eighteenth-century bookseller Francis Noble (d. 1792) who, with his brother John, was a pioneer in the circulating library business; they traded first in St Martin's Court in 1737.[13] However, James Raven notes others of this surname who were active in the early eighteenth-century book trade including an 'S. Noble' who was publishing and selling books in Long Walk, Cheapside, between at least 1713 and 1717.[14] Details of acquisition are much clearer in the case of Harley 2322, the copy of the *Pore Caitif*: Harley bought this from the printer William Bowyer the younger (1699–1777) on 11 September 1725, along with five other manuscripts.[15] These volumes had previously been the property of Ambrose Bonwicke (1652–1722), headmaster of the Merchant Taylors' School between 1686–91, and were in his hands before 1697 at least.[16]

OXFORD, BODLEIAN LIBRARY, MSS RAWLINSON C. 299 AND C. 894

Thomas Roberts's remedy book and Edmund Roberts's anthology of devotional texts are both now part of the Rawlinson collection at the Bodleian Library. The remedy book (Rawlinson C. 299) has been much used, but has no owners' names apart from that of Thomas Roberts himself. One indication that it remained in the family's hands throughout much of the seventeenth century is the presence of a seal impression on f. 51^v. The applied circular seal is in red wax and under magnification the letters 'W R' can be made out, set beneath what seems to be a design of a prancing horse, the head facing towards the right. From its miniature size the impression would seem to have been made from a signet ring, and the initials 'W R' almost certainly stand for William Roberts. However, in the seventeenth century there were three generations of men who had this name: Sir William Roberts, the

---

[12] Plomer, *A Dictionary of the Printers and Booksellers*.
[13] On the Noble brothers see Raven, 'The Noble Brothers'.
[14] Raven, 'The Noble Brothers', p. 298, and see also discussion of a Samuel Noble on pp. 299–300.
[15] For details see Wright, *Fontes Harleiani*, p. 76.
[16] See Sharp, 'Bonwicke, Ambrose'. A catalogue of Bonwicke's manuscripts was printed by Bernard, *Catalogi*, ii.250, nos. 8719–8727; BL, MS Harley 2322 is listed as no. 8727.

grandson and heir of Francis Roberts (d. 1662), his son Sir William Roberts, Bt. (d. 1688), and his son Sir William Roberts (d. 1698), as well as a cousin, also named William Roberts (d. 1700), to whom the estate passed. The anthology of devotional texts (Rawlinson C. 894) clearly also remained in family hands throughout much of this period. The records in the added quire at the front of this volume give information about the children and grandchildren of Sir William Roberts (d. 1662), with birth dates running into the 1670s, and the very latest record seems to be that which notes the death of his wife, Eleanor Aty, in 1678. On the pastedown of this volume is the bookplate of Richard Rawlinson (1690–1755).[17] Rawlinson had connections with the Inns of Court, and from 1712 onwards travelled extensively in England, copying monumental inscriptions and making antiquarian notes.[18] He collected books and manuscripts whilst travelling and at London book sales between 1715 and 1755. It seems likely that these two small Roberts manuscripts passed into his collection without intervening owners, and after Rawlinson's death into the Bodleian Library in 1756.

MANCHESTER, JOHN RYLANDS LIBRARY, MS ENGLISH 98

The Roberts copy of Nicholas Love's *Mirror of the Blessed Life of Jesus Christ* effectively passed into the hands of another family at an early stage through the marriage of Thomas Roberts's eldest daughter Dorothy to the lawyer Alan Horde. Thereafter the manuscript remained in the Horde family for at least two generations, as demonstrated by the addition of the list of births of Dorothy and Alan's grandchildren through their second son, Edmund Horde. It is not clear what happened to the book after this period, though various early modern inscriptions indicate that it had probably passed out of the family's possession. The name 'Brindley' has been written in the top margin of f. 61^r by a sixteenth-century hand, with the name 'John' added before it by a seventeenth-century hand. Another seventeenth-century inscription on f. 138^v reads: 'Robert Knyuett oweth this booke'. Whilst this individual has not been identified, one possible candidate might be the Robert Knyvett, gentleman, described as of Westminster and of Stanwell in Middlesex, whose name occurs

---

[17] Clapinson, 'Richard Rawlinson', and Enright, 'I Collect and I Preserve'.
[18] His notes relating to Middlesex are in BodL Rawlinson B. 389b and c (2 vols).

in bonds and receipts between 1610–11.[19] Another candidate might be Sir Robert Knyvett, baronet, of Buckenham Norfolk who died in 1699.[20] The name 'Knyvett' is a well-known one in terms of book-collecting, but there seem to be no links with the Knyvetts of Ashwellthorpe in Norfolk, nor with the library of Sir Thomas Knyvett (1539–1618).[21] The manuscript then effectively disappears from sight until the nineteenth century when it was in the library of Thomas William Evans (1821–92) of Allestree Hall, Derby (his armorial bookplate is set on its inside back cover).[22] Evans, who was made a baronet in 1887, was Member of Parliament for South Derbyshire. He had no children, and bequeathed his estate to his brother-in-law William Gisborne. When Gisborne died in 1898 the property passed to his son, Lionel Guy Gisborne, who rented it out after 1902 and sold it in 1913. At least some of the contents of the library had been sold before this point. The copy of Nicholas Love was purchased in 1905 by the John Rylands Library: they bought it from the Bloomsbury book dealers Bull and Auvache on 12 July 1905, paying £25 for it.[23]

CAMBRIDGE, MA, UNIVERSITY OF HARVARD, HOUGHTON LIBRARY, MS RICHARDSON 22

This compilation of devotional texts was the last of the Roberts family books to enter public ownership. It is not clear how or when this volume left the family's possession, but its progress through the hands of a series of private owners may be charted through the salerooms from the mid nineteenth century onwards. In 1859 it was part of the collection of Guglielmo Libri (1802–69), the Italian scientist, bibliophile, and notorious book thief.[24] Libri spent much of his life in France but fled in 1848 to escape investigation for book theft; he lived in London until 1868 and was an active dealer in books and manuscripts during this time. Sotheby's held ten auctions of his material between 1849 and 1865, and this manuscript surfaces in their sale of 28

---

[19] See Norfolk Record Office, KNY 473 372X1, KNY 474 372X1, KNY 475 372X1.
[20] Burke and Burke, *A Genealogical and Heraldic History of the Extinct and Dormant Baronetcies*, p. 295.
[21] See discussion of MSS Ii.6.2 and Ii.6.7 above.
[22] Burke, *A Genealogical and Heraldic History of the Landed Gentry*, i.522.
[23] Ker, *MMBL*, iii.416, and de Hamel, 'The Selling and Collecting', p. 96.
[24] On Libri see Harris, 'Libri, Guglielmo'.

March 1859.[25] Although the stated reason for the sale was that the collector was 'obliged to leave London in consequence of ill health, and for that reason to dispose of his literary treasures', Libri did not in fact move abroad until 1868. Other aspects of the catalogue description are also mendacious: it claims that the manuscript was formerly in the library of Henry VIII, and that it was rebound for him with 'the Tudor rose and Royal Arms impressed on the cover'. The Tudor rose and crown are blind stamped four times on both the front and back covers, but the royal arms do not appear, and this seems little more than an attempt to inflate the fetching price. The manuscript next appears in the sale of manuscripts of the industrialist William Bragge (1823–1884) in June 1876, though it is not clear whether Bragge had bought it directly from Libri's sale, or whether there had been an intervening owner.[26] Its next owner was Thomas Brooke (1830–1908) of Armitage Bridge House near Huddersfield. It is listed in the catalogue of his manuscripts and printed books that was published in 1891, and Brooke commented in the preface that the books had 'nearly all been bought by myself since 1854'.[27] Brooke was succeeded by his younger brother, John Arthur Brooke (1844–1920) of Fenay Hall in Huddersfield. After John Arthur died in 1920 his library was sold over seven days between 25 May and 3 June 1921, and this manuscript was lot number 49, offered on the first day.[28] The purchaser was William King Richardson (1859–1951), who paid £90 for it. Richardson, who was a graduate of Harvard and Balliol College, Oxford, was a prominent Boston lawyer and bibliophile who bequeathed a large number of books and manuscripts to the Harvard College Library.[29] Richardson was the manuscript's last private owner, and as well as being a keen collector of old books he was also a reader of them: his copious annotations in light pencil may be observed in the margins throughout the volume.

---

[25] Sotheby, *Catalogue of the Extraordinary Collection of Manuscripts, formed by M. Guglielmo Libri*, p. 26, no. 111.

[26] Sotheby's, *Catalogue of a Magnificent Collection of Manuscripts*, p. 5, no. 23. On Bragge see Smith, 'Bragge, William'.

[27] Ellis, *A Catalogue of the Manuscripts and Printed Books*, i.34.

[28] Sotheby's, *Catalogue of the Valuable and Extensive Library*, no. 49, p. 10. The relevant extract from the sale catalogue is pasted onto the first flyleaf beneath Richardson's bookplate.

[29] On Richardson's collection see Jackson, 'The William King Richardson Library', 328–37.

Appendices

APPENDIX I

Timeline of Key Events During the Lifetimes of Thomas and Edmund Roberts

1470	Birth of Thomas Roberts; deposition of Edward IV; Henry VI restored as king
1471	Edward IV returns, defeats the Lancastrians at Barnet and Tewkesbury; death of Henry VI
1476	William Caxton's first printed book in England: *The Canterbury Tales*
1483	Death of Edward IV; accession of Edward V, his deposition and death; accession of Richard III
1485	Death of Richard III at Bosworth; accession of Henry VII; first outbreak of the sweating sickness
1486	Marriage of Henry VII to Elizabeth of York, daughter of Edward IV
1487	Yorkist rising of Lambert Simnel and its defeat at the battle of Stoke
1497	Perkin Warbeck captured by Henry VII; John Cabot discovers Newfoundland
1502	Death of Arthur, Prince of Wales
1508	Second outbreak of sweating sickness
1509	Death of Henry VII; accession of Henry VIII and his marriage to Catherine of Aragon
1513	Battle of Flodden Field; James IV of Scotland killed
1515	Thomas Wolsey created cardinal
1516	Birth of Princess Mary
1517	Martin Luther's ninety-five theses; outbreak of sweating sickness
1520	Birth of Edmund Roberts; Field of the Cloth of Gold; Leo X promulgates a ban on the writings of Martin Luther
1521	Burning of Lutheran books in London; confirmation of the title 'Defender of the faith' for Henry VIII
1527	Henry VIII begins proceedings to annul his marriage with Catherine of Aragon
1528	Outbreak of sweating sickness
1529	Meeting of the Reformation parliament
1533	Annulment of the marriage of Catherine of Aragon and Henry VIII; marriage to Anne Boleyn; birth of Princess Elizabeth; Act to restrain appeals to Rome
1534	First Act of Succession; first Act of Supremacy; Acts abolishing payments to Rome

1535   Valor ecclesiasticus; Thomas More and John Fisher executed for refusing to acknowledge Henry as head of the Church in England and take the oath of succession

1536   Second Act of Supremacy; king incorporates title of Supreme Head in royal title; execution of Anne Boleyn; Henry VIII marries Jane Seymour; first dissolution Act begins the dissolution of lesser religious houses

1537   Birth of Prince Edward; death of Jane Seymour

1540   Henry VIII's marriage to Anne of Cleves (January), annulled (July); marriage to Catherine Howard

1542   Death of Thomas Roberts; execution of Catherine Howard

1543   Henry VIII's marriage to Catherine Parr

1547   Death of Henry VIII; accession of Edward VI

1553   Death of Edward VI; accession of Lady Jane Grey and her deposition; accession of Mary Tudor

1554   Mary's marriage to Philip of Spain, king of Naples and Jerusalem

1558   Death of Mary Tudor; accession of Elizabeth I

1577   Death of Dorothy Roberts Horde Taylard

1585   Death of Edmund Roberts

APPENDIX II

Summary List of Contents of the Manuscripts Owned by the Roberts Family

CAMBRIDGE, UNIVERSITY LIBRARY, MS Ii.6.2

Book of Hours (Use of Sarum) with twenty-one full-page miniatures; many prayers and other items in English and Latin added to originally blank leaves.

ff. 4^r–9^v Calendar
ff. 11^r–31^r Commemorations
ff. 34^r–73^v Hours of the Virgin
ff. 76^r–83^r Penitential Psalms
ff. 85^r–93^r Office of the Dead
ff. 95^v–102^r *Commendatio animarum*

CAMBRIDGE, UNIVERSITY LIBRARY, MS Ii.6.7

Book of Hours (Use of Sarum) with four full-page miniatures.

ff. 1ʳ–6ᵛ Calendar
ff. 8ʳ–44ʳ Hours of the Virgin
f. 45ʳ Penitential Psalms
f. 63ʳ Psalms of the Passion
f. 76ʳ–81ᵛ The Fifteen Oes
f. 85ʳ–113ʳ Office of the Dead
f. 114ʳ *Commendatio animarum*
f. 127ᵛ Hymn to the Virgin

LONDON, BRITISH LIBRARY, MS HARLEY 1859

ff. 2ʳ–217ʳ *Registrum Brevium*

LONDON, BRITISH LIBRARY, MS HARLEY 2322

ff. 1ʳ–152ʳ *Pore Caitif*

(includes: f. 1ʳ Prologue to the Pater Noster; f. 4ʳ Pater Noster; f. 18ʳ Ave; f. 23ʳ Creed; f. 37ᵛ Prologue to the Ten Commandments; f. 39ʳ Ten Commandments; f. 87ʳ 'Answeris to hem that seien that we schulde not speke of holy writt'; f. 88ᵛ The Counsel of Christ; f. 92ʳ Of Virtuous Patience; f. 95ᵛ On Temptation; f. 96ᵛ The Charter of Our Heavenly Heritage; f. 104ᵛ The Horse or Armour of Heaven; f. 115ʳ The Name of Jesus; f. 119ʳ The Love of Jesus; f. 124ᵛ Of Meekness; f. 127ᵛ Of Man's Will; f. 129ᵛ Of Active Life and Contemplative Life; f. 132ᵛ The Mirror of Chastity)

MANCHESTER, JOHN RYLANDS LIBRARY, MS ENGLISH 98

Nicholas Love, *Mirror of the Blessed Life of Jesus Christ*

OXFORD, BODLEIAN LIBRARY, MS RAWLINSON C. 299

Remedy book containing a collection of 314 Middle English medical recipes and 4 charms, with the addition of a further 43 recipes.

Appendices

OXFORD, BODLEIAN LIBRARY, MS RAWLINSON C. 894

ff. 1^{r-v} *Six Masters on Tribulation*
ff. 1^v–2^v *Nota de paciencia infirmitatis* (Latin)
ff. 2^v–18^r *The Twelve Profits of Tribulation*
ff. 18^v–33^r *The Boke of Crafte of Dying*
ff. 33^r–48^r *A Tretyse of Gostly Batayle*
ff. 48^r–54^v extract from Walter Hilton, *On the Mixed Life*
ff. 55^{r-v} extracts from the *Abbey of the Holy Ghost*
ff. 55^v–56^r extracts from Walter Hilton, *Scale of Perfection*
ff. 56^r–58^r extract from *Contemplations of the Dread and Love of God* (part of chapter AB)
ff. 58^r–59^v 'A good contemplacion for a prest or he go to masse'
ff. 59^v–65^r extracts from Walter Hilton, *Scale of Perfection*
ff. 65^r–67^v *Twelve Degrees of Humility*
ff. 68^r–74^r Walter Hilton, *Eight Chapters on Perfection*
ff. 74^r–86^v English translation of Pseudo-Bernard *Meditationes Piissime*
ff. 86^v–91^r *The Counsels of Saint Isidore*
ff. 91^v–97^v extract from the *Epistle of Pelagius / Jerome to Demetrias*
ff. 97^v–106^r Anonymous treatise against fleshly affections

CAMBRIDGE, MA, HARVARD UNIVERSITY, HOUGHTON LIBRARY, MS RICHARDSON 22

ff. 1^r–52^r Middle English translation of Pseudo-Augustine, *Soliloquiorum animae ad deum*
ff. 52^v–68^v *A Tretyse of þe Stodye of Wysdome þat Men Clepen Benjamin*
f. 68^v Seven deeds of mercy, bodily and ghostly (*NIMEV* 3459)
ff. 68^v–69^r Erased English rubric to following Latin prayer
ff. 69^r–71^r Prayer to Christ (Latin)
ff. 71^v–72^r Short Charter of Christ (*NIMEV* 4184)
ff. 72^r–78^r A Song of Love to our Lord Jesus Christ (*NIMEV* 1732.5)
ff. 78^r–82^v Verse prayer on the 'Ave Maria' (*NIMEV* 454.5)
ff. 82^v–89^v Long Charter of Christ (*NIMEV* 4154)
ff. 89^v–90^v English prose meditation *Reliquie cogitationis diem festum agent tibi*

APPENDIX III

Manuscripts and Printed Books of Uncertain Association

MANUSCRIPTS

Glasgow, Glasgow University Library, MS Hunter 117

A fifteenth-century collection of medical recipes that belonged to Richard Nix, Bishop of Norwich 1501–35 (f. 1ᵛ, bottom margin: *Richardus nix possedet hunc librum medecine*; f. 55ʳ, bottom margin: *Ricardus nix possidet hunc librum medesine*).[1] On a rear flyleaf is a list of names in sixteenth-century hands: 'George Tybye, Adome Stavane, John Bowton, R. Jenkins (?), Thomas Roberts'. The hand is not that of Thomas Roberts, and again these are names that do not occur amongst his known associates. The only connection I can find between Thomas Roberts and Nix is a tangential one, through the lawyer Richard Bellamy: Bellamy, who had died by 1538, acted as attorney to Nix who was related to him by marriage (Bellamy's wife was Nix's niece).[2]

London, British Library, MS Additional 73518

Book of Hours (Use of Sarum) owned by the Roberts family of Little Braxted, Essex; see discussion in Appendix IV below.

London, British Library, MS Harley 1915

Latin commentaries (Bede, Jerome) on the Acts of the Apostles and the Apocalypse. Owned in the late seventeenth century by Mrs Roberts of Holborn, and has the dates 1555 and 1535 on f. 1ʳ.

London, British Library, MS Harley 2729

Eleventh-century collection of works of Roman history (Sextus Julius Frontinus, *Strategemata*; Flavius Eutropius, *Breviarium ab urbe condita*), that has the name 'Richard Roberts', perhaps a later member of the family; see discussion in Chapter 2 above.

---

[1] Described by Young and Aitken, *A Catalogue of the Manuscripts*, p. 117.
[2] See Paxton, 'The Nunneries of London', pp. 288–89.

London, British Library, MS Harley 4273

Collection of legal works (*Modus tenendi parliamentum*), with the name 'Edro Roberts' written by a seventeenth-century hand in the top margin of f. 3^r. Venn and Venn, *Alumni Cantabrigiensis*, list six men of this name, but none seem to be connected with the Robertses of Willesden. However, there were men named Edward in later generations of the family: a son of Francis Roberts who was born in 1578, and a son of William Roberts who was born in 1642 and died in 1662, so it is possible that this volume was connected with the family.

London, British Library, MS Royal 8. C. XI

Jacobus de Theramo (Giacomo Palladini), *Belial*, or *Peccatorum consolatio*: the report of a canon law process brought by infernal powers against Christ, early fifteenth century.

The name 'Sampson Roberttes' occurs in an inscription on f. 1^r: *Et titulo permutationis a Sampsono Roberttes anno salutis 1565 1595*. There are no other inscriptions with the Roberts name in the volume which is very clean and almost entirely free from annotation. The name 'Sampson Roberts' does not occur amongst the family records in BodL, MS Rawlinson C. 894. Venn and Venn, *Alumni Cantabrigiensis*, have two entries for men of that name (perhaps the same?) who matriculated in 1564.

Book of Hours, Use of Sarum, Sold by Sotheby's, 7 December 1992, lot 59

Sold to Schuster. Previously sold by Sotheby's on 30 June 1921, lot 595, as part of the sale of the property of the Reverend Nathaniel C. S. Poyntz of Dorchester on Thames, Oxfordshire. *Circa* 1400 and perhaps produced in London. The catalogue records an early sixteenth-century inscription on one of its preliminary leaves: 'This is Thomas Robards Booke, Witnes by me John Benfylld and Jone Russell and Walter Crayes and John Hayward the baylay'. I have not been able to identify these names which do not occur amongst Thomas Roberts's associates.

New Haven, Yale University, Beinecke Library, MS 483.20

A fragment of a fourteenth-century Italian manuscript of Dynus de Mugello, *Super infortiato et digesto novo* (a commentary on Justinian, *Digesta*). This single parchment folio has been folded in half and used as a wrapper around another volume. There are several sixteenth-century inscriptions on the recto, including *Westhall, supervisio manorii*, and the names 'Robert', 'Thomas', 'Alsoppe'. On the verso are accounts written by a sixteenth-century hand. None of the writing is in the hand of Thomas Roberts, but the location suggests a possible connection with the Roberts family through his Sadler in-laws. Another record in London, BL, MS Additional Charter 25487, is a writ that names William Sadler and his wife Bridget, and Christopher Sadler and his wife Johanna, in connection with lands at Westhall in Suffolk in Elizabeth's reign.

Stockholm, Royal Library, Library X.90

Fifteenth-century collection of medical recipes that has the inscribed name 'Nicholas Robertus' in an early sixteenth-century hand. No 'Nicholas' occurs amongst the Roberts family records in BodL, MS Rawlinson C. 894.

PRINTED BOOKS

Oxford, Bodleian Library, Antiq.d.F.9 (1)

A copy of Ovidian commentaries that has the inscription *Possidet hunc Roberts* in a sixteenth-century hand, not attributable to either Thomas or Edmund Roberts; see Postscript.

Printed Hours, Sold at Sotheby's 2 July 1963, lot 338.[3]

STC 16042. Has the name 'Henri Roberte' and the date 1546.

APPENDIX IV

Other Families Named Roberts

The surname 'Roberts' is not an uncommon one and at least three other prominent families with this name flourished in the sixteenth century. Furthermore, in each of these families there was a Thomas Roberts who was contemporaneous with Thomas Roberts of Willesden, and all of these men had links with the capital (or at least with the court and royal household), meaning that distinguishing the records which relate to Thomas Roberts of Willesden requires considerable effort, and occasionally it has proved impossible to be sure of the evidence. Details of records that clearly relate to these three other families, whose principal land holdings were in Wales, Kent, and Essex respectively, and a note of some other men named 'Thomas Roberts' or who had the surname 'Roberts', are outlined below.

---

[3] See *Catalogue of Valuable Printed Books, Autograph Letters … 1 July 1963*, p. 55.

Appendices

THE ROBERTSES OF USK

The first of these other families, and the easiest to separate out, is the Roberts family of Usk in Monmouthshire. The name of the Welsh Thomas Roberts (properly Thomas ap Robert, but this form is not invariably used), occurs in the public record during the first quarter of the sixteenth century, a period exactly contemporary with Thomas Roberts of Middlesex, and much potential confusion arises from the fact that both men were appointed to the role of auditor of lands in their respective regions. The earliest mention of this Thomas Roberts I have found dates from 12 April 1504 when the names of 'Thomas Robertes and Maurice ap John, both of Uske, gentlemen', occur in a recognizance to the king. In the same record Thomas is further noted as being required to pay yearly, before 15 February, all sums due from him as a general receiver of the lordships of Usk, Caerleon, and Trelleck.[4] The father of Thomas ap Robert was Robert ap Jankin, one of the gentleman ushers of the chamber to Henry VII; a record of 1509 notes that he and his son John had been murdered in Usk.[5] By the early 1520s Thomas ap Robert had succeeded his father in his role in the royal household; records from 1522, 1524, and 1526 describe him as 'gentleman usher of the Chamber'.[6] William ap Roberts, recorded as a member of Henry VIII's household in 1516 in the role of esquire for the body extraordinary, was probably a relative.[7] Thomas was the auditor of South Wales from 1510; a commissioner of the peace for Usk, Caerleon, and Trelleck; and the receiver of various grants and lordships pertaining to this area.[8] A grant of March 1530 notes him as deceased. The grant was to James Wytteney, one of the sewers of the chamber who had been listed as such in 1516.[9] In 1530 James was to be 'receiver-general of the lordships of Uske, Kererlion, and Tryllok, parcel of the earldom of March, S. Wales; constable of the lordship of Tregruke; beadle and coroner of Edlegon; and receiver of the lordships of Newport, Wenloge, and Maghen, in the marches of S. Wales, *vice* Thomas. ap Robert, deceased'; the phrasing suggests that all of these offices had been previously fulfilled by Thomas ap Robert.[10] Thomas in fact may have died at a relatively young age since his son

---

[4] *CCR Henry VII* 2.131 (19 Henry VII, no. 377).

[5] *LPFD Henry VIII* vol. 1, part 3, p. 30 (1 Henry VIII, no. 54: Grants in May 1509, no. 43 'Thomas Roberts').

[6] *LPFD Henry VIII*, 3.ii.864 (13 Henry VIII, no. 2016, grant 12); *LPFD Henry VIII*, 4.i.196 (16 Henry VIII, no. 464, grant 20); and *LPFD Henry VIII*, 4.i.868 (17 Henry VIII, no. 1526).

[7] *LPFD Henry VIII*, 2.i.872 (8 Henry VIII, no. 2735).

[8] For references to him as auditor see *LPFD Henry VIII* (2nd ed.), 1.i.293 (2 Henry VIII, no. 485, grant 37) and p. 422 (3 Henry VIII, no. 784, grant 21); *LPFD Henry VIII* (2nd ed.), 1.ii.1114 (5 Henry VIII, no. 2535, grant 11); *LPFD Henry VIII*, 2.i.165 (7 Henry VIII, no. 602); *LPFD Henry VIII*, 4.i.428 (16 Henry VIII, no. 976). For reference to him as a commissioner of the peace see *LPFD Henry VIII*, 2.i.216 (7 Henry VIII, no. 815). For grants, leases, and so on see, amongst other examples: *LPFD Henry VIII*, 2.ii.1402 (10 Henry VIII, no. 4585); *LPFD Henry VIII*, 3.ii.864 (13 Henry VIII, no. 2016, grant 12); and *LPFD Henry VIII*, 4.i.124 (15–16 Henry VIII, no. 297, grant 8).

[9] *LPFD Henry VIII*, 2.i.873; 8 Henry VIII, no. 2735, 'Jas. Whitney'.

[10] *LPFD Henry VIII*, 4.iii.2831 (21 Henry VIII, no. 6301, grant 12).

THE ROBERTSES OF KENT

and heir, Clement, was a still a minor. A long-standing associate, John Peryent, who had been auditor with Thomas since 1510, was granted Clement's wardship and marriage, and had his own status as auditor renewed in 1539.[11]

THE ROBERTSES OF KENT

Another Roberts family that was seemingly unconnected with the Middlesex family is the Roberts family of Kent. Members of this gentry family are associated with properties in the areas around Cranbrook in west Kent and Ticehurst in east Sussex, but the sense of distance implied by these different county designations is misleading since Cranbrook and Ticehurst lie only six miles apart.[12] The John Roberts who died *circa* 1495, and who is commemorated with his wife in a brass at Hawkshurst, presumably belonged to a branch of this family.[13] In the second half of the fifteenth century Walter Roberts, son of John Roberts (died 1461), had his seat at Glassenbury, close to Cranbrook. Walter's name, clearly designated as Walter 'of Cranebrooke, Kent, esq.', occurs in a general pardon granted by Henry VIII in 1509, and this record helpfully details a number of accepted variations of the Roberts surname: 'Roberth, Robarth, Roberd or Robard'.[14] Walter Roberts was one of the most trusted retainers of Sir Richard Guildford, the influential loyalist and Bosworth companion of Henry VII.[15] Walter served as sheriff of Kent in 1488, and was actively involved in local administration for the next thirty years: his name appears repeatedly in Commissions of the Peace during this period, and – somewhat less frequently – in Commissions for Gaol Delivery at either Maidstone or Canterbury.[16] He was also part of the Commission for Muster and Array in Kent in 1490 and again in April 1496 on account of the warlike preparations of the King of Scots near to Berwick.[17] Walter Roberts was married twice and had eight surviving children: by his first wife,

---

[11] *LPFD Henry VIII*, 12.i.353 (28 Henry VIII, no. 795, grant 43); *LPFD Henry VIII*, 14.i.157 (30 Henry VIII, no. 403, grant 2).

[12] For a brief explanation of this family's history and development see Tittler, *Accounts of the Roberts Family*, pp. xv–xviii; some of the detail in this section is drawn from this source.

[13] See the rubbing in BL, MS Additional 32490 T.70.

[14] *LPFD Henry VIII* (2nd ed.), 1.i.212 (1 Henry VIII, no. 438).

[15] For some discussion of Walter Roberts's connection with the Guildford affinity see Penn, *Winter King*, pp. 126–31.

[16] For his service as sheriff of Kent see *CFR Henry VII 1485–1509*, no. 193 (p. 90). For commissions of the peace see *CPR Henry VII vol. i: 1485–94*, pp. 489–90; *CPR Henry VII vol. ii: 1494–1509*, pp. 644–45. *LPFD Henry VIII*, 2nd ed., 1.ii.1539 (1509–14); 2.i.2 (6 Henry VIII, no. 6), p. 179 (7 Henry VIII, no. 677), p. 198 (7 Henry VIII, no. 747), p. 349 (7 Henry VIII, no. 1302); 2.ii.1179 (9 Henry VIII, no. 3748); 3.i.552 (13 Henry VIII, no. 1379, grant 16). For commissions of gaol delivery see *CPR Henry VII vol. i: 1485–94*, pp. 320, 348, 351, 358. *CPR Henry VII vol. ii: 1494–1509*, pp. 209, 357; and *LPFD Henry VIII*, 2nd ed., 1.i.137 (1 Henry VIII, no. 289, grant 43).

[17] *CPR Henry VII vol ii: 1494–1509*, p. 67.

Margaret Penn, he had a son, John, and three daughters, Mercy (or Mary), Elizabeth, and Jane; by his second wife, Alice, widow of Lord Abergavenny, he had three sons: Thomas, William, Clement, and a daughter Joan; he died in 1522.[18]

The 'John Roberde' who was granted the manor and rectory of Brenchley in 1526 was presumably Walter's eldest son from his first marriage; John is then described as of 'Brenchysley' in records of 1529 given at Horsmonden (both places were close to Cranbrook).[19] This John Roberts, described as 'the elder', died in 1532.[20] Walter's eldest son by his second marriage, Thomas Roberts, was sheriff for Kent in 1533, and part of the Tenths of Spiritualities Commission in Kent in 1535;[21] he also served on the Commission of the Peace for Kent five times (in 1537, 1538, 1539, 1540, and 1542).[22] He is styled as 'Thomas Robertes of Crambroke' in the Commission of Oyer and Terminer for Rye in October 1539, and the following month was amongst the retinue of the duke of Suffolk when the latter formally received Anne of Cleves at Dover; he is also named in the Commission of Sewers in Kent in 1540–41.[23] The signature of this Thomas Roberts survives on a document from 13 June 1539 and may be contrasted with the signature of Thomas Roberts of Middlesex.[24] Thomas Roberts of Cranbrook died in 1558.[25] He and his wife Elizabeth had five children: their eldest son, Walter, inherited Glassenbury, and lived there until his death in 1580; their second son, Thomas (born 1523), inherited the property of Boarzell at Ticehurst on his marriage in 1553. This younger Thomas served as justice of the peace in Sussex once or twice, and either he or perhaps his father is recorded as having served Mary Tudor loyally during the uprising of 1554 led by Thomas Wyatt.[26] His adherence to Catholicism may explain his lack of preferment in terms of public service. Thomas Roberts the younger married Margaret (or Margery), daughter of Thomas Pigott of Whaddon, Buckinghamshire, in 1553. Margaret had been married

---

[18] As recorded in the seventeenth century, see Hovenden, *The Visitations of Kent*, pp. 93–94. For Walter Roberts's will see TNA, PROB 11/20/22.

[19] *LPFD Henry VIII*, 4.i.989 (18 Henry VIII, no. 2217) and 4.iii.2704 (21 Henry VIII, no. 6058).

[20] For his will see TNA, PROB 11/24/324.

[21] *LPFD Henry VIII*, 6.598 (25 Henry VIII, no. 1481, grant 29 'Sheriff Roll'); *LPFD Henry VIII*, 8.49 (26 Henry VIII, no. 149, no. 40).

[22] *LPFD Henry VIII*, 12.ii.471 (29 Henry VIII, no. 1311, grant 28); *LPFD Henry VIII*, 13.i.568 (30 Henry VIII, no. 1519, grant 60); *LPFD Henry VIII*, 14.i.535 (31 Henry VIII, no. 1192, grant 25); *LPFD Henry VIII*, 16.173 (32 Henry VIII, no. 379, grant 14); *LPFD Henry VIII*, 17, p. 633 (34 Henry VIII, no 1154, grant 22).

[23] *LPFD Henry VIII*, 14.ii.158 (31 Henry VIII, no. 435, grant 46); *LPFD Henry VIII*, 14.i.200 (31 Henry VIII, no. 572); *LPFD Henry VIII*, 16.14 (32 Henry VIII, no. 46) and p. 330 (no. 678, grant 55).

[24] *LPFD Henry VIII*, 14.i.504 (31 Henry VIII, no. 1109), and see Chapter 1, section titled 'Father and Son: John Roberts (d. 1476) and Thomas Roberts (1470–1542)'; both documents are accessible via *State Papers Online*.

[25] His will is East Sussex Record Office, DUN 49/5.

[26] *CPR Philip and Mary*, III (1555–57), p. 43.

three times previously, all without surviving issue, and was the widow of Sir Walter Hendley. Hendley (or Henley) had been a prominent member of the Kentish gentry, a landowner in the Cranbrook area, and a former high official in the Court of Augmentations.[27] Thomas Roberts the younger died in 1567 and his wife Margaret in 1587.[28] The Boarzell estate passed to another Walter Roberts, the son of Thomas's brother John and his wife Elizabeth, and was enlarged by additional properties that John Roberts acquired at Snave, near Appledore in Kent. In this later period more potential confusion with members of the Middlesex family arises because, following the marriage of Edmund Roberts's eldest son Francis to Mary Barne in 1575, some properties in Kent came into their hands.[29]

THE ROBERTSES OF ESSEX

A third Roberts family of this period had lands at Little Braxted, just east of Witham in Essex, but were also associated with London. The Thomas Roberts who made his will on 3 October 1535, leaving his manor at Little Braxted to his wife Anne, was resident at Elsingspital in London (the Hospital or Priory of St Mary within Cripplegate).[30] This Thomas Roberts left various pious bequests to the prior and canons of Elsingspital and to the parish church at Little Braxted, stipulating that the latter were for repairs and building work; monies were also left for repairs at his manor at Little Braxted which was to pass to his son, Clement, when he attained his majority. Later in the sixteenth and seventeenth centuries some members of this family were London lawyers: Thomas Robertes, son and heir of Thomas Robertes, of Little Braxted, Essex, esquire, was admitted to the Middle Temple on 29 June 1593.[31] Another Thomas Roberts, probably the third generation of this family, matriculated at St Catharine's College, Cambridge in the Easter term of 1634, and was admitted to Gray's Inn on 10 February 1636–37.[32] There are various sources of potential confusion between members of this family and members of the Willesden Robertses. The Thomas Roberts who died in 1535 was exactly contemporaneous with Thomas Roberts of Willesden, and both had bases in London; later members of both families were active in London legal circles. Yet another point of overlap which is directly relevant to this study is that the Essex family owned a late fifteenth-century manuscript book of hours in which they recorded details of their family history. Until very recently this manuscript was in private hands and inaccessible to scholars; it made

---

[27] Richardson, *History of the Court of Augmentations*, p. 43 and p. 492.
[28] His will was proved in 1576, see TNA, PROB 11/58/469.
[29] *CPR Edward VI 1575–78*, no. 2835 notes a property transfer by John Barne in favour of his married daughters Mary Roberts and Elizabeth Altham.
[30] TNA, PROB 11/25/462.
[31] Sturgess, *Register of Admissions*, i.65.
[32] He died in 1680; Venn and Venn, *Alumni Cantabrigiensis*, i.466, describe him as 'doubtless son and heir of Thomas, of Little Braxted, Essex'.

several brief appearances in the salerooms during the twentieth century and the related catalogue entries have provided the only access to it.[33] The combination of its original contents (a book of hours of the use of Sarum) and its additional annotations, on flyleaves and blank pages, recording births in the Roberts, Tymperley, and Strangman families, plausibly suggested an association with the Robertses of Willesden who owned two similar fifteenth-century hours which they annotated in much the same manner. However, now that this manuscript has come fully into public view this supposed association can be shown to be false. Subsequent to its sale to Sam Fogg Rare Books and Manuscripts in 1992 the manuscript was purchased by the British Library and accessioned as MS Additional 73518.[34] It is now apparent that this book of hours was owned by William Roberts of Little Braxted, or by a member of his immediate family. William was the father of the Thomas Roberts who died at Elsingspital in 1535. He died in 1508, and his first wife Joyce, the daughter of Edward Peryent, had predeceased him in 1483; her obit, on 27 February 1483, has been added to the volume's calendar. A memorial brass to Joyce and William (and his second wife, Margaret, daughter of Sir William Pyrton) survives in the church of St Nicholas, Little Braxted.[35] On the first flyleaf of the book of hours is a record of the births of William's six children: four with Joyce (Thomas 1476, Grace 1478, Elisabeth 1480, Walter 1481), and two with Margaret (Margaret 1495, Fabian 1497/8).[36] The births of five children to Thomas Roberts (i.e. William's eldest son) are recorded on a blank leaf at the end of the book (Elizabeth 1509 and Thomas 1511, Clement 1525, Elisabeth junior 1526, and Philipe 1530; the long gap in the dates suggests two wives).[37] Despite this list it seems that the book passed not to Thomas but instead to his sister, Margaret, who married first John Tymperley, by whom she had three children between 1511–13, and secondly Edward Strangman, with whom she had a further seventeen children between 1516–35; the names and dates of birth of all of these children are recorded in entries added to originally blank leaves at the end of the Hours of the Virgin.[38]

---

[33] Sotheby, *Catalogue of Valuable Printed Books ...* 24–25 January 1949, p. 29, lot 315; Sotheby, *Catalogue of Western MSS and Miniatures* 10 December 1969, p. 61, lot 79; Sotheby, *Western Manuscripts and Miniatures* 23 June 1992, p. 120, lot 92.

[34] See the catalogue description at www.searcharchives.bl.uk.

[35] Recorded by Haines, *A Manual of Monumental Brasses*, p. 53, and listed by Stephenson, *A List of Monumental Brasses in the British Isles*, p. 110, who also noted another brass of William and Joyce in shrouds at Digswell, Hertfordshire (p. 184). There is a rubbing of the Little Braxted brass in BL Additional 32490 DD9.

[36] f. i^v, written in black ink; the entries are in Latin and record both time of day and day of the week, as well as the date.

[37] f. 127^r.

[38] ff. 45^r–46^v; see further discussion of this manuscript in Connolly, 'Late Medieval Books of Hours'.

Appendices

Other Thomas Robertses and Men with the Surname Roberts

City records from fifteenth-century London show a number of men with the surname 'Roberts' involved with various crafts and trades; these include William Roberts, brewer, in 1436; Richard Roberts, skinner, in 1447; Thomas Roberts, skinner in 1474; John Roberts, vintner in 1450; Henry Robert, 'browderer' (embroiderer), in 1444, 1457, and 1468, and Thomas Roberts, tailor in 1420, 1461, 1470, and 1474.[39] Any or none of these men might have been scions of the Middlesex family, and direct evidence of connections is mostly lacking. Henry Robert's gift of goods and chattels to William Robert, 'husbondman' of the parish of Wye (near to Ashford) in Kent, almost certainly indicates a blood relationship between the two men, and the family concerned may have been the Kentish Roberts family later associated with Cranbrook.[40] Although it would be unwise to press such fragile connections too far, it may be worth noting that some of the associates of the London tailor Thomas Robert had links with Middlesex. In September 1470 he was named as the recipient of the gift of goods and chattels of a fellow tailor, Thomas Leonard, 'of St Mary Matfelon parish without Algate co. Middlesex'.[41] In a similar transaction four years later, this time by Robert Clement, citizen and 'inholder' of London, Thomas Robert was amongst five named recipients, one of whom was Henry Walshe, yeoman of Fynesbury (Finsbury).[42] This Thomas Robert lived in the parish of St Vedast, Foster Lane, but tailoring was the most commonly attested occupation in London in the fifteenth century and tailors lived all over the city, though their numbers were particularly high in the environs of Fleet Street due to the proximity of their legal and civil servant customers.[43]

A few more individuals with the name 'Thomas Roberts' who may be eliminated from further consideration include Thomas Roberts of Long Compton in Warwickshire who was liable for a bill of 40s in the loan ordered by the king in 1523;[44] Thomas Swynnerton 'otherwise Robertes' who wrote a theological treatise 'The Tropes and Figures of Scripture' addressed to Thomas Cromwell in 1536;[45] Thomas Roberts of Minterne in Dorset, whose house was burgled and whose wife Alice was assaulted by the tailor, Hugh Whitewode, in

---

[39] For William see *CCR Henry VI*, 3 (1435–41), p. 97; for Richard see *CCR Henry VI*, 4 (1441–47), p. 494; for Thomas the skinner see *CCR Edward IV*, 2 (1468–76), p. 363; for John see *CCR Henry VI*, 5 (1447–54), p. 185; for Henry see *CCR Henry VI*, 4 (1441–47), p. 210, *CCR Henry VI*, 6 (1454–61), p. 261 and *CCR Edward IV*, 2 (1468–76), p. 45 (no. 175); for Thomas the tailor see *CCR Henry V*, 2 (1419–22), p. 115, and below.

[40] *CCR Henry VI*, 4 (1441–47), p. 210.

[41] *CCR Edward IV*, 2 (1468–76), p. 131, no. 515.

[42] *CCR Edward IV*, 2 (1468–76), p. 361 no. 1298.

[43] *CCR Edward IV*, 1 (1461–68), p. 62. On London tailors in the fifteenth century see Barron, *London in the Later Middle Ages*, p. 69.

[44] *LPFD Henry VIII*, 3.ii.1524 (15 Henry VIII, no. 3685).

[45] *LPFD Henry VIII*, 11.568 (28 Henry VIII, no. 1422).

1537;[46] and the Thomas Roberts who was granted a licence to alienate lands, specified as lying in Gloucestershire, in 1544 (Thomas Roberts of Willesden was dead by this date).[47] Two records of 1545 signal other men by the same name: one who was a tenant of a messuage in the parish of St Sepulchre without Newgate in London, and another who was captain of the ship *Mary George of Rye*.[48] The first of these was probably related to the Henry Roberts, citizen and brewer of London, whose inquisition post mortem was taken at the Guildhall on 27 January 1566.[49] That inquisition refers to various properties in Knightrider Street, in the parish of the Holy Trinity, and others in the parish of St Sepulchre without Newgate. Henry's beneficiaries were his wife, Elizabeth, and (though the wording is confusing), his great-nieces, Helen and Margaret, daughters of his nephew Richard Roberts, and his nephews Anthony and Henry Roberts, the last styled as 'of Lincolnshire'. It is not clear if the testator was the same man as the Henry Robardes mentioned in an account of a burglary in the latter part of Henry VIII's reign, but the reference to relatives in Lincolnshire may indicate a connection with the William Roberts (Roberdes or Robertz) who served on a number of commissions in Holland, Lincolnshire in the 1520s, 1530s, and 1540s.[50] The activities of this William Roberts in the public service seem very similar to those of his contemporary, Thomas Roberts of Willesden, but there is no reason to connect the two men and their parallel careers may simply have been coincidental.[51]

Although I have not found any evidence that indicates that these families were consanguineous with the Roberts family of Willesden, scattered references, such as Henry Roberts's remembering of his Lincolnshire nephews in 1566, remind us that in the sixteenth century, as now, individuals might move away from their initial communities for a variety of reasons related to work, business, marriage, or inheritance. Thus the Thomas Robert who is described in a recognizance of 1462 as a merchant of Bristol should not be too readily dismissed from consideration; developing commercial interests meant that Bristol and London were well-connected in this period, with members of some mercantile families setting up establishments in both

---

[46] *LPFD Henry VIII*, 12.83 (29 Henry VIII, no. 191, grant 47).

[47] *LPFD Henry VIII*, 19.283 (35 Henry VIII, no. 443, grant 10).

[48] See, respectively, *LPFD Henry VIII*, 20.i.122–23 (36 Henry VIII, no. 282, grant 19) and *LPFD Henry VIII*, 20.ii. 41–42 (37 Henry VIII, no. 88).

[49] Madge, *Abstracts of Inquisitions Post Mortem*, pp. 68–70.

[50] *LP Henry VIII Addenda* 1.ii. 609 (no. 1861); this undated entry is attributed by the editors to the latter half of Henry VIII's reign (see note on p. 592).

[51] See, however, the mention of lands in Lincolnshire in the possession of Francis Roberts below, suggestive of some family connection. For the Lincolnshire William Roberts see *LP Henry VIII Addenda* 1.i.131 (no. 408); *LPFD Henry VIII*, 3.ii.1365 (15 Henry VIII, no. 3282); *LPFD Henry VIII*, 4.i.238 (16 Henry VIII, no. 547); *LPFD Henry VIII*, 12.i.515 (28 Henry VIII, no. 1104, grant 10); 12.ii.405 (29 Henry VIII, no. 1150, grant 16); *LPFD Henry VIII*, 15, p. 106 (31 Henry VIII, no. 282, grant 19); *LPFD Henry VIII*, 16.52 (32 Henry VIII, no. 107, grant 7); *LPFD Henry VIII*, 17.566 (34 Henry VIII, no. 1012, grant 31).

places.⁵² Another William Roberts who flourished in the first half of the sixteenth century was the William Roberdes who was professed at the house of Augustine canons at Missenden, Buckinghamshire and who received a pension of 106s 8d at the dissolution.⁵³ There is no reason to connect him with the Robertses of Willesden, but it is nevertheless possible that he might have been a distant member of the family. Other research into medieval biography, such as Robert Adams's investigation of William Langland, argues that people who bore the same surname probably *were*, at some level, related to each other (or thought that they were), even though their consanguinity had been apparently diluted by time, location, and relative prosperity, and modern genetic findings apparently support this conclusion.⁵⁴ Certainly details of the family history of the Willesden Robertses in the fourteenth and fifteenth centuries are very sketchy, and there may well have been collateral branches whose descendants cannot now be easily linked to the main line. For this reason it is unwise to assume that there were no links at all between the Robertses of Lincolnshire (or Essex, Kent, or Monmouthshire) and the Robertses of Willesden: the connections may have been so long distant as to have become barely perceptible.

---

⁵² *CCR Edward IV*, 1 (1461–68), p. 153. On personal links between the mercantile elite of Bristol and London see Burgess, 'Educated Parishioners', pp. 286–89.

⁵³ *LPFD Henry VIII*, 14.ii.98 (31 Henry VIII, no. 262).

⁵⁴ *Langland and the Rokele Family*, p. 34.

Bibliography

PRIMARY SOURCES

Almeida, Francisco Alonso (ed.), *A Middle English Medical Remedy Book*, Middle English Texts, 50 (Heidelberg: Winter, 2014)

Armytage, George J. (ed.), *Middlesex Pedigrees as Collected by Richard Mundy in Harleian MS No. 1551*, Publications of the Harleian Society, 61 (London: Harleian Society, 1914)

Baker, J. H., *The Notebook of Sir John Port*, Publications of the Selden Society, 102 (London: Selden Society, 1986)

Bannerman, W. Bruce (ed.), *The Registers of St Mary the Virgin, Aldermanbury, London*, 3 vols., Publications of the Harleian Society, 61–62, 65 (London: Harleian Society, 1931–35)

Bannerman, W. Bruce (ed.), *The Visitations of the County of Surrey, Made and Taken in the Years 1530 by Thomas Benolte; 1572 by Robert Cooke; and 1623 by Samuel Thompson and Augustin Vincent, Marshals and Deputies to William Camden*, Publications of the Harleian Society, 43 (London: Harleian Society, 1899)

Beadle, Richard and Colin Richmond (eds.), *Paston Letters and Papers of the Fifteenth Century, Part III*, EETS s.s. 22 (Oxford: Oxford University Press, 2005)

Bernard, Edward, *Catalogi librorum manuscriptorum Angliae et Hiberniae in unum collecti* (Oxford, 1697)

Bestul, Thomas H. (ed.), *Walter Hilton: The Scale of Perfection* (Kalamazoo, MI: Medieval Institute Publications, 2000)

Biggs, Brendan J. H. (ed.), *The Imitation of Christ*, EETS o.s. 309 (Oxford: Oxford University Press, 1997)

Brown, Carleton (ed.), *Religious Lyrics of the Fourteenth Century* (Oxford: Clarendon Press, 1924)

Caley, J. and J. Hunter (eds.), *Valor Ecclesiasticus temp. Henrici VIII, Auctoritate Regia Institutus*, 6 vols. (London: Record Commissions, 1810–34)

Chew, Helena M. (ed.), *London Possessory Assizes: A Calendar*, London Record Society, 1 (London: London Record Society, 1965)

Chew, Helena M. and W. Kellaway (eds.), *London Assize of Nuisance, 1301–1431*, London Record Society, 10 (London: London Record Society, 1973)

Bibliography

Cicchetti, A. and R. Mordenti (eds.), *I libri di famiglia in Italia, Vol 1: Filologia e storiografia letteraria* (Roma: Edizioni di Storia e Letteratura, 1985)

Connolly, Margaret (ed.), *Contemplations of the Dread and Love of God*, EETS o.s. 303 (Oxford: Oxford University Press, 1994)

Curtis, G. W. S. (ed. & trans.), *The Passion and Martyrdom of the Holy English Carthusian Fathers: The Short Narration by Dom Maurice Chauncy* (London: Church Historical Society, 1935)

Darlington, Ida (ed.), *London Consistory Court Wills 1492–1547*, London Record Society, 3 (London: London Record Society, 1967)

Davies, Matthew, Catherine Ferguson, Vanessa Harding et al. (eds.), *London and Middlesex 1666 Hearth Tax*, 2 vols. (London: British Record Society, 2014)

Davis, Norman (ed.), *Paston Letters and Papers of the Fifteenth Century, Parts 1 and 2*, EETS s.s. 20 and 21 (Oxford: Oxford University Press, 2004; repr. with corrections from the Clarendon edition of 1971 and 1976)

Ellis, Henry (ed.), *The Visitation of the County of Huntingdon, under the Authority of William Camden, by his Deputy Nicholas Charles*, Camden Society Publications, 43 (London, Camden Society, 1849)

Fry, G. S. (ed.), *Abstracts of Inquisitions Post Mortem, Relating to the City of London Returned into the Court of Chancery. Part I. 1 Henry VIII to 3 Elizabeth, 1485–1561*, 3 vols. (London: British Record Society, 1896)

Griffin, Carrie (ed.), *The Middle English Wise Book of Philosophy and Astronomy: A Parallel-Text Edition*, Middle English Texts, 47 (Heidelberg: Winter, 2013)

Hamer, Richard, with Vida Russell (eds.), *Gilte Legende*, 3 vols., EETS o.s. 327, 328, and 339 (Oxford: Oxford University Press, 2006, 2007, 2012)

Hamilton, W. D. (ed.), *A Chronicle of England during the Reigns of the Tudors, from A.D. 1485 to 1559, by Charles Wriothesley, Windsor Herald*, 2 vols., Camden Society, n.s. 11 and 20 (Westminster: J. B. Nichols, 1875–77)

Hassall, W. O. (ed.), *Cartulary of St Mary Clerkenwell*, Camden Society, 3rd ser., 71 (London: Royal Historical Society, 1949)

Hayward, Maria, *The Great Wardrobe Accounts of Henry VII and Henry VIII*, London Record Society, 47 (London: D. S. Brewer, 2012)

Hodgett, G. A. J. (ed.), *The State of the Ex Religious and Former Chantry Priests in the Diocese of Lincoln 1547–1574*, Publications of the Lincoln Record Society, 53 (Hereford: The Hereford Times, 1959)

Hodgson, P. (ed.), *The Cloud of Unknowing and Related Treatises*, Analecta Cartusiana, 3 (Salzburg: Institut für Anglistik und Amerikanistik, Universität Salzburg, 1982)

Hodgson, P. (ed.), *Deonise Hid Diuinite*, EETS o.s. 231 (London: Oxford University Press, 1955)

Bibliography

Hopper, C. (ed.), 'London Chronicle', in *The Camden Miscellany*, 4 (London: Camden Society, 1859), pp. 1–21

Horstman, C. (ed.), *Yorkshire Writers: Richard Rolle of Hampole and His Followers*, 2 vols. (London: Macmillan, 1895–96)

Hovenden, Robert (ed.), *The Visitations of Kent . . . 1619 and 1621*, Publications of the Harleian Society, 42 (London: Harleian Society, 1898), pp. 93–94

Hughes, Paul L. and James F. Larkin (eds.), *Tudor Royal Proclamations*, 3 vols. (New Haven and London: Yale University Press, 1964)

James, N. W. and V. A. James (eds.), *The Bede Roll of the Fraternity of St Nicholas*, 2 vols. (London: London Record Society, 2004)

Jones, E. A. (ed.), *The 'Exhortacion' from Disce Mori, edited from Oxford, Jesus College, MS 39*, Middle English Texts, 36 (Heidelberg: Winter, 2006)

Kirchberger, C., 'Te Deum Laudamus', *The Life of the Spirit*, August–September (1952), 106–10

Kirchberger, C., 'Veni Creator Spiritus', *The Life of the Spirit*, June (1950), 549–54

Kitching, C. J. (ed.), *London and Middlesex Chantry Certificate, 1548*, London Record Society, 16 (London: London Record Society, 1980)

Kuriyagawa, Fumio and Toshiyuki Takamiya (eds.), *Two Minor Works of Walter Hilton* (Tokyo: Privately Printed, 1980)

Lang, R. G. (ed.), *Two Tudor Subsidy Assessment Rolls for the City of London: 1541 and 1582*, London Record Society, 29 (London: London Record Society, 1993)

List of the Lands of Dissolved, Religious Houses, 7 vols. (New York: Kraus Reprint, 1964)

Loengard, Janet Senderowitz (ed.), *London Viewers and Their Certificates, 1508–1558*, London Record Society, 26 (London: London Record Society, 1989)

Madge, Sidney J. (ed.), *Abstracts of Inquisitions Post Mortem Relating to the City of London Returned into the Court of Chancery*, Part II, 4–9 Elizabeth (1561–1577) (London: British Record Society, 1896)

Matthew, F. D. (ed.), *The English Works of Wyclif, Hitherto Unprinted*, EETS o.s. 74 (London: Trübner & Co., 1880)

McCann, Timothy J. (ed.), *Recusants in the Exchequer Pipe Rolls, 1581–1592, Extracted by Dom Hugh Bowler* (Southampton: Catholic Record Society, 1986)

Nichols, John Gough (ed.), *The Diary of Henry Machyn, Citizen and Merchant-taylor of London: From A.D. 1550 to A.D. 1563*, Camden Society Publications, 42 (London: Camden Society, 1848)

Noble, W. M., *Calendars of Huntingdonshire Wills 1479–1652* (London: British Record Society, 1911)

Ogilvie-Thomson, S. J., *Walter Hilton's Mixed Life. Edited from Lambeth Palace MS 472*, Salzburg Studies in English Literature, Elizabethan and Renaissance Studies

92.15 (Salzburg: Institut für Anglistik und Amerikanistik Universität Salzburg, 1986)

Powell, Susan (ed.), *John Mirk's Festial*, EETS o.s. 334 and 335 (Oxford: Oxford University Press, 2009 and 2011)

Riley, Henry Thomas (ed. and trans.), *Liber Albus: the White Book of the City of London* (London: Richard Griffin & Co., 1861)

Robbins, Rossell Hope, *Secular Lyrics of the XIVth and XVth Centuries* (Oxford: Oxford University Press, 1952)

Sargent, Michael G., *Nicholas Love: The Mirror of the Blessed Life of Jesus Christ, A Full Critical Edition* (Exeter: University of Exeter Press, 2005)

Schuster, Louis A., Richard C. Marius, James P. Lusardi, and Richard J. Schoeck (eds.), *The Complete Works of St Thomas More, vol. VIII*, 3 vols. (New Haven: Yale University Press, 1973)

Sharpe, Reginald R., *Calendar of the Letter-Books A–L of the City of London*, 11 vols. (London: Corporation of the City of London, 1899–1912)

Sharpe, Reginald R. (ed.), *Calendar of Wills Proved and Enrolled in the Court of Husting, London, AD 1258–AD 1688: Preserved among the Archives of the Corporation of the City of London, at the Guildhall*, 2 vols. (London: Corporation of the City of London, 1889–90)

State Papers Online: the Government of Britain, 1509–1714, Part 1: The Tudors, 1509–1603: State Papers Domestic (Hampshire: Gale Cengage Learning)

Steane, J. B. (ed.), *Christopher Marlowe: The Complete Plays* (London: Penguin, 1969)

Steer, Francis W. (ed.), *Scriveners' Company Common Paper 1357–1628*, London Record Society, 4 (London: London Record Society, 1968)

Tittler, Robert (ed.), *Accounts of the Roberts Family of Boarzell, Sussex, c. 1568–1582*, Sussex Record Society, 71 (Lewes: Sussex Record Society, 1977–79)

Turner, G. J. (ed.), *Year books of Edward II, vol. VI: 4 Edward II, AD 1310–1311*, Publications of the Selden Society, 26 (London: Quaritch, 1914 for 1911)

Wordsworth, Christopher, *Horae Eboracenses: The Prymer of Hours of the Blessed Virgin Mary, according to the Use of the Illustrious Church of York*, Publications of the Surtees Society, 132 (London: Bernard Quaritch, 1920)

SECONDARY LITERATURE

Adams, Reginald H., *The Parish Clerks of London: A History of the Worshipful Company of Parish Clerks of London* (London: Chichester, Phillimore, 1971)

Adams, Robert, *Langland and the Rokele Family: The Gentry Background to Piers Plowman* (Dublin: Four Courts, 2013)

Bibliography

Alford, John A., *Piers Plowman: A Glossary of Legal Diction* (Cambridge: D. S. Brewer, 1988)

Almeida, Francisco Alonso, 'Finding-information Aids in Mediaeval English Medical Manuscripts: The Cases of MS Hunter 117 and MS Hunter 185', in Ana Bringas López, Dolores González Álvarez, Javier Pérez Guerra, Esperanza Rama Martínez, and Eduardo Varela Bravo (eds.), *Woonderous Ænglissce, Selim Studies in Medieval English Language*, 14 (Vigo: Servizo de Publicacions da Universidade de Vigo, 1999), pp. 21–31

Anderson, Andrew H., 'The Books and Interests of Henry, Lord Stafford (1501–1563)', *The Library*, 5th series, 21 (1966), 87–114

[Anon], 'Victoria and Albert Museum: The Reid Gift, I', *The Burlington Magazine for Connoisseurs*, 1.3 (1903), 389–90

Arnold-Forster, Frances, *Studies in Church Dedications*, 3 vols. (London: Skeffington, 1899)

Arnould, Alain and Jean Michel Massing, *Splendours of Flanders* (Cambridge: Cambridge University Press, 1993)

Ashe, Laura, 'The "Short Charter of Christ": An Unpublished Longer Version, from Cambridge University Library, MS Add. 6686', *Medium Aevum*, 72 (2003), 32–48

Axton, Richard and Peter Happé (eds.), *The Plays of John Heywood* (Cambridge: D. S. Brewer, 1991)

Baildon, W., *The Records of the Honorable Society of Lincoln's Inn: Admissions*, 2 vols. (London: Lincoln's Inn, 1896)

Bainbridge, Virginia, 'Syon Abbey: Women and Learning c.1415–1600', in E. A. Jones and Alexandra Walsham (eds.), *Syon Abbey and Its Books, Reading, Writing and Religion c. 1400–1700* (Woodbridge: Boydell, 2010), pp. 82–103

Baker, J. H., 'Baldwin, Sir John (*bap.* before 1470, *d.* 1545)', in *Oxford Dictionary of National Biography* (Oxford: Oxford University Press, 2004), www.oxforddnb.com/view/article/1166

Baker, J. H., 'The Books of the Common Law', in Lotte Hellinga and J. B. Trapp (eds.), *The Cambridge History of the Book in Britain: Volume III, 1400–1557* (Cambridge: Cambridge University Press, 1999), pp. 411–32

Baker, J. H., 'Broke, Sir Richard (*d.* 1529)', *Oxford Dictionary of National Biography* (Oxford: Oxford University Press, 2004), www.oxforddnb.com/view/article/3496

Baker, J. H., 'Cordell, Sir William (1522–81)', *Oxford Dictionary of National Biography* (Oxford: Oxford University Press, 2004), www.oxforddnb.com/view/article/6306

Bibliography

Baker, J. H., *The Order of Serjeants at Law*, Selden Society Supplementary Series, 5 (London: Selden Society, 1984)

Baker, J. H., *The Oxford History of the Laws of England, Volume VI: 1483–1558* (Oxford: Oxford University Press, 2003)

Baker, J. H., 'Packington, Sir John (*b.* in or before 1477, *d.* 1551)', *Oxford Dictionary of National Biography* (Oxford: Oxford University Press, 2004), www.oxforddnb.com/view/article/21143

Baker, J. H., *Readers and Readings in the Inns of Court and Chancery*, Selden Society Supplementary Series, 13 (London: Selden Society, 2001 for 2000)

Baker, J. H., 'Spelman, Sir John (*c.* 1480–1546)', *Oxford Dictionary of National Biography* (Oxford: Oxford University Press, 2004), www.oxforddnb.com/view/article/26105

Barratt, Alexandra, *Anne Bulkeley and Her Book: Fashioning Female Piety in Early Tudor England* (Turnhout: Brepols, 2009)

Barratt, Alexandra, 'Singing from the Same Hymn-Sheet: Two Bridgettine Manuscripts', in Margaret Connolly and Linne R. Mooney (eds.), *Design and Distribution of Late Medieval Manuscripts in England* (York: York Medieval Press, 2008), pp. 139–60

Barron, Caroline M., *London in the Later Middle Ages: Government and People 1200–1500* (Oxford: Oxford University Press, 2004)

Barron, Caroline M., 'The Will as Autobiography', in Julia Boffey and Virginia Davis (eds.), *Recording Medieval Lives: Proceedings of the 2005 Harlaxton Symposium* (Donington: Shaun Tyas, 2009), pp. 141–81

Barron, Caroline M. and Anne F. Sutton (eds.), *Medieval London Widows 1300–1500* (London and Rio Grande: Hambledon, 1994)

Barron, Caroline M. and Matthew Davies, *The Religious Houses of London and Middlesex* (London: Institute of Historical Research, 2007)

Bartlett, Robert, *Why Can the Dead Do Such Great Things? Saints and Worshippers from the Martyrs to the Reformation* (Princeton, NJ and Oxford: Princeton University Press, 2013)

Baskerville, G., 'Married Clergy and Pensioned Religious in Norwich Diocese, 1555', *English Historical Review*, 48 (1933), 43–64 and 199–228

Beaven, Alfred B., *The Alderman of the City of London: temp. Henry III – 1908: With Notes on the Parliamentary Representation of the City, the Aldermen and the Livery Companies, the Aldermanic Veto, Aldermanic Baronets and Knights, etc.* (London: Corporation of the City of London, 1908)

Benskin, Michael, 'In Reply to Dr Burton', *Leeds Studies in English*, 22 (1991), 209–62

Bettey, J. H., 'The Suppression of the Carthusian Priory at Hinton Charterhouse', *Avon Past*, 15 (1990), 8–13

Bibliography

Bindoff, S. J. (ed.), *The History of Parliament: The House of Commons 1509–1558*, 3 vols. (London: History of Parliament Trust, 1982)

Binski, Paul and Patrick Zutshi, with Stella Panayatova (eds.), *Western Illuminated Manuscripts: A Catalogue of the Collection in Cambridge University Library* (Cambridge: Cambridge University Press, 2011)

Blake, N. F. (ed.), *Middle English Religious Prose*, York Medieval Texts (London: Arnold, 1972)

Bland, D. S., *A Bibliography of the Inns of Court and Chancery*, Selden Society Supplementary Series, 3 (London: Selden Society, 1985)

Blanton, Virginia, *Signs of Devotion: The Cult of St Æthelthryth in Medieval England, 695–1615* (University Park, PA: Penn State University Press, 2007)

Blyth, William, *Historical Notices and Records of the Village and Parish of Fincham in the County of Norfolk* (Kings Lynn: Thew and Son, 1863)

Boffey, Julia, 'London Books and London Readers', in Brian Cummings and James Simpson (eds.), *Cultural Reformations: Medieval and Renaissance in Literary History* (Oxford: Oxford University Press, 2010), pp. 420–37

Boffey, Julia, *Manuscript and Print in London c. 1475–1530* (London: British Library, 2012)

Boffey, Julia, 'Reading in London in 1501: A Micro-Study', in Mary C. Flannery and Carrie Griffin (eds.), *Spaces for Reading in Later Medieval England* (Houndmills: Palgrave Macmillan, 2016), pp. 51–61

Boffey, Julia, 'Some London Women Readers and a Text of *The Three Kings of Cologne*', *The Ricardian*, 10 (1996), 387–96

Boffey, Julia, and A. S. G. Edwards, 'Unrecorded Middle English Verse Texts in a Canterbury Cathedral Library Manuscript', *Medium Aevum*, 72 (2003), 49–62.

Boffey, Julia and Virginia Davis (eds.), *Recording Medieval Lives: Proceedings of the 2005 Harlaxton Symposium*, Harlaxton Medieval Studies, 17 (Donington: Shaun Tyas, 2009)

Borland, Catherine R., *A Descriptive Catalogue of the Western Medieval Manuscripts in Edinburgh University Library* (Edinburgh: T. A. Constable, 1916)

Bossy, John, *The English Catholic Community, 1570–1850* (London: Darton, Longman, and Todd 1975)

Brady, Mary Teresa, 'The Apostles and the Creed in Manuscripts of *The Pore Caitif*', *Speculum*, 32 (1957), 323–25

Brady, Mary Teresa, 'Lollard Interpolations and Omissions in Manuscripts of *The Pore Caitif*, in Michael G. Sargent (ed.), *De Cella in Seculum: Religious and Secular Life and Devotion in Late Medieval England* (Woodbridge: D. S. Brewer, 1989), pp. 183–203

Bibliography

Brady, Mary Teresa, 'The Pore Caitif: An Introductory Study', *Traditio*, 10 (1954), 529–48

Brady, Mary Teresa, 'Rolle and the Pattern of Tracts in "The Pore Caitif"', *Traditio*, 36 (1980), 456–65

Brady, Mary Teresa, 'The Seynt and His Boke: Rolle's *Emendatio vitae* and *The Pore Caitif*', *14th Century English Mystics Newsletter*, 7.1 (1981), 20–31

Brewer, D. S. and A. E. B. Owen (eds.), *The Thornton Manuscript (Lincoln Cathedral MS 91)* (London: Scolar, 1975)

Brewer, J. S., J. Gairdner and R. H. Brodie (eds.), *Letters and Papers, Foreign and Domestic, of the Reign of Henry VIII*, 22 vols. in 38 (London: HMSO, 1862–1932)

Brigden, Susan, *London and the Reformation* (Oxford: Clarendon Press, 1989)

Brigden, Susan, 'Tithe Controversy in Reformation London', *Journal of Ecclesiastical History*, 32 (1981), 285–301

Brown, Carleton, and R. H. Robbins (eds.), *The Index of Middle English Verse* (New York: Index Society, 1943)

Burgess, Clive, 'Educated Parishioners in London and Bristol on the Eve of the Reformation', in Caroline M. Barron and Jenny Stratford (eds.), *The Church and Learning in Later Medieval Society: Essays in Honour of R. B. Dobson, Proceedings of the 1999 Harlaxton Symposium*, Harlaxton Medieval Studies, 11 (Donington: Shaun Tyas, 2002), 286–304

Burke, Bernard, *A Genealogical and Heraldic History of the Landed Gentry of Great Britain and Ireland*, 6th edn, 2 vols. (London: Harrison, 1879)

Burke, John, and John Bernard Burke, *A Genealogical and Heraldic History of the Extinct and Dormant Baronetcies of England, Ireland and Scotland* (London: Scott, Webster, and Geary, 1841)

Burton, T. L., 'On the Current State of Middle English Dialectology', *Leeds Studies in English*, 22 (1991), 167–262

Cambers, Andrew, 'Readers' Marks and Religious Practice: Margaret Hoby's Marginalia', in John N. King (ed.), *Tudor Books and Readers: Materiality and the Construction of Meaning* (Cambridge: Cambridge University Press, 2010), pp. 211–31

Carley, James P., 'The dispersal of the monastic libraries and the salvaging of the spoils', in Elisabeth Leedham-Green and Teresa Webber (eds.), *The Cambridge History of Libraries in Britain and Ireland, Volume 1: To 1640* (Cambridge: Cambridge University Press), pp. 265–91

Carley, James P., *The Libraries of King Henry VIII*, Corpus of British Medieval Library Catalogues, 7 (London: British Library and British Academy, 2000)

Carley, James P. (ed.), *The Library* on the Post Dissolution Wandering of Books from England's Medieval Libraries, *The Library*, Virtual Issue no. 4 https://academic.oup.com/library/pages/medieval_libraries_virtual_issue

Bibliography

Catalogue of a Magnificent Collection of Manuscripts, Formed by a Gentleman of Consummate Taste & Judgment ... which will be Sold by Auction by Messrs. Sotheby, Wilkinson & Hodge ... on Wednesday, the 7th of June 1876 and Three following Days (London: Sotheby, Wilkinson & Hodge, 1876)

Catalogue of the Extraordinary Collection of Splendid Manuscripts, Chiefly upon Vellum, in Various Languages of Europe and the East, formed by M. Guglielmo Libri, the Eminent Collector, who is obliged to leave London in consequence of ill health, and for that reason to dispose of his literary treasures ... which will be sold by Auction by Messrs. S. Leigh Sotheby & John Wilkinson ... on Monday, 28th of March, 1859, and Seven following Days (London: Sotheby and Wilkinson, 1859)

Catalogue of the Valuable and Extensive Library of the Late Sir John Arthur Brooke, Bt (of Fenay Hall, Huddersfield), Comprising Many Valuable Illuminated and Historical Manuscripts ... which will be Sold by Auction by Messrs. Sotheby, Wilkinson & Hodge ... on Wednesday May 25th, 1921, and Two Following Days; and on Monday, May 30th, 1921, and Four Following Days (London: Sotheby, Wilkinson, and Hodge, 1921)

Catalogue of Valuable Printed Books and Important Illuminated Other Manuscripts, Comprising the Property of Sir John Trelawny, Bt. and the Property of the Rev. N. C. S. Poyntz (Deceased) ... which will be Sold by Auction by Messrs. Sotheby, Wilkinson & Hodge ... on Tuesday, 28th of June, 1921, and Two Following Days (London: Sotheby, Wilkinson, and Hodge, 1921)

Catalogue of Valuable Printed Books, Autograph Letters and Historical Documents ... which will be Sold by Auction by Messrs. Sotheby & Co. ... on the 1st July, 1963 and the Following Day (London: Sotheby, 1963)

Catalogue of Valuable Printed Books and Manuscripts, Autograph Letters and Historical Documents, 24–25 January 1949 (London: Sotheby, 1949)

Catalogue of Western Manuscripts and Miniatures, 10 December 1969 (London: Sotheby, 1969)

Catalogue of Western Manuscripts and Miniatures, 23 June 1992 (London: Sotheby, 1992)

Catalogue of Western Manuscripts and Miniatures, 7 December 1992 (London: Sotheby, 1992)

Clapinson, Mary, 'Richard Rawlinson (1690–1755)', *Oxford Dictionary of National Biography* (Oxford: Oxford University Press, 2004) www.oxforddnb.com/view/article/23192

Clark, L. G., *Collectors and Owners of Incunabula in the British Museum* (Bath: Harding and Curtis, 1962)

Bibliography

Coatalen, Guillaume, 'Unpublished Elizabethan Sonnets in a Legal Manuscript from the Cambridge University Library', *The Review of English Studies*, 54 (2003), 553–65

Coates, Alan, Kristian Jensen, Cristina Dondi et al., *A Catalogue of Books Printed in the Fifteenth Century Now in the Bodleian Library*, 6 vols. (Oxford: Oxford University Press, 2005)

Cockburn, J. S. (ed.), *Calendar of Assize Records, Surrey Indictments, Elizabeth I* (London: HMSO, 1980)

Colker, Marvin L., *Trinity College Library Dublin, Descriptive Catalogue of the Medieval and Renaissance Latin Manuscripts*, 2 vols. (Aldershot: Scolar Press, 1991)

Connolly, Margaret, 'Books for the "helpe of euery persoone þat þenkiþ to be saued": Six Devotional Anthologies from Fifteenth-Century London', *Yearbook of English Studies*, 33 (2003), 170–81

Connolly, Margaret, 'Compiling the Book', in Alexandra Gillespie and Daniel Wakelin (eds.), *The Production of Books in England 1350–1500* (Cambridge: Cambridge University Press, 2011), pp. 129–49

Connolly, Margaret, 'Evidence for the Continued Use of Medieval Medical Prescriptions in the Sixteenth Century: A Fifteenth-Century Remedy Book and Its Later Owner', *Medical History*, 60 (2016), 133–54

Connolly, Margaret, *Index of Middle English Prose Handlist XIX: Manuscripts in the University Library, Cambridge (Dd-Oo)* (Cambridge: D. S. Brewer, 2009)

Connolly, Margaret, 'Late Medieval Books of Hours and Their Early Tudor Readers In and Around London', in Tamara Atkin and Jaclyn Rajsic (eds.), *Manuscript and Print in Late Medieval and Early Tudor Britain: Essays in Honour of Prof. Julia Boffey* (Woodbridge: D. S. Brewer, forthcoming)

Connolly, Margaret, 'Practical Reading for Body and Soul in Some Later Medieval Manuscript Miscellanies', *Journal of the Early Book Society*, 10 (2007), 151–74

Connolly, Margaret, 'Sixteenth-Century Readers Reading Fifteenth-Century Religious Books: The Roberts Family of Middlesex', in Nicole R. Rice (ed.), *Middle English Religious Writing in Practice: Texts, Readers, and Transformations* (Turnhout: Brepols, 2013), pp. 239–62

Connolly, Margaret and Linne R. Mooney (eds.), *Design and Distribution of Late Medieval Manuscripts in England* (York: York Medieval Press, 2008)

Connolly, Margaret and Raluca Radulescu (eds.), *Insular Books: Vernacular Manuscript Miscellanies in Late Medieval Britain*, Proceedings of the British Academy, 201 (Oxford: Oxford University Press, 2015)

Cooke, W. H. (ed.), *Students Admitted to the Inner Temple 1547–1660* (London: William Clowes & Sons, 1877)

Bibliography

Croenen, Godfried, Kristen M. Figg, Andrew Taylor, 'Authorship, Patronage, and Literary Gifts: The Books Froissart Brought to England in 1395', *Journal of the Early Book Society*, 11 (2008), 1–42

Daniell, Christopher, *Death and Burial in Medieval England 1066–1550* (London and New York: Routledge, 1997)

Davies, Matthew and Andrew Prescott (eds.), *London and the Kingdom: Essays in Honour of Caroline M. Barron* (Donington: Shaun Tyas, 2008)

Davis, V., 'Medieval English Clergy Database', *History and Computing*, 2 (1990), 75–87

de Hamel, Christopher, 'The Selling and Collecting of Manuscripts of Nicholas Love's *Mirror of the Blessed Life of Jesus Christ* since the Middle Ages', in S. Oguro, R. Beadle, and M. G. Sargent (eds.), *Nicholas Love at Waseda* (Woodbridge: D. S. Brewer, 1997), 87–97

de Hamel, Christopher, *Syon Abbey: The Library of the Bridgettine nuns and Their Peregrinations after the Reformation* (Otley: The Roxburghe Club, 1991)

de Ricci, Seymour, with the assistance of W. J. Wilson, *Census of Medieval and Renaissance Manuscripts in the United States and Canada*, 3 vols. (New York: H. W. Wilson, 1935–40)

Dillon, Anne, *The Construction of Martydom in the English Catholic Community, 1535–1603* (Aldershot: Ashgate, 2002)

Doe, Norman, 'Frowyk, Sir Thomas (c. 1460–1506)', *Oxford Dictionary of National Biography* (Oxford: Oxford University Press, 2004), www.oxforddnb.com/view/article/10206

Doyle, A. I., 'Remarks on Surviving Manuscripts of *Piers Plowman*' in Gregory Kratzman and James Simpson (eds), *Medieval English Religious and Ethical Literature. Essays in Honour of G. H. Russell* (Cambridge: D. S. Brewer, 1986)

Doyle, A. I., 'Stephen Dodesham of Witham and Sheen', in P. R. Robinson and R. Zim (eds.), *Of the Making of Books: Medieval Manuscripts, Their Scribes and Readers; Essays Presented to M. B. Parkes* (Aldershot: Scolar, 1997), pp. 94–115

Doyle, A. I., (ed.), *The Libraries of the Carthusians*, in Vincent Gillespie (ed.), *Syon Abbey*, Corpus of British Medieval Library Catalogues, 9 (London: British Library and British Academy, 2001)

Doyle, A. I., 'The Library of Sir Thomas Tempest: Its Origins and Dispersal', in G. A. M. Janssens and F. G. A. M. Aarts (eds.), *Studies in Seventeenth-Century English Literature, History, and Bibliography* (Amsterdam: Rodopi, 1984), pp. 83–93

Drogon, Marc, *Anathema!: Medieval Scribes and the History of Book Curses* (Totowa and Montclair, NJ: Allanheld and Schram, 1983)

Duffy, Eamon, *Marking the Hours: English People and Their Prayers 1240–1570* (New Haven, CT: Yale University Press, 2006)

Duffy, Eamon, *The Stripping of the Altars: Traditional Religion in England c. 1400–c.1500* (New Haven and London: Yale University Press, 1992)

Duffy, Eamon and David Loades (eds.), *The Church of Mary Tudor* (Aldershot: Ashgate, 2006)

Edwards, A. S. G., 'Reading John Walton's Boethius in the Fifteenth and Sixteenth Centuries', in Mary C. Flannery and Carrie Griffin (eds.), *Spaces for Reading in Later Medieval England* (Houndmills: Palgrave Macmillan, 2016), pp. 35–49

Eire, Carlos and Ronald Truman (eds.), *Reforming Catholicism in the England of Mary Tudor* (Aldershot: Ashgate, 2005)

Ellis, G. I., *A Catalogue of the Manuscripts and Printed Books Collected by Thomas Brooke, F.S.A., and Preserved at Armitage Bridge House, Near Huddersfield*, 2 vols. (London: Ellis and Elvey, 1891)

Ellis, Roger H., *Catalogue of Seals in the PRO: Personal Seals*, 2 vols. (London: HMSO, 1981)

Ellis, William Smith, 'Hoard or Howard of Ewell and Guildford, Co. Surrey', *Miscellanea genealogica et heraldica*, n.s. 4 (1884), 137–43, 267–68, 273, 288–90, 296–99

E[llis], W[illiam] S[mith], 'Pedigree of the Family of Hord of Salop, Oxon and Surrey', *The Topographer and Genealogist*, 1 (1846), 33–42

Elvin, C. N., *A Hand-book of Mottoes Born by the Nobility, Gentry, Cities, Public Companies* (London: Heraldry Today, 1963)

Enright, B. J., 'I Collect and I Preserve': Richard Rawlinson, 1690–1755, and Eighteenth-Century Book Collecting: Portrait of a Bibliophile, XXVIII', *The Book Collector*, 39 (1990), 27–54

Erler, Mary C., 'Devotional Literature', in Lotte Hellinga and J. B. Trapp (eds.), *The Cambridge History of the Book in Britain: Volume III, 1400–1557* (Cambridge: Cambridge University Press, 1999), pp. 495–525

Erler, Mary C., 'The Laity', in Vincent Gillespie and Susan Powell (eds.), *A Companion to the Early Printed Book in Britain 1476–1558* (Cambridge: D. S. Brewer, 2014), pp. 134–49

Erler, Mary C., *Reading and Writing during the Dissolution: Monks, Friars, and Nuns 1530–1558* (Cambridge: Cambridge University Press, 2013)

Erler, Mary C., *Women, Reading, and Piety in Late Medieval England* (Cambridge: Cambridge University Press, 2002)

Farmer, D. H., *The Oxford Dictionary of Saints*, 2nd edn (Oxford: Oxford University Press, 1987)

Fein, Susanna G., 'Literary Scribes: The Harley Scribe and Robert Thornton as Case Studies', in Margaret Connolly and Raluca Radulescu (eds.), *Insular Books: Vernacular Manuscript Miscellanies in Late Medieval Britain*, Proceedings of the British Academy, 201 (Oxford: Oxford University Press, 2015), pp. 61–79

Fein, Susanna, 'The Contents of Robert Thornton's Manuscripts', in Susanna Fein and Michael Johnston (eds.), *Robert Thornton and His Books: Essays on the Lincoln and London Thornton Manuscripts* (York: York Medieval Press, 2014), pp. 13–65

Fisher, R. M., 'Thomas Cromwell, Dissolution of the Monasteries, and the Inns of Court 1534–40', *Journal of the Society of Public Teachers of Law*, 14 (1976–79), 103–17

Fitch, Marc (ed.), *Index to Testamentary Records in the Commissary Court of London (London Division), Now Preserved in the Guildhall Library, London, Vol. I, 1374–1488* (London: HMSO, 1969)

Fitch, Marc (ed.), *Index to Testamentary Records in the Commissary Court of London (London Division), Now Preserved in the Guildhall Library, London, Vol. II, 1489–1570* (London: HMSO, 1974)

Fitch, Marc (ed.), *Index to Testamentary Records in the Commissary Court of London (London Division), Now Preserved in the Guildhall Library, London, Vol. III, 1571–1625* (London: British Record Society, 1985)

Flannery, Mary C. and Carrie Griffin (eds.), *Spaces for Reading in Later Medieval England* (Houndmills: Palgrave Macmillan, 2016)

Ford, Margaret Lane, 'Private Ownership of Printed Books', in Lotte Hellinga and J. B. Trapp (eds.), *The Cambridge History of the Book in Britain: Volume III, 1400–1557* (Cambridge: Cambridge University Press, 1999), pp. 205–28

Gadd, Ian and Alexandra Gillespie (eds.), *John Stow (1524–1605) and the Making of the English Past: Studies in Early Modern Culture and the History of the Book* (London: British Library, 2004)

Gayk, Shannon, *Image, Text, and Religious Reform in Fifteenth-Century England* (Cambridge: Cambridge University Press, 2010)

Gibbons, Katy, *English Catholic Exiles in Late Sixteenth-Century Paris* (Woodbridge: Boydell Press, 2011)

Gillespie, Alexandra and Daniel Wakelin (eds.), *The Production of Books in England 1350–1500* (Cambridge: Cambridge University Press, 2011)

Gillespie, Vincent and Susan Powell (eds.), *A Companion to the Early Printed Book in Britain 1476–1558* (Cambridge: D. S. Brewer, 2014)

Gottfried, R. S., *Doctors and Medicine in Medieval England 1340–1530* (Princeton: Princeton University Press, 1986)

Gray, A., 'A Carthusian *Carta Visitationis* of the Fifteenth Century', *Bulletin of the Institute of Historical Research*, 40 (1967), 91–101

Bibliography

Green, Richard Firth, *A Crisis of Truth: Literature and Law in Ricardian England* (Philadelphia: University of Pennsylvania Press, 1999)

Griffiths, Jane, 'Editorial Glossing and Reader Resistance in a Copy of Robert Crowley's *Piers Plowman*', in Carol M. Meale and Derek Pearsall, *Makers and Users of Medieval Books: Essays in Honour of A. S. G. Edwards* (Cambridge: D. S. Brewer, 2014), pp. 202–213

Griffiths, Jeremy and Derek Pearsall, *Book Production and Publishing in Britain 1375–1475* (Cambridge: Cambridge University Press, 1989)

Grigson, F., 'Pedigree of Roberts of Willesden', *The Genealogist* 5 (1881), 300–307

Gunn, S. J., 'Lovell, Sir Thomas (*c.* 1449–1524)', *Oxford Dictionary of National Biography*, Oxford: Oxford University Press, 2004, www.oxforddnb.com/view/article/17065

Haines, Herbert, *A Manual of Monumental Brasses: Comprising an Introudction to the Study of These Memorials, and a List of Those Remaining in the British Isles: with Two Hundred Illustrations* (Oxford: J. H. and Jas. Parker, 1861)

Hall, T. W. and A. H. Thomas, *Descriptive Catalogue of the Charters, Rolls, Deeds, Pedigrees, Pamphlets, Newspapers, Monumental Inscriptions, Maps and Miscellaneous Papers Forming the Jackson Collection at the Sheffield Public Reference Library* (Sheffield: J. W. Northend, 1914)

Hanna, Ralph, 'Analytical Survey 4: Middle English Manuscripts and the Study of Literature', in Rita Copeland, David Lawton, and Wendy Scase (eds.), *New Medieval Literatures*, 4 (Oxford: Clarendon Press, 2001), pp. 243–64

Hardwick C., and H. R. Luard, *A Catalogue of Manuscripts Preserved in the Library of the University of Cambridge*, 5 vols. (Cambridge, 1856–67)

Harris, P. R., 'Libri, Guglielmo (1802–1869)', *Oxford Dictionary of National Biography*, (Oxford: Oxford University Press, 2004), www.oxforddnb.com/view/article/73791

Harvey, Barbara, *Westminster Abbey and Its Estates in the Middle Ages* (Oxford: Clarendon Press, 1977)

Hellinga, Lotte and J. B. Trapp (eds.), *The Cambridge History of the Book in Britain, Volume III: 1400–1557* (Cambridge: Cambridge University Press, 1999)

Heseltine, Peter, *The Brasses of Huntingdonshire* (Peterborough: Cambridgeshire Libraries, 1987)

Heyworth, Peter, 'Wanley, Humfrey (1672–1726)', *Oxford Dictionary of National Biography* (Oxford: Oxford University Press, 2004), www.oxforddnb.com/view/article/28664

Hill, Gabriel, 'Pedagogy, Devotion, and Marginalia: Using the *Pore Caitif* in Fifteenth-Century England', *The Journal of Medieval Religious Cultures*, 41 (2015), 187–207

Bibliography

Hofmann, Theodore, Joan Winterkorn, Frances Harris, and Hilton Kelliher, 'John Evelyn's Archive at the British Library', *The Book Collector*, 44 (1995), 147–209

Hornbeck, J. Patrick II, *What Is a Lollard?: Dissent and Belief in Late Medieval England* (Oxford: Oxford University Press, 2010)

Horobin, Simon, 'Stephan Batman and His Manuscripts of *Piers Plowman*', *The Review of English Studies*, 62 (2011), 358–72

Howard, J. J., 'Genealogical Notes of the family of Roberts of Willesden', *Miscellanea et Genealogica Heraldica*, n.s. 3 (1880), 25–28

Hudson, Anne, 'A Chapter from Walter Hilton in Two Middle English Compilations', *Neophilologus*, 52 (1968), 416–21

Hunt, T., *Popular Medicine in Thirteenth-Century England* (Cambridge: Brewer, 1990)

Hutchison, Ann M., 'Beyond the Margins: The Recusant Bridgettines', in *Studies in St Birgitta and the Brigittine Order*, 2 vols., Analecta Cartusiana 35.19 (Salzburg: Institut für Anglistik und Amerikanistik, Universität Salzburg, 1993)

Ives, E. W., *The Common Lawyers of Pre-Reformation England. Thomas Kebell: A Case Study* (Cambridge: Cambridge University Press, 1983)

Jackson, Deirdre, 'Humfrey Wanley and the Harley Collection', *The Electronic British Library Journal* (2011), art. 2, pp. 1–20, www.bl.uk/eblj/2011articles/article2.html

Jackson, H. J., *Marginalia: Readers Writing in Books* (New Haven: Yale University Press, 2001)

Jackson, William H., 'The William King Richardson Library', *Harvard Library Bulletin*, 5 (1951), 328–37

Jardine, Lisa and Anthony Grafton, '"Studied for Action": How Gabriel Harvey Read His Livy', *Past and Present*, 129 (1990), 30–78

Jewers, A. J., 'Grants and Certificates of Arms', *The Genealogist*, n.s. 16 (1899–1900), 263–70

Jolliffe, P. S., *A Check-List of Middle English Prose Writings of Spiritual Guidance* (Toronto: Pontifical Institute of Mediaeval Studies, 1974)

Jones, E. A., 'The Compilations of Two Late-Medieval Devotional Manuscripts', in Helen Barr and Ann M. Hutchison (eds.), *Text and Controversy from Wyclif to Bale: Essays in Honour of Anne Hudson*, Medieval Church Studies, 4 (Turnhout: Brepols, 2004), pp. 79–97

Jones, E. A., 'The Heresiarch, The Virgin, The Recluse, The Vowess, The Priest: Some Medieval Audiences for Pelagius's *Epistle to Demetrias*', *Leeds Studies in English*, n.s. 31 (2000), 205–27

Jones, E. A. and Alexandra Walsham (eds.), *Syon Abbey and Its Books, Reading, Writing and Religion c. 1400–1700* (Woodbridge: Boydell, 2010)

Jones, M. C., 'Formula and Formulation: Efficacy Phrases in Medieval English Medical Manuscripts', *Neuphilologische Mitteilungen*, 99 (1998), 199–209

Bibliography

Jones, Michael K. and Malcolm G. Underwood, *The King's Mother: Lady Margaret Beaufort, Countess of Richmond and Derby* (Cambridge: Cambridge University Press, 1992)

Jones, Norman, *The English Reformation: Religion and Cultural Adaptation* (Oxford: Blackwell, 2002)

Jones, Peter Murray, 'Crophill, John (d. in or after 1485)', *Oxford Dictionary of National Biography* (Oxford: Oxford University Press, 2004), www.oxforddnb.com/view/article/6780

Keen, Laurence, 'Documentary Evidence for the Medieval Fabric of S. Mary's Parish Church, Willesden', *London and Middlesex Archaeology Society Transactions*, 22 (1968–70), 37–40

Keene, D. and V. Harding, *A Survey of Documentary Sources for Property Holding in London before the Great Fire*, London Record Society, 22 (London: London Record Society, 1985)

Keiser, George R., 'Works of Science and Information', in Albert E. Hartung (ed.), *A Manual of the Writings in Middle English 1050–1500*, vol. X (New Haven, CT: Connecticut Academy of Arts and Sciences, 1998)

Kelen, Sarah A., *Langland's Early Modern Identities* (Houndmills: Palgrave Macmillan, 2007)

Kelen, Sarah A. (ed.), *Renaissance Retrospections: Tudor Views of the Middle Ages* (Kalamazoo: Medieval Institute Publications, Western Michigan University, 2013)

Kennedy, Kathleen E., 'Reintroducing the English Books of Hours or "English Primers"', *Speculum*, 89 (2014), 693–723

Ker, Neil R. (ed.), *Medieval Libraries of Great Britain: A List of Surviving Books*, 2nd edn (London: Royal Historical Society, 1964)

Ker, Neil R. (ed.), *Medieval Manuscripts in British Libraries*, 4 vols. (Oxford: Clarendon Press, 1969–92)

Ker, Neil R., *Records of All Souls College Library, 1437–1600*, Oxford Bibliographical Society, n.s. 16 (1971)

Ker, Neil R., 'The Migration of Manuscripts from the English Medieval Libriares', *The Library*, 4th series, 23 (1942), 1–11

Knighton, C. S. (ed.), *Calendar of State Papers, Domestic Series, Mary I (1553–1558)* (London: Public Record Office, 1998)

Knowles, David, *The Religious Orders in England*, 3 vols. (Cambridge: Cambridge University Press, 1948–59)

Knowles, David and R. Neville Hadcock, *Medieval Religious Houses, England and Wales* (Longman: London, 1971)

Lacey, Kay, 'Margaret Croke (d. 1491)', in Caroline M. Barron and Anne F. Sutton (eds.), *Medieval London Widows 1300–1500* (London: Hambledon, 1994), pp. 143–64

Lagorio, Valerie M. and Michael G. Sargent, 'English Mystical Writings', in Albert E. Hartung (ed.), *A Manual of the Writings in Middle English 1050–1500*, vol. IX (New Haven, CT: Connecticut Academy of Arts and Sciences, 1993), pp. 3049–3137

Lay, Jenna, 'Sander, Elizabeth (*d.* 1607)', *Oxford Dictionary of National Biography* (Oxford: Oxford University Press, 2004), www.oxforddnb.com/view/article/105928

LeJacq, Seth Stein, 'The Bounds of Domestic Healing: Medical Recipes, Storytelling and Surgery in Early Modern England', *Social History of Medicine*, 26 (2013), 451–68

Lemon, Robert (ed.), *Calendar of State Papers Domestic Series, of the Reigns of Edward VI, Mary, Elizabeth, 1547–80* (London: HMSO, 1856)

Leong, Elaine, 'Collecting Knowledge for the Family: Recipes, Gender and Practical Knowledge in the Early Modern Household', *Centaurus*, 55 (2013), 81–103

Linnell, C. L. S., *Norfolk Church Dedications*, St Antony's Hall Publications, 21 (York: St Anthony's Press, 1962)

Loades, David, 'Tonge [née White], Susan [*known as* Susan Clarencius] (*b.* before 1510, *d.* in or after 1564), courtier, *Oxford Dictionary of National Biography* (Oxford: Oxford University Press, 2006), www.oxforddnb.com/view/article/94978

Lovatt, R. W., 'John Blacman: Biographer of Henry VI', in R. H. C. Davis and J. M. Wallace-Hadrill (eds.), *The Writing of History in the Middle Ages: Essays presented to R. W. Southern* (Oxford: Clarendon Press, 1981), pp. 415–44

Lovatt, R. W., 'The Library of John Blacman and Contemporary Carthusian Spirituality', *Journal of Ecclesiastical History*, 43 (1992), 195–230

Lysons, Daniel, *The Environs of London: Being an Historical Account of the Towns, Villages, and Hamlets, within Twelve Miles of That Capital*, 4 vols. (London: A. Strachan for T. Cadell, Jun. and W. Davies, 1795–96)

MacCulloch, D., *The Chorography of Suffolk*, Suffolk Records Society Publications, 19 (Ipswich: Boydell for Suffolk Records Society, 1976)

MacCulloch, D., *Thomas Cranmer* (New Haven: Yale University Press, 1996)

McIntosh, Angus, Michael L. Samuels, and Michael Benskin, *A Linguistic Atlas of Late Mediaeval English*, 4 vols. (Aberdeen: Aberdeen University Press, 1986)

McKisack, M., *Medieval History in the Tudor Age* (Oxford: Clarendon Press, 1971)

McKitterick, D. J., *The Library of Sir Thomas Knyvett of Ashwellthorpe, c. 1539–1618* (Cambridge: Cambridge University Library, 1978)

Bibliography

Maddern, Philippa, '"Best Trusted Friends": Concepts and Practices of Friendship among Fifteenth-Century Norfolk Gentry', in Nicholas Rogers (ed.), *England in the Fifteenth Century: Proceedings of the 1992 Harlaxton Symposium* (Stamford: Paul Watkins, 1994), pp. 100–117

Malden, H. E., *The Victoria History of the County of Surrey*, Vol. III (London: Constable, 1911)

Manly, John M. and Edith Rickert, *The Text of the Canterbury Tales*, vol. I (Chicago: University of Chicago Press, 1940)

Marshall, Peter, *Religious Identities in Henry VIII's England* (Aldershot: Ashgate, 2006)

May, Stephen W. and Arthur F. Marotti, *Ink, Stink Bait, Revenge, and Queen Elizabeth: A Yorkshire Yeoman's Household Book* (Ithaca and London: Cornell University Press, 2014)

Mayer, T. F., 'Sander, Nicholas (*c.* 1530–1581)', *Oxford Dictionary of National Biography* (Oxford: Oxford University Press, 2004), www.oxforddnb.com/view/article/24621

Meadows, Peter, 'Moore, John (1646–1714)', *Oxford Dictionary of National Biography* (Oxford: Oxford University Press, 2004), www.oxforddnb.com/view/article/19126

Meale, Carol M., ' ... alle the bokes that I haue of latyn, englische, and frensch': laywomen and their books in late medieval England', in Carol M. Meale, *Women and Literature in Britain 1150–1500* (Cambridge: Cambridge University Press, 1993), pp. 128–58

Meale, Carol M., 'Amateur Book Production and the Miscellany in Late Medieval East Anglia: Tanner 407 and Beinecke 365', in Margaret Connolly and Raluca Radulescu (eds.), *Insular Books: Vernacular Manuscript Miscellanies in Late Medieval Britain*, Proceedings of the British Academy, 201 (Oxford: Oxford University Press, 2015), pp. 157–73

Meale, Carol M., '"oft siþis with grete deuotion I þought what I miȝt do plesyng to god": The Early Ownership and Readership of Love's *Mirror*, with Special Reference to Its Female Audience', in Shoichi Oguro, Richard Beadle, and Michael G. Sargent (eds.), *Nicholas Love at Waseda* (Cambridge: D. S. Brewer, 1997), pp. 19–46

Middleton-Stewart, Judith, *Inward Purity and Outward Splendour: Death and Remembrance in the Deanery of Dunwich, Suffolk, 1370–1547* (Woodbridge: Boydell Press, 2001)

Mooney, Linne R., *Index of Middle English Prose, Handlist XI: Manuscripts in the Library of Trinity College, Cambridge* (Cambridge: D. S. Brewer, 1995)

Mooney, Linne R., 'A Scribe of Lydgate's *Troy Book* and London Book Production in the First Half of the Fifteenth Century', in Simon Horobin and Aditi Nafdi (eds.), *Pursuing Middle English Manuscripts and Their Texts: Essays in Honour of Ralph Hanna* (Turnhout: Brepols, 2017), pp. 19–42

Mooney, Linne R. and Estelle Stubbs, *Scribes and the City: London Guildhall Clerks and the Dissemination of Middle English Literature 1375–1425* (York: York Medieval Press, 2013)

Moreton, C. E., 'The "Library" of a Late Fifteenth-Century Lawyer', *The Library*, 6th Series, 13 (1991), 338–46

Moreton, C. E., *The Townshends and Their World: Gentry, Law, and Land in Norfolk c. 1450–1551* (Oxford: Clarendon Press, 1992)

Nelson, Alan H. and John R. Elliott, Jr, *The Inns of Court*, 3 vols., Records of Early English Drama, 23 (Cambridge: D. S. Brewer, 2010)

Neville-Sington, Pamela, 'Pynson, Richard (*c.* 1449–1529/30)', *Oxford Dictionary of National Biography* (Oxford: Oxford University Press, 2004), www.oxforddnb.com/view/article/22935

New, Elizabeth A., *Seals and Sealing Practices* (London: British Records Association, 2010)

Oates, J. C. T., 'English Bokes Concernyng to James Morice', *Transactions of the Cambridge Bibliographical Society*, 3.2 (1960), 124–32

Oguro, Shoichi, Richard Beadle, and Michael G. Sargent (eds.), *Nicholas Love at Waseda* (Cambridge: D. S. Brewer, 1997)

Oliva, Marilyn, *The Convent and the Community in Late Medieval England* (Cambridge: Boydell, 1998)

Orlemanski, Julie, 'Thornton's Remedies and the Practices of Medieval Reading', in Susanna Fein and Michael Johnston (eds.), *Robert Thornton and His Books: Essays on the Lincoln and London Thornton Manuscripts* (York: York Medieval Press, 2014), pp. 235–55

Page, William (ed.), *The Victoria History of the County of Middlesex, Vol. II* (London: Constable, 1911)

Page, William (ed.), *The Victoria History of the County of Somerset, Vol. II* (London: Constable, 1911)

Park, John James, *The Topography and Natural History of Hampstead* (London: White, Cochrane & Co., 1814)

Parkes, Malcolm B., 'The Influence of the Concepts of *Ordinatio* and *Compilatio* on the Development of the Book', in J. J. G. Alexander and M. T. Gibson (eds.), *Medieval Learning and Literature: Essays Presented to Richard William Hunt* (Oxford: Clarendon Press, 1976), pp. 115–41

Parkes, Malcolm B., 'Punctuation in Copies of Nicholas Love's *Mirror of the Blessed Life of Jesus Christ*' in Shoichi Oguro, Richard Beadle, and Michael G. Sargent (eds.) *Nicholas Love at Waseda* (Cambridge: D. S. Brewer, 1997), pp. 47–59

Bibliography

Parmiter, Geoffrey de C., 'Elizabethan Popish Recusancy in the Inns of Court', *Bulletin of the Institute of Historical Research*, Special Supplement 11 (London: University of London 1976)

Patterson, Lee, *Negotiating the Past: The Historical Understanding of Medieval Literature* (Wisconsin: University of Wisconsin Press, 1987)

Peikola, Matti, '"And after all, myn Aue-Marie almost to the ende": Pierce the Ploughman's Crede and Lollard Expositions of the Ave Maria', *English Studies*, 4 (2000), 273–92

Peikola, Matti, *Congregation of the Elect: Patterns of Self-Fashioning in English Lollard Writings*, Anglicana Turkuensia (Turku: University of Turku, Finland, 2000)

Penn, Thomas, *Winter King: The Dawn of Tudor England* (London: Allen Lane, 2011)

Pine, L. G., *A Dictionary of Mottoes* (London: Routledge & Kegan Paul, 1983)

Plomer, Henry Robert, *A Dictionary of the Printers and Booksellers Who Were at Work in England, Scotland and Ireland from 1668 to 1725* (London: Oxford University Press for the Bibliographical Society, 1922)

Pollock, Linda, *With Faith and Physic: The Life of a Tudor Gentlewoman – Lady Grace Mildmay 1552–1620* (London: Collins and Brown, 1993)

Powell, Edgar, 'Roberts and Horde Families', *The Genealogist*, n.s. 2 (1885), 46–47

Power, Eileen, *Medieval English Nunneries c. 1275 to 1535* (Cambridge: Cambridge University Press, 1922)

Putnam, B. H., *Early Treatises on the Practice of the Justices of the Peace in the Fifteenth and Sixteenth Centuries*, Oxford Studies in Social and Legal History, 7 (Oxford: Clarendon Press, 1924)

Radulescu, Raluca and Alison Truelove (eds.), *Gentry Culture in Late Medieval England* (Manchester: Manchester University Press, 2005)

Ramsay, Nigel and James M. W. Willoughby, *Hospitals, Towns, and the Professions*, Corpus of British Medieval Library Catalogues, 14 (London: British Library and British Academy, 2009)

Rand, Kari Anne, *The Index of Middle English Prose, Handlist XX: Manuscripts in the Library of Corpus Christi College, Cambridge* (Cambridge: D. S. Brewer, 2009)

Raven, James, 'The Noble Brothers and Popular Publishing', *The Library*, 6th series, 12 (1990), 292–345

Raymo, Robert R., 'Works of Religious and Philosophical Instruction', in Albert E. Hartung (ed.), *A Manual of the Writings of Middle English 1050–1500*, vol. VII (New Haven, CT: The Connecticut Academy of Arts and Sciences, 1986), pp. 2255–2378 and 2467–2582

Revard, Carter, 'Scribe and Provenance', in Susanna G. Fein (ed.), *Studies in the Harley Manuscript: The Scribes, Contents, and Social Contexts of British Library MS Harley 2253* (Kalamazoo, MI: Medieval Institute Publications, 2000), pp. 21–109

Bibliography

Revell, Peter, *Fifteenth Century English Prayers and Meditations: A Descriptive List of Manuscripts in the British Library* (New York and London: Garland, 1975)

Rice, Nicole, 'Reformist Devotional Reading: The *Pore Caitif* in British Library, MS Harley 2322', in E. A. Jones (ed.), *The Medieval Mystical Tradition in England: Exeter Symposium VIII* (Cambridge: D. S. Brewer, 2013), pp. 177–93

Richardson, W. C., *History of the Court of Augmentations 1536–1554* (Baton Rouge: Louisiana State University Press, 1961)

Ringler, W. A., Jr, *Bibliography and Index of English Verse in Manuscript 1501–1558* (London, New York: Mansell, 1992)

Ringrose, Jayne, 'The Royal Library: John Moore and His Books', in Peter Fox (ed.), *Cambridge University Library The Great Collections* (Cambridge: Cambridge University Press, 1998), pp. 78–89

Robbins, Rossell Hope, 'The Gurney Series of Religious Lyrics', *PMLA*, 54 (1939), 369–90

Robbins, Rossell Hope, 'Levation Prayers in Middle English Verse', *Modern Philology*, 40 (1942), 131–46

Robbins, Rossell Hope, 'Popular Prayers in Middle English Verse', *Modern Philology*, 36 (1939), 337–50

Robbins, Rossell Hope and John L. Cutler, *Supplement to the Index of Middle English Verse* (Lexington, KY: University of Kentucky Press, 1965)

Robinson, Pamela R., 'The "Booklet": A Self-Contained Unit in Composite Manuscripts', *Codicologica*, 3 (1980), 46–69

Rogers, Nicholas, 'Patrons and Purchasers: Evidence for the Original Owners of Books Produced in the Low Countries for the English Market', in B. Cardon, I. van der Stock and D. Vanwijnsberge (eds.), *'Als Ich Can': Liber Amicorum in Memory of Professor Dr Maurits Smeyers,* Corpus of Illuminated Manuscripts vols. 11–12, Low Countries Series 8 (Louvain: Peeters, 2002), vol. 12, pp. 1165–81

Rogers, Nicholas, 'Some *Curiosa Hagiographica* in Cambridge Manuscripts Reconsidered', in Lynda Dennison (ed.), *The Legacy of M. R. James* (Donington, Lincs: Shaun Tyas, 2000), 194–210

Royal Commission on Historical Monuments (England), *An Inventory of the Historical Monuments in Huntingdonshire* (London: HMSO, 1926)

Royal Commission on Historical Monuments (England), *An Inventory of the Historical Monuments in Middlesex* (London: HMSO, 1937)

Rudy, Kathryn M., 'Dirty Books: Quantifying Patterns of Use in Medieval Manuscripts Using a Densitometer', *Journal of Historians of Netherlandish Art*, 2 (2010), 1–26

Rudy, Kathryn M., *Piety in Pieces: How Medieval Readers Customized Their Manuscripts* (Cambridge: Open Book Publishers, 2016) https://doi.org/10.11647/OBP.0094

Bibliography

Sainty, Sir John, *A List of English Law Officers, King's Counsel and Holders of Patents of Precedence*, Selden Society, Supplementary Series, 7 (London: Selden Society, 1987)

Sargent, Michael G., 'The Transmission by the English Carthusians of some Late Medieval Spiritual Writings', *Journal of Ecclesiastical History*, 27 (1976), 225–40

Sargent, Michael G., 'What Do the Numbers Mean? A Textual Critic's Observations on Some Patterns of Middle English Manuscript Transmission', in Margaret Connolly and Linne R. Mooney (eds.), *Design and Distribution of Late Medieval Manuscripts in England* (York: York Medieval Press, 2008), pp. 205–44

Savine, Alexander, *English Monasteries on the Eve of the Dissolution*, Oxford Studies in Social and Legal History, 1 (Oxford: Clarendon Press, 1909)

Scase, Wendy, 'John Northwood's Miscellany Revisited', in Margaret Connolly and Raluca Radulescu (eds.), *Insular Books: Vernacular Manuscript Miscellanies in Late Medieval Britain*, Proceedings of the British Academy, 201 (Oxford: Oxford University Press, 2015), 101–20

Scattergood, John and Guido Latré, 'Trinity College Dublin MS 75: A Lollard Bible and Some Protestant Owners', in John Scattergood and Julia Boffey (eds.), *Texts and Their Contexts: Papers from the Early Book Society* (Dublin: Four Courts, 1997), 223–40

Schaap, Tanya, 'From Professional to Private Readership: A Discussion and Transcription of the Fifteenth- and Sixteenth-Century Marginalia in *Piers Plowman* C-Text, Oxford, Bodleian Library, MS Digby 102', in Kathryn Kerby-Fulton and Maidie Hilmo (eds), *The Medieval Reader: Reception and Cultural History in the Late Medieval Manuscript* (New York: AMS Press, 2001), pp. 81–116

Schofield, B. (ed.), *Muchelney Memoranda*, Somerset Record Society, 42 (London: printed for subscribers, 1927), pp. 55–56

Scott, Kathleen L., 'The Illustration and Decoration of Manuscripts of Nicholas Love's *Mirror of the Blessed Life of Jesus Christ*', in Shoichi Oguro, Richard Beadle, and Michael G. Sargent (eds.), *Nicholas Love at Waseda* (Cambridge: D. S. Brewer, 1997), pp. 61–86

Scott, Kathleen L., *Later Gothic Manuscripts 1390–1490 A Survey of Manuscripts Illuminated in the British Isles, 6*, 2 vols. (London: Harvey Miller, 1996)

Scott, Kathleen, L., *Tradition and Innovation in Later Medieval English Manuscripts* (London: British Library Press, 2007)

Selwyn, David G., *The Library of Thomas Cranmer* (Oxford: The Oxford Bibliographical Society, 1996)

Sharp, Richard, 'Bonwicke, Ambrose (1652–1722)', *Oxford Dictionary of National Biography* (Oxford: Oxford University Press, 2004), www.oxforddnb.com/view/article/2862

Bibliography

Sharpe, Kevin, *Reading Revolutions: the Politics of Reading in Early Modern England* (New Haven, CT: Yale University Press, 2000)

Sherman, William H., *John Dee: the Politics of Reading and Writing in the English Renaissance* (Amherst, MA: University of Massachusetts Press, 1995)

Sherman, William H., *Used Books: Marking Readers in Renaissance England* (Philadelphia, PA: University of Pennsylvania Press, 2008)

Simpson, James (ed.), *The Index of Middle English Prose, Handlist VII: A Handlist of Manuscripts Containing Middle English Prose in Parisian Libraries* (Cambridge: D. S. Brewer, 1989)

Slights, William W. E., *Managing Readers: Printed Marginalia in English Renaissance Books* (Ann Arbor, MI: University of Michigan Press, 2001)

Smeyers, Maurits, *Flemish Miniatures from the 8th to the Mid-16th century: The Medieval World on Parchment* (Turnhout: Brepols, 1999)

Smith, D. M., and V. C. M. London, *The Heads of Religious Houses: England and Wales, III: 1377–1540* (Cambridge: Cambridge University Press, 2008)

Smith, G. B., 'Bragge, William (1823–84)', rev. Carl Chinn, *Oxford Dictionary of National Biography* (Oxford: Oxford University Press, 2004), www.oxforddnb.com/view/article/3223

Somerset, Fiona, 'Censorship', in Alexandra Gillespie and Daniel Wakelin (eds.), *The Production of Books in England 1350–1500* (Cambridge: Cambridge University Press, 2011), pp. 239–58

Somerset, Fiona, *Feeling Like Saints: Lollard Writings after Wyclif* (Ithaca and London: Cornell University Press, 2014)

Spalding, Mary Caroline, *The Middle English Charters of Christ* (Philadelphia, PA: Bryn Mawr College, 1914)

Speck, W. A., 'Harley, Robert, First Earl of Oxford and Mortimer (1661–1724)', *Oxford Dictionary of National Biography* (Oxford: Oxford University Press, 2004), www.oxforddnb.com/view/article/12344

Spencer, Brian, *Pilgrim Souvenirs and Secular Badges* (London: HMSO, 1998)

Squibb, G. D., *Doctors Commons. A History of the College of Advocates and Doctors of Law* (Oxford: Clarendon Press, 1977)

Steiner, Emily, *Documentary Culture and the Making of Medieval English Literature* (Cambridge: Cambridge University Press, 2003)

Stephenson, Mill, *A List of Monumental Brasses in the British Isles* (London: Headley, 1926)

Stephenson, Mill, *A List of Monumental Brasses in Surrey* (Surrey: Surrey Archaeological Society, 1921; reprinted Bath: Kingsmead Reprints, 1970)

Bibliography

Stoker, David, 'Harley, Edward, Second Earl of Oxford and Mortimer (1689–1741)', *Oxford Dictionary of National Biography* (Oxford: Oxford University Press, 2004), www.oxforddnb.com/view/article/12337

Sturges, Robert S., 'Anti-Wycliffite Commentary in Richardson MS 22', *Harvard Library Bulletin*, 34 (1986), 380–95

Sturges, Robert S., 'The Middle English Pseudo-Augustinian *Soliloquies* and Its Anti-Wycliffite Commentary', in Anne Clark Bartlett and Thomas H. Bestul (eds.), *Cultures of Piety: Medieval English Devotional Literature in Translation* (Ithaca: Cornell University Press, 1999), pp. 41–63 and 166–80

Sturges, Robert S., 'A Middle English Version of the Pseudo-Augustinian *Soliloquies*', *Manuscripta*, 29 (1985), 73–9

Sturgess, H. A. C. (ed.), *Register of Admissions to the Honourable Society of the Middle Temple from the Fifteenth Century to the Year 1944*, 3 vols. (London: Butterworth & Co., 1949)

Sutton, Anne F., 'Lady Joan Bradbury (d. 1530)', in Caroline M. Barron and Anne F. Sutton (eds.), *Medieval London Widows 1300–1500* (London: Hambledon, 1994), pp. 209–38

Sutton, Anne and Livia Visser-Fuchs, 'The Cult of Angels in Late Fifteenth-Century England', in Lesley Smith and Jane H. M. Taylor (eds.), *Women and the Book: Assessing the Visual Evidence* (London: British Library, 1996), pp. 230–65

Sutton, Anne and Livia Visser-Fuchs, *The Hours of Richard III* (Stroud: Sutton, 1990)

Sutton, Anne and Livia Visser-Fuchs, 'The Making of a Minor London Chronicle in the Household of Sir Thomas Frowyk', *The Ricardian*, 10 (1994), 86–103

Sutton, Anne and Livia Visser-Fuchs, *Richard III's Books* (Stroud: Sutton, 1997)

Talbert, C. H. and E. A. Hammond, *The Medical Practitioners in Medieval England: A Biographical Register* (London: Wellcome Historical Medical Library, 1965)

Talbert, Ernest W., 'The Notebook of a Fifteenth-Century Practising Physician', *Texas Studies in English*, 21 (1942), 5–30

Tavormina, M. Teresa, 'The Twenty-Jordan Series: An Illustrated Middle English Uroscopy Text', *ANQ*, 18.3 (2005), 43–67

Tavormina, M. Teresa, *Uroscopy in Middle English: A Guide to the Texts and Manuscripts, Studies in Medieval and Renaissance History*, Third Series, no. 11 (2014)

Thomas, David Richard (ed.), 'Extracts from Old Wills Relating to Wales', *Archaeologia Cambrensis*, 9.34 (1878), 148–56

Thompson, E. M., *The Carthusian Order in England* (London: Society for Promoting Christian Knowledge, 1930)

Bibliography

Thompson, John J., 'Love in the 1530s', in Carol M. Meale and Derek Pearsall (eds.), *Makers and Users of Medieval Books: Essays in Honour of A. S. G. Edwards* (Cambridge: D. S. Brewer, 2014), pp. 191–201

Thompson, S., 'Fitzjames, Richard (*d.* 1522)', *Oxford Dictionary of National Biography* (Oxford: Oxford University Press, 2004), www.oxforddnb.com/view/article/9612

Tite, Colin G. C., *The Manuscript Library of Sir Robert Cotton* (London: British Library, 1994)

Torre, V. J. B., 'An Unrecorded Lady at Willesden, Middlesex', *Transactions of the Monumental Brass Society*, 7 (1939), 284–86

Trivedi, Kalpen, '"Trewe techyng and false heritikys": Some 'Lollard' Manuscripts of the *Pore Caitif*', in David Matthews (ed.), *In Strange Countries: Middle English Literature and Its Afterlife: Essays in Memory of J. J. Anderson* (Manchester: Manchester University Press, 2011), pp. 132–58

Troup, F., 'Biography of John Bodley, Father of Sir Thomas Bodley', *Transactions of the Devonshire Association*, 35 (1903), 167–97

Tyson, Moses, 'Handlist of the Collection of English Manuscripts in the John Rylands Library, 1928', *Bulletin of the John Rylands Library*, 13 (1929), 152–219

Unwin, G., *The Gilds and Companies of London*, 4th edn (London: Cass, 1963)

Valentine, K. J., *Our Lady of Willesdon*, 2nd edn ([n.p.]: [n. pub.], 2005)

Valentine, K. J., 'The Roberts Family of Willesden', *London and Middlesex Archaeological Society Transactions*, 36 (1985), 183–88

Venn, John and J. A. Venn, *Alumni Cantabrigienses: a Biographical List of All known Students, Graduates and Holders of Office at the University of Cambridge from the Earliest Times to 1900, Part I (to 1751)*, 4 vols. (Cambridge: Cambridge University Press, 1922–27)

Voigts, Linda E., 'A Handlist of Middle English in Harvard Manuscripts', *Harvard Library Bulletin*, 33 (1985), 56–60

Voigts, Linda E. and Patricia D. Kurtz, *Scientific and Medical Writings in Old and Middle English: An Electronic Reference*, CD-ROM (Ann Arbor: University of Michigan Press, 2000)

Wadsworth, Cliff (ed.), *A Walk Round St Mary's Willesden Churchyard* (London: Willesden Local History Society, 1998)

Wadsworth, Cliff (ed.), *The Church of St Mary, Willesden: A History and Guide* (London: Willesden Local History Society, 1996)

Ward, H. L. D. and J. A. Herbert (eds.), *Catalogue of Romances in the Department of Manuscripts in the British Museum*, 3 vols. (London: Longmans, 1883–1910)

Warner, Lawrence, *The Myth of Piers Plowman: Constructing a Medieval Literary Archive* (Cambridge: Cambridge University Press, 2014)

Watson, Andrew G. (ed.), *Supplement to the Second Edition of Medieval Libraries of Great Britain: A List of Surviving Books, edited by Neil R. Ker* (London: Royal Historical Society, 1987)

Watson, Rowan, *Western Illuminated Manuscripts: A Catalogue of works in the National Art Library from the Eleventh to the Early Twentieth Century, with a Complete Account of the George Reid Collection*, 3 vols. (London: V&A Publications, 2011)

Webb, E. A., *The Records of St Bartholomew's Priory and of the Church and Parish of St Bartholomew the Great, West Smithfield*, 2 vols. (Oxford: Oxford University Press, 1921)

Weightman, Christine, *Margaret of York, Duchess of Burgundy 1446–1503* (Gloucester: Alan Sutton, 1989)

Wieck, Roger S., *Time Sanctified: The Book of Hours in Medieval Art and Life* (New York: George Braziller Inc., 1988)

Wiggins, Alison, 'What did Renaissance Readers Write in Their Printed Copies of Chaucer?', *The Library*, 7th series, 9 (2008), 3–36

Williamson, J. Bruce, *The Middle Temple Bench Book*, 2nd edn (London: Chancery Lane Press, 1937)

Winston, Jessica, *Lawyers at Play: Literature, Law, and Politics at the Early Modern Inns of Court* (Oxford: Oxford University Press, 2016)

Wogan-Browne, Jocelyn, Nicholas Watson, Andrew Taylor, and Ruth Evans (eds.), *The Idea of the Vernacular: An Anthology of Middle English Literary Theory 1280–1520* (Exeter: University of Exeter Press, 1999)

Wormald, F. and P. M. Giles, *Descriptive Catalogue of the Additional Illuminated Manuscripts in the Fitzwilliam Museum acquired between 1895–1979* (Cambridge: Cambridge University Press, 1982)

Wormald, Francis and Cyril Ernest Wright (eds.), *The English Library before 1700* (London: Athlone Press, 1958)

Wright, Cyril Ernest, 'The Dispersal of the Libraries in the Sixteenth Century', in Francis Wormald and Cyril Ernest Wright (eds.), *The English Library Before 1700* (London: Athlone Press, 1958), pp. 148–75

Wright, Cyril Ernest, *Fontes Harleiani: A Study of the Sources of the Harleian Collection of Manuscripts Preserved in the Department of Manuscripts in the British Museum* (London: British Museum, 1972)

Wright, C. J. (ed.), *Sir Robert Cotton as Collector: Essays on an Early Stuart Courtier and his Legacy* (London: British Library, 1997)

Young, John, and P. H. Aitken, *A Catalogue of the Manuscripts in the Library of the Hunterian Museum in the University of Glasgow* (Glasgow: James Maclehose, 1908)

Youngs, Deborah, 'Entertainment Networks, Reading Communities, and the Early Tudor Anthology: Oxford, Bodleian Library, MS Rawlinson C.813', in Margaret Connolly and Raluca Radulescu (eds.), *Insular Books: Vernacular Manuscript Miscellanies in Late Medieval Britain*, Proceedings of the British Academy, 201 (Oxford: Oxford University Press, 2015), pp. 231–46

Youngs, Deborah, *Humphrey Newton (1466–1536): An Early Tudor Gentleman* (Woodbridge: Boydell, 2008)

Youngs, Deborah, 'The Late Medieval Commonplace Book: the Example of the Commonplace Book of Humphrey Newton of Newton and Pownall, Cheshire (1466–1536), *Archives*, 25 (2000), 58–73

Zupko, R. E., *A Dictionary of English Weights and Measures from Anglo-Saxon Times to the Nineteenth Century* (Madison, Milwaukee: Longon, 1968)

UNPUBLISHED WORKS

Ayoub, L. G., 'John Crophill's Books. An Edition of British Library MS Harley 1735', unpublished D.Phil. thesis, Centre for Medieval Studies, University of Toronto (1994)

Brady, Mary Teresa, 'The Pore Caitif, Edited from MS Harley 2336, with Introduction and Notes', unpublished Ph.D. thesis, Fordham University (1954)

Davidson, Alan, 'Roman Catholicism in Oxfordshire c. 1580–1640', unpublished Ph.D. thesis, University of Bristol (1970)

Doyle, A. I., 'A Survey of the Origins and Circulation of Theological Writings in English in the Fourteenth, Fifteenth and early Sixteenth Centuries with Special Consideration of the Part of the Clergy Therein', 2 vols., unpublished Ph.D. thesis, University of Cambridge (1953)

Hunt, S., 'An Edition of Tracts in Favour of Scriptural Translation and of Some Texts Connected with Lollard Vernacular Biblical Scholarship', unpublished D.Phil. thesis, University of Oxford (1994)

Jones, M. C., 'Vernacular Literacy in Late Medieval England: The Example of East Anglian Medical Manuscripts', unpublished Ph.D. thesis, University of Glasgow (2000)

Morgan, Gerald R., 'A Critical Edition of Caxton's *The Art and Craft to Know Well to Die* and *Ars Moriendi* Together with the Antecedent Manuscript Material', 2 vols., unpublished D.Phil. thesis, University of Oxford (1972)

Murray, V., 'An Edition of a Tretyse of Gostly Batayle and Milicia Christi', unpublished D.Phil. thesis, University of Oxford (1970)

Paxton, Catherine, 'The Nunneries of London and Its Environs in the Later Middle Ages', unpublished D.Phil. thesis, University of Oxford (1992)

Rogers, Nicholas John, 'Books of Hours Produced in the Low Countries for the English Market in the 15th century', unpublished M.Litt. thesis, University of Cambridge (1984)

Index of Manuscripts and Early Printed Books

Manuscripts
Bristol
  Public Library
    MS 8, 147
Cambridge
  Corpus Christi College
    MS 142, 131
    MS 296, 94
  Fitzwilliam Museum
    MS 40–1950, 211
    MS 49, 205
  Queen's College
    MS 12, 147
  Trinity College
    MS B.15.16, 146
    MS R.14.32, 177
  University Library
    MS Additional 6578, 146
    MS Ee.2.15, 127
    MS Ff.5.35, 69
    MS Ff.6.8, 211
    MS Gg.6.25, 170
    MS Hh.3.8, 167
    MS Ii.3.26, 127
    MS Ii.6.2, 10, 15, 34, 36, 37, 42, 96, 168, 169, 171, 174, 184, 185, 193–199, *198*, 200–217, *218*, 227, 231, 240, 241, 243, 247–248, 254
    MS Ii.6.26, 97
    MS Ii.6.7, 34, 169, 187–193, *192*, 247–248, 254–255
    MS Ll.4.3, 146
    MS Oo.7.45(i), 146
Cambridge, MA
  Harvard University, Houghton Library
    MS Richardson 22, 14, 78, 79, 90, 94, 100–128, *109*, *126*, 148, 149, 251–252, 256
Canterbury
  Canterbury Cathedral
    MS Additional 46, 127
Dublin
  Trinity College
    MS 75, 170
    MS 352, 162
Durham
  University Library
    MS Additional 754, 83
  Ushaw College
    MS 10, 214
Edinburgh
  Edinburgh University Library
    MS 39, 131, 170
  National Library of Scotland
    MS Advocates' 18.1.7, 145
    MS Advocates' 19.2.1, 9
Glasgow
  Glasgow University Library
    MS General 1130, 146
    MS Hunter 77, 146
    MS Hunter 117, 178, 257
Leeds
  Catholic Diocese of Leeds, Diocesan Archives
    Mirror MS, 146

Index of Manuscripts and Early Printed Books

Lincoln
  Lincoln Cathedral Library
    MS 91, 170, 204
London
  British Library
    MS Additional 15857, 35
    MS Additional 22285, 164
    MS Additional 32490, 46, 154, *155*, 261, 264
    MS Additional 37049, 115
    MS Additional 37657, 69
    MS Additional 37659, 62, 69
    MS Additional 37787, 110
    MS Additional 73518, 186, 257, 264
    MS Additional 74210, 35
    MS Additional 82370, 167
    MS Additional Charter 25487, 259
    MS Arundel 23, 69
    MS Arundel 197, 128
    MS Cotton Cleopatra E. IV, 158
    MS Cotton Titus C. XIX, 104, 149
    MS Egerton 3245, 210
    MS Hargrave 210, 69
    MS Harley 494, 214
    MS Harley 674, 107
    MS Harley 1062, 153
    MS Harley 1551, 38
    MS Harley 1859, 13, 45, 48, 49, *50*, *50*, *52*, 56, 67–76, 102, 174, 175, 184, 248, 255
    MS Harley 1915, 257
    MS Harley 2253, 2, 116
    MS Harley 2322, 14, 79–100, *81*, *89*, *91*, 102, 243, 249, 255
    MS Harley 2445, 110
    MS Harley 2729, 57, 257
    MS Harley 3432, 154
    MS Harley 4273, 258
    MS Lansdowne 465, 62
    MS Lansdowne 874, 30
    MS Royal 8 C. XI, 258
    MS Royal 13 B. I, 67
    MS Royal 17 B. XVII, 75
    MS Royal 17 C. XVIII, 149, 150, 151
    MS Sloane 2515, 160, 161
    MS Sloane 2683, 204
    MS Stowe 862, 20, 22, 23, 27, 28, 29, 45, 165
  Lambeth Palace Library
    MS 474, 111
  Victoria and Albert Museum
    MS Reid 44, 31
Manchester
  John Rylands Library
    MS English 98, 14, 32, 34, 55, 79, 101, 103, 129–139, *136*, 143, *144*, 146, 147, 148, 151–153, 160, 169, 174, 193, 250–251, 255
New Haven
  Yale University, Beinecke Library
    Beinecke MS 324, 146
    Beinecke MS 483.20, 258
    Beinecke MS 535, 146
    Takamiya MS 20, 147
    Takamiya MS 110, 83
New York
  Pierpont Morgan Library
    MS M 648, 146
Norwich
  Norwich Castle Museum
    MS 158.926/4g.1, 31
Oxford
  Balliol College
    MS 354, 121
  Bodleian Library
    MS Additional B. 66, 85, 97
    MS Ashmole 61, 113
    MS Ashmole 189, 113
    MS Bodley 423, 128
    MS D.D. All Souls c 124/85a, 21
    MS Digby 230, 147
    MS Rawlinson A. 387B, 146

Index of Manuscripts and Early Printed Books

MS Rawlinson B. 389b, 30, 250
MS Rawlinson B. 389c, 250
MS Rawlinson C. 299, 15, 21, 24, *25*, 33, 72, 75, 82, 83, 174, 175–185, *182*, 228, 249–250, 255
MS Rawlinson C. 446, 147
MS Rawlinson C. 506, 73
MS Rawlinson C. 894, 15, 16, 36, 37, 56, 77, 92, 149–151, 171–174, *173*, 217–230, *226*, 238, 240, 241, 243, 250, 256, 258, 259
MS Selden Supra 53, 147
MS Tanner 397, 170
MS Top Oxon C 757, 170
Princeton, NJ
  Princeton University, University Library
    MS Kane 21, 146
San Marino, CA
  Huntington Library
    MS HM 127, 108
    MS HM 46980, 167
Sheffield
  Sheffield Archives
    Jackson Collection JC/14/17 (formerly JC/901), 69
Shrewsbury
  Shrewsbury School
    MS 37, 154
Stockholm
  Royal Library
    MS X.90, 178, 259
Unlocated
  Book of Hours, use of Sarum, sold Sotheby's 7 December 1992, lot 59, 247, 258
  Book of Hours, Use of Sarum, sold Sotheby's 7 December 1992, lot 59, 247, 258

Printed Books

Oxford
  Bodleian Library
    Antiq.d.F.9 (1), 246, 259
Unlocated
  Printed Hours, sold Sotheby's 2 July 1963, lot 338, 201, 259

General Index

'A good contemplacion for a prest or he go to masse', 149, 219, 221
A Good Tretys of a Notable Chartour of Pardoun of Oure Lorde Ihesu Crist, 98
A London Chronicle, 233
'A lytil tretise ayence fleischly affeccyoneȝ & alle vnþrifti loves', 149, 219, 223, 229
A Prymer in Englyshe, 201
'A songe of loue to owre lorde Ihesu Christe', 92, 115–116
A Tretyse of Gostly Batayle, 92, 131, 219, 220, 224, 225
A Tretyse of þe Stodye of Wysdome þat Men Clepen Benjamin. See Richard of St Victor: *Benjamin Minor*
Abbey of the Holy Ghost, 219, 221
acrostics, in English verse, 117, 119
Act of Supremacy and Succession, 156, 157, 160
Acton, Middlesex, 23, 26
  Fosters, manor of, 21, 22, 35, 141
Adam of Dryburgh
  De Instructione Anime, 146
Adam, Humphrey, lawyer, 32, 33
  Anne, daughter of, 32, 33
  Henry, son of, 33
  will of, 32, 69, 143
Adam, Nicholas, 33, 69
Adesto domine supplicacionibus nostris, 208, 214
Adoramus te, 210, 215
Adyf, George, cleric, 26
Alderton, Thomas, of London, citizen, 26
Alexander VI, pope, 212

Altham, Elizabeth, 263
Altham, James, of Mark Hall, 67, 172
  Mary, wife of, 172
Altham, Thomas, 67
Ambrose, St, 162
  De bono mortis, 160
An vniforme and catholyke prymer in latin and Englishe, 201
anathema (book curse), 120
Angele qui meus es custos pietate superna, 208, 214
Anima Ihesu christi sanctifica me, 209
Anne of Cleves, 262
'Anno quartodecimo virgo concepisti', 211
Anselm, St
  Prayer and Meditations, 149
'Answeris to hem þat seien þat we schulde not speke of holy writt', 79, 82, 84, 97, 243
anthologies, devotional, 148–149, 217–230
Antwerp, 238
Aperton, Middlesex, 61
Ardern, Sir Peter, 130
arma Christi, 112
Armyster, John, Master of the Temple, 56, 172, 238
Ars Moriendi, 160, 220
Arundel, Thomas, Archbishop of Canterbury, 129, 147
Arundel, Thomas, *fl.* 1540, 158, 159
Ashill, Norfolk, 33
Atkynson, William, translator, 130
Atte Hall, John, 27
Atte Wood, John, 22
Aty, Robert, of Kilburn Priory, 23

General Index

Eleanor, daughter of, 16, 23, 171
Auchinleck manuscript (NLS, Advocates' 19.2.1), 9
auditor, office of, 64, 140, 260, 261
Augmentations, Court of, 142, 164, 239, 263
Augustine, St, 162
   Confessions, 103
   prayers attributed to, 110
   Soliloquies, 103
Ave et gaude mater domini nostri ihesu christi, 208
Ave gemma preciosa, 194
Ave Maria, 86, 117, 119, 210, 213
   commentary on, 94–96
   in English verse, 117
   in *Pore Caitif*, 79, 80, 84, 86
'Ave quene of heven ladi of erþe welle of all bownte', 117–119
Ave virgo graciosa stella sole clarior, 206, 212

Babham, Thomas, of London, grocer, 131, 170
   Margaret, wife of, 131
badges, pilgrim, 42
Badingham, Suffolk, 195
Baker, Sir John, lawyer, 66, 235
Baldwyn, John, lawyer, 49
Bale, John, 99
Ball, John, chaplain, 26
ballads, 167
Balland, Nicholas, monk, 159
Barking Abbey, abbess of, 147
Barnes, John, of Willesden, 23, 38, 67, 263
   Jane, wife of, 40
   Mary, daughter of, 23, 40, 171, 263
Barnesdale, Anne, 217
Barnet, Battle of, 24, 174
Barnet, Herts., 24
Batmanson, John, 156
Beaufort, Lady Margaret, 9, 130, 245
Bede, St, commentaries by, 257
Bellamy, Richard, lawyer, 69, 141, 257
Benfylld, John, 247, 258

Benjamin Minor. See Richard of St Victor
Bernard, Edward
   Catalogi librorum manuscriptorum Angliae et Hiberniae, 248
Bernard, St, 133, 134, 222
   De duodecim gradibus humilitatis, 222
   'Verses of St Bernard', 187
bibles, 142
   bequests of, 33, 70, 143
   vernacular translations, 105, 170
bindings, of manuscripts, 101, 161
Blackborough Priory, 31
Blacman, John, scribe, 160
Blakmare, John, 159
Blundeville, Thomas
   The fower chiefyst offices belongyng to horsemanshippe, 74
Bodley, Beatrice, widow, 29, 34, 131, 132
Bodley, Francis, of London, grocer and fishmonger, 131, 132, 170
Bodley, Richard, of London, grocer, 130, 131
Bodley, William, of London, grocer, 29, 131, 132
   wives of, 131
Boethius
   De Consolatione Philosophiae, 8
Boke of Crafte of Dying, 219, 220, 225, 227–228
Bolton, William, cleric, 26
Bonde, William, 59
Bonwicke, Ambrose, 249
books of hours, 10, 77, 185–199, 200–217, 247, 257
   additions to, 199, 204–217, 231, 242
   calendars in, 31, 174, 189–193, 201
   family records in, 15, 34, 131, 168–170, 193, 263
   from the Low Countries, 194, 202
   miniatures in, 187, 194, 204
   printed, 186, 201
books, early printed
   prices of, 201
   print runs, 130
books, of law, 62, 69, 153, 166, 167

General Index

Boone, Nicolas. *See* Bowne, Nicolas
Boorde, Andrew, monk, 157
Bourne family, 170
Bowes, Sir Martin, 151
   Elizabeth Harlowe, wife of, 151
   William, son of, 151
Bowne, Nicolas, 59
Bowton, John, 257
Bowyer, William, the younger, printer, 249
Bracton, Henry de
   De legibus et consuetudinibus Angliae, 125
Bragge, William, industrialist, 252
Brentford, chapel at, 58
breviaries, bequests of, 33, 70, 143
Brevis tractatus de arte moriendi, 160
Brewood White Ladies Priory, 156
Bridgnorth, Shropshire, 154
Broke, Sir Richard, lawyer, 62
Broke, Sir Robert, lawyer, 66, 239
Brooke, John Arthur, of Fenay Hall, 252
Brooke, Thomas, of Armitage House, 252
Brown, John, lawyer, 64
Browne, Anne, nun, 141
Browne, Sir Humfrey, lawyer, 66, 235
Browne, William, 29, 34, 141
   Alice, wife of, 29, 34
Browne, William, alderman
   Alice, wife of, 29
Brut, chronicle, 142
Bryce, Alice, 29
Brydeman, Mistress, 172
Bugon, John, 64, 140
Bulkeley, Anne, 9
Bull and Auvache, booksellers, 251
Burgon, Thomas, 64
Burgoyne, John. *See* Bugon, John
Busshop, John, priest, 22, 35, 233

Calais, 65
Cambridge, university of, 57, 248
   Christ's College, 57
   Emmanuel College, 58
   Peterhouse, 57
   Queen's College, 58
   St Catharine's College, 263
Carbonell family, 199
Carbonell, Elizabeth, daughter of
   Margery, 195
Carbonell, Richard, 195
   Elizabeth, wife of, 195
Carbonell, Sir John, of Badingham, 195
   Margery, wife of, 195, 199
Careley, John, of Willesden, 20, 26, 27
Carthusians, libraries of, 147, 160, 161
Catalogus eruditorum Thome Becket, 69
Catewodes. *See* Roberts family, of Willesden, main residence
Caxton, William, printer, 130
Chambers, Middlesex, prebend of, 21
chancery, scribes of, 2
chantries, 41, 233
Chantries Act, of Edward VI, 233
charms, 167, 183, 207, 214
   against fevers, 214
   Flum Jordan charm, 184
   for toothache, 184
   for worms, 74
   'God was Born in Bethlehem charm', 184
   'Three Good Brothers' charm, 184
   to extinguish fire, 207
   'Uncorrupted Wounds of Christ' charm, 184
Charters of Christ, 92, 112–127
   Long Charter of Christ, 119–127
   Short Charter of Christ, 112–115, 125
charters, format of, 113, 123
Chaucer, Geoffrey, 2, 8
   Canterbury Tales, 127
   The Man of Law's Tale, 127
Chauncy, John, 69
Chauncy, Maurice, 160
Cheseman family, of Dormer's Wells, 58
Cheseman, Edward, lawyer, 58

General Index

Eleanor, daughter of, 61
Elizabeth, daughter of, 150
Cheseman, John, 58, 61
Cheseman, Robert, brother of Edward, 58
Cheseman, Robert, son of Edward, 58, 59, 60, 61, 63, 65, 150
Chester, Sir Robert, 36, 239
　Katherine, wife of, 36, 172, 239
Chewton, Somerset, 158
Cheyne, Sir Thomas, 51
　Frideswide, wife of, 51
Chidleye, Robert, lawyer, 66
Cholmeley, Nicolas, 59
Cholmeley, Sir Richard, 59
Cholmeley, Sir Roger, lawyer, 61, 63, 66
Christ
　life of, 111, 122
　Passion of, 111, 112, 115, 204
　verses to, 115
　words of, 120, 121, 124, 187
Chrysostom, St John, 162
Civil War, English, 23, 244
Clarence, Susan, 239
Clement, Robert, innkeeper, 265
Clerkenwell Priory, 150
Cok, John, scribe, 142
Coldhill, Constance, 191
Coldhill, Roger, 191
Colet, John, 105
Commendatio animarum. See Commendations
Commendations, 187, 194, 202, 203
Commission, to search properties (London), 63, 175
Commission, to seize property (of Scots), 59, 69
commonplace books, 162
Confessionem derelicti pauperis. See Pore Caitif
Contemplations of the Dread and Love of God, 219, 221, 225
Cook, George, *fl.* 1656, 23
Copped Hall, Waltham, 64

Cordell, Sir William, lawyer, 66, 237
Cordewell family, 171
coroner, office of, 59
corrections, scribal, 86, 188, 190
Cotton, Robert, book collector, 8
Counsels of Saint Isidore, 219, 222, 227, 229
Court of Arches, 156, 238
Coventry Priory, 159
Coverdale, Miles, 105
Cranbrook, Kent, 261
Cranmer, Thomas, Archbishop of Canterbury, 56
Crayes, Walter, 247, 258
Cristede, Anne, 26
Cromwell, Thomas, 34, 64, 156, 157, 265
Crophill, John, of Wix, 177
curse, on book thieves, 120
Curson, Robert, clerk, 20
Customs House, London. *See* Woolwharf, London

Da nobis domine auxilium de tribulacione, 128
Daunce, Sir John, 60, 62, 236
Daunsey, Anne, nun, 236
David of Augsburg
　De exterioris et interioris hominis compositione, 223
De duodecim utilitatibus tribulationis, 220
De regali stupe nata Frideswida nobilis, 205
Deane, John, 140
decoration, of manuscripts, 79, 100, 108, 137–139, 186, 187–188, 246
Dedisti domine habitaculum martiri tuo Clementi, 207
Dee, John, 10
Denysell, John, lawyer, 63
Derham, Thomas, 170
Deus qui beate Frideswide virgini tue felicitatem, 206
Deus qui es vera felicitas et requies beatorum, 206

General Index

Deus qui nos anima beati Clementes martiris tui, 207
Deus qui nos beati Georgii martiris tui meritis, 208
diagrams, 106, 216
Dies caniculares, 189
diet, advice on, 176, 178
Disce Mori, 219, 228
Divine Office, 186, 201
Doctors Commons, 156
Docwra, Sir Thomas, 62
Dodesham, Stephen, scribe, 146, 147
dog days. *See Dies caniculares*
Domine Ihesu Christe qui in hunc mundum propter nos peccatores de sinu patris, 110
Dormer, Joanna (Jane), 236, 240
Dormer, Robert, of Ascott, 149, 236
Dormer's Well, Middlesex, 61
Dorset, William, 27
Downer, Henry, 140
Drake, William, 10
Dulcissime domine ihesu christe, qui de sinu patris omnipotentis, 110
Dynus de Mugello
  Super infortiato et digesto novo, 258
Dyvers sightes of uryne, 177

Edgware (Edgworth), Middlesex, 61, 65
Edmonton, Middlesex, 61, 62
Edward I, king of England, 19
Edward II, king of England, 20, 153
Edward IV, king of England, 11, 18, 24
Edward V, king of England, 11, 18
Edward VI, king of England, 11, 18, 241
  legislation against books, 241
  reign of, 16, 66, 235
  religious reforms, 233, 234
Elizabeth I, queen of England, 11, 18, 67, 237
  reign of, 15, 16, 235
Elizabeth of York, wife of Henry VII, 42
Ellryngton, Edward, 236
Elrington, Thomas, 67, 236

Elryngton, Robert, 60, 63, 236
Elsingspital. *See* St Mary within Cripplegate, Hospital
Enfield, Middlesex, 61
Epistle of Pelagius / Jerome to Demetrias, 219
erasures, in manuscripts, 101, 102, 108, 168, 202
Eton School, 154
Euge dicta sanctis oraculis antequam nata visu, 211
Eutropius
  Breviarium historiae Romanae, 57
Evans, Thomas William, of Allestree Hall, 251
Ewell, Surrey, 55, 152
  Fitznell, manor of, 154
  St Mary's church, 55, 154

Fairsire, Ralph, 41
Fane, Mary, 170
Felton, Sibille de, nun, 147
Fesaunt, Jasper, 65, 235
Fifteen Oes, 186, 187, 188
Finchley, Middlesex, 61
Fitzjames, Richard, Bishop of London, 211
Flavius Eutropius
  Breviarium ab urbe condita, 257
Folowynge of Cryste. *See* Kempis, Thomas à: *Imitation of Christ*
Forms of Confession, 131, 204, 232
Fowler, John, 69
Framlingham, Suffolk, 196
Frampton, Robert
  Lettice, widow of, 27
Franklyn, Richard, 38, 171
  Frances, wife of, 38, 171
  John, son of, 171
fraternities, 11, 58
Fraternity of St Nicholas, 32
Frende (Frene), Roger, of Willesden, 26
Frendes, property, 35
Frontinus, Julius
  Stratagemata, 57

General Index

Frowick, Frowik(e). *See* Frowyk
Frowyk family, 61
Frowyk, Henry, 59, 60, 61
    Elizabeth, daughter of, 62
    Henry, son of, 61
Frowyk, Sir Thomas, 21, 26, 59, 60, 69
    books of, 62, 68
    Elizabeth, wife of, 68
    Frideswide, daughter of, 51
    will of, 51
Frowyk, Sir Thomas, chronicler, 59
Fryssheney, Stephen, 58
Fulham, Middlesex, 26, 59
Fyncham (Fincham), Norfolk, 30
Fyncham, Elizabeth, nun, 32
Fyncham, John, d. 1496, 31
    Margaret (Margerie), daughter of, 31
Fyncham, John, d. 1541, 31, 32
    Ela, daughter of, 31
    Ela, wife of, 31
Fyncham, Margaret (Margerie), nun, 31
Fyncham, Robert, 30, 148
    Margaret, daughter of, 30
Fyncham, Robert, of Westwynch, 32
Fyncham, Simeon, 30
    John, son of, 31
Fyncham, Thomas, 31
Fyndons, 35

Gabriel, archangel, 96, 117
Gage, Sir John, of Firle Place, 147
Gaol Delivery, Commission of, 65, 261
Garrard, William, 233
Gate, Sir Henry, 170
Gaude pia magdalena spes salutis uite uena, 202
gentry, 11, 12, 23, 48, 60, 64, 139, 263
    books of, 78, 167, 175, 246
George deo care salvatorem deprecare, 205
George I, king of England, 248
Gerson, Jean
    Opusculum tripartitum, 220
Gibbs family, 171

Gilte Legende, 224
Gisborne, Lionel Guy, 251
Gisborne, William, 251
Gloucester, John, 27
Glynn, Maurice, Archdeacon of Bangor, 156, 237
Glynne, Sir Stephen Richard, antiquary, 40
Goldwell, Agnes, 147
Gonson, Benjamin, treasurer of the Navy, 35, 37, 197
    Ursula, wife of, 35, 36
Goodere family, of Hadley, 60
Goodere, Francis, 60, 65
Goodere, Thomas, 60
    widow of, 62
Goodman, Thomas, of London and Essex, 56
Gore, Hundred of, Middlesex, 61
Gower, John, 2
Gregory, St, 222
    Sermons, 160
Gressham, Mr T, 172
Griffin, Edward, lawyer, 66
Guildford, Sir Richard, 261
Guildhall, London, 266
    chapel of, 32
    scribes of, 2
guilds, 11, 131
Gunnersbury, Middlesex, 61

Hackney, Middlesex, 61, 66
Hairolde, George, of London, 127
Hales, Christopher, 64
Hales, John, lawyer, 64, 235
Hales, John, of Totnam Hiecrosse, 67
Halle, John, of Willesden, 26
Halliwell Priory, 63, 150, 236
    prioress of, 150
Hanson, John, of Rastrick, 9, 167
Hare, Sir Nicholas, lawyer, 66
Harfield, Middlesex, 61
Harlesden, Middlesex, 21, 22, 35, 59
    Brays, 21

General Index

Harlesden, Middlesex (cont.)
   Dorans, 21
   Downes, 21
   Panyermane, 21
   Robertes Crofte, 21
Harley lyrics, scribe of, 2
Harley, Edward, 2nd Earl of Oxford, 248
Harley, Robert, 1st Earl of Oxford, 248
Harlowe, William, 151
   Elizabeth, daughter of, 151
Harman, John, of Pynnore (Pinner), 60
Harman, William, *fl.* 1656, 23
Harrison family, 171
Harrow Wylde, Middlesex, 61
Harrow, Middlesex, 36, 58, 61
Harvey, Gabriel, 10
Hawkes (Hawkys), Richard, 61, 62, 63
Hawkes, Robert, 69
Hawkins, Mary, 38
Hawley, Francis, lawyer, 127
Hayward, John, bailiff, 247, 258
Hede, Beda, of Kyngesbury, 26
'Heil and holi ay be þi name', 119
Hendley, Sir Walter, 263
Hendon, Middlesex, 22, 35, 61
Henry VI, king of England, restoration of, 18
Henry VII, king of England, 11, 18
   Elizabeth of York, wife of, 42
   household officials of, 58, 260
Henry VIII, king of England, 9, 11, 18, 67, 232, 242
   Anne Boleyn, wife of, 156
   Anne of Cleves, wife of, 262
   Assertio septem sacramentorum, 162
   dispute with Rome, 102, 105, 241
   household officials of, 260
   in France, 59
   reign of, 56, 66, 233
   religious reforms, 10, 16, 163
heraldry, 196
heralds, 30

Hereford, Use of, 185
Hese, Middlesex, 58
Heveningham, Sir John, 195
   Margaret, wife of, 195, 199
Heveningham, Suffolk, 195
Hewlot, William, of London, citizen, 26
Heywood, John
   The Four P.P., 42
Hill, Richard, 121
Hille, Margaret, widow, 27
Hilton, Walter
   Eight Chapters on Perfection, 219, 222
   On the Mixed Life, 149, 219, 221
   Scale of Perfection, 129, 130, 219, 221
Hinton Priory, 14, 156–160, 164
Hoccleve, Thomas
   Regiment of Princes, 146
Holy Name, devotions to, 92, 118
Holy Trinity Priory, London, 150
Honorius Augustodunensis
   De cognitione verae vitae, 160
Hoorde, Thomas, lawyer, 55
Hord, George, lawyer, 55
Horde family, 151–164
Horde family, of Horde Park, Shropshire, 55
   books of, 15, 154
Horde, Alan, of Ewell, 54, 154, 157, 158, 250
   children of, 55, 153
   Dorothy, wife of, 34, 55, 154, 237
   will of, 154, 159, 163, 237, 242
Horde, Alan, son of Alan Horde of Ewell, 164
Horde, Anne, 164
Horde, Barbara, 164
Horde, Edmund, prior of Hinton, 14, 15, 154, 156–164
Horde, Edmund, son of Alan Horde of Ewell, 55, 152, 153, 250
   children of, 153
Horde, Elizabeth, nun, 156
Horde, Elizabeth, of Ewell, 154

General Index

Horde, John, of Horde Park, 154
Horde, Richard, son of John Horde of Horde Park, 55, 154
    Francis, son of, 55
    Jerome, son of, 156
    John, son of, 154
Horde, Robert, son of John Horde of Horde Park, 154, 158
Horde, Thomas, of London and Weston, 164
Horde, Thomas, son of Alan Horde of Ewell, 54, 152
Horde, Thomas, son of John Horde of Horde Park, 154
Horde, Ursula, nun, 149, 164, 237
Horde, William, 164
Hornsey, Middlesex, 36
Hours of the Cross, 186, 187
Hours of the Holy Ghost, 186
Hours of the Virgin, 187, 202, 205, 206
Hugh of St Victor, 105
    De arrha animae, 103
Hulet, William. *See* Hewlot, William, of London, citizen
Hull Priory, 161
Hungerford, Sir Walter, 156, 158, 159
Huse, Anthony, 35, 55, 238
    arms of, 197
    Catherine, wife of, 56
    Margaret, sister of, 56
    Ursula, daughter of, 55
Huse, Matthew, 56
Hussey. *See* Huse
Hyll, Anne, widow, 159
Hyll, Peter, of London, notary, 26

Iesu dulcis memoria, hymn, 116
'Iesu suete is þe loue of þe', 116
images, religious
    destruction of, 42, 105, 233
    veneration of, 105
In quacumque domo nomen fuint vel imago, 208

indexes, in manuscripts, 82, 180
indulgences, 96, 102, 110, 167
    for reciting *Ave Maria*, 212
    for saying the name of Jesus, 96, 212
    to Ralph Roberts, 43–45, 75, 175
Injunctions, royal
    of 1536, 90
    of 1538, 102, 202
    of Edward VI, 233
Inns of Chancery, 32
    Clement's Inn, 32, 48, 174
    Lyon's Inn, 32, 70
    Staple Inn, 57, 62
Inns of Court, 11, 32, 47
    Gray's Inn
        members of, 57, 58, 62, 64
    Inner Temple
        members of, 13, 49, 57, 59, 64, 75, 166, 174
    libraries of, 68,
    Lincoln's Inn
        members of, 62, 64
        records of, 31
    Middle Temple
        members of, 54, 55, 56, 57, 60, 64, 127, 153
        records of, 67
    performances at, 95, 245
    Temple church, 56
    Temple, Master of. *See* Armyster, John
Invictissima cristi martiri & virgo sancta Dorothea, 207
Ipswich, shrine at, 241

Jacobus de Theramo (Giacomo Palladini)
    Belial or *Peccatorum consolatio*, 258
Jakes (Jakys), Thomas, lawyer, 59, 69
    books of, 62, 68, 69
    Elizabeth, wife of, 68
    will of, 68
Jakes, Robert, 59
    Maud, wife of, 59

James IV, king of Scotland, 59, 261
Janitor celi qui accepisti claves, 208
Jenyns, Nicholas, of London, 63
Jerome, St, 162, 222
    commentaries by, 257
    Meditatio, 160
Jesse, tree of, 107
Joan, Countess of Kent, 130
John XXII, pope, 96, 212
John, St (the Evangelist)
    De Fine Mundi, 75
Johnson, Richard, 67
'Joye in god whoes grace is beste', 216
Justinian, *Digesta*, commentary on, 258
Juvenal
    Satires, 154

Kebell, Thomas, lawyer, 16, 68, 245
Kempis, Thomas à
    Imitation of Christ, 129, 130
Kensington, Middlesex, 27
Kentish Town, Middlesex, 61
Keynsham Abbey, 157
Kilburn Priory, 23, 140, 141, 150, 236
    library of, 142
    prioresses of, 141
Kilburn, Middlesex, 37, 63
King's Bench, officers of, 58
Kingsbury, Middlesex, 23, 61
Kirke, Sybil, nun, 141
Kirkton, John. *See* Kyrton, John
Knights of St John, 141
Knightsbridge, Middlesex, 27
Knyvett, Robert, of Westminster and Stanwell, 250
Knyvett, Sir Robert, of Buckenham, 251
Knyvett, Sir Thomas, of Ashwellthorpe, 248, 251
Kyng, Henry, 36
Kyng, Nicholas, 36
Kynge, John, of Willesden, 20

Kyrketon, John, of Edelmeton. *See* Kyrton, John
Kyrton, John, 60, 62, 63
    Ann, wife of, 60
    Margaret, daughter of, 60
    William, son of, 60

La Légende Dorée, 224
Lady Jane Grey, queen of England, 18, 241
Langland, William, 2, 267
    Piers Plowman, 7, 69
Langrige, John, priest, 147
Lant, Richard, printer, 98
law, language of, 124
lawyers, 11, 32
    books of, 13, 67, 69, 127, 245
Lay Folk's Mass Book, 75
Lee, Edward, Archbishop of York, 157
leechbooks, 177
Leek, Jasper, 60
    Margaret, wife of, 60
Leek, John, of Edmonton, 60
    Ann, wife of, 60
Legenda Aurea, 142, 224
Leonard, Thomas, tailor, 265
Libri, Guglielmo, book collector, 251
Life of St Katherine, 131
Life of St Margaret, 131
Life of St Nicholas, 131
Litany, of Saints, 186, 187, 201
Little Braxted, Essex, 263
Little Stanmore. *See* Stanmer Parva, Middlesex
liturgy, 121, 185
livery, 125
livery companies, 11
Lodisman, Henry, 63
lollard interpolations, in texts, 79, 93
lollards, 79
    beliefs of, 93, 97, 98, 99
    persecution of, 105

General Index

London
  churches
    St Bride, Fleet Street, 183
    St Clement Danes, 42, 65, 70, 207
    St Dunstan in the West, 26, 70
    St Mary, Aldermanbury, 151
    St Nicholas in the Shambles, 26
    St Stephen, Colman Street, 37
  districts
    Bishopsgate, 32
    Charing Cross, 63
    Clerkenwell, 63
    Fleet Street, 70, 265
    Islington, 63
    Knightrider Street, 266
    Paternoster Row, 56
    St John's Street, 63
    Temple Bar, 32, 48, 63
  parishes
    All Hallows, Barking, 131
    St Andrew Undershaft, 183
    St Clement Danes, 18, 22, 32, 35, 48, 70
    St Giles in the Field, 33
    St Mary Abchurch, 34
    St Mary Matfelon without Algate, 265
    St Michael, Basinghawe, 37
    St Sepulchre without Newgate, 266
    St Stephen, 63
    St Vedast, Foster Lane, 265
London Charterhouse, 156, 161
London, bishopric of, 67
Long Charter of Christ. *See* Charters of Christ
Longe, Sir Henry, sheriff of Wiltshire, 158
Losse, Hugh, 65, 141, 239
  Agnes, wife of, 65
Louvain, 159
Love, Nicholas, 146
  Mirror of the Blessed Life of Jesus Christ, 14, 34, 78, 83, 129–139, 147, 219, 243, 250
  Memorandum, 137
  Treatise on the Sacrament, 137
Lovell, Sir Thomas, lawyer, 62

Ludlow, 2
Luther, Martin, 162
Luyt, Joan, widow, 58
Lydgate, John
  Lives of St Edmund and St Fremund, 127
  Troy Book, 146
lyric poetry, 167
Lyster, John, of Wakefield, lawyer, 60
  Richard, son of, 60

Machyn, Henry, 239
Mandeville, John
  The Book of John Mandeville, 69
manuals, devotional, 85, 108
manuscripts
  annotations in, 137, 179, 189, 199, 223–227
  extensions to, 180
  losses from, 101, 137, 145, 180, 202
  unfinished aspects of, 114, 188
'Many knoweth many thynges & knoweth not hem selfe', 222
Margaret of York, Duchess of Burgundy, 9
Marham Abbey, 195
Mark Hall. *See* Altham, James
Markyate Priory, 150
Mary George of Rye, ship, 266
Mary I, queen of England, 11, 18, 234, 241
  reign of, 15, 16, 66, 163, 234, 242
Mary, the Virgin, 95, 113, 115
  Annunciation to, 119, 168, 187, 197
  devotion to, 78, 232, 241
  feasts of, 117
  Little Office, 186, 201
  prayers to, 14, 128, 186, 206, 208, 211
  verses on the life of, 204, 211
  verses to, 92, 94, 102, 117
Mass of St Gregory, miniature of, 187
Masset, Elizabeth, 131
Maurice ap John, of Uske, 260
meditations (English), 128, 222
meditations (Latin), 210
memoriae. *See* prayers:to saints

General Index

'Mi good Lord & merciful fader almyȝty, whan I wreche', 128
Michell, Robert, of London, citizen, 26
Middleton, John de, citizen of London, 19, 20
Mildmay, Grace, 170
Mileward, John Le, of Willesden, 19
Mirk, John
   The Festial, 127
Missenden Abbey, 267
Modus tenendi parliamentum, 258
monasteries, dissolution of, 10, 32, 102, 141, 147, 156, 233, 236, 242
Moore, John, Bishop of Ely, 193, 248
Mordaunt, Margaret, 238
Mordaunt, William, 58
More, Sir Thomas, 60, 129, 130, 132, 162, 237
Morice, James, 245
Mount Grace Priory, 146, 157
Mundy, Richard, 38, 58
Muster and Array, Commission of, 261
Myldemay, Thomas, 64

Napier family, 170
Narborough, Norfolk, 62
Neasden House. *See* Roberts family, of Willesden, main residence
Neasden, Middlesex, 11, 18, 20, 21, 22, 45, 59, 165, 174
   Barnhaw, 22
   Bower Lane, 19, 23
   Brentcroft, 19
   Bucklands, 29, 35
   Littlecroft, 28
   Lyttel's, 22, 165
   Sheeproad, 19, 20
   Sherrick, 20
   Sherrick Green, 19
   Taylors, 20
   Thorncroft, 19
Neudegate. *See* Newdigate
Nevell, Mary, nun, 236
Nevill, Sir Thomas, 60, 236

Newdigate family, 62
Newdigate, George, son of John d. 1528, 150
Newdigate, Joanna. *See* Dormer, Joanna (Jane)
Newdigate, John, d. 1528, 60, 62, 63, 149, 236,
   Amphilis, wife of, 149
   children of, 149
Newdigate, John, son of John d. 1528, 149
   John, son of, 66, 67, 172, 236
Newdigate, John, under-steward at Halliwell, 150
Newdigate, Mary, nun, 149
Newdigate, Sebastian, son of John d. 1528, 149, 236
Newdigate, Sybil, nun, 150
Neweton, Nicholas, gentleman, 51
Newgate Gaol, 65
Newland, William, 29, 35, 166
   Alyce, wife of, 29
Newton, Humphrey, of Wilmslow, 9, 167
Nix, Richard, Bishop of Norwich, 178, 257
Noble, Francis, bookseller, 249
Noble, John, bookseller, 249
Noble, Thomas, printer, 249
Northcote, Middlesex, 58
Northolt, Middlesex, 36, 37
Nota de paciencia infirmitatis, 219
Notary, Julian, printer, 130
notebooks, personal, 166–168, 230
Notte, John, 64
Nova Statuta Angliae, 31
Nuthows, Middlesex, 36

'O Ihesus lorde wellcum thu be', 209
O intemerata et in eternum benedicta, 186, 187
O lilium odiferum spergens ubique vivificum, 206
'O my sovereyn lord Iesu', 210
Oakington, Middlesex, 140, 141
Obsecro te domina sancta maria, 186, 187
Office of the Dead, 186, 187, 188, 201, 202
Office of the Vernicle (Holy Face), 202

General Index

Office of the Virgin, 186, 201
Officium Parvum Beatae Virginis Mariae, 186
Omnipotens sempiterne deus cuius nomine gloriosa virgo, 207
Omnipotens sempiterne deus te adore, 208
Orchard of Syon, 154
orthodoxy, in Middle English texts, 100–128
Osulstone, Hundred of, Middlesex, 61
Oune (Onne), manor of, Staffs., 158
'Oure most mercyfull fader, Lord God, knowyng oure frelite', 208
Ovid, commentaries, 246, 259
Oxford, university of, 160
   All Souls College, 156
Oyer and Terminer, Commission of (Kent), 262
Oyer and Terminer, Commission of (Middlesex), 65

Paddington, Middlesex, 20, 27
Page family, of Harlesden, 193
Page, Robert, 192
Page, William, of Harlesden, 21, 51
   John, son of, 21
   Margaret, wife of, 51
Pagnell family, 170
Pagnell, Isabell, 170
Pakyngton (Packyngton) family, 61
Pakyngton (Packyngton), John, lawyer, 49, 60, 63
Palmer family, 61
Palmer, John, 61, 63, 236
   Eleanor, wife of, 61
Palmer, Katherine, nun, 236
pardons, 96, 167, 212
Parker, Matthew, 8
Parnyll. *See* Pernell
Paston, John, 175, 195
Paten, William, of Stoke Nuyngton, 67
Pater Noster, 124, 210
Pattenson, John, of London, 37
Peace, Commission of (Kent), 261, 262

Peace, Commission of (Middlesex), 63, 65, 66, 235
Peche, Lady Elizabeth, 147
Pelagius
   Epistula ad sacram Christi virginem Demetriadem, 222
Penn, Margaret, 262
pensions, of former religious, 141, 158, 267
Pepwell, Henry, printer, 106
Per crucis hoc signum fugiat, 208
Pernell, Thomas, of London, citizen, 26
Persye, Thomas, of Islington, 67
Peryent, Edward, 264
   Joyce, daughter of, 264
Peryent, John, 261
Peter of Blois, 220
Petre, William, 157
Piers Plowman. *See* Langland, William
Pigott, Thomas, of Whaddon, Bucks, 262
pilgrimage, 13
   souvenirs of, 102
Pink Canopies Group (artists), 194
Pinner, Middlesex, 61
plague, outbreaks of, 183
plague, prayers against, 214
plays, religious, 95, 128
Plomer, John, *fl.* 1656, 23
poor relief, 46
Pore Caitif, 14, 78, 83–100, 219, 243, 248, 249
   'Charter of Our Heavenly Heritage, 83, 90, 92, 98
   'Counsel of Christ', 83
   'Creed', 79, 83, 84, 86, 88, 93
   'Desire of Jesus', 83, 92
   'Horse or Armour of Heaven', 83, 92
   'Mirror of Chastity', 83, 84, 90
   'Name of Jesus', 83, 92
   'Of Active Life and Contemplative Life', 83
   'Of Man's Will', 83
   'Of Meekness', 83
   'Of Virtuous Patience', 83

Pore Caitif (cont.)
  'On Temptation', 83, 90
  'Pater Noster', 79, 80, 83, 84, 85, 86,
  'Ten Commandments', 79, 80, 83, 84, 85, 86, 87, 93, 94, 98
  'The Name of Jesus', 90, 92
  'Virtuous Patience', 82
Pore Caitif, heterodoxy of, 93–100
Port, Sir John, lawyer, 166, 167
Poyntz, Nathaniel C. S., 258
Pra quis omnipotens deus ut qui beati herasimi, 208
prayers, 92, 208, 214, 231
  against plague, 214
  at the elevation, 207, 209
  for communion, 209
  for protection from enemies, 203
  for remission from purgatory, 110
  of Richard III, king of England, 110
  to a guardian angel, 214
  to aid conception, 207, 214
  to Christ, 14, 110–112, 207, 210
  to saints, 202
  to St Botolph, 206, 208
  to St Clement, 206, 207
  to St Cornelius, 206, 209
  to St Dorothy, 207, 208
  to St Erasmus, 204, 208
  to St Etheldreda, 194, 206
  to St Frideswide, 205, 206
  to St George, 205, 208
  to St John the Baptist, 205
  to St Katherine, 131
  to St Peter, 208
  to the Trinity, 202
prophecies, 167
Protestantism, 16
proverbs, 167
Psalms, 201, 203, 215
  Fifteen Gradual Psalms, 186, 187
  Psalms of the Passion, 187
  Seven Penitential Psalms, 186, 187, 188, 202

Pseudo-Augustine
  De spiritu et anima, 160
  Soliloquies, 83, 103–105, 148, 219
Pseudo-Bernard
  Meditationes Piissime, 219, 222
Pynson, Richard, printer, 70, 130
Pyrton, Sir William, 264
  Margaret, daughter of, 264

Rawlinson, Richard, book collector, 250
recipes, for ink, 167
recipes, medical, 15, 24, 72, 167, 175–185, 204, 257, 259
records, family, 29, 37, 55, 168–174, 203, 230
  baptisms, 171, 241
  godparents, 171, 238
  lists, 34, 131, 143, 151–153, 193, 196, 217, 238, 246, 250, 263
Registrum Brevium, 13, 45, 47, 48, 50, 56, 70, 72, 151, 248
  De Curia claudendi, 72
  De forsifactum maritagum, 72
  De herede rapto et abducto, 72
Reliquie cogitationis diem festum agent tibi, 128
remedy books, 170, 177
Restoration (of monarchy in England), 23, 244
Reynes, Robert, 9
Rich, Richard, 64
Richard III, king of England, 9, 11, 18, 110, 111
Richard of St Victor, 105
  Benjamin Major, 106
  Benjamin Minor, 105–107
Richardson, William K., book collector, 103, 252
Robard, Richard, of Willesden, 20
Robartes, John, *fl.* 1580, lawyer, 57
Roberd, John, 20
Roberd, John, *fl.* 1421, 20
Roberd, Thomas, 19, 20
Roberd, Thomas *fl.* 1406, 20
Roberd, William, 20

General Index

Robert, Henry, 259
Robert, Henry, embroiderer, 265
Robert, John, *fl.* 1448, 27
Robert, John, of Langford, miller, 27
Robert, Richard, *fl.* 1421, 20
Robert, William, *fl.* 1421, 20
Roberts family, of Bristol, 57
    Roberts, John, 57
    Roberts, Thomas, merchant, 266
    Roberttes, John, lawyer at Middle Temple, 57
Roberts family, of Essex, 57, 257, 263–264
    Robertes, Thomas, lawyer at Middle Temple, 57, 263
    Roberts, Margaret, 264
    Roberts, Thomas, lawyer at Gray's Inn, 263
    Roberts, Thomas, of Elsingspital, 263, 264
        Anne, wife of, 263
        children of, 264
        Clement, son of, 263
    Roberts, William, of Little Braxted, 264
        wives and children of, 264
Roberts family, of Kent, 261–263, 265
    Roberts, Edmund, merchant, 67
    Roberts, John, d. 1461, 261
    Roberts, John, d. 1495, 261
    Roberts, John, of Brenchley, 262
    Roberts, John, of Snave, 263
        Elizabeth, wife of, 263
    Roberts, Thomas, of Cranbrook, 64, 262
        Elizabeth, wife of, 262
    Roberts, Thomas, the younger, of Boarzell, 262
        Margaret, wife of, 262
    Roberts, Walter, of Boarzell, 263
    Roberts, Walter, of Cranbrook, 261
        children of, 261
    Roberts, Walter, of Glassenbury, 262
Roberts family, of Usk, 260–261
    Robert ap Jankin, 260
        John, son of, 260
    Thomas ap Robert (Thomas Roberts), 260
        Clement, son of, 261
    William ap Roberts, 260
Roberts family, of Willesden, 11, 13, 18–45, 48
    ancestry, 12, 13
    arms of, 197
    estate, 16, 18, 22, 23, 244, 247
    heraldry, 41, 45
    main residence, 19, 22, 23, 35, 165
    Roberts, Antony, of Lincolnshire, 266
    Roberts, Barne. *See* Roberts, Francis, son of Edmund
    Roberts, Dorothy, daughter of Thomas, 33, 34, 152
        betrothal of, 40, 51
        marriage to Alan Horde, 14, 54
        marriage to Lawrence Taylard, 55, 238
    Roberts, Edmund, son of Thomas, 16, 18, 22, 34, 35–38, 65, 154
        book of hours, 15, 38, 46, 200–217
        books of, 13, 15, 46, 71, 78, 151, 171, 200–230
        career of, 56, 66–67, 141
        children of, 36, 37, 240
        children, godparents of, 56, 240
        death of, 174, 217
        Katherine, daughter of, 172, 241
        lands of, 21, 22, 35
        legal dispute with Ursula Gonson, 22, 37, 197
        memorial brass, 30, 37, 38, 42, 45, 244
        memorial verses, 45
        Thomas, son of, 172
        wives of
            1 Frances Welles, 36, 37, 171, 240
            2 Faith Pattenson, 37, 46, 172
    Roberts, Edward, 258
    Roberts, Francis, son of Edmund, 23, 36, 57, 199, 217, 239, 241, 247
        Barne, son of, 23, 57, 171
        children of, 172
        Frances, daughter of, 38, 171
        James, son of, 57

General Index

Roberts, Francis, son of Edmund (cont.)
   Mary, wife of, 23, 38, 40, 171, 263
   memorial, 38
   Robert, son of, 57, 151
   Thomas, son of, 57
   William, son of, 151
Roberts, Henry, of Lincolnshire, 266
Roberts, Henry, of London, brewer, 266
   Elizabeth, wife of, 266
Roberts, John, ancestor of Thomas, 22, 28
Roberts, John, d. 1476, father of Thomas, 20, 24–27, 48
   death of, 24, 174
Roberts, John, *fl.* 1420s, 27
Roberts, John, lawyer, *fl.* 1519, 57
Roberts, John, senior, of Willesden, 20, 27
Roberts, John, son of Thomas, 21, 34, 35, 65, 66, 90, 242
   career as lawyer, 56
   lands of, 21, 35, 141
Roberts, John, vintner, 265
Roberts, Michael, son of Thomas, 21, 22, 34–35, 55, 65, 66, 152, 197, 208, 235
   burial place of, 42
   Ursula, wife of, 22, 35, 36, 197, 238 *See* Huse, Anthony
   will of, 22, 29, 35, 56, 232
Roberts, Mrs, of Holborn, 257
Roberts, Nicholas, 178, 259
Roberts, Ralph, 20, 43, 44, 45, 75, 175
   Johanna, wife of, 43, 44, 45, 75
   Thomas, son of, 27
Roberts, Richard, 257, 266
Roberts, Richard, lawyer at the Inner Temple, 57
Roberts, Richard, skinner, 265
Roberts, Richard, son of Barne, 57, 58
Roberts, Sampson, 258
Roberts, Sir William, 2nd Baronet, d. 1698, 23, 38, 250
Roberts, Sir William, Baronet, d. 1687, 23, 38, 250
   Sarah, wife of, 38
Roberts, Sir William, d. 1662, 23, 57, 244, 247, 250
   Eleanor, wife of, 23, 171, 250
Roberts, Thomas, 13, 18, 24–35, 45
   Alice, daughter of, 22, 33, 35,
   Anne, daughter of, 21, 22, 33, 34
   associates of, 58–65
   birth of, 24, 174
   burial place of, 42, 65
   career as lawyer, 13, 47, 48–51, 75, 113, 175
   connections with religious houses, 14, 140–142
   death of, 174
   Dorothy, daughter of. *See* Roberts, Dorothy
   lands in Essex, 64
   monogram, 96, 102, 143–145, 151, 196, 203, 204, 219
   public commissions, 13, 49, 58–65
   servants of, 33
   will of, 21, 29, 34, 152, 232
   wives of, 34, 48, 51
     1 Margaret Fyncham, 29, 40, 148
     2 Anne Adam, 32, 33, 152
     3 Katherine Sadler, 29, 34, 36, 152
Roberts, Thomas, *fl.* 1393, 20
Roberts, Thomas, *fl.* 1544, 266
Roberts, Thomas, of Long Compton, Warks., 265
Roberts, Thomas, of Minterne, Dorset, 265
   Alice, wife of, 265
Roberts, Thomas, of Willesden, husbandman, grandfather of Thomas, 27
Roberts, Thomas, skinner, 265
Roberts, Thomas, tailor, 265
Roberts, William, brewer, 265
Roberts, William, d. 1700, 38, 250
   William, son of, 38

General Index

Roberts, William, monk, 267
Roberts, William, of Lincolnshire, 266
Roberts, William, seal of, 181
Roger de Ramis, 140
Rolle, Richard
   Emendatio Vitae, 92
   Form of Living, 92
Roper, William, lawyer, 66, 237
Roxeth, Middlesex, 37, 61
Royston, Herts., 36, 240
Russell, Jone, 247, 258
Ryman, James, 121

Sadler, Christopher, 259
   Johanna, wife of, 259
Sadler, John, draper and alderman, 34, 66
   Gresill (Griselda), wife of, 34, 172, 237
Sadler, Roger, draper, 33, 152
   Beatrice, daughter of, 29, 132
   John, son of, 34
   Katherine, daughter of, 29, 132
Sadler, Willam
   Bridget, wife of, 259
Sadler, William, 259
Saints, 233, 237 *See* prayers: to saints
   Alphege, 190, 194
   Anne, 212
   Antony, 224
   Apollonia, 184
   Bridget, 186
   Christopher, 187
   Elizabeth, 96
   Etheldreda, 190
   Frideswide, 190, 194
   George, 205
   John the Baptist, 205
   John the Evangelist, 113, 205
   Margaret, 187, 205
   Mary Magdalene, 202
   Michael, 210
   Peter, 214
   St Anne, 202
   Thomas of Canterbury, 202
   suppression of feasts, 102, 202, 234
   Winwaloe, 190
Salisbury, Nicholas, suffragan bishop of, 43
Salter, Thomas, 233
Sampson, Elizabeth, lollard, 42
Sancte Johannes Baptista electe dei tu es angelus, 205
Sancte Johannes Baptista qui mervisti salvatorem, 205
Sander, Elizabeth, nun, 164
Sander, Nicholas, 162, 164
Sarum, Use of, 185
Sciencia utilissima homini mortali, 160
Scotte, John, 58
Scrope, Margaret, nun, 147
'Seint Iorge þat ys our lady knyʒth', 73
Selden scribe, 146
serjeant, office of, 51
   oath of, 50, 74, 175
Seven Words, of Christ, 187
Sewers, Commission of (Kent), 262
Sewers, Commission of (Middlesex), 59, 66, 151
Sextus Julius Frontinus
   Strategemata, 257
Sheen Priory, 146, 156, 158
   restoration of, 159, 163
Shordyche, Robert, 58
   George, son of, 58
   Margaret, wife of, 58
Short Charter of Christ. *See* Charters of Christ
Shouldham Priory, prioress of, 31
Shrewsbury, Earl of (John Talbot), 211
shrines, 191, 211, 234, 241
Six Masters on Tribulation, 219, 225
Skewes, John, lawyer, 64
Smythson, Thomas, 21
   Anne, wife of, 21, 22, 35
Sol vertet in tenebras et luna, 75
Soliloquiorum animae ad deum. *See* Pseudo-Augustine
Sopwell Priory, 150

General Index

Southall, Middlesex, 58
Southcote, John, lawyer, 66
Speculum stultorum. See Witeker (Wireker), Nigel
Spelman (Spilman), Sir John, lawyer, 32, 60, 61, 62
St Albans Abbey, 150
St Albans, Herts., 22, 35, 37
St Bartholomew's Priory, 140, 141
   library of, 142
St Helen's Priory, Bishopsgate, 141
St Mary within Cripplegate, Hospital, 263
St Victor, Abbey of, Paris, 105
Stafford, Lord Henry, 16
Stafford, Morys (Maurice), scribe/illuminator, 70
Stanford, Sir William, lawyer, 66
Stanmer Magna, Middlesex, 61
Stanmer Parva, Middlesex, 61, 65, 140, 141
Stanmore the Less. *See* Stanmer Parva, Middlesex
Stapleton, Anthony, lawyer, 66
Stavane, Adome, 257
Stawell, Ralph, lawyer, 167
Stella celi extirpavit, 209
Stow, John, 8
Strangman, Edward, 264
Strangman, family, 264
Stratford, Middlesex, 66
Stratford-at-Bow Priory
   prioress of, 141
Subsidy, Commission of (Middlesex), 60, 61, 62, 66
Subsidy, Commission of (Norfolk), 31
Sudbery, Middlesex, 61
Suffolk, Duke of (Charles Brandon), 262
Sutton family, arms of, 196
Swaffham, Norfolk, 33
Swynnerton, Thomas, *alias* Robertes

The Tropes and Figures of Scripture, 265
Syon Abbey, 9, 149–150, 237
   in exile at Lisbon, 164
   in exile at Rouen, 164
   prioresses of, 150, 236, 237
   restoration of, 163, 236
Syon Martyrology, 164, 237

tailor's yard, measure of, 75, 174
Talbot, John, Earl of Shrewsbury, 211
Tanner, Thomas, 248
Tawe, John, lawyer, 235
Taylard, Sir Lawrence, lawyer, 55, 238
Taylor, Edward, of Hadley
   Eleanor, widow of, 61
Te Deum Laudamus, 128
Te veneranda caro cristi, 207, 209
Tenths of Spiritualities, Commission of (Kent), 262
Tenths of Spiritualities, Commission of (Middlesex), 64, 140
textual criticism, 2
'The merites of mas who can expresse', 208
The primer set foorth by the kynges maiestie, 201
Thornton, Robert, 9, 170, 175, 204
Thorpe family, arms of, 196
Thousand Aves, devotion of, 213–215
Thyrwhitt, Sir Robert I (1504–72), 239
Ticehurst, Sussex, 261, 262
Tilney of Ashwellthorpe, arms of, 196
Tilney scroll, 196
tokens, legal, 125
Tokyngton. *See* Oakington, Middlesex
Tokyngton, Ralph, 140
Tonge, Thomas, Clarencieux King of Arms, 239
Towkar, George, 127
Townshend, John, 31

Townshend, Sir Roger, lawyer, 31, 68, 245
Tractatus de tribulacione, 220
Tregonwell, John, 157
Turnour, Richard, of Hendon, 35
Twelve Degrees of Humility, 219, 222, 223
'Twelve Degrees of Meekness', 149
Twelve Profits of Tribulation, 219, 220, 222, 224, 229
Twyforde, John, the elder, 26
Tybye, George, 257
Tymperley, family, 264
Tymperley, John, 264
Tyrrell, Maud, 239
Tyrwhitt, Sir Robert II (c. 1510–81), 239

Umpton, Jesper, lawyer, 238
universities, 57, 237, 245
Urban IV, pope, 96, 212
Urban V, pope, 96, 212
urine, texts on, 177, 181

Veni Creator Spiritus, 128
Virgo pia Dorothea polleus miraculis, 208
Virgo templum trinitatis, 203
Vita S. Eustachii, 69

Wade, Armygell, 238
Walshe, Henry, of Finsbury, 265
Walsingham, shrine at, 211, 241
Waltham Abbey, 64
Waltham Forest, Keeper of, 67, 234
Waltham, Essex, 64
Walton, John, 8
Wanley, Humfrey, 248
Ward, Thomas
    Christopher, son of, 183
Warde, Thomas, surgeon, 183
Ware, Herts., 59
Warwick, Earl of (John Dudley), 141
Watton, manor of, Norfolk, 195

Webbe, Catherine, 56
Welles, Richard, of Ware, 36
    Frances, daughter of, 36
Wembley, Middlesex, 61, 140, 141
Westbourne, Middlesex, 27
Westhall, Suffolk, 259
Westminster, 174
    Pety France, 22
    Tothill Street, 21, 22, 63, 233
Westminster Abbey, 21, 140, 150, 242
Westminster, Bishop of
    Court of, 34
Wesynham, Thomas, 27
Wethers, Nicholas, 65
Whitchurch. *See* Stanmer Parva, Middlesex
White, Henry, lawyer, 64
White, Richard, of Hutton Hall, 239
White, Susan. *See* Clarence, Susan
Whitewode, Hugh, tailor, 265
'Whoso wole ouer rede þis booke', 119
Whytford, Richard, translator, 130
Willesden, 35, 37
    Edgware Road, 45
Willesden, Middlesex, 11, 18, 59, 61, 63
    Middletons, manor of, 22
    Oxgate, manor of, 23, 59
    pilgrimage to, 13, 42, 105
    shrine, 42, 105, 241
    St Mary's church, 13, 30, 38–46, 240, 241
        chapel of St Katherine, 41, 42
        memorials, 37, 40, 52
        Roberts family pew, 41
    vicars of, 22, 233
William IV, Landgrave of Hesse-Cassel, 67
Willoughby d'Eresby, Robert, Lord, 130
Witeker (Wireker), Nigel
    Speculum stultorum, 69
Witham Priory, 161
Wolley, Emmanuel, 67
woodcuts, 102

General Index

Woodville, Anthony, 31
Woolwharf, London, 37
Worcester, shrine at, 241
Worde, Wynkyn de, printer, 130, 221
works of mercy, 107, 111
Wroth family, 61
Wroth, Robert, lawyer, 60, 62, 63
   Margaret, mother of, 61
   wife of, 62
Wroth, Thomas, 65

Wyatt, Thomas, 262
Wycliffe, John, 79, 99
Wytteney, James, 260

'Ye shall say a ml tymes Ave Maria', 213
Yellyng, Middlesex, 26
York, Use of, 185

Zenck, Adolph, 67
zodiac, signs of, 177, 189

Ingram Content Group UK Ltd.
Milton Keynes UK
UKHW032352050723
424457UK00021B/344